REVOLUTIONARY JUSTICE IN PARIS, 1789–1790

This book examines how France's revolutionary authorities handled political opposition in the year following the fall of the Bastille. Though demands for more severe treatment of the enemies of the new regime were frequently and loudly expressed, and though portents and warning signs of the coming unwillingness to tolerate opposition were hardly lacking, political justice in 1789–90 was in fact characterized by a remarkable degree of indulgence and forbearance. Through an investigation of the judicial affairs which attracted the most public attention in Paris during this period, this study seeks to identify the factors which produced a temporary victory for policies of mildness and restraint.

Though much recent historical research has been guided by Michel Foucault's contention that the benevolent slogans of the late eighteenth-century judicial reform movement masked a hidden agenda which stressed "social control," this study's analysis of early revolutionary judicial practices indicates that traditional conceptions about Enlightenment "humanitarianism" should be taken more seriously than they are sometimes taken by current historians. For rather than seeing the Terror of 1793–4 as being implicitly embedded in pre-revolutionary ideology, as François Furet and others argue, this study emphasizes the restraining influence of ideology and locates the source of pressure for the future Terror in popular demands for justice and vengeance and in the political dynamics generated by these demands. In this work, the most important link between the revolutionary justice of 1789–90 and the Terror is the loss of political credit suffered by the moderate Fayettist politicians who pursued the lenient and conciliatory judicial policies that marked the Revolution's first phase.

REVOLUTIONARY JUSTICE IN PARIS, 1789–1790

BARRY M. SHAPIRO

Allegheny College, Pennsylvania

CAMBRIDGE
UNIVERSITY PRESS

Published by the Press Syndicate of the University of Cambridge
The Pitt Building, Trumpington Street, Cambridge CB2 1RP
40 West 20th Street, New York, NY 10011–4211, USA
10 Stamford Road, Oakleigh, Victoria 3166, Australia

First published 1993

Printed in Great Britain at the University Press, Cambridge

A catalogue record for this book is available from the British Library

Library of Congress cataloguing in publication data
Shapiro, Barry M.
Revolutionary justice in Paris, 1789–1790/Barry M. Shapiro.
p.   cm.
ISBN 0 521 41598 5
1. Paris (France) – History – Revolution, 1789–1799.
2. Humanitarianism – Political aspects.   3. Conspiracies – France –
– Paris – History – 18th century.   4. Justice, Administration of –
– France – Paris – History – 18th century.   I. Title.
DC 194.S52 1993
944.04′1 – dc20   92–10280   CIP

ISBN 0 521 41598 5 hardback

To my mother,
and in memory of my father

Contents

Preface		*page* ix
Acknowledgments		xvi
List of abbreviations		xvii
Introduction		1
1	Revolutionary justice in 1789–1790: the Comité des Recherches, the Châtelet, and the Fayettist coalition	14
2	The judicial aftermath of the July Revolution	35
3	The Besenval affair: amnesty or prosecution?	59
4	Lafayette, Orléans, and the October Days	84
5	The post-October Days campaign against the left	99
6	The Favras conspiracy	124
7	The Favras–Besenval judicial transaction	148
8	The Maillebois conspiracy	175
9	The October Days affair and the radicalization of the Comité des Recherches	188
10	The Maillebois and October Days affairs: mutual amnesty and the breakup of the Fayettist coalition	204
Conclusion		221
Notes		227
Select bibliography		281
Index		296

Preface

On the eve of the French Revolution, few subjects were capable of arousing more indignation in "enlightened" circles in France than the miscarriages of justice allegedly being perpetrated by an irrational and inhumane judicial system.[1] Responding to a sustained campaign by an energetic group of publicists and reformers, the "tribunal of public opinion" had ruled almost unanimously by the 1780s that French justice was too severe, too arbitrary, and, in general, scandalously and shamefully "barbaric," considering that it was almost the end of the eminently civilized eighteenth century. As Condorcet put it in 1793:

> A strongly expressed demand for ... the abolition of torture and barbarous punishments, the desire for a more lenient criminal justice system, and for a jurisprudence which would provide complete security to the innocent ... These principles, gradually filtering down from philosophical works to every group in society whose education went further than the catechism and the alphabet, became the common faith and emblem of all those who were neither Machiavellians nor fools.[2]

Yet, these words were written, as is well known, by a man who at that very moment was being hunted and tracked down by a regime which was in the process of making a mockery of the supposed "principles" of this supposed "common faith." Classified by the Montagnards as a leading Girondin, Condorcet was arrested in March 1794 and apparently committed suicide soon afterwards to avoid almost certain execution.[3] By the end of the "barbarous" Reign of Terror, in which more than half the victims were dispatched without benefit of even the most elemental procedural guarantees,[4] all the pre-revolutionary talking and writing about judicial reform must have seemed to have been little more than a silly parlor game.

Confronted by the stark contrast between the "temples to clemency" imagined by pre-revolutionary reformers and the harsh

realities of the Revolutionary Tribunals of the year II,[5] the "classical" school of French revolutionary historiography sought to direct
attention away from this contrast by stressing the "circumstances"
faced by the "terrorists." Thus, Albert Mathiez invoked foreign and
civil war in trying to explain why a man like Robespierre, "whose
soul was sweet and humane," was unable to act in accordance with
his 1784 declaration that "it is better to spare a thousand guilty
persons than to sacrifice a single innocent." "Attacked on all sides by
monarchical Europe and torn apart from within by some of her own
children who conspired with the enemy," Mathiez wrote, "revolutionary France had to either conquer or perish. In a supreme effort,
she concentrated all her forces and organized the Terror, the necessary instrument of victory."[6]

However, though the dangers faced by the Jacobin government
certainly accelerated and intensified the deterioration of legal guarantees and humanitarian assumptions, the classical school's exclusive focus on "circumstances" as *the* cause of the Terror should
probably be regarded as more of a rationalization than an explanation. For in taking the crisis of 1793–4 as a given, the *thèse des
circonstances* ignores the problem of how this crisis developed in the
first place, thereby glossing over the considerable role that those who
are presented as merely "responding" to a critical situation had
themselves played in creating the polarized political climate that
ultimately produced this situation. As a consistent advocate of rigorous punishment for counter-revolutionary conspirators from the
very beginning of the Revolution, the "sweet and humane" Robespierre, for example, was not without influence in undermining the
political viability of the conciliatory efforts of the early revolutionary
authorities.

While the classical school implicitly accepted the notion that
Enlightenment thinking had fostered a widespread demand for
humanitarian judicial reform which then had to be put on hold until
the nation was out of danger, the now dominant "revisionist" school
of revolutionary historiography has taken a very different view of the
relationship between pre-revolutionary thought and revolutionary practice. For rather than attempting to sever the connection
between thought and practice, most revisionist historians tend to see
the Terror as a logical outgrowth of pre-revolutionary "Rousseauian" ideas.[7] In thereby stressing the "unitarian," "communi-
tarian," and even "proto-totalitarian" aspects of late eighteenth-

century political culture and thought, these historians have, in fact, been mounting a systematic challenge to traditional historiographical tendencies to emphasize the liberal and humanitarian dimensions of Enlightenment thinking. Hence, though the pre-revolutionary judicial reform movement itself has not yet been subjected to thoroughgoing revisionist analysis, it is clear that the basic thrust of the revisionist position entails a dismissal of the significance of this movement or, alternatively, a calling into question of the supposedly liberal and humane nature of its goals.

Thus, a revisionist analysis might argue that support for the reform movement has been grossly exaggerated, or that its support was largely superficial and the voicing of liberal slogans did not at all reflect an inclination to act upon them. Or, as a variant of the latter option, it might be argued, as a group of legal historians has done recently, that the goals of the movement were not really liberal or humanitarian. But regardless of what line of argument might be pursued, it is obvious that Condorcet's "common faith" will never figure very prominently in a revisionist discussion of the impact of late eighteenth-century thought upon the Revolution. For as one observer at a major revisionist-oriented conference reported, there is general agreement among this group of historians that "an ideology fully as hostile to personal freedoms as absolutist theory... [was] preeminent before the Revolution."[8] With such an ideology already in place before 1789, moreover, it is hardly surprising that much recent revisionist scholarship has tended to relegate the early revolutionary period to the status of being, at one and the same time, a logical extension of authoritarian pre-revolutionary thought and a rehearsal for the bloody events to come.[9]

Although not explicitly directed towards the debate on the origins of judicial severity in the French Revolution, the point of view of a group of contemporary legal historians dovetails nicely with the "Rousseauian" thrust of the revisionist position. Strongly influenced by Michel Foucault, these historians have sought to debunk the traditional notion that eighteenth-century judicial reformers were primarily interested in protecting the rights of individuals accused of crimes and in securing more humane treatment for those convicted of them. Instead, as Joanne Kaufmann has asserted, the real concern of these reformers was "transforming a collection of individuals into a well-ordered society ... [and] fashioning a more effective system of obedience, a rational system of social control."[10] Thus, Foucault

himself argued that the shift from a system of physical punishment
to one of penal confinement resulted in a rationalization and an
augmentation of state control over the individual. Rather than
being tortured and maimed, the criminal became "the property of
society," thereby becoming the object of a continual process of
"inspection," "observation," "training," and "correction."[11]

Furthermore, just as revolutionary revisionist historians tend to
see the obsessive concern with moral purity and virtue in revolutionary discourse as being intimately connected to the need for
power and control,[12] so do the "Foucauldians" view the moralistic
stress of eighteenth-century judicial reformers on their own "humanity" and "benevolence" as masking an obsessive interest in
domination and discipline. As Foucault put it: "Our philanthropy
prefers to recognize the signs of a benevolence ... where there is only
a condemnation of idleness." Or as Michael Ignatieff has com-
mented with respect to British reformers: "Humanitarianism was
inextricably linked to the process of domination."[13] Thus, just as
François Furet bemoans the tendency for historians to see the
Revolution "through the eyes of its participants," so do the Foucauldian "legal revisionists" insist that ideas like "leniency" and
"benevolence" are misleading when "divorced from their context or
taken at face value."[14]

But if such ideas cannot be taken entirely "at face value," the goal
of this study is to show that they should not be entirely discounted
either. For a detailed examination of how revolutionary justice
operated in 1789–90 reveals that the early revolutionary authorities
treated their political opponents of both right and left with a degree
of restraint and indulgence that was remarkably consistent with the
liberal and humanitarian ideals of the pre-revolutionary judicial
reform movement. While portents and warning signs of the coming
unwillingness to tolerate opposition were by no means absent during
this period, the dominant theme of this work will be the ability of the
leaders of the Constituent Assembly and the Fayettist municipality
in Paris to remain surprisingly faithful to the principles of Condorcet's "common faith."

This is not to say that these principles did not sometimes operate
at cross purposes with one another. Thus, the tension between the
desire for "humane" justice and the desire for "rational" justice will
become readily apparent as we observe numerous potential victims
escaping rigorous punishment through "arbitrary" or "irregular"

procedures. Nor is it to say that an ideological commitment to this "common faith" was the only major determinant of the early Revolution's indulgent judicial policies. For as we will soon see, these policies also resulted from strategic decisions to seek political support from anti-revolutionary elements. Yet, on the whole, the self-described ideals of the eighteenth-century reformers had far more impact on revolutionary judicial policies than either the "Furétistes" or the "Foucauldians" might care to admit. Indeed, by furnishing a set of limits beyond which the early revolutionary authorities were simply not prepared to go, these ideals can be seen as providing the foundation for a level of tolerance and forbearance towards political opponents that will permit us to reaffirm the now somewhat discredited notion that there really was a liberal phase of the French Revolution.[15]

In examining the manner in which political opposition was handled during 1789–90, we will repeatedly find ourselves confronted with the problem of what Otto Kirchheimer called "the use of legal procedure for political ends."[16] For if the early revolutionary authorities tended to behave in accordance with the principles of Condorcet's "common faith," they obviously did not do so in a political vacuum. Consequently, it will hardly be surprising to discover that their actions in the major politico-judicial affairs of the period were often largely rooted in considerations which can be considered "political" in the narrowest sense of that term. However, as we explore the political maneuvers and tactics that surrounded the unfolding of these affairs, one important theme that will emerge throughout will be the general tendency for ideological and "political" considerations to complement each other as determinants of judicial policy. Thus, for example, the Fayettist municipal regime's manipulation of judicial machinery to insure lenient treatment for a string of royal officials enabled the regime to remain faithful to its ideological proclivities towards "humanity" and, at the same time, to pursue a conciliatory and accommodationist political strategy. In fact, the frequent appearance of this particular pattern will lead us to speculation about the possibility that ideological tendencies towards restraint helped generate and shape conciliatory strategies. Certainly the opposite pattern seemed to prevail in the year II, when a rigidly moralistic ideology combined with a non-conciliatory strategy to produce a policy of "using legal procedure" to systematically eliminate political opponents.

NOTES

Throughout the book, translations from French works are the author's, unless otherwise indicated.

1 See W. Doyle, *Origins of the French Revolution*, (Oxford, 1980), 86–7.
2 M. J. Condorcet, *Esquisse d'un tableau historique des progrès de l'esprit humain*, (Paris, 1970), 164. The virtual unanimity of support for this "common faith" is registered in the *cahiers* of winter–spring 1789. (See A. Desjardins, *Les Cahiers des Etats-Généraux et la Législation Criminelle*, [Paris, 1883]; E. Seligman, *La Justice en France pendant la Révolution*, [Paris, 1901], I: 174–7; and J. Godechot, *Les Institutions de la France sous la Révolution et l'Empire*, [Paris, 1962], 141–2.)
3 See L. Cahen, *Condorcet et la Révolution Française*, (Paris, 1904), 523–41.
4 See D. Greer, *The Incidence of the Terror*, (Cambridge, Mass., 1935), 37.
5 For a prediction of future "temples to clemency," see L. S. Mercier, *Memoirs of the Year 2,500*, (Boston, 1977), 32.
6 A. Mathiez, *Etudes sur Robespierre*, (Paris, 1973), 63. For Robespierre's pre-revolutionary statement, see "Discours sur les peines infamantes couronné par l'Académie de Metz en 1784," *Oeuvres complètes de Maximilien Robespierre*, (Paris, 1912), I: 37.
7 See especially F. Furet, *Interpreting the French Revolution*, tr. E. Forster, (Cambridge, 1981); F. Furet, "Terror," in *A Critical Dictionary of the French Revolution*, ed. F. Furet and M. Ozouf, tr. A. Goldhammer, (Cambridge, Mass., 1989), 137–50; K. M. Baker, *Inventing the French Revolution*, (Cambridge, 1990), 252–305; and C. Blum, *Rousseau and the Republic of Virtue*, (Ithaca, 1986). For a study which takes the "Rousseauian" argument to its most extreme point, see J. Talmon, *The Origins of Totalitarian Democracy*, (London, 1952).
8 J. Censer, "The Coming of a New Interpretation of the French Revolution," *Journal of Social History* (Winter 1987): 302. (The statement cited represents the author's summary of the research presented.) The proceedings of this conference have been published in K. M. Baker, ed., *The French Revolution and the Creation of Modern Political Culture: The Political Culture of the Old Regime* (Oxford, 1987).
9 See especially F. Furet and R. Halévy, "L'Année 1789," *Annales E.S.C.* (January 1989), 3–24; Baker, *Inventing the French Revolution*, 301–5; R. M. Andrews, "Boundaries of Citizenship: The Penal Regulation of Speech in Revolutionary France," *French Politics and Society* 7 (Summer 1989): 90–109; and S. Schama, *Citizens: A Chronicle of the French Revolution*, (New York, 1989), 859–61.

10 J. Kaufmann, "In Search of Obedience: The Critique of Criminal Justice in Late-Eighteenth Century France," *Proceedings of the Sixth Annual Meeting of the Western Society for French History* (1979): 188.
11 M. Foucault, *Discipline and Punish: The Birth of the Prison*, tr. A. Sheridan, (New York, 1977), 109, 195, 203. Also see J. Langbein, *Torture and the Law of Proof*, (Chicago, 1977), 27–44; and R. Morgan, "Divine Philanthropy: John Howard Reconsidered," *History* 62 (1977): 388–410.
12 See Furet, *Interpreting the French Revolution*, 59–60.
13 M. Foucault, *Madness and Civilization*, tr. R. Howard, (New York, 1965), 46; and M. Ignatieff, *A Just Measure of Pain: The Penitentiary in the Industrial Revolution, 1750–1850*, (New York, 1978), 214.
14 See Furet, *Interpreting the French Revolution*, 9; and Kaufmann, "In Search of Obedience," 188.
15 For other recent correctives to the tendency to equate 1789 and 1793–4, see I. Woloch, "On the Latent Illiberalism of the French Revolution," *American Historical Review* 95 (1990): 1452–70; and D. Bien, "François Furet, the Terror, and 1789," *French Historical Studies* 16 (1990): 777–83.
16 See O. Kirchheimer, *Political Justice: The Use of Legal Procedure for Political Ends*, (Princeton, 1961).

Acknowledgments

It is a great pleasure to acknowledge the help so many people have given me in the years that this study has progressed from a dissertation proposal into a book. First and foremost, Edward Berenson, my dissertation adviser at UCLA, served throughout as a discerning and discriminating critic and an understanding and sympathetic friend. In addition, Peter Reill, Elizabeth Perry, Geoffrey Symcox, and David Rapoport all deserve recognition for having helped guide me through the minefields of graduate school.

Bruce Clayton, my colleague in the History Department at Allegheny College, read the entire manuscript and provided invaluable suggestions. While it is impossible to mention all the other colleagues at Allegheny who offered me help and encouragement, I must at least say thanks to Demerie Faitler, Paula Treckel, Philip Wolfe, Amelia Carr, Jean Paulhan, and to the Faculty Development Committee for timely financial support.

Among other colleagues, Jack Censer deserves special recognition for the helpful criticism and support he has given me over the years. I am also particularly grateful to Laetitia Argenteri, Dale Clifford, Philip Dawson, Sylvia Neely, Gary Kates, and Léonore Loft.

Abbreviations

AHRF	*Annales Historiques de la Révolution Française*
AN	Archives Nationales
AdP	*Ami du Peuple*
AP	*Archives Parlementaires de 1787 à 1860*, series 1, ed. M. J. Mavidal and M. E. Laurent, (Paris, 1867–96)
APL	*Annales patriotiques et littéraires*
BN	Bibliothèque Nationale
CdP	*Courrier de Paris*
CdV	*Courrier de Versailles* (pre-October Days edition of *Courrier de Paris*)
Chronique	*Chronique de Paris*
JCV	*Journal général de la cour et de la ville*
JU	*Journal universel*
LaCroix	*Actes de la Commune de Paris pendant la Révolution*, ed. S. LaCroix, series 1, (Paris, 1895–1914)
PdJ	*Point du jour*
PF	*Patriote français*
PV	*Procès-verbal des séances et délibérations de l'Assemblée Générale des Electeurs de Paris* (Paris, 1790)
RdP	*Révolutions de Paris*
RFB	*Révolutions de France et de Brabant*

Introduction

As the deputies to the Estates-General gathered in Versailles in the spring of 1789, their mandate to help institute a systematic reform of the criminal justice system could hardly have been clearer. Speaking of the reforms "we have been thirsting after for so long," one confident pamphleteer asserted that "the representatives of the Nation will assist in the completion of an absolutely necessary task. This desire is in every heart and is echoed by every mouth." Or, as one nineteenth-century student of the *cahiers* of 1789 explained, "it was the entire nation which demanded reform." Moreover, if we are to believe a Parisian magistrate who was destined to play a prominent role in administering revolutionary justice during 1789–90, public opinion had been solidly behind such demands for some time. Writing in 1781, Châtelet judge André-Jean Boucher d'Argis declared that "criminal law reform is being called for by everyone, by Magistrates as well as by Citizens." And even the recalcitrant Parlement de Paris had to acknowledge in 1786 that a "general cry" had been raised against the existing procedures, now seen as nothing but "a remnant of ancient barbarism."[1]

But what was the nature of this "reform" that everyone wanted, or at least everyone whose views somehow registered in what passed for pre-revolutionary public opinion? What kinds of attitudes towards crime and punishment were reflected in the calls for an end to a system which "makes the innocent groan and aggravates the torments of the guilty," and how might these attitudes have influenced the course of early revolutionary justice?[2] In particular, can we innocently accept Condorcet's assertion that "the desire for a more lenient criminal justice system" was part of the pre-revolutionary "common faith," and then attempt to trace the impact of this desire on the treatment of political opposition during the early Revolution?

1

Or is it first necessary, as would insist the legal revisionists discussed in the Preface, to "unpack" the meaning of the term "lenient"?

In the most comprehensive study to date of the thought of late eighteenth-century French judicial reformers, Joanne Kaufmann reaffirms the well-established notion that a clear consensus had developed concerning the kinds of changes seen as necessary in the criminal justice system. However, unlike earlier historians who also emphasize the homogeneous and repetitive nature of pre-revolutionary judicial reform literature, Kaufmann does not, as already noted, see the reformers as being primarily interested in establishing a more lenient, more humane, or more benevolent judicial system, at least not in the sense ordinarily attributed to these words. Instead, their main goal, in her view, was to build a more secure foundation for an orderly society through the institution of more effective and more efficient punitive measures. Or, to use Foucault's words, the aim was "not to punish less, but to punish better."[3]

Take, for example, the notion that the degree of punishment inflicted on an offender should be "proportional" to the seriousness of the crime committed. First popularized by the Tuscan reformer Beccaria, a call for some form of proportionality was virtually obligatory in all late eighteenth-century judicial reform texts.[4] But should proportionality be seen as a means of generating milder punishments, of eliminating the savagery and cruelty of the indiscriminate use of the death penalty? Or should it be seen as a means of providing a more satisfactory deterrence by lending more certainty and legitimacy to the punitive process? According to Kaufmann: "Unproportionality led to variation, inequality, and caprice in sentencing, thus robbing the law of its punitive threat as criminals would usually count on leniency." Thus, the journalist and littérateur Delacroix argued against the death penalty for domestic theft because it created a reluctance to prosecute: "In advocating public works as the appropriate penalty Delacroix hopes that such 'leniency' would produce greater severity in law enforcement." In the same vein, the reformers used what might be described as an early form of Orwellian "double-speak" to think of themselves as "humane": "Humane justice would be proportional, more rational – as much in terms of 'ratio' as of reason – but it would be a strict undeviating justice. It was humane, even when severe, because it was comprehensible and predictable, thus providing a certain amount of psychological security."[5]

In a similar way, "Foucauldian" legal historians have also been re-interpreting another of the favorite themes of the pre-revolutionary judicial reformers: the demand for an end to "inquisitorial justice."[6] Hence, Kaufmann argues that statements like "every imaginable precaution must be taken so that life, liberty, and property are never put at risk without good cause" or "the accused has lost all the means accorded him by Natural Right" were fueled not so much by a desire to protect innocent defendants as by the idea that a fair trial would help legitimate the punitive process and "renew confidence in the system of justice."[7] In the same vein, Richard Andrews has recently attempted to unmask the claims of reformers that their attacks on lengthy trial procedures were motivated by humane concern for the rights of imprisoned defendants. For Andrews, these attacks were rooted in an overwhelming desire to see criminals convicted and punished as quickly and as efficiently as possible.[8]

Thus, like the revolutionary revisionist historians discussed above, legal revisionist historians have also been directing their efforts towards exposing the authoritarian or even proto-totalitarian dimensions of late eighteenth-century political and social thought.[9] However, if such efforts have provided a welcome corrective to traditional tendencies to celebrate uncritically the pre-revolutionary movement for judicial reform as a "liberal crusade,"[10] might they not also have raised the spectre of a new form of reductionism? Does a preoccupation with disorder and a desire to establish more effective methods of social control preclude a sense of compassion towards those who are disorderly? Is the urge to regulate behavior totally incompatible with the inclination to be tolerant towards those who resist regulation? Or, recognizing the inevitability of a certain degree of tension between these two modes of feeling, could a genuine desire to "punish better" have coexisted with an equally genuine desire to "punish less"?

In 1781, the future Girondin leader Brissot de Warville, one of the best known of the pre-revolutionary judicial reformers, dramatically depicted the plight of those unjustly accused of crimes:

Oh you, the accused, whom a rigorous law holds in irons, oh my brothers, I have also felt the fatal indifference which has taken away your liberty and left you suspended. I have been with you as you stretched out on your bed of pain. I have seen your tears flow, and my own tears have followed. I have seen the anger in your heart, and mine has shared your emotions.[11]

Furthermore, Brissot, who will frequently be encountered during the course of this study, voiced similar sentiments regarding the way even the guilty were treated: "How sickened one becomes when one sees the bloody penalties faced everywhere by the guilty, ... when one sees justice arming itself blindly with a dangerous severity against disorders which arise out of the defects of society, ... trying to make up for the shedding of blood by shedding blood and to repair losses by causing losses."[12] And along the same lines, another leading reformer, the Provençal lawyer Bernardi, declared: "How can anyone look on with composure as citizens are so relentlessly pursued for crimes which are either minor or imaginary, locked up in infected and unhealthy cells through a long and rigorous procedure, and forced to spend a great part of their lives in the most cruel uncertainty and amidst tears and despair."[13]

In thereby presenting themselves as "sensitive souls crying hot tears upon their manuscripts,"[14] Brissot and Bernardi were reflecting the currents of sentimentality which suffused much of late eighteenth-century culture and thought. However, if late eighteenth-century sentimentality can be taken as an advanced stage in what Norbert Elias described as the "civilizing process," the widespread presence of "sensitive souls" (or at least of would-be "sensitive souls") during the pre-revolutionary period could have triggered a paradoxical reaction to issues of crime and punishment. According to Elias, a fundamental characteristic of the "civilizing process" is that people "become more sensitive to the impulses of others," while developing a "sharper understanding of what is going on in others."[15] But sensitivity towards those accused of being criminals, including those charged with committing political crimes, can cut in two different ways. On the one hand, the "sensitive soul," as we have just seen in the effusions of Brissot and Bernardi, will feel compassion for others, and such compassion will constitute part of the very definition of being civilized. Or, if it cannot quite bring itself to feel the proper sympathy or empathy, the "sensitive soul" will at least know what it is *supposed* to feel, and it may seek to compensate by trying to tolerate undesirable behavior or opinions. Yet, its greater sensitivity to others will also render the "sensitive soul" more easily offended by what it perceives to be distasteful behavior or opinions, thereby generating greater pressures for more effective enforcement of what are seen as civilized standards.

Thus, we can now differentiate between two equally meaningful senses in which pre-revolutionary judicial reformers employed the epithet "barbarous" to describe Old Regime criminal justice: it was "barbarous" because it was cruel and inhumane towards offenders, but it was also "barbarous" because it was crude and unrefined in its efforts to deter offenses. Since the "sensitive souls" who developed this twofold critique of traditional justice were obviously far more eager to proclaim their vaunted "humanity" than to highlight their less unequivocally admirable urge to control or "civilize" others, it has apparently been left to the current generation of revisionist legal historians to fully uncover the critique's repressive implications. However, when we observe the early revolutionary authorities wrestling with the problem of how to deal with their political enemies, we will see that the leaders of both the Constituent Assembly and the Fayettist municipal regime in Paris had indeed absorbed the "lessons in humanity" taught by eighteenth-century reformers. While revolutionary turbulence certainly reinforced the authoritarian and rationalistic aspects of eighteenth-century judicial thought, thereby creating a certain amount of pressure for the implementation of vigilant "public safety" measures, this study will emphasize the extent to which pre-revolutionary humanitarianism operated as an effective countervailing force. For the inclination to be lenient towards political offenders ultimately had a decisive impact on judicial policies during the first year of the Revolution.

In tracing the links between pre-revolutionary judicial thought and early revolutionary political justice, one facet of the critique of traditional criminal justice merits particular attention: its treatment of political crime. Though not addressed nearly as often nor with the same degree of quasi-unanimity as ordinary crime, the subject of political crime elicited a stream of thought which, in seeking to narrow the very definition of what was considered criminal behavior, can in itself be seen as encouraging indulgent attitudes towards political opponents.

Expanding upon Montesquieu's celebrated comment that "for a government to degenerate into despotism, it is enough that the crime of *lèse-majesté* [high treason] be vaguely defined," the prolific Brissot declared in 1781 that "high treason is a crime that Monarchs often make use of to get rid of subjects they hate and whose ruin they have sworn."[16] And in another work published in the same year, he stated that "the petty despotism of some ministers has, through an absurd logic, even understood treason to include conspiracies which have no other goal but that of displacing them, conspiracies which, in the eyes of the impartial observer, are only simple intrigues."[17] As the leader of the Paris Comité des Recherches of 1789–90, the first major French revolutionary institution with the specific responsibility of combatting conspiracies against the new regime, Brissot would have ample opportunity to demonstrate that the commitment to a "de-criminalization" of political opposition that is implied in these remarks was more than empty rhetoric. Moreover, his willingness to distinguish between "treason" and "simple intrigue" is especially interesting in light of his later reputation, at least among his revolutionary opponents, as a consummate "intriguer."[18] As someone with a penchant for what today would be called "playing politics," Brissot would never be able to adapt comfortably to the moralistic and doctrinaire aspects of the emerging revolutionary culture.

In addition to advocating restrictions on the definition of treason, the pre-revolutionary Brissot also insisted that if treason trials were necessary, they should follow "the ordinary forms and rules of justice." Furthermore, at least when being published outside France, he endorsed a total abolition of the death penalty, even for regicides.[19] Regarding other political crimes, as a dissident writer with a strong personal interest in free expression, it is hardly surprising to see him suggest that monarchs apply the following formula to subversive literature: "If their authors are motivated by frivolity, we scorn them; if they are insane, we pity them; and if they intend to be harmful, we pardon them." However, his tendency to favor leniency towards political offenders also extended to sedition and popular revolt. Wise governments, he asserted, will focus on eliminating the causes of sedition, and even rebels can usually be pardoned.[20]

While other pre-revolutionary judicial reformers usually devoted less attention to political crime than Brissot, the idea that a loose definition of treason could easily become an instrument of tyranny was, as Giovanna Cavallaro has recently put it, one of the "common-place" notions of late eighteenth-century judicial thought.[21] Thus, Bernardi proclaimed that "there is scarcely any word which has served to torment wretched humanity more than *lèse-majesté*," and, following Beccaria, he lamented the "art of odious interpretation" to which this word had lent itself. "Only crimes which lead directly to the destruction of society," he stated, "can be considered treason." Similarly, the legal scholar Roussel de la Bérardière explicitly excluded "court intrigues, fantasies, and other trivialities" from his discussion of treason and declared that "it is indeed very dangerous to use this detestable word without discrimination." And the littérateur and future Paris National Guardsman Chaussard praised the Tuscan Grand Duke Leopold for eliminating from the Criminal Code "this multitude of crimes, improperly called *lèse-majesté*, which were invented in perverted epochs and which have led to unheard-of refinements in cruelty."[22]

Going beyond the specific question of defining treason, it is possible to identify the presence of a vibrant current in late eighteenth-century thought which attempted to extend the general maxims advanced by Montesquieu and Voltaire concerning the need to limit the prosecution and punishment of political and religious behavior.[23] Thus, Valazé, another future Girondin, carefully differentiated between "political vices" and "political crimes," with "contempt for the Constitution of one's country" and "refusal of a post in which one might be useful" being listed as among the vices which presumably should not become subject to judicial pursuit.[24] And Delacroix, voicing an early version of the nineteenth-century notion that political offenders could sometimes be treated more leniently than ordinary criminals,[25] defended the rights of "distinguished writers who could embrace false systems without being criminals and who, without having the intention of disrupting society, only seek to propagate what they think is the truth."[26]

Regarding the impact of such attitudes, it is, as already implied, obviously far easier for dissenting intellectuals to advocate principles of toleration than for those with power and responsibility to embody these principles in actual policies. And certainly the revolutionary behavior of some pre-revolutionary reformers made it clear that they had only been paying lip-service to the defense of political and religious liberties.[27] Yet, the course of events of 1789–90 indicates that, in contrast to those who would succeed them, the early revolutionary authorities operated with a kind of instinctual inclination to pursue policies which would be consistent with the liberal views of political crime enunciated by pre-revolutionary reformers. One might even say they acted as if one of their greatest fears was that some future Montesquieu or Voltaire would add them to some future list of history's greatest tyrants.

However, if early revolutionary leniency towards political opponents can indeed be seen as resulting from a sincere effort to
transfer late eighteenth-century judicial thought into the revolutionary arena, it can also be viewed as a logical continuation of
eighteenth-century practice. Whereas the turbulent sixteenth and
seventeenth centuries were filled with examples of executed and
imprisoned ex-ministers, the worst fate that seems to have befallen a
disgraced minister in the relatively peaceful and politically stable
eighteenth century was that of a polite exile to the offender's own
provincial estates.[28] In fact, so far as I can determine, there was only
one execution of an important public official during the entire pre-
revolutionary eighteenth century.[29] Moreover, to take another genre
of political crime, the relatively lenient treatment accorded contro-
versial eighteenth-century writers (i.e. short prison stays for the likes
of Voltaire, Diderot, and Brissot) contrasts sharply with the more
savage punishment meted out to earlier critics of French society.[30]
While evidence on the question of whether ordinary crime was
actually being punished less severely in the late eighteenth century
remains mixed,[31] there can no doubt that political offenders, particularly those who were either aristocrats or intellectuals, were
being treated in what may be thought of as a more civilized manner.
In this sense, at least, it can be said that the tolerant and forbearing
currents in eighteenth-century social thought were already having a
substantial impact on social reality.

Moreover, whatever the actual state of progress towards "enlightened" judicial practices, there seems to have been, as the century
approached its end, a widespread perception that "barbarism" was
rapidly disappearing. "Humanity is being ushered in by the age,"
wrote Chaussard in 1788, "the progress of the laws is following the
progress of knowledge, and in proportion as a piece of the veil of
truth is lifted, the veil of error falls."[32] In the same vein, Brissot
spoke of a general "softening of manners" and contrasted the
"happy age in which we live" with "these horrible centuries in which
France ... saw the blood of its own children flow from everywhere,"
while his future rival Robespierre celebrated "this enlightened century ... in which the voice of reason and humanity resounds with so
much force" and in which people were "becoming more sensitive
and more refined because of the progress of our knowledge."[33]
Assuring the victims of judicial abuses that changes were imminent,
Lacretelle, another soon-to-be member of the Paris Comité des

Recherches of 1789–90, declared: "I dare to promise this to them in the name of the Reason of this century."[34]

Given the pervasiveness of a general sense of pride in the advanced nature of the age, the periodic appearances during the early Revolution of a "ferocity" that was both a reminder of the past and a portent of the future often produced an expression of shock and surprise. "The spirit of Monarchical Courts is still teaching ferocity in such an advanced age," lamented the future Girondin Carra in a report on the Maillebois conspiracy, one of the early counter-revolutionary plots that will be examined in this study.[35] And the right-wing deputy Maury, while attacking attempts by various National Assembly deputies to justify the house arrest of one of their colleagues, shouted: "It is at the end of the eighteenth century that they dare to utter maxims which would scarcely find a place in the instructions given to the executioners charged with carrying out the judgments of Tiberius and Phalaris."[36] While there was certainly an element of exaggeration and political grandstanding in such declamations, the sense of shock that was frequently expressed upon observing the savage judicial rituals carried out by the revolutionary crowd was perhaps more genuine. "Will future generations believe," asked Gouy d'Arcy after one of the popular massacres of July 1789, "that in such an enlightened century, the entrails of a man were torn open and his heart carried on the end of a lance, that his head was passed from hand to hand in triumph through the streets and his cadaver dragged all through the capital?"[37]

In an effort to shed some light on the process through which the humanitarian ideals of the pre-revolutionary judicial reform movement, so influential in 1789–90, came to have less and less influence in determining judicial policies as the Revolution unfolded, this study will place a great deal of emphasis on the role of popular demands and popular pressure. While the impact of "the People" upon the course of revolutionary justice was not always as "barbaric" as that depicted by Gouy d'Arcy, an insistence on judicial severity was, from the very beginning, a central item in the political program of the revolutionary popular movement. With the question of how to treat the enemies of the Revolution serving as a major focal point of early revolutionary political conflict, "the People," or at least those who passed for being its spokesmen, would constitute the most significant force opposing the indulgent inclinations of the early revolutionary authorities. Throughout 1789 and 1790, both the National Assembly and the Fayettist municipal regime in Paris were, as will be made clear in the chapters to come, largely successful in turning aside popular demands for the prosecution and punishment of anti-revolutionary elements. However, as the Revolution traced its familiar route leftward and the popular movement assumed more and more political weight, the pressure for investigatory rigor and judicial harshness would become more and more difficult to resist.[38]

As already indicated, one of the key aims of this study is to demonstrate that both revisionist revolutionary historians and revisionist legal historians have been underestimating the scope and impact of pre-revolutionary liberal thought. However, the attention that will be paid to popular visions of revolutionary justice will provide a means of achieving something of a reconciliation with revisionist ideas, or at least a means of understanding why the commitment of the pre-revolutionary "enlightened elite" to the humanitarian thrust of Condorcet's "common faith" proved to be so fragile and transitory. With "the People" emerging during the early revolutionary period as the only really viable source of political legitimacy,[39] those members of the "enlightened elite" who could successfully put forward claims to speak for this newly sacred entity automatically assumed a measure of political credibility out of all proportion to their influence within the elite. Of course, in the crucible of the early Revolution, a new conception of "the People" was itself being forged, as the idea of *le peuple* as the popular classes became confounded with and evolved into the notion of *le peuple* as equivalent to *la nation*.[40] But on a day-to-day basis, the most tangible embodiment of both of these conceptions of "the People" was that quintessential French revolutionary protagonist, the Parisian revolutionary crowd. And since whatever else it may have wanted, the crowd was clearly demanding that its enemies be punished, one of the most revealing tests of the credentials of an aspiring popular spokesman quickly became the willingness to discard the liberal and humane assumptions of the pre-revolutionary "common faith."

With pre-revolutionary judicial reformers like Robespierre and Marat presenting themselves as strong advocates of judicial severity from the very beginning of the Revolution, it is evident that, for whatever reasons, at least a portion of the "enlightened elite" was ready to take this step.[41] However, through the first year of the

Revolution, most of the elite, or at least those members of it who exercised political authority, were far from ready to embrace the crowd's perspectives on revolutionary justice. Yet, even as their loyalty to the humanitarian thrust of pre-revolutionary judicial thought led them to oppose the popular urge for punitive rigor and the popular impatience with legal guarantees, other facets of pre-revolutionary judicial thought led these early revolutionary legislators and officials to take positions which were by no means incompatible with certain aspects of what François Furet calls the "ideology of pure democracy."[42]

Thus, for example, one of the most common demands of the judicial reformers had been that all secret proceedings be abolished and that all relevant documents in a criminal action be made available to both the accused and the public itself.[43] At first glance, such a demand might seem to be primarily based on a concern for the rights of the defendant, who would obviously have an enormous interest in acquiring such material and who could, at times, also benefit from the publicity generated by a free press and public trials. But if we consider Brissot's assertion that "Society itself demands this publicity" and his subsequent contention that "the vigilant eye of the public will only frighten those monsters who look for dark places to hide their odious crimes," we realize that the call for judicial publicity was also rooted in a deep concern for social order and "public safety."[44] Or, to put it another way, though the "glare of publicity" may sometimes intimidate repressive governments which seek to limit public knowledge of their repressive acts, it can also serve to impede the secret pursuit of private interest, a pursuit which, from the standpoint of the emerging "ideology of pure democracy," was coming to seem less and less legitimate.[45] Though Brissot and the Paris Comité des Recherches of 1789–90 would actually do more to protect counter-revolutionary conspirators than to turn the "glare of publicity" upon them or to mobilize the "vigilant eye of the public" against them, the establishment of public judicial proceedings in October 1789, which was widely hailed as a triumph of "philosophy," helped contribute to the creation of the feverish atmosphere in which the Comité operated.[46] Furthermore, always sensitive to the importance of maintaining popular confidence, the Comité sought to adapt to this heated atmosphere by cultivating an image of itself as a vigorous prosecutor and investigator, even as it acted quite differently behind the scenes.

On November 11, 1789, for example, Brissot informed his friend Bancal des Issarts that "the Comité des Recherches is taking up all my time, and it is certainly important to uncover old plots and those which are taking shape." "However," he confided, "there do not really seem to be any dangerous ones now." Yet, in sharp contrast to the rather relaxed tone of this letter, his newspaper was insisting at virtually the same moment that "we must spy upon and watch over the traitors who prepare new catastrophes for us in the darkness."[47] While Brissot sometimes argued that this kind of public denunciation of secret evil-doing was actually designed to calm popular fears by convincing "the People" that the Comité was maintaining proper surveillance,[48] it is easy to see how such a statement might also have served to intensify and encourage popular alarms and rumors, an ambiguity in the Comité's activities to which we will repeatedly return in the chapters to come. But whatever impact the Comité may have had in either soothing or exciting revolutionary passions, Brissot would certainly find that the fulfillment of his pre-revolutionary demand for judicial publicity would operate as a constraining factor upon his own actions, making it, as we will see, more difficult for him to give free rein to his indulgent inclinations.

Another aspect of pre-revolutionary judicial thought that was especially compatible with democratic ideology was the demand expressed by many reformers that each citizen be given the right to make official accusations. Bernardi, for example, enthusiastically recalled Rousseau's statement that "in the good times of Rome, citizens maintained careful surveillance over each other and accused each other publicly because of their zeal for justice."[49] While it was sometimes argued that such a procedure would protect defendants against the abuses of secret denunciations, it is not difficult to see how this proposed reform could also become a weapon in the arsenal of "public safety" proponents. And while the pre-revolutionary tendency to advocate "democratic denunciation" was somewhat tempered by a distaste for Old Regime "spies" and "snitches," Comité des Recherches member Agier argued in November 1789 that such "prejudices" were no longer applicable under the "Reign of Liberty":

Let us stop applying, because of a fatal prejudice, standards which belong only to the Old Regime and not to the present, and let us not dishonor the Reign of Liberty by the stains of slavery. To be silent when it is a question of denouncing someone is a virtue under despotism, but it is a crime, yes it really is one, under the Empire of Liberty.[50]

In short, though this study will stress the links between pre-revolutionary judicial thought and the generally indulgent and non-vigilant nature of early revolutionary justice, it must also be kept in mind that there were facets of pre-revolutionary thought and early revolutionary practice that reflected the concern with maintaining order and enforcing obedience noted by legal revisionists. Moreover, at least with respect to the threats posed by counter-revolutionaries, it can be said that this concern with control and obedience dove-tailed more easily with popular perspectives on revolutionary justice than did humanitarian inclinations inherited from the pre-revolutionary period. Indeed it can perhaps be said that the rationalistic currents of late eighteenth-century judicial thought, which looked to uniform, regular, and public procedures, were, in general, easier to reconcile with the "ideology of pure democracy" than its humanitarian and liberal aspects, which were often seen as leading to special treatment for privileged evil-doers.

Finally, the gingerly manner with which popular demands for judicial severity were treated by the early revolutionary authorities who opposed them can itself be taken as indicative of the deepening impact of democratic ideology on the enlightened elite. In part, of course, the authorities' preoccupation with appeasing or satisfying "the People" represented a response to the newly revealed physical power of the revolutionary crowd. But beyond this, even as they were being thwarted and shunted aside during the period covered in this study, popular demands for judicial severity were accorded a certain measure of respect and legitimacy simply because they were seen as emanating from "the People." And as the Revolution proceeded, it would become harder and harder to resist the judicial implications of popular sovereignty.[51]

Revolutionary justice in 1789–1790: the Comité des Recherches, the Châtelet, and the Fayettist coalition

During the first year of the French Revolution, responsibility for political justice was largely shared by two institutions, the Paris Comité des Recherches, an investigatory and prosecutory agency which served as the capital's political police, and the Châtelet, an ancient royal court which held temporary authority over all *lèse-nation* cases in France.[1] Though their formal powers derived from separate sources, the Comité being a creation of the Paris municipal council and the Châtelet being designated as *lèse-nation* tribunal by the National Assembly, these two institutions actually functioned as the central components of a single system of political justice, a system which operated under the aegis of the Commandant-General of the Paris National Guard, the Marquis de Lafayette.[2]

The first year of the Revolution was, as Georges Lefebvre put it, "Lafayette's year."[3] With his dominance of the Parisian municipality already established during the summer of 1789, the "Hero of Two Worlds" was able to turn that curious episode known as the October Days to his own advantage and induce both Louis XVI and the National Assembly to move from Versailles to Paris.[4] Having thereby consolidated and enhanced his position as the most powerful man in France, Lafayette moved, towards the end of October, to protect his authority against enemies on both the right and the left by instituting the system of political justice that would remain in place until his own ascendancy began to fade. Before the creation of this system, "official" revolutionary justice had essentially consisted, as will be seen in chapters 2 and 3, of efforts by the revolutionary authorities to save as many "aristocrats" as possible from being massacred by the revolutionary crowd. But on October 21, in what was, in all likelihood, a co-ordinated operation, the newly arrived National Assembly and the Paris municipal council each took separate action to set up the mechanisms through which the enemies of

14

the revolutionary regime could be legally punished. By that evening, a Fayettist political police (the Comité des Recherches) and a Fayettist political tribunal (the Châtelet) were ready to assume their duties.[5]

Though Lafayette's political abilities are often derided and his early revolutionary prominence is frequently presented as largely accidental or fortuitous,[6] the sophisticated manner in which the complementary activities of the Comité des Recherches and the Châtelet served to enhance the Parisian General's political credit has been heretofore ignored by historians. Dominated, as we will see shortly, by key Lafayette allies and associates, each of these institutions appealed to a fundamentally different political constituency, thereby contributing to the establishment of an always tenuous but at least temporarily workable governing coalition. Thus, the primary function of those who could be called the "left Fayettists" of the Comité des Recherches was to bolster the new regime's standing among radical and popular elements, while the parallel assignment of those who could be called the "right Fayettists" of the Châtelet was to reconcile and reassure conservative and royalist elements. Yet, even as the handling of political justice operated on this essentially strategic level, it also reflected the humanitarian assumptions of the pre-revolutionary judicial reform movement. For the Comité's fire-breathing denunciations of counter-revolutionary "enemies of the People" were launched into a system in which the judges of the Châtelet constituted a veritable "safety net," insuring lenient treatment for those whom the Comité accused. Hence, the inclusionary and conciliatory strategy practiced by the Fayettist regime went hand in hand with and, to a certain extent, might even be seen as being derived from or shaped by its ideological inclinations towards punitive mildness.[7] Moreover, this combination of conciliation and punitive restraint also prevailed in the treatment of radical opposition, though here the Comité des Recherches and the Châtelet reversed roles, with the "left Fayettists" of the Comité acting to obstruct investigations being pursued by Châtelet "right Fayettists."

Through the autumn and winter of 1789–90, the double-edged system of political justice over which Lafayette presided functioned fairly effectively as the Comité and the Châtelet were able to keep their considerable differences under wraps. Thus, for example, though the Comité had pressed hard for the conviction of the Baron

de Besenval, the commander of the royal troops which had surrounded Paris and Versailles during the crisis of July 1789, it was
careful not to criticize publicly the Châtelet's decision to release this
old friend of Marie-Antoinette, thereby lending a certain measure of
legitimacy to what radicals called a "simulated trial."[8] By the spring
of 1790, however, the members of the Comité had begun to edge
away from their collaboration with the Fayettist regime and its
conciliatory policies towards the right. Anxious to preserve their
credentials as "advanced patriots," Brissot and his colleagues
moved to dissolve their implicit partnership with the Châtelet,
thereby depriving Lafayette of an important source of political support on his left and helping to set in motion the political dynamic
which would come to fruition on the Champ-de-Mars in July 1791.
With Comité "left Fayettists" and Châtelet "right Fayettists" publicly denouncing each other through the summer and autumn of
1790, the breakdown of the judicial system instituted by the Parisian
General heralded the impending disintegration of the Fayettist
regime itself.

THE COMITÉ DES RECHERCHES

The Paris Comité des Recherches should not be confused with the
Comité des Recherches created in July 1789 by the National Assembly. While these two committees often worked closely together, a
brief comparison between them will make it clear why the municipal
Comité was by far the more important of the two. For one thing, the
Paris Comité had the advantages of institutional continuity.
Whereas the composition of the national committee changed almost
monthly until the summer of 1790, the membership of the municipal
committee remained the same from October 1789 until December
1790, even staying intact for two months after the replacement of its
discredited parent body by an entirely new municipal council.[9]

More importantly, the duties and powers assigned to the two
committees were vastly different. The Paris Comité was directed to
"receive denunciations and depositions on the plots and conspiracies which could be discovered, to arrest, if necessary, persons who
are denounced, to interrogate them, and to acquire and assemble the
evidence necessary to make a case against them." In contrast, the
decree creating the national Comité made no reference to any police
or prosecutorial powers; instead, this committee was commissioned

to "receive all possible information and opinions on the conspiracies
... that threaten the security of the State and its citizens, and report
this information to the National Assembly, which will then take
appropriate action." As the radical journalist Loustalot, who from
its very inception saw the Paris Comité as a tool of the "municipal
aristocracy" of Lafayette and his mayoral colleague Bailly, observed: "This institution cannot be excused ... simply because its
name is similar to that of the National Assembly's Comité des
Recherches. The latter does not have the power to arrest denounced
persons ... and the appropriate name for it is really Comité
d'Instruction."[10]

Though the wording of legislative decrees does not always indicate future reality, this is one instance in which it did. While the
national committee would continue to function almost exclusively as
an information-gathering panel,[11] the Paris Comité would become
an important administrative agency. Consequently, as just indicated in Loustalot's comment, it was the Paris Comité rather than the
national one that usually found itself the target of intense criticism
from the left and, more frequently, from the right. In a mixture of
political sophism and sincere but exaggerated concern, it was seen as
a blasphemous violation of the Declaration of the Rights of Man, as a
return to the spirit of the Bastille, as a revival of the Old Regime's
police, and as a modern inquisition.[12] Then, when the real Terror
had made the Comité's activities seem like child's play, it was
resurrected by conservative nineteenth-century historians as a
"model for all those revolutionary committees which would soon
cover France with blood and scaffolds" and as a "prototype of all of
the committees of vigilance, surveillance, police, general security,
and public safety."[13] We will find, however, that these rhetorical
flourishes have little value as historical analysis.

THE MEMBERS OF THE COMITÉ

The history of the Paris Comité des Recherches of 1789–90 can, in
many respects, be regarded as an episode in the "pre-history" of the
Girondins of 1791–3. As Gary Kates has recently shown, the origins
of the Girondins can, in large measure, be traced to the early
revolutionary activities of a group of Parisian municipal politicians
who, while continually trying to steer a middle course between
Enlightenment elitism and the direct democracy of the Parisian

districts, constituted a "radical" or "democratic" faction within the generally quite moderate Paris municipal council. With the Comité's two leading members (Brissot and Garran de Coulon) appearing on Kates' list of ten men at the core of this group and with two of the Comité's other four members (Agier and Perron) also apparently having had ties to it, the Comité des Recherches was one of the principal mechanisms through which this "proto-Girondin" group participated in the coalition that governed the capital (and, to a large extent, the nation itself) during the first year of the Revolution.[14]

The son of a relatively prosperous innkeeper from Chartres, Jacques-Pierre Brissot de Warville (1754–93), who would, of course, emerge as the generally acknowledged leader of the Girondins, was clearly the most influential of the Comité's members. With respect to revolutionary justice, Brissot and the Girondins are usually portrayed as heroic martyrs whose commitment to legalism and non-violence put them at a fatal disadvantage in their struggle with the Mountain, or as opportunistic politicians who were just as willing to spill blood as their rivals.[15] Such ambiguity is not surprising, for it mirrors the ambiguous legacy left by Brissot's Comité des Recherches, an institution which operated on the cutting-edge of the tension between the ideals of Enlightenment humanitarianism and the realities of democratic political practice.

An energetic spokesman and organizer for various pre-revolutionary causes, the ubiquitous Brissot had found the prestigious and wealthy Marquis de Lafayette to be a valuable supporter of his anti-slavery Société des Amis des Noirs. In addition, he had enlisted Lafayette's aid for a series of projects relating to the new American republic. Having also been closely associated since about 1785 in the Kornmann group, which combined interest in mesmerism with oppositional political activity, the two men were apparently on fairly good terms and had clearly laid the groundwork for close revolutionary collaboration.[16] Already assuming the stance that he would take *vis-à-vis* the Parisian General during the early Revolution, Brissot attempted, even during the pre-revolutionary period, to prod Lafayette into adopting more radical positions, warning him that "the art of circumspection, the need always to keep one's options open and to avoid possible traps, the desire to have only friends and to caress one's enemies ... all these timid maxims will, in the end, extinguish virtue itself."[17] At the same time, Brissot was enthusiastically promoting "this young and brave Frenchman" as "the hope of our Nation."[18] With public opinion taking on more and more political significance as the end of the eighteenth century approached, Lafayette was in a unique position to translate his celebrity status into potential political influence, and, as Louis Gottschalk notes, he was by no means unaware of the need to create "the correct impression of his share in America's glory." As one of the first publicists to contribute to "the cultivation of the Lafayette legend," Brissot was instrumental in nurturing the popularity that would soon carry the "Hero of Two Worlds" to a position of power.[19]

Moreover, Brissot was also well placed to help Lafayette secure what was to become the structural source of his power, his military control of Paris. During the crisis of July 1789, Brissot was President of the well-to-do Filles-Saint-Thomas District. On July 14, this district passed a decree committing itself to vote for Lafayette as Paris National Guard Commander and to seek support for him from the other districts.[20] As the actual impact of this decree remains veiled in mystery, Gottschalk and Margaret Maddox's description of Brissot as a "prime mover" behind Lafayette's supposedly spontaneous election the next day may be somewhat premature.[21] But whatever its impact, the passage of this decree could only have tightened the pre-revolutionary links between the two men, links which were certainly solidified even further when Brissot's *Patriote français* quickly established itself as one of the leading organs of the Fayettist press, dispensing ample helpings of praise for "our cherished General" and the municipal government which he dominated.[22]

In addition to their long-standing political ties, Lafayette and Brissot also shared a strong interest in judicial reform. During the Assembly of Notables of spring 1787, Lafayette served as a kind of mouthpiece for the reform movement by proposing a comprehensive revision of the "barbarisms" contained in the Criminal Code, and in October 1789 he was apparently the moving spirit behind a National Assembly decree which guaranteed legal counsel for defendants and established public procedures.[23] As his friend Brissot had been one of the leading pre-revolutionary judicial reformers, it seems likely that the future Girondin provided some input on both occasions. Furthermore, with respect to the specific issue of how political opponents should be treated, both men shared an apparent willingness to forgive their enemies. "If we want to be free," Brissot declared on July 21, 1789, "we must be just towards everyone... Since we are the victors, have the generosity to pardon everything." Along the same lines, anticipating that an early completion of the Constitution being prepared by the Assembly would lead to reconciliation with those "conspirators" who had fled France after the fall of the Bastille, Lafayette stated that "this great moment will bring about a general forgiveness of all discord and all parties, and the return of all those who have left."[24]

Given Brissot's solid connections to the Parisian General and his pre-revolutionary reputation as an expert in questions of crime and punishment and given his emergence as one of the most visible members of the Paris municipal council,[25] it is hardly surprising to find him placed in a key position within the political police when the Fayettist regime moved to consolidate its authority following the October Days. However, as a member of the Comité des Recherches, we will find Brissot perpetually torn between his moderate and "philosophic" tendencies and his growing realization that his association with Lafayette was compromising his credentials as an "advanced patriot." Thus, while he functioned as an important component of the Fayettist coalition until the spring of 1790, it is probably best to think of Brissot as a "left Fayettist," continually seeking, as he later explained, "to sustain in [Lafayette] some breaths of Liberty, and to prevent him from succumbing to the seductions of men who had sworn our ruin."[26] But if by the end of the period covered in this study, Brissot had already begun the process which would eventually culminate in a total rupture between the two men, he could never completely erase the memory of his connection with his former friend and ally. For the ultimate failure of the Girondins to secure the support of the Parisian popular movement can, to at least some degree, be traced to the positions of responsibility and authority that Brissot and other "left Fayettists" had held during the period of Lafayette's ascendancy.

In an influential article written in 1968, Robert Darnton depicted Brissot as a pre-revolutionary failure and literary hack who was able to "make it" through a career in the Revolution.[27] While this description may be something of an exaggeration for a man who clearly achieved at least a measure of pre-revolutionary recognition and respectability,[28] Darnton's characterization can certainly be applied

with more accuracy to Comité des Recherches member Jean-
Philippe Garran de Coulon (1748–1816). The son of a provincial tax
collector, Garran had "come to Paris to join a crowd of starving
authors and client-less lawyers."[29] And though he was the author of
no less than forty-three pre-revolutionary literary and philosophical
works (including one entitled *Mes ennuis, ouvrages ennuyeux, dédiés à
l'ennui*), none of them was apparently ever published.[30] But despite
being, as childhood friend and National Assembly deputy Creuzé-
Latouche put it, "almost unknown" before the Revolution, Garran
quickly established himself as an important Parisian activist in the
crucial months of May, June, and July 1789. On April 22, his local
district had only selected him as a supplemental delegate to the
Assembly of Third Estate Electors. Yet, benefitting, in all likelihood,
from his close ties to Creuzé-Latouche (also on Kates' list of leading
"proto-Girondins"), he rapidly attained city-wide recognition and
was almost elected in late May to the Estates-General itself.[31]

It was in the Assembly of Electors that Garran came into his own
as a key member of the municipality's "democratic" faction.[32] Originally convened to elect Paris' Third Estate deputies, this Assembly
continued to meet as the events of June and July unfolded, finally
assuming revolutionary responsibility for the affairs of the capital on
July 13.[33] As one of the leading Electors, we will see Garran playing
an especially significant role on July 14 itself. By the time the Comité
des Recherches was formed in October, he was one of Brissot's most
important allies in the Assemblée des Représentants, the municipal
council which replaced the Electors on July 30.[34]

As the author of most of the reports issued by the Comité on the
various cases with which it became involved, Garran was probably
the one man most closely identified with it in the public mind.
(Though certainly influential behind the scenes, Brissot was better
known during this period as the editor of the *Patriote français*.) Hence,
it was Garran who was largely responsible for the political cover that
the Comité's aggressive public image provided for the indulgent
policies of the Fayettist regime. Aided, no doubt, by his identifi-
cation with the Comité, Garran was the first deputy elected from
Paris to the Legislative Assembly in 1791,[35] and he remained closely
linked to Brissot and his other former colleagues from the municipality through the brief life of that body. In the Convention,
however, being perhaps more keenly attuned to the direction of the
political winds and/or more directly motivated by considerations of

personal survival, he was somehow able to disassociate himself from his old friends. Though sometimes placed on the Mountain and sometimes in the Plain, the *Biographie Universelle* probably came closest to the truth when it said that he "no longer seemed to think about anything except making himself forgotten."[36] Having perfected the ability to adjust to the tides of political fortune, Garran served in the Thermidorian Convention, the Directory's Council of 500, and the Bonapartist Senate. He was also made a Count of the Empire, but when the Bourbons returned, he went into a discreet and reputedly well-heeled retirement.

Of the six members of the Comité des Recherches, the one who had achieved the most pre-revolutionary prominence was Pierre-Louis Lacretelle (1751–1824), the son of a prosperous attorney from Nancy.[37] A successful lawyer and versatile man of letters who, like Brissot, specialized in critiques of the judicial system, Lacretelle was on friendly terms with such luminaries as D'Alembert, Turgot, Malesherbes, and Suard. With this impressive array of references, he was appointed to a 1787 royal commission on criminal law reform that might be seen as a response to Lafayette's initiative at the Assembly of Notables. He was also tied to Necker, and was the author of pro-Necker pamphlets during both the pre-revolutionary and early revolutionary periods.

As will be seen below, Lacretelle quickly recoiled from the "left Fayettist" tilt of the Comité des Recherches, remaining a nominal member but barely participating in its activities. Elected to the Legislative Assembly in 1791, he became one of the most hated of the Feuillants, and when the Monarchy fell, he was proscribed and went into hiding. Resurfacing after the fall of Robespierre, he remained generally aloof from politics until the Restoration, when he attained some recognition as part of the liberal opposition.

In perusing Lacretelle's pre-revolutionary work on judicial reform, it is possible to detect some of the roots of his rapid estrangement from his colleagues on the Comité des Recherches. In contrast to Brissot, Lacretelle opposed democratic denunciation and argued that the abuses this system had produced in Rome could have been avoided if the public prosecutor had been able to censor irresponsible accusations.[38] In addition, while concurring with the demand of most reformers for the abolition of judicial secrecy, he envisioned one result of public trials that was scarcely compatible with the "ideology of pure democracy." "I see the People surrounding the Tribunal of its Magistrates," he wrote, "just as children come to hear the lessons of their father."[39] In this classic defense of "enlightened authority" by one of the last direct disciples of the philosophes, Lacretelle demonstrated the paternalistic inclinations that would lead him to cling to the Constitutional Monarchy even as it became increasingly evident that the People did not want to listen to its "lessons." Perhaps his disillusionment with the Comité des Recherches can be largely attributed to the realization that this revolutionary prosecutor would be taking lessons from the People rather than giving lessons to it.

The son of a Parlement de Paris *procureur*, Pierre-Louis Agier (1748–1823) was a prominent pre-revolutionary lawyer best known for strong Jansenist views.[40] He was a close associate of the influential National Assembly deputy Armand Camus, whose unsuccessful candidacy for Mayor of Paris in summer 1790 would serve as a rallying point for growing "proto-Girondin" dissatisfaction with the municipal administration of Bailly and Lafayette.[41] During the 1780s, Camus and Agier worked together on a massive legal compendium which echoed the standard pre-revolutionary opinion that French criminal law "was always looking for a victim to sacrifice to public tranquillity." And Agier further indicated his adherence to the general precepts of the criminal law reform movement by asserting in 1788 that procedures must be changed in order to "approach the holy and impartial rules of Nature."[42]

As a respected expert on jurisprudence with ties to Camus, Agier was a logical choice for inclusion on the Comité des Recherches and, while he garnered less public recognition than Garran, the Comité seems to have occupied most of his time during the Revolution's first year. In November 1790, he was elected to one of the newly created tribunals in the capital. However, following the insurrection of August 1792, he refused to swear a loyalty oath to the new Montagnard Commune and was forced to withdraw from public life, though he escaped prosecution. After Robespierre's fall, he was reinstated as a judge, eventually presiding over the Thermidorian Revolutionary Tribunal that condemned Fouquier-Tinville. This quick reinstatement and prestigious assignment further suggest "Girondin" or at least "republican" credentials, as Feuillants and other Constitutional Monarchists did not generally return to public service until well into the Directory period.

Agier continued to serve as a judge under all succeeding regimes, ending his career as head of the Royal Appeals Court. Yet, in contrast to Garran, who is usually presented as an unprincipled opportunist, this devout Jansenist had a reputation for great integrity. Still, Agier and Garran did share one distinction which sets them apart from their four colleagues on the Comité des Recherches of 1789–90: they were the only members of the Comité not defined as criminals by at least one post-1789 government.

The least-known member of the Comité des Recherches, Alexandre-César Perron (?–1792) was a Parisian lawyer who quickly established himself as one of the most trusted of the municipal Représentants, having received several important assignments before being appointed to the Comité.[43] Though he never wrote any of its published reports and never appeared in public as a Comité spokesman, Perron seems to have done much of its day-to-day work, or at least his signature is ever present on what remains of its paperwork. After the replacement of the Représentants by a new municipal council in October 1790, he was chosen as an Administrator of Police, a position he would hold for almost two years. In this post, he continued to fulfill the political police functions he had exercised on the Comité.[44]

As Administrator of Police, Perron facilitated preparations for the insurrection of August 1792 by signing orders for the delivery of arms and munitions to the insurgents. Yet, he was regarded with intense suspicion by the new revolutionary Commune, an attitude that indicates that he was (or at least was seen as) an ally of Brissot and the Girondins. On August 21, he was arrested and sent to the Abbaye Prison. Two weeks later, he became one of the victims of the September Prison Massacres.[45]

In contrast to Lacretelle's position to the right of the Comité des Recherches' "proto-Girondin" core, Nicolas Oudart (1750–?), a lawyer from Champagne, was the Comité's most radical member.[46] Though he never manifested any opposition to the Comité's early activities, he seems to have taken a more peripheral role than Garran, Agier, or Perron. However, as will be seen below, he emerged to play a leading part in the Comité's eventual repudiation of the Châtelet in the spring and summer of 1790, a period when the Comité was negotiating a sharp left turn.

Like Agier, Oudart was elected to one of the new Parisian tribunals which began to operate at the end of 1790.[47] But unlike Agier, his judicial career prospered after the establishment of the Republic. In January 1793, the same Parisian electoral assembly that had recently elected an all-Montagnard slate to the Convention chose Oudart to head the capital's central criminal court.[48] Moreover, his presence at the Hôtel-de-Ville on the night of 9 Thermidor also indicates a Robespierrist inclination. After Robespierre's fall, Oudart was harassed by the Thermidorians and then arrested and imprisoned for two months following the Prairial revolt.[49]

Oudart resurfaced as a judge during the Consulate and the Empire, but the return of the Bourbons once again brought about his forced retirement.[50] However, in 1819, an essay on criminal justice by a "M. Oudart" appeared. This essay, which is probably the work of an elderly Nicolas Oudart, spoke at length about the "infamous" and "barbarous" judicial system of the Old Regime and repeated many of the standard humanitarian slogans of the pre-revolutionary reform movement. Yet, M. Oudart also declared that the National Assembly's 1791 judicial reform laws "did not provide sufficient guarantees for insuring public safety," a comment that reminds us that its probable author was not only a member of the generally restrained Comité des Recherches of 1789–90 but also a judge in Paris during the year II.[51]

THE CHÂTELET

The 700-year-old Châtelet de Paris was the principal royal court for the Parisian area and the immediate subordinate of the Parlement de Paris.[52] In putting all *lèse-nation* cases into the hands of this Old Regime tribunal on October 21, 1789, the National Assembly had delivered a powerful and, as it would turn out, a decisive signal of its essential lack of interest in inflicting punishment on the enemies of the Revolution. For while it appeared at the time that the selection of the Châtelet was only a temporary expedient, it would be a full year before the Assembly acted to rescind this crucial decision and even then, as we will see, the deputies took steps to insure that the lenient practices of the Châtelet would continue under the new Haute Cour Nationale created in March 1791. In fact, the Representatives of the Nation appear to have approached the whole question of setting up a *lèse-nation* court with a certain measure of reluctance.

Ever since the fall of the Bastille had triggered the capital's first exposure to popular revolutionary justice, those responsible for maintaining order in Paris had argued that the creation of a *lèse-nation* tribunal was necessary, as Bailly put it, "to prevent the atrocious acts of justice to which a People that has been led astray has been carried." Or as Brissot, already bowing to the imperatives of the revolutionary process, declared: "The people of Paris are dangerous; they must be appeased."[53] On July 22, fearing that the arrest of two particularly hated royal officials, the Paris Intendant Berthier and his father-in-law Foulon, would produce more violence, the Paris Electors demanded that the National Assembly institute a *lèse-nation* court. In the same decree, the Electors, apparently hoping to produce a talismanic effect on a vengeful crowd, ordered that a placard announcing "Prisoners Put Under the Protection of the Nation" be hung on the door of the Abbaye Prison. But neither Foulon nor Berthier ever reached the Abbaye. Before the day was out, both had been seized and massacred.[54]

It was only after this new explosion of popular wrath that the Assembly first agreed to take up the question of a *lèse-nation* tribunal. In the debate which ensued, some deputies associated with the Monarchien faction, a group of influential moderates who had backed the Third Estate through the pre-July 14 crisis but who were already attracting suspicion among "advanced patriots," argued that the existing courts sufficed and reminded the Assembly that the *cahiers* had unanimously opposed tribunals of exception. As the Comte de Virieu declared, a special *lèse-nation* court would "recall the most dreadful abuses of arbitrary power and must not be employed by the defenders of liberty."[55] However, a number of more conservative deputies had no objections to a special tribunal as long as the "proper" people were placed on it. Thus, they proposed a new court composed of judges from the three Parisian Sovereign Courts, the Parlement, the Chambre des Comptes, and the Cour des Aides.[56]

On the other hand, some of the Assembly's "advanced patriots" argued for a special tribunal made up of genuine supporters of the Revolution, asserting that such a panel was necessary "to calm the People's hatred and assure it legal vengeance."[57] In calling for such a "national" tribunal, Anthoine indicated an inclination towards a unitary vision of sovereignty that was destined to become especially prominent during the period of the Jacobin Republic:

Yes, when perverse ministers established, in the King's name, these ephemeral tribunals to give their assassinations an appearance of legality, it was correct to speak out against this odious form, an enemy of Law itself. But here, gentlemen, it is the assembled Nation which exercises the fullness of its power. It is the legislative power ... which momentarily seizes the portion of judicial power which is necessary to maintain order, or rather which constitutes a new judicial power.[58]

Yet, while a number of deputies echoed Anthoine's call for a "national" court, the only specific proposal to that effect was made by a delegate from one of the Paris districts who presented a plan for a tribunal to be composed of sixty "citizen-jurors," one from each of the capital's districts. But the only deputy recorded as having endorsed this proposal was Brissot's close friend and schoolmate from Chartres, Pétion, and indeed the proposal had emanated from Brissot's Filles-Saint-Thomas District.[59]

Finally, there was a motion drafted that day which contained the seeds of the compromise that would emerge three months later, a motion declaring that the Châtelet should take the lead in pursuing all those accused of crimes against the Nation.[60] Thus, the delegation of authority over political justice to the Châtelet, which for reasons that will be discussed shortly was less compromised than the hated Sovereign Courts, was already being seen as a way to bypass these courts without creating a "national" tribunal. But rather than taking any definite action at that time, the Assembly opted for further delay, promising only that a *lèse-nation* court would be created in the near future.[61]

However, the authorities in Paris, who were always more responsive to popular unrest than the Assembly, were not at all happy with this decision. As Brissot put it: "It is not with promises that one stops the fury of the People ... Perhaps blood will again flow illegally if this Tribunal is not instituted."[62] On July 31, September 3, and September 30, an exasperated Assemblée des Représentants sent delegations to the National Assembly to ask for the creation of a *lèse-nation* court.[63] But the question was not taken up again until after severed heads had once again been paraded on pikes.

The immediate context surrounding the resumption of discussion on a *lèse-nation* tribunal in mid-October was the impending October 19 transfer of the National Assembly from Versailles to Paris, a transfer which provided tangible confirmation of Lafayette's newly strengthened hold on the threads of national political power. With the Assembly preparing to follow the royal family into the Parisian General's bailiwick, the deputies seem to have acquired a suddenly heightened appreciation of the need to heed the requests of municipal officials. On October 10, speaking in the name of the Assemblée des Représentants, Brissot, who was about to take up his duties with the Comité des Recherches, assured the skittish deputies that order would be maintained in Paris and, at the same time, focused their attention on the explosive quality of the momentous recent events: "The storm is far from us, this storm which threatened to crush the capital and France itself. It has passed as a flash of lightning and it has vanished just as quickly... Forget this moment of delirium, there will be no more of them."[64] However, the ability of the Fayettist municipal regime to make good such a promise rested, to a large degree, on the fulfillment of its call for the establishment of a tribunal that could help discourage both counter-revolutionary and radical activity.

Thus, whereas the Assembly had ignored all the municipality's previous demands, it finally declared on October 14 that the Châtelet would handle preliminary proceedings in all *lèse-nation* cases,[65] and, as noted above, it authorized this court to judge these cases one week later. Compared to the relatively extended debate of July 23, the debates of October 14 and 21 were extremely limited and, one senses, almost perfunctory. For it seems likely that Lafayette had let it be known that he wanted political justice to be in the hands of the Châtelet, a tribunal with whose leaders he had, as we will see shortly, already established close relations. Hence, one of the few deputies recorded as speaking against the decrees of October 14 and 21 was one of Lafayette's leading rivals Mirabeau, who, whether attacking from the left or the right, consistently opposed the Parisian General through the first two years of the Revolution. And appropriately enough, Mirabeau's comments on October 21 contained a judicious mixture of radical and royalist rhetoric, an ambiguity which reflected his simultaneous flirtation at that time with both the Duc d'Orléans and the King's brother, the Comte de Provence.[66]

However, there was no such ambiguity in the October 21 remarks of a still relatively unknown deputy from Arras who had been demanding vigorous action against the enemies of the Revolution since July: "We must take measures to choke the conspiracy which threatens us. We cannot allow the Attorney-General of the Châtelet to assume the function of Attorney-General of the Nation. Only the representatives of the Nation or the Nation itself can judge this type of crime."[67] But, like all of Robespierre's early interventions, this call to "étouffer la conjuration" was better appreciated outside the Assembly than by the deputies themselves.[68] Apart from Mirabeau and Robespierre, opposition to the Châtelet was almost non-existent, and even the "advanced patriots" of the Duport–Barnave–Lameth faction adhered to the consensus which had formed in its favor. "This dignified and virtuous tribunal," said Duport, "already has all the attributes necessary to win the People's confidence."[69]

Though less enthusiastic than Duport, most patriotic journalists expressed satisfaction that the Assembly had at last established some form of legal mechanism for trying and judging *lèse-nation* suspects. As the future Girondin Carra put it: "We must certainly hope that impartial justice will finally take action against these culprits without the Court's favor being able to save them." Or as the more radical Loustalot observed: "It was not possible to make a worse choice . . . Yet, it is better to have venal judges who are used to practicing the ambidextrous maneuvers of the old judicial order than not to have any judges at all." Only a fugitive Marat, who was, as we will see in chapter 4, already being pursued by the Châtelet in its capacity as an ordinary criminal court, was unwilling to take at least a "wait-and-see" attitude towards the new *lèse-nation* tribunal. "The Assembly," he declared, "has delivered the friends of Liberty and the People, hands and feet bound, to the creatures of the Parlement and the Court. What hope can there be now for good patriots!"[70]

As for the Parisian districts, which had already established themselves as a point of access for a more democratically oriented style of politics, the historian Georges Garrigues asserted that "assigning the task of judging political crimes to a tribunal as discredited as the Châtelet awakened many suspicions in the districts, suspicions which were soon manifested."[71] However, the only evidence provided for this statement was two district decrees demanding that the Châtelet judges swear an oath of loyalty to the Nation. While the districts would certainly play an important role in the Châtelet's eventual downfall a year later, two mildly suspicious decrees do not add up to "many suspicions" and it appears that Garrigues exaggerated the amount of initial grass-roots opposition to the Assembly's decision. It would not be long, to be sure, before the Châtelet came to be known as the "Queen's wash-house."[72] But for the moment at least, it appears that most district activists were willing to lend an ear to the soothing and optimistic words of one anonymous pamphleteer: "The Châtelet [is] always a stranger to intrigues, cabals, and sundry interests, and it always does its duty ... It will examine the crimes and the evidence; and sure that the Law will avenge us of real crimes, we will put our trust in it, and not look for imaginary ones."[73]

THE LEADERS OF THE CHÂTELET

On July 13, 1789, three prominent Parisian magistrates, Talon, Sémonville, and Boucher d'Argis, came to the Hôtel-de-Ville to join the Assembly of Electors. In thereby giving their blessing to what amounted to a revolutionary municipal government, these Old Regime officials had essentially committed an act of rebellion. It is true, as will be seen in the next chapter, that the actual physical dangers faced by the Electors had been greatly diminished by the retreat the previous evening of most of the royal troops within Paris. But if the Court had somehow managed to regain control of the situation, these judges would certainly have been quite badly compromised. As Bailly put it, in a statement that would ring even truer if they had acted a day earlier, "it was beautiful to have them arrive at the moment of peril."[74]

Of the three rebellious magistrates, the only one attached to the Châtelet at that time was Boucher d'Argis. Both Talon and his close friend Sémonville were then Parlement de Paris judges. However, the patriotic credentials earned by these men on July 13 must be seen as a key factor in determining the eventual designation of the Châtelet as the Revolution's first political tribunal. For on September 30, 1789, Talon was appointed as head of the Châtelet.[75] And when he resigned in June 1790, he was succeeded by Boucher d'Argis, who led it until its dissolution in January 1791.[76]

Though Antoine-Omer Talon (1760–1811) belonged to one of the most powerful parlementary families in France, his judicial career had stalled in the decade preceding the Revolution. Having been

promised the important post of Avocat-Général au Parlement, he
found himself passed over three times in favor of rivals with more
influential patrons. In compensation for these disappointments, he
was informed in 1786 that he would succeed the 71-year-old Angran
d'Alleray as Châtelet lieutenant-civil.[77] On July 13, 1789, the very
day he joined the Paris Electors, Talon wrote to the Minister of
Justice Barentin to remind him that he (Talon) was still awaiting
"His Majesty's kindness when the occasion presents itself."[78] Could
Talon have been hedging his bets? Or might he have been calculat-
ing that a victory by the insurgents would hasten Angran's departure without endangering the judicial institutions themselves?

In any event, Angran finally left his post on September 6. According to two of his fellow magistrates, he resigned because he didn't
want to have anything to do with the Châtelet's impending responsibility for political justice.[79] It seems more likely, however, that the
Châtelet's selection as *lèse-nation* court was itself contingent on the
more or less forced resignation of Angran and the accession of the
more politically reliable Talon. As Angran's designated successor,
Talon could be moved to the Châtelet without creating the appearance of an undue disturbance of the normal procedures of judicial
appointment. At the same time, it is clear that patriotic support
could never have crystallized around the Châtelet until someone
with at least some degree of revolutionary credibility had become its
leader.

Moreover, Talon's political standing in the post-October Days
period was based on more than the general commitment that he had
made to the patriot cause during the July crisis. For even as the
Assembly was preparing to delegate *lèse-nation* cases to the Châtelet,
Talon and his inseparable partner Sémonville were already serving
as Lafayette's principal agents in a complicated and ultimately futile
effort to construct an alliance with the ever present Mirabeau.[80] In
fact, Talon and Sémonville carried out important though unspecified behind-the-scenes assignments for the Parisian General through
most of the first year of the Revolution and, as Mirabeau's friend
LaMarck later wrote, "they added greatly to [Lafayette's] authority
through their maneuvers."[81] However, in October 1790, with Lafayette's influence now waning, the versatile duo deserted him and
offered their services to Mirabeau, who by this time was firmly
established as an adviser to the royal family. Though he detested
Talon and Sémonville, Mirabeau respected and feared their political

talents and, as part of an elaborate and idiosyncratic counter-revolutionary scheme, recommended that they head an "atelier de police" which would co-ordinate all secret royalist activity in the capital. Explaining why it was necessary to employ such notorious "intriguers," LaMarck reminded Marie-Antoinette that Talon had already performed similar duties for Lafayette: "We will find he has ways of getting things done in Paris that cannot be matched by anyone else. Thus, I believe it is almost impossible to do without him."[82]

Although Mirabeau never had the Court's full confidence, the "atelier de police" was established, and shortly before the insurrection of August 1792, Talon informed Louis XVI that "the enterprise that I formed has remained hidden and impenetrable and has left Your Majesties with a kind of little army in Paris still ready to act in your interest."[83] When the Monarchy fell, Talon fled to America. He returned to France in the late 1790s, but was arrested as a royalist conspirator in 1803 and transported to the island of Saint-Marguerite, where he reportedly went mad.[84]

In contrast to Talon, whose flair for political intrigue seems to have been largely devoid of any concern with ideas, André-Jean Boucher d'Argis (1751–94) was yet another French revolutionary philosopher-politician. In fact, he was a second-generation *philosophe*, as his father had written many of the legal articles in Diderot's *Encyclopédie*.[85] Also in contrast to Talon, Boucher d'Argis did not belong to a prominent *noblesse de robe* family. In this, however, he was quite typical of the Châtelet's judges, most of whom seem to have come from either bourgeois or recently ennobled families, another consideration which probably helped make the Châtelet appear more palatable as a potential *lèse-nation* court.[86] As one former magistrate recalled: "Châtelet judges, who came from a less elevated social class than Sovereign Court magistrates, generally had less antipathy for the Revolution."[87]

During the pre-revolutionary period, Boucher d'Argis had built a solid reputation as the most progressive and "enlightened" of the Châtelet's magistrates. A well-known publicist for criminal law reform, he was also the founder and moving spirit of L'Association de Bienfaisance Judiciaire, a philanthropic society which provided legal counsel to indigents and compensation to acquitted defendants.[88] In seeking official recognition from the Estates-General in

May 1789, this group relied on the influence of its most celebrated member, the Marquis de Lafayette, whose sustained backing for the principle of guaranteed legal defense would finally bear fruit in the National Assembly reforms passed that October.[89]

As will be seen below, Boucher d'Argis was the presiding judge in the Revolution's first major political trial, the trial of the royal military commander Besenval. He was also a central figure in the judicial attack mounted against Marat in the autumn and winter of 1789–90. In March 1790, he was named Châtelet second-in-command, and, as already noted, he succeeded Talon as Châtelet head in June. Can these important assignments and promotions be attributed to Boucher d'Argis' position in the Châtelet's pre-revolutionary hierarchy? While this is certainly possible, it seems more reasonable to ascribe them to his patriotic credentials and political connections. In addition to his co-operation with the Paris Electors, Boucher d'Argis' close ties with the municipal authorities are also indicated by the fact that he served as a Battalion Commander in Lafayette's National Guard.[90] With Boucher d'Argis playing a key role, the Châtelet acted as the judicial arm of the Fayettist regime until the point when its leniency towards counter-revolutionaries had so totally undermined its political credit that the Parisian General had to accept its repudiation.

Extremely unpopular due to his recent high visibility at the Châtelet, Boucher d'Argis was resoundingly defeated at the end of 1790 in the elections to the new tribunals established by the National Assembly.[91] Instead, he returned to one of his earlier preoccupations and became a kind of self-appointed "public defender." He also remained active in local politics, and was president of the conservative Fraternité section as late as May 1793. However, with the triumph of the Mountain and of his old enemy Marat, his proscription was virtually inevitable. Having been arrested as "one of the chiefs of the federalist faction" and having been brought to trial after the passage of the Draconian law of 22 Prairial, this late eighteenth-century champion of the right to legal counsel went to his death without being allowed to defend himself.[92]

As a pre-revolutionary judicial publicist, Boucher d'Argis, presenting himself as a "humane judge" who trembled at the very thought of the "excess of cruelty" contained in the Criminal Code, echoed many of the standard themes of the reform movement, especially those relating to the need to provide legal guarantees to defendants.[93] Moreover, in November 1788, he persuaded the Châtelet to appoint a committee to suggest ways of establishing fairer criminal procedures and a system of proportional punishments, a step which undoubtedly further improved the Châtelet's image in enlightened circles.[94] However, there was one part of the pre-revolutionary consensus on judicial reform to which Boucher d'Argis did not subscribe: its insistence on the need for public proceedings. Instead, he saw open courtrooms as "tumultuous tribunals where reason does not always preside" and where "a man who might be unjustly accused would be exposed to public scorn." In comparison to Lacretelle, who foresaw nice little children coming for their civics lessons, Boucher d'Argis had a far more prophetic vision of how public trials would actually unfold: "We would see the Temple of Justice become each day a murderous arena, with the Magistrates themselves forced to descend from their Tribunal to defend their lives and their edicts."[95] Though written in 1781, this passage could easily serve as a description of the atmosphere surrounding the first major political trial held after the establishment of public judicial proceedings. This trial was the Besenval trial, and, as we have seen, its Presiding Magistrate was Boucher d'Argis himself.

2

The judicial aftermath of the July Revolution

With Comité des Recherches prosecutors and Châtelet judges now finally in place, the new Fayettist system of political justice was immediately confronted with an important piece of unfinished business left over from the previous summer. For by putting off the creation of a *lèse-nation* tribunal until after the October Days, the National Assembly had, in effect, been suspending judgment on the "aristocratic conspiracy" that had provoked the Paris Revolution of July 12–14. In the next two chapters, I will look into the controversies that developed after July 14 around the question of whether the defeated "conspirators" should be punished by the victorious revolutionaries, controversies that would be inherited by the Châtelet and the Comité. In doing so, I will pay particular attention to the case of the Swiss-born military commander Pierre-Victor-Joseph Baron de Besenval (1721–91), who, for reasons that will soon be made clear, would be the only major "July conspirator" actually put on trial. In examining the Besenval case and a group of associated cases, I will trace the emergence of a dialogue between two competing conceptions of revolutionary justice: a conciliatory and indulgent justice that reflected the humanitarian assumptions of the pre-revolutionary judicial reform movement, and a repressive and punitive justice that would become increasingly dominant as the Revolution unfolded. However, before turning to this dialogue, let us briefly explore a parallel dialogue that had been carried on within court circles prior to the July Revolution. For pre-July 14 royal justice was, in many ways, a mirror image of post-July 14 revolutionary justice.

THE JULY CONSPIRACY: MYTHS AND REALITIES

From the opening of the Estates-General until the point at which it had lost whatever punitive powers it might once have possessed, the

Court was continually torn between a policy of repression and a policy of accommodation. On the one hand, a powerful faction led by the Comte d'Artois (the younger of the King's two brothers) and perhaps also by Marie-Antoinette attempted to convince Louis XVI to take drastic military and judicial measures to preserve royal authority.[1] According to a July 9 diplomatic dispatch, the parlementary militant d'Eprémesnil, who had drawn close to Artois during this period, had designed a plan to "break up the Estates-General, arrest its most outspoken members, and send them, along with M. Necker, to the Parlement so they could all be tried and executed as criminals guilty of high treason."[2] Moreover, if we are to believe the Duc des Cars, one of Artois' closest associates, this type of plan was more than a hypothetical project being pushed by isolated extremists. For according to des Cars, Artois himself was the sponsor of a proposal to arrest the most rebellious of the deputies and "send them to the Parlement which will be sure to make quick work of them."[3] In addition, a dispatch from the Austrian Ambassador Mercy-Argenteau reported a "crazy idea proposed by M. le Comte d'Artois" to have Necker arrested, a report which is especially credible because Mercy was Marie-Antoinette's most trusted political adviser.[4] And while it is true that it is a long way from the arrest of Necker to the batch of executions envisioned by d'Eprémesnil, even that one arrest would have been the first arrest of a minister since the days of Louis XIV.

Although none of these projects of judicial repression was ever implemented, the hardline faction did persuade the King to assemble some 30,000–40,000 troops and to place them under the command of the Baron de Besenval, an old friend of both Artois and the Queen.[5] What did Louis XVI intend to do with these troops? That is something we will probably never know with any certainty, for as the historian who has studied this problem most closely put it: "The plan of counter-revolution, if there really was one, was elaborated behind closed doors, and compromising indiscretions appear to have been avoided."[6] Furthermore, according to an often cited remark of Necker, the King himself may not have been totally aware of why he had been asked to summon the troops: "There were secrets and there were secrets behind the secrets, and I believe that the King himself did not know everything. Perhaps they intended, according to developing circumstances, to lead the Monarch to measures which they had not yet dared to speak to him about."[7] Yet, whatever the ultimate aim, the assembling of such a force is not, to say the least, the way one goes about pursuing a policy of conciliation. If not explicitly designed for repression, this "petite armée" was, at the very minimum, designed for intimidation. Moreover, as will be seen shortly, the fear of what the troops might do soon proved to be more important than what they actually did. If there were approved plans to use them against Paris and the National Assembly, these plans were short-circuited by the insurrection of July 12–14.

As for the conciliatory response to the belligerent position emanating from the Artois faction, it can be found in the accommodationist strategy of Necker and in Louis XVI's unwillingness to be responsible for bloodshed. Regarding Necker, we will soon see him trying to persuade the victorious revolutionaries that Besenval and other defenders of the traditional monarchy were not traitors. But before July 14, with the shoe of authority still resting precariously on the other foot, his role was to attempt to convince the King that the Third Estate deputies were not rebels. Thus, des Cars explained how, at some point before Necker's July 11 dismissal, the Minister was able to force a "pale and disfigured" Artois to concede at least temporary defeat: "I told the King everything; I begged and conjured him, but the cursed Genevan [Necker] was opposed to it all. He has the gall to assure us that the intentions of the Jeu de Paume are pure and that the Third Estate is totally loyal to the King."[8]

Regarding Louis XVI, his unwillingness to "unsheathe the sword against his subjects" is legendary and is simply taken for granted by most historians of the period. Pierre Caron, for example, wrote that: "They were able to get him to approve the calling of the troops ... and the dismissal of Necker, but they despaired at ever being able to get him to accept the idea of force and bloodshed." Or as Emmanuel Vingtrinier put it: "The King did not want to have recourse to violence. He pushed away all proposals of this nature with horror."[9] And while one might be inclined to be skeptical about such seemingly formulaic claims, they are supported by both specific contemporary reports and by general comments on the King's personality. Perhaps the most striking example from the first category is Necker's already cited remark that the Artois faction did not "dare" to speak to Louis about their true intentions. In addition, after speaking with the hardline Prince de Condé, the Saxon Ambassador noted that "despite the arrival of the troops, I realized they had little hope of striking the blow they desired. They seemed convinced that what they called the King's lack of firmness would prevent them from doing what they wished."[10]

As for Louis' personality, Marie-Antoinette's First Lady-in-Waiting noted that the King "from the very beginning of the Revolution had shown in every crisis the fear he entertained of giving any order which might cause the effusion of blood." And Madame de Staël, another friendly but more balanced witness, wrote that Louis XVI was "religiously scrupulous about not exposing the lives of Frenchmen for his own personal defense." Moreover, the magistrate Sallier, a much less friendly but for that very reason perhaps an especially credible source, stated: "He never accepted the idea that he was supposed to fulfill the duties of a King. Hence, he was courageous about accepting humiliation. Covering his cowardice with the veil of humanity, it pleased him to say, 'I do not want a single man to perish for my sake'."[11]

Given that nearly every faction or political group had its own reasons for wanting to promote the image of a feeble but humane king, it is difficult to separate legend from fact on this issue. But short of embarking on a detailed study of his personality, I believe that the best evidence that a non-violent strain in Louis XVI's character did indeed influence the course of events in the summer of 1789 can be found in the events themselves. For despite heavy pressure from the Artois camp, the King never did unsheathe his sword. Apart from some minor skirmishing on July 12, the assembled troops were never employed and no judicial repression was ever attempted.[12] It is true that almost half of the regiments ordered to Paris were still on the march on July 12, and it might be argued that the "conspirators" were preparing to strike only to have their plans interrupted by the uprising in the capital.[13] Yet, there was a considerable number of troops available when the Paris Insurrection broke out and the fact remains that next to nothing was done with them. In fact, most of the troops in the capital were actually withdrawn on the night of July 12.[14] As Georges Lefebvre wrote: "Since 1789, there have been political parties with a much stronger organization than the patriots of that time, but none has ever met with as little resistance on the part of a government."[15]

Still, one might argue that, rather than being rooted in humanitarian considerations, the lack of resistance of July 1789 can actually be explained by apprehensions regarding troop loyalty.[16] But while this factor undoubtedly had some impact in generating the final failure to act, it also seems reasonable to assume that it could not have been entirely accidental that this virtual abdication by a "pacifist-king" who was jealous of his authority but who would not fight to preserve it took place at the tail-end of the civilized and refined eighteenth century.[17] Or to put it another way, the same currents of *sensibilité* and *humanité* which contributed to the development of the pre-revolutionary judicial reform movement also seem to have influenced Louis XVI. Thus, just as early revolutionary judicial indulgence may be traced to the sentimental rather than to the rationalistic aspects of late eighteenth-century judicial thought, Cornwall Rogers has argued that the King's resistance was sapped by his susceptibility to the sentimental rather than to the rationalistic facets of late eighteenth-century culture:

While Louis partially abandoned the Enlightenment on its analytical or more rational side, he became progressively a product of the emotional or sentimental impulses of the movement. Indeed, certain of his traits which are traditionally pictured as personal, and hence purely individual, may, it seems to me, be understood as an expression of that vast system of feeling that undermined the intellectual and social conventions of the old regime.[18]

Moreover, given Louis' pacifist tendencies, concerns about troop loyalty and unwillingness to shed blood can be seen as interconnected rather than as mutually exclusive factors. On a practical level, the lack of decisive action early in the crisis provided time for any already existing tendencies towards disaffection to become more pronounced, with reports and rumors regarding the King's hesitations serving to encourage and solidify the notion that the troops should not fire upon the People. If Artois' faction finally did succeed in overcoming the King's scruples in early July, it may by then have been too late. Beyond this, there is the question of perceived versus actual disaffection. According to Samuel Scott, the officers in the field seem to have greatly underestimated the potential loyalty of the troops.[19] Since confidence is a very delicate psychological mechanism, these harried officers, shaken by an awareness that the King's support for their endeavors was only lukewarm, could easily have exaggerated the degree of disaffection in the ranks. In addition, the King's own confidence in his troops was probably undermined by his less than wholehearted commitment to the repressive purposes for which they had presumably been summoned. As any loyal reader of modern psychological "self-help" manuals knows, the absence of belief in the validity of one's purpose is hardly conducive to confidence in one's ability to accomplish that purpose.

In any event, though some combination of humanitarian scruples and anxiety about troop disloyalty would ultimately prevent the Court from actively pursuing a repressive policy, the "patriots" watching the military build-up around Paris and Versailles did not have the benefit of this information. On the contrary, they feared and expected some kind of attack, especially after the King finally sent Necker into exile on July 11 and asked the hardline Baron de Breteuil to form a new ministry. With respect to the National Assembly, rumors of the Court's plans ran the gamut from simple dissolution to various forms of massacre. Among the latter, some unnamed deputies believed that plans had been made "to point cannon at the hall of the Estates-General, to have the troops enter and slaughter almost 200 deputies, and then force those that remained either to disperse or to do as they are told."[20] Even more extreme were rumors that cannon were going to bombard the Assembly or that the Assembly was going to be mined.[21] As for Paris, weeks of rumors regarding an impending attack came to a climax on July 14 with a feverish series of reports at the Hôtel-de-Ville that troops were going into action. At 7 a.m., for example, it was announced that a massacre had already taken place in the Faubourg Saint-Antoine and that "everyone there has been slaughtered, regardless of age or sex."[22] Then, after all these alarms had been proven false, rumors continued to circulate that an attack *had* been planned, and one of the first journalists to put these rumors into printed form was future Comité des Recherches member Brissot, who was already focusing on the need to "shed some light on the trials which will no doubt take place."[23]

On August 5, Brissot's *Patriote français* published the text of a plan for an attack on Paris that was to have been carried out on the night of July 14, an attack in which the entire city was to have been bombarded by cannon from the heights of Montmartre and "riddled by fire and blood." But having warned only one week earlier that "turbulent or credulous souls are still spreading false alarms," Brissot was anxious not to create the impression that he was himself guilty of such "rumor-mongering." Thus, his presentation of the text of this plan was laced with a string of qualifications: "It *appears* certain there was a plan for attacking Paris;" "it is my duty to gather all the facts which *could* have *some* authenticity;" and rather apologetically, "we admit, in reporting this plan, that we do not have the courage to believe in its existence."[24]

For what, however, is he apologizing? For publishing something he did not believe to be true, or for not believing? Despite all the epistemological scruples expressed by this would-be *philosophe* and author of a book called *De la vérité*,[25] it "appears certain" that the main effect and indeed the very purpose of publishing the text of the supposed attack plan was to propagate and encourage belief in the existence of a horrible and barbaric conspiracy against the capital. For how many of Brissot's readers would have noticed that the phrase "it appears certain there was a plan for attacking Paris" referred only to the existence of *some* plan, not to those hair-raising details of the published plan which were sure to cause the most sensation? How many readers, for that matter, would have noticed any of the qualifications, to say nothing of those who had only heard of the plan's terrible details via word-of-mouth circulation? Beyond all the qualification, the August 5 *Patriote français* represents a hesitant early attempt by Brissot to present himself as a true revolutionary journalist, disseminating popular rumors, encouraging popular fears, and denouncing popular enemies.

Combined with his call the previous day for a district-based *lèse-nation* tribunal,[26] Brissot's report on the Paris attack plan helped to establish him as one of the leaders in the campaign to prosecute and convict Besenval, the commander of the troops that would have carried out the supposed assault. Thus, this report also included the text of an intercepted and already notorious order sent by Besenval to the Governor of the Bastille on July 14: "M. de Launay will defend himself until the last extremity; I have provided him with sufficient forces." The juxtaposition of this quite genuine order with the more dubious text of the attack plan appears to have been designed to help the reader associate Besenval with the bloody details of the supposed plan. Furthermore, few readers would have payed much attention to Brissot's scrupulous use of the conditional in his conclusion: "[Such a plan] would suppose the soul of a Nero in the monsters who would have conceived it, and no punishment would be sufficient to expiate their crime."[27] As will be seen in more detail in the next chapter, the events surrounding the arrest and detention of Besenval, who was at that moment the only possible "monster" available for punishment, had already led Brissot to back away from his recommendation of two weeks earlier that the defeated agents of monarchical power be pardoned.[28]

The attack plan published by Brissot was also printed, with almost identical wording, in at least two other places and was widely circulated all through the capital.[29] However, though it is probable that some kind of action against Paris was in the works (perhaps the arrest of some Electors and some Palais-Royal agitators), it is inconceivable that the King had approved anything even remotely resembling this plan. Though it might be argued that the published plan was only someone's proposal, what is most suspicious about it is the supposed date of the planned attack, the night of July 14. If, as is often asserted, the Court was awaiting the arrival of all the summoned troops, it could not have struck on that night. It would, instead, have had to wait until at least July 16.[30] But the night of July 14 is exactly the date one would use if one wanted to concoct a scenario to help solidify the already emerging consensus that only the timely uprising of July 14 had prevented the "aristocratic plot" from swinging into operation. While it might still be argued that the published plan had been proposed by an underling unaware of the details of the troop movements, it seems more likely that it was a fake or, at the very least, that someone had affixed a fraudulent date to a real proposal. Though Georges Lefebvre's emphasis on the spontaneous nature of rumor transmission during the summer of 1789 may remain generally well founded,[31] here is one case in which the conscious manipulation of information seems to have played an important role.

Confronted with the appearance that the Court was going to act against Paris and the Assembly, the supporters of the Revolution reacted with a combination of legitimate anxiety and exaggerated fear, anxiety and fear that was partly spontaneous and partly manipulated. But the manner in which supporters of the Monarchy viewed the designs of the revolutionaries was remarkably similar. For here too we find a core of realistic anxiety fueled by the threats of patriotic analogues of extremists like Artois and d'Eprémesnil, along with an uncontrolled growth of layers of exaggerated fear that was to some extent the product of conscious manipulation.

As early as mid-June 1789, the political scene was inundated with threats and rumors of systematic proscriptions and massacres of "traitors." The Monarchien leader Mounier, for example, reported that "they made a list of all those who voted against the abbé Sieyès' motion [that the Third Estate call itself the National Assembly] and they circulated this list throughout Paris. Everyone named there found himself represented as a traitor." And a June 28 letter from the conservative deputy Ferrières was even more explicit: "They speak openly at the Palais-Royal of massacring us. Our houses were marked for assassination, and my door had a black 'P' on it."[32]

While such threats and accusations were obviously hardly conducive to the development of a liberal and pluralistic political system, it must be noted that, like the royal army which served to intimidate but which was never used, none of the early revolutionary threats against conservative and moderate deputies was ever carried out. Moreover, even those popular massacres that did occur during the Revolution's early stages were quite limited in number and more or less spontaneous in nature.[33] But this did not prevent so-called "moderate" politicians from trying to exploit the fear of horrors worse than those that were actually going to occur during the Terror and analogous to the worst projects attributed to the Court. Thus, in a typical version of the standard Monarchien assertion that their parliamentary defeats resulted from "mob intimidation," Lally-Tolendal inadvertently revealed his own political strategy in describing what was purportedly the strategy of his opponents: "It was always to remind the deputies of the idea of danger, always to show them, just as they voted, the sword hanging over their heads."[34]

This climate of mutual fear and mutual exaggeration, a climate which permits us to speak of anti-popular as well as popular demagoguery, must always be kept in mind as we turn now to the dispensing of revolutionary justice itself. But while the pressures that would eventually produce systematic violence and judicial terror can be observed very early on, we will see that late eighteenth-century tendencies towards more civilized and more restrained behavior also came into play, thereby helping to insure that these pressures would, for a surprisingly long period of time, be kept largely under control.

GARRAN DE COULON AND THE FOURTEENTH OF JULY

Anticipating the tendency of modern historians to emphasize the symbolic rather than the real importance of the fall of the Bastille, the nineteenth-century poet-historian Lamartine saw the virtually empty old prison as a metaphor for an already dead Old Regime: "The cells, the dungeons, the carcans, and the chains were all nothing more than the outdated vestiges of mysteries, tortures, and burial places which themselves enclosed nothing more than memories."[35] Yet, for the actors themselves, for victors and vanquished alike, each unaware of the insignificance of mere *événements* in the face of "historical continuities" and the "longue durée," the fourteenth of July marked the turning point of history. And for the student of political justice, July 14, whatever other significance it may or may not have had, marks the day on which the identity of those who feared being punished and those responsible for doing the punishing abruptly switched, the day on which the leaders of the National Assembly were converted from potential victims of royal justice into the final arbiters of what would now be thought of as "revolutionary justice."

Just one day before this abrupt switch occurred, the Assembly had registered its protest against the newly installed Breteuil ministry by declaring that "the ministers and civil and military agents of the government are responsible for all actions contrary to the rights of the Nation and to the decrees of this Assembly."[36] Suddenly enforceable the next day, this decree would become the legal basis for the prosecution of Besenval and some of his fellow "July conspirators." But decree or no decree, legality or no legality, the ill-fated "ministry of thirty-six hours" and all the other presumed leaders of the Artois faction knew they were in danger and quickly decided their only safety lay in flight. Led by Artois himself, the roads leading out of Paris and Versailles were soon filled with what was to become the first wave of French revolutionary *émigrés*.[37]

As we will see shortly, the vast majority of these high-ranking fugitives were able to escape, and the reason that so much attention became focused on Besenval was that he was the most prominent of those unable to do so. However, there were other "conspirators" who also failed to escape, and one of these was the Paris Prévôt des Marchands, Jacques de Flesselles, who had been entangled in a tense relationship with the Assembly of Electors since late April.[38] On July 13 and 14, this tension came to a boiling point when Flesselles, after finally agreeing to work with the Electors, sent several delegations on what seem to have been diversionary searches for nonexistent weapons.[39] Following all these wild-goose chases, this royal official's own goose was cooked on July 14 by rumors that an incriminating note from him had been found in the possession of the massacred Bastille Governor de Launay: "I amuse the Parisians with ribbons and promises. Hold out until evening. You will be reinforced."[40] Chased from the Hôtel-de-Ville, Flesselles was shot to death just outside, and his head was paraded in the streets with de Launay's as one of the two main trophies of the day.

For our purposes in this study, the most significant aspect of the Flesselles affair is the part played in it by future Comité des Recherches member Garran de Coulon. Here, for example, is an early nineteenth-century account from the anti-revolutionary *Biographie Universelle*, an account which, in its essential points, is repeated in several other sources of varying political persuasions:

Garran got himself noticed at the July 14 Electors' meeting by a vehement reprimand of Flesselles, who presided. "You have betrayed your country," he said furiously, "your country abandons you." And the unfortunate Flesselles, frightened and losing his composure, left his place and threw himself into the middle of the populace, which assassinated him.[41]

Not content, however, with a version which restricted Garran's role to this final and seemingly spontaneous act of the Flesselles drama, the turn-of-the-century historian Gustave Bord added a new twist to the Garran–Flesselles story. Discussing one of the earlier diversionary weapon searches, Bord appears to have gratuitously added Garran's name to a passage from the *Procès-verbal des Electeurs* which described a group of unnamed Electors angrily denouncing Flesselles.[42] Moreover, Bord performed a similar cut-and-paste operation in a discussion of the Electors' July 20 order that the just-arrested Paris Intendant Berthier be brought to the capital, a move which led to Berthier's death two days later and which, in Bord's view, had been planned for that very purpose. Here again, Bord took a passage from the *Procès-verbal* in which unnamed Electors were angrily attacking a royal official and, seemingly without any evidence, deftly inserted Garran's name.[43]

But there was method to this apparent methodological madness. Eager to demonstrate that all of the violent eruptions of summer 1789 were part of a carefully orchestrated Masonic plot and equally eager to connect the Comité des Recherches to this plot, Bord was trying to persuade his readers that Garran, the author of the Comité's published brief against those servants of the Monarchy who had escaped the July violence, was a "point man" in a well-planned effort to eliminate a host of top royal officials.[44] For, having helped dispose of Flesselles and Berthier, Garran's next assignment, in Bord's eyes, was to engineer the judicial assassination of Besenval:

> At each event, he launches the word or phrase which compromises the man in the hot seat... Garran de Coulon was certainly partly responsible for the assassinations of the Prévôt des Marchands and the Intendant de Paris, and now he is given the task of rendering a legal opinion on the question of whether those in authority in July were guilty.[45]

By adding his "evidence" linking Garran to the Flesselles and Berthier assassinations to his extravagant vision of the Comité des Recherches as "the model for all these revolutionary committees which, in a few months, will put the executioner to work on a full-time basis,"[46] Bord was able construct the following equation: July Massacres = Comité des Recherches = Terror. And this equation provided some support, at least in his own mind, for his *idée fixe*, the idea that from start to finish the entire Revolution was nothing but a blood-bath, an idea which, in less dramatic and less exaggerated form, has reappeared in recent scholarly efforts to assimilate 1789 to the year II.

However, let us now put Garran aside for a moment and return to Flesselles' July 14 departure from the Hôtel-de-Ville. According to the Electors' *Procès-verbal*, a mounting deluge of denunciations of Flesselles finally coalesced into a "general consensus" that "it was necessary that he come to the Palais-Royal to be judged," following which he responded: "All right, gentlemen, let's go to the Palais-Royal."[47] Let us first note that the *Procès-verbal* discreetly avoids any mention of the physical force which had almost certainly accompanied this "general consensus."[48] But beyond this, a distinction should be made between the accusations made against Flesselles earlier in the day by Electors, accusations which could presumably have been taken up at a future trial, and this final "voeu général," which clearly amounted to little more than a summary death sentence. For whereas the earlier accusations had been made in the presence of a relatively limited audience, by the time of Flesselles' departure, which occurred not long after the surrender of the Bastille, the Electors' meeting-hall had been invaded by a huge crowd which threatened "to set the Hôtel-de-Ville on fire, and to slit the throats of the Prévôt des Marchands, his assistants, the members of the Permanent Committee, and even all the Electors."[49]

Now what implications can be drawn from the presence of this crowd, interchangeably identified in the *Procès-verbal* as "la foule," "la multitude," or "le peuple"? As already indicated, this study will place a great deal of emphasis on the distinction between a punitive "People" and an indulgent "revolutionary elite," and the *Procès-verbal* of July 14 is a text that provides many striking illustrations of this distinction. In the late afternoon, for example, some Electors "seeing [some captured Bastille defenders] as nothing more than unfortunate victims who had to be saved from an impulse of furor and prejudice" managed to convince the crowd that it should not "sacrifice" these captives. Then, just before Flesselles' departure, about thirty more Bastille defenders "whose death was loudly demanded by the multitude" were led into the Electors' meeting room. Despite efforts by some Electors and by the temporary National Guard Commander La Salle to appeal to "la générosité française," two of the captives who were thought to have been Bastille cannoneers were seized and quickly hanged. Finally, immediately after Flesselles' exit, Elie, a military officer who was one of the heroes of the Bastille siege, was able to persuade the crowd to allow the release of the rest of the captives. As the *Procès-verbal* put it, the "impulse for grace captured everyone's heart, and the words 'grace', 'grace' resounded through the entire room." Thus, invoked by members of the revolutionary elite, the sentiments of humanity and forgiveness retained some influence even at the height of the anger and vengefulness that dominated the fourteenth of July.[50]

But then what are we to make of the "general consensus" which had sent Flesselles to his death only moments before? Can it be argued that, beset by fears for their own safety, many Electors were reluctant to oppose this "general consensus," that the Electors were indeed subject, at least at that moment, to a kind of "mob intimidation"? As much as such a formula has been put to unfortunate use by two centuries of anti-democratic thinkers, this, in my view, is exactly the kind of argument that needs to be made at this point. Or to put it another way, it might be said that the Electors' "abandonment" of the obviously compromised Flesselles constituted a kind of "sacrificial offering" to the People, an "offering" which not only helped insure their own safety but also facilitated the subsequent pardon of the less personally responsible Bastille defenders.

However, while words like "intimidation," "abandonment," and "sacrifice" underline the essentially passive role that the Electors seem to have played in the death of the Prévôt des Marchands, it is certainly likely that there were some Electors who, whether from personal conviction or political calculation, helped generate and encourage the "general consensus" that determined Flesselles' fate. Moreover, it also seems likely that Garran's emergence as the most recognizable of these *durs* helped him to establish a reputation as a politician in whom those inclined to a punitive approach to revolutionary justice could have confidence, a reputation that might well have helped lead to his selection as a member of the Comité des Recherches and, within the Comité, to his designation as its expert on the July conspiracy. While the always hesitant Brissot found it difficult to take a strong position against the enemies of the Revolution without adding a string of qualifications, the man who had chased Flesselles out of the Hôtel-de-Ville on July 14 was particularly well positioned to become a valuable "left Fayettist" ally of a regime that would often be leaving itself open to the charge that it was protecting conspirators.

THE PRIVACY OF LETTERS

If the rapid oscillations between punishment and clemency taking place on July 14 reflected the tension between repressive and indulgent conceptions of justice and, by extension, the tension between notions of public safety and notions of individual rights, these tensions were also revealed in the Electors' handling of another issue that arose during the July crisis. On July 13, the newly formed Paris National Guard had begun to intercept all "suspicious" correspondence. Deciding that "under such dangerous circumstances, the common interest must take precedence over particular interests," the Electors, in an early use of "circumstances" as a justification for rigorous public safety measures, decreed that all these letters would be opened and read publicly.[51] With rumors of a military attack reaching a climax and with Paris taking on the appearance of a "ville en guerre,"[52] this decision can hardly be considered surprising. Rather, what is somewhat surprising is the hesitation that preceded it. For the Electors had to be polled three times before finally overcoming their scruples and ratifying what Bailly called "the imperious requirement" of "the People assembled" that these letters be read.[53] As the Elector Dusaulx put it: "We agreed that the letters contained in these packets should not be opened and that we would send them to the National Assembly. But we were forced ... to satisfy the curiosity of the citizens who were present."[54]

During the next two days, many intercepted letters were read publicly, including Besenval's promise of reinforcements for the Bastille, the reading of which greatly intensified the crowd's anger towards the old general.[55] However, on the morning of July 15, with the emergency slightly eased and with the Electors not wanting to spend their time listening to a rapidly accumulating backlog of letters, a five-man committee (which included Garran) was assigned the task of examining the letters and deciding if any merited further attention.[56] But this committee operated for less than six hours. After hearing the Comte d'Ogny, the head of the Royal Postal Service, complain that the interception of correspondence was "a deadly attack upon all branches of Commerce," the Electors ordered that letters no longer be intercepted by National Guard patrols. Instead, they created a new committee which was sent to the Hôtel-des-Postes and instructed "to look at those which appear suspect and, above all, to prevent the violation of personal secrets with respect to those that do not carry any indication of endangering public tranquillity." Moreover, they also decreed that all letters which had not yet been read by the first committee would be immediately handed over to the new panel, thus putting the original committee out of business.[57] Thus, whether primarily impelled by pressure from the business–financial community or by an ideological commitment to individual rights, the Electors had, in effect, repudiated their own postal surveillance committee and replaced it with one that would operate under Ogny's supervision at the Hôtel-des-Postes. Less than twenty-four hours after the fall of the Bastille, with tensions at a somewhat reduced but still extremely high level,[58] they had already indicated a desire to relax revolutionary vigilance.

It would not be long before private correspondence would be routinely inspected by revolutionary officials, despite much less dangerous immediate circumstances. Hence, on October 9, 1789, Talleyrand complained that "the only letters which arrive via the ordinary post are those in which nothing is written."[59] And on November 2, the ten-day-old Paris Comité des Recherches began to examine all letters addressed to a list of leading Orleanists.[60] But on July 15, if a distinction can be made between the "duration" and "intensity" of revolutionary circumstances, it appears that the habit of living in a revolutionary situation had not yet begun to take its full toll. Thus, despite the crisis atmosphere of that day, the Electors were able to register at least some degree of support for the principle of the inviolability of letters, a principle which, according to the Duc de Castres, was part of the "code d'honneur" of the refined eighteenth century.[61]

On the other hand, the Electors' lack of vigilance on this issue may have had something to do with their failure to retain the confidence of the more democratically oriented Parisian districts, a failure which soon led to the formation of an entirely new municipal council, the Assemblée des Représentants.[62] Moreover, the order forbidding the interception of letters hardly put an end to the practice. The *Procès-verbal* of late July reports several examples of letters being seized by National Guard patrols. In one of these cases, the tension between the Electors and the districts was strikingly demonstrated when some delegates from the Saint-Séverin District demanded that a letter seized by its National Guard battalion be opened, though "after some difficulties, they agreed to send the letter back without reading it."[63] This incident is particularly interesting because this letter was thought to have been written by the Comte de Saint-Priest, one of the ministers who had been dismissed and then re-called along with Necker. It marks the first recorded indication of popular suspicion of Saint-Priest, who would play a prominent role in several of the affairs we will examine in this study.

But the intercepted letter that attracted the most attention at the end of July was one which never reached the Assembly of Electors. On July 23, the Baron de Castelnau, a top aide of Artois, was arrested by a patrol from the Petits-Augustins District. As he was being taken into custody, Castelnau attempted to tear up a letter he was carrying. Tired, no doubt, of the laxity of the Electors, the district authorities sent the pieces of this letter and Castelnau himself (along with some other correspondence he was carrying) to the new mayor Bailly, who, in a power-play of his own, was at that moment temporarily allied with the districts against the Electors. However, Bailly and the Electors' Permanent Committee were "embarrassed" by the request that they read the seized correspondence. Hoping to foist the unpleasant responsibilities associated with public safety onto a higher authority, they ordered Castelnau's release and sent the suspicious correspondence to the President of the National Assembly, the Duc de Liancourt. But the latter, whose "delicacy made the very idea of having open letters in his hands repugnant to him," was equally unsettled by the offending package and returned it to the Hôtel-de-Ville. At this point, recalled Bailly, one of the suspicious letters was finally opened "and we didn't find anything in it except personal compliments."[64]

However, the controversy aroused by the Castelnau correspondence did not end here. Apart from the problem of its contents (to which I will return shortly), Liancourt's unilateral decision to return it to the municipality generated considerable discontent within the Assembly. Liancourt lamely explained that Bailly's package had arrived so late at night and the principles of inviolability of letters and legislative incapacity to exercise executive powers were so self-evident that he "took it upon himself to interpret the sentiments of the Assembly." However, the self-evidence of these two liberal principles was belied by the fact that the Assembly felt it necessary to engage in a full-scale debate on a proposal to create a national postal surveillance committee.[65]

In what was destined to become a depressingly familiar argument, the supporters of this proposal argued that, as future Committee of Public Safety member Barère put it, "when the Nation is put in danger ... the universal maxim *salus populi suprema lex* takes its widest scope and reigns supreme over all rights." And, according to Gouy d'Arcy, that moment had arrived: "In a state of war, opening letters is permitted. And in these times ... of slanders and schemes, we can consider ourselves as being, and, in fact, we really are in a state of war."[66] Or as Robespierre stated:

Certainly letters are inviolable. I know it, I am convinced of it. But when an entire Nation is in danger, when there are plots against its liberty, when respectable citizens are proscribed, that which is a crime in other times becomes praiseworthy ... The most fundamental law is the safety of the People. If this is an obligatory law, it is certainly so now for we are faced with the most terrible crisis in which a Nation can find itself.[67]

Included among the opponents of postal surveillance was a parade of moderate deputies who were developing a Cassandra-like capacity to envision a major flood being produced from the slightest breach in the dike of inalienable rights. As Dupont de Nemours argued: "Once it is known that letters will be opened, they will be able to immolate whomever they want, and save whomever they want. They will be able to create the most false impressions and the most frivolous alarms, and satisfy their private animosities." But moderates like Dupont were joined on this occasion by some of the most influential "advanced patriots." Thus, Agier's friend Camus declared that "the seals of letters cannot be broken without openly violating the most sacred rights." And the characteristically more practical Mirabeau, apparently forgetting that the debate had been sparked by Castelnau's arrest, sarcastically asked if "it is really thought that conspirators send their messages through the ordinary post?"[68]

Some of the opponents of the proposed committee tried to meet the advocates of vigilance on their own grounds. "We are no longer surrounded by the dangers that threatened us," declared the Monarchien Bishop de Langres, referring to the King's dismissal of Besenval's troops. And an unidentified but certainly overly optimistic deputy launched what may well have been the first of many futile attempts to declare that the Revolution was over by stating that extraordinary measures were no longer justified because "peace appears to be firmly established, and schism and division no longer exist."[69] However, in direct response to this line of argument, another unnamed deputy demonstrated the marvelous flexibility of "circumstances" as a justification for security measures, particularly when it is a question of secret plots, which are never easily discernible to the uninstructed: "It is useless to tell us we are enjoying calm. Who can say for sure that the conspiracy has been stamped out? Who can answer for what will follow? Perhaps the evil is greater than ever."[70] Or as Camusat de Belombre put it: "Though some are trying to persuade us that we are safe, we are not. I believe, on the contrary, that the danger is growing every day, that extremely violent projects are being hatched, and that it has never been more necessary to take precautions to ward off the new blows being prepared."[71]

The debate on postal surveillance was summarized in somewhat flippant terms by the littérateur Garat: "Some see the question as it should be seen in times of peace, others as it should be seen in times of war. There is thus really only a question of fact to examine: are we at war or are we at peace?"[72] Reflecting the eighteenth century's extravagant faith in science and learning, Garat was implying that, after judicious debate and analysis, a conclusive answer to this question would emerge. But there was clearly no "question of fact" at issue here, only conflicting perspectives, conflicting temperaments, and conflicting ambitions and interests. It was, that is, not a question of fact, but rather one of politics, and the problem was not to define peace and war, but rather to define the political community. Or to put it another way, the question at issue was not "are we at war or at peace," but rather "who is this 'we'?" For radicals like Robespierre, the assertion that "we are at peace" or perhaps even the very posing of the question was an indication that the speaker or writer was not one of "us," but, in reality, one of "them." For it is exactly those who had spoken of peace whom the Incorruptible must have been thinking about when he made the most striking remark in the postal surveillance debate. Asking whether the Assembly could refuse to pursue information that could lead to "the elucidation of the most fatal conspiracy ever contrived," Robespierre declared: "I do not believe it can. *Making arrangements for the benefit of the conspirators is a treasonous betrayal of the People.*"[73] In thus expanding the definition of treason to include those who were in any way contributing to the protection or defense of the "conspirators," this "alchemist of revolutionary opinion-making" was envisioning a soon-to-be-realized state of affairs in which all attempts at reconciliation and compromise would themselves be seen as crimes.[74]

With this in mind, let us now return to the Castelnau correspondence. As we have seen, Bailly indicated that a letter was finally "opened" and found to contain only "compliments." But this letter, which turned out to be a note to Artois from the English Ambassador, could not have been the letter that Castelnau had tried to destroy since a letter torn into pieces would not have had to be opened. As for the torn-up letter itself, Bailly, who may still have had reasons for discretion when he wrote his *Mémoires* in 1792, acknowledged its existence but said nothing further about it.[75] However, it appears that the pieces of this letter were actually reassembled and read. Thus, a number of newspapers reported that the Monarchien leader Clermont-Tonnerre, present at the Hôtel-de-Ville when the Castelnau package was examined, told the National Assembly that "the reassembling of the scattered parts of the torn-up letter, which at first was presumed to contain something important, has shown that this letter does not have any significance."[76] Since no further information about this letter ever seems to have surfaced, Clermont's announcement is the closest thing we have to an "official report" regarding its contents.

But how can such a report be believed? For what could have been more suspicious than Castelnau's attempt to destroy this letter, a letter which, in all likelihood, was either written by or addressed to Artois himself? While there may have been nothing overtly or directly dangerous to the new regime in this letter, the fact that its contents were never publicly revealed suggests that there must have been something in it that was embarrassing to someone. To mention only one possibility of what this "something" may have been, it appears that Talleyrand, the Vicomte de Noailles (Lafayette's brother-in-law), and several other liberal nobles had been engaged in feverish negotiations with the Artois camp up to the very moment of Artois' flight from France, a piece of information that would have caused these gentlemen considerable discomfort if it had surfaced in late July.[77] But whether designed to protect "lukewarm" patriots who may have been negotiating with the hardliners or to avoid further embarrassment to the Artois faction in the interest of a possible future reconciliation, it seems likely that the municipal authorities, in collaboration with the leadership of the National Assembly, decided to suppress the contents of this letter.[78]

If such a "cover-up" did indeed occur, its purpose would have been to allow for as extended a definition of the political community as possible, in contrast to Robespierre who was already eager to "purge" or "purify" it. This "inclusionary" attitude was aptly expressed in another remark attributed to Clermont: "We found some opinions in it [the Castelnau correspondence] which are contrary to general sentiment, but no trace of an offense worthy of the Assembly's attention," a statement which suggests a willingness to accept the existence of a "gray zone" between "virtue" and "crime."[79] But while early revolutionary judicial policies generally reflected the conciliatory strategy and tolerant attitude implied in Clermont's remark, justifications for a more "exclusionary" position were also being developed. Thus, one writer, upset that counter-revolutionary journals were being allowed to circulate so freely, would soon argue that Noah had been too tolerant and should not have allowed all the animals into his ark: "The presence of too many unclean animals does not produce anything of value for the inhabitants of a house. By dirtying the walls, these animals only breed degradation."[80]

As for the outcome of the Assembly debate on the privacy of letters, the motion to create a postal surveillance committee was defeated on July 27, thereby providing something of a vote of confidence for the non-vigilant manner in which the Castelnau affair had been handled. However, as the deputies were sufficiently divided for it to become necessary to go beyond a voice vote,[81] it also appears that there was a certain degree of uneasiness with the complacency exhibited by the municipality and by Assembly President Liancourt. Thus, on the very next day, the Assembly created what can be regarded as a watered-down version of the surveillance committee it had just refused to institute. Authorized not to open and read correspondence but rather merely to receive information on plots and conspiracies, this panel would soon come to be known as the National Assembly's Comité des Recherches.[82]

LA CHASSE AUX BÊTES

While the interception and seizure of correspondence certainly aroused a good deal of interest and controversy in July 1789, the interception and seizure of persons aroused even more. As the July crisis reached its climax, proscription lists calling for the arrest and punishment of the leading "conspirators" circulated freely in the Palais-Royal and throughout Paris, and the violent events of July 14 demonstrated that these lists had to be taken more seriously than the lists of anti-patriotic deputies circulated in June.[83] One of these lists appeared in the form of a pamphlet which announced a *Chasse aux bêtes puantes et féroces* and facetiously offered bounties to the "chasseurs" who could "consummate the total destruction, which we have already begun, of these carnivorous and venomous beasts." The most lucrative offerings on this list were 40,000 *livres* for "a Panther escaped from the Court of Germany [Marie-Antoinette]" and 35,000 *livres* for "a Tiger raised in the Menagerie of Versailles [Artois]."[84]

Yet, despite Georges Lefebvre's assertion that "France became covered [in late July] with a tightly knit network of committees, militias, and investigators without mandate, thus rendering movement almost as difficult for several weeks as it would be in the year II,"[85] the fact is that the summer of 1789 was not really a very good "hunting season." For one thing, due to a combination of naiveté, inexperience, and a general lack of vigilance, Lefebvre's "network" was a rather ineffective one. Thus, when a carriage containing the hated Duchesse de Polignac, a close friend of both Besenval and the Queen, was stopped at Sens, a quick-thinking abbé reportedly managed to satisfy the "investigators" by shouting: "Good news,

M. Necker has been recalled, the Ministers and the Army sent away, and all the Polignac riff-raff is in flight." The carriage was allowed to proceed, and it was only later that "[the People] saw that it had been tricked, and that its prey had escaped."[86] As Lefebvre himself put it: "If the People was suspicious in 1789, it was evidently not very rigorous regarding marks of conformity and one passed for a 'patriot' without a great deal of difficulty."[87] Here again, we can see that revolutionary circumstances had not yet taken their full toll.

Another reason why the summer of 1789 was not a good "hunting season" was the unwillingness of some of the leaders of the National Assembly to co-operate with the "chasseurs." On July 29, a Captain Roussel of the Petits-Augustins District's National Guard Battalion, the same battalion that had arrested Castelnau a week earlier, notified Assembly President Liancourt that Breteuil, the head of the "ministry of thirty-six hours," was hiding somewhere in the district. Roussel wanted Liancourt to send orders indicating "the means to be employed to discover the hiding-place of this apparent fugitive."[88] Perhaps opinion was divided within the district as to whether an attempt to arrest Breteuil should be made, and it may have been thought that an endorsement of this project by the prestigious Liancourt would weigh heavily in its favor.

But Roussel should have known by then that Liancourt, one of Lafayette's closest allies in the National Assembly during the early revolutionary period, was hardly the right man to whom to address such a request. Displaying all the *délicatesse* that he had just shown in the Castelnau affair and sounding rather like a virtuous maiden who has been asked to do terrible things, Liancourt indignantly replied that "it is more than indiscreet to make such a vague and undefined denunciation to the National Assembly." Informing Roussel that he was "strangely mistaken" if he thought it was the function of the Assembly or of any of its members to search for and arrest fugitives, he declared that such an activity would "lower the august representatives of the Nation to the vile ministry of espionage."[89]

In Liancourt's chaste words, we can hear a clear echo of the liberal and humanitarian sentiments which had fueled the pre-revolutionary judicial reform movement, sentiments which would continue to have an important influence on the National Assembly's handling of political justice in the months to come. For, as we will see throughout this study, the Assembly would generally try to exercise as much judicial indulgence and as little investigatory rigor as seemed politically possible at a given moment. As for Breteuil, there does not seem to have ever been any attempt by the Petits-Augustins District to arrest him. Eventually, he would reach the Swiss border and later resurface as one of the main architects of the royal family's June 1791 flight from Paris.[90]

Finally, the general lack of success of the "chasse aux bêtes" of July 1789 can also be attributed to the military escorts that protected many of the fugitives. Thus, the deposed War Minister Broglie was threatened by a furious crowd at Verdun and was only saved by his own troops. Similarly, the Prince de Lambesc, especially hated because of exaggerated reports regarding his celebrated charge into the Tuileries on July 12, also required his regiment's protection to escape from an angry crowd. In the mean time, Artois himself left Versailles with an enormous armed escort. In this way, the troops whose presence had ignited the July crisis finally proved to be of some use to the "conspirators" who had summoned them.[91]

For various reasons, then, virtually all the leading members of the Artois faction were able to elude their pursuers and join the first wave of emigration. Besides those already mentioned (Artois, Broglie, Breteuil, Lambesc, and Polignac), this group included such hated figures as Artois' best friend, the Comte de Vaudreuil; the Captain of Artois' Guards, the Prince de Hénin; the Prince de Condé; Condé's top military attaché, the Marquis d'Autichamp; the Prince de Conti; the ex-ministers Barentin and Villedeuil; and the infamous abbé Vermont, a close confidant of the Queen.[92] With all these presumed accomplices in what Robespierre was calling "the most fatal conspiracy ever contrived" having eluded the grasp of judicial pursuit, we can now begin to understand why the arrest and detention of Besenval attracted so much attention. However, before proceeding to an examination of his case, the fate of a handful of other well-known hardliners who were arrested in late July should at least be mentioned. In Paris itself, the massacre of the Intendant Berthier and his father-in-law Foulon and the arrest and release of Castelnau have already been noted. In addition, two other notorious anti-revolutionaries, the Maréchal de Castries and the ex-War Ministry official Lambert were also arrested by district battalions and then released almost immediately by municipal authorities.[93] Moreover, three other objects of popular animus were arrested by provincial militias but quickly released by order of the National Assembly: the abbé Maury, a deputy arrested at Peronne; the abbé

Calonne, brother of the ex-Finance Minister, arrested at Nogent; and the ex-Foreign Affairs Minister Vauguyon, arrested at Le Havre.

Regarding Maury, it was easy for the Assembly to justify its non-punitive inclinations. As a deputy, he became the beneficiary of a declaration of parliamentary immunity issued on June 23.[94] Though originally designed to protect patriot deputies from the Court, this declaration was now invoked to protect Maury, probably the Assembly's most hated member, from the People. As for Calonne, who was an alternate deputy, the Assembly considered the argument that he too was covered by parliamentary immunity, but the formula finally settled on was that he should be released because there were no formal charges against him. Although Brissot reported that the July 27 release of Maury and Calonne "seems to have displeased the true friends of liberty," opposition within the Assembly was, with one curious exception, apparently non-existent. Even Robespierre does not seem to have voiced any objections.[95]

However, the Vauguyon case posed more difficulties. By the time his arrest came to the Assembly's attention on August 1, it had just ordered, as will be seen in the next chapter, that Besenval remain under arrest despite the fact there were no formal charges against him either. Therefore, another formula had to be found, and the one eventually hit upon was that, as an ex-Minister and as current Ambassador to Spain, Vauguyon's fate should be decided by the King, a decision which, of course, was tantamount to ordering his release.[96] But regardless of the official reasons provided by this Assembly of rhetoricians and lawyers which could usually find some legalistic explanation to justify its actions, the common denominator of the decisions on Maury, Calonne, and Vauguyon appears to have been a basic inclination to avoid rigorous public safety measures. Yet, when the Assembly was forced to make a decision on Besenval, this inclination had to give way to another consideration, the need to retain popular confidence. For Besenval, after all, had been the commander of the troops which had threatened Paris and the Assembly and, as such, had to be treated as a central figure in the supposed "July conspiracy." As the most important fugitive whose case did not abruptly end in either escape or death, he would soon become the focal point for the first major test of French revolutionary justice.

3

The Besenval affair: amnesty or prosecution?

Having withdrawn from Paris with most of his troops on the evening of July 12, the Baron de Besenval had returned to Versailles where he found himself besieged by rumors that he would be arrested or assassinated. Yet, his self-described devotion to duty and the royal family was so great that he only agreed to flee when Louis XVI "ordered" him to do so. But once the decision to try to escape was made, attention needed to be given to the problem of eluding the revolutionary "chasseurs":

> The entire kingdom being in arms, with all outlets closed, it was doubtful I could go far without being arrested. Suggestions were made that I disguise myself and I rebuffed them impatiently. But they kept hounding me. Finally, I agreed to dress myself as a gendarme. The Prévôt-Général gave me two cavaliers as an escort, and I left Versailles at dusk.[1]

The problem with this account, however, is that it doesn't explain why one of the French army's highest ranking officers was left to flee the country without the kind of military protection made available to many of the other fugitives. Broglie, Lambesc, and many of the other top military leaders had gone to Saint-Denis (where most of the troops had been sent after July 14) and had then left for the eastern frontier.[2] Why didn't Besenval go there? Or why wasn't he furnished with a more substantial escort of his own? We have just seen that the King had "ordered" him to leave, an order which Besenval later presented as concern for the safety of a loyal officer and as a face-saving device designed to cover the "dishonor" of flight. But perhaps it would be more accurate to view this order more literally: as something approaching a formal order of dismissal and exile. Or, to take a less extreme version of this line of thought, the events of July 12–14 had, it can be suggested, so discredited Besenval that no one at

59

Versailles was willing to take the steps necessary to provide him with anything more than the token escort he was finally given.

As commander of the troops whose performance (or non-performance) had sealed a major defeat for the Monarchy, Besenval would soon be accused of treason by royalist writers who, like the terrorists of the year II, were unable to distinguish between military failure and crime. Alluding to the old general's reputation for sensuous dissipation, the satirist Rivarol wrote that he had "let the Invalides be taken because he was afraid that if rioting became too widespread, they would pillage his house, in which he had just had an entire apartment painted and charming baths installed. These are the kind of men who served the King!"[3] Similarly, Montjoie stated that "no officer of the King served the Revolution better than M. le Baron de Besenval," while an anonymous pamphleteer charged that he had "knowingly neglected" to fulfill the Court's wishes because he favored the Revolution.[4]

While such accusations were encouraged by the extraordinary efforts that we will soon see Necker make on his behalf, Besenval's behavior during the Parisian Insurrection was sufficiently equivocal to generate royalist suspicion well before this Minister's intervention. In Besenval's own words, the rumors of arrest and assassination that surrounded him at Versailles reflected the fact that "I had become the target of a party that was perhaps stronger at Versailles and in the house of the King than at Paris itself."[5] But while he implies here that there was a single pro-revolutionary party threatening him at both Paris and Versailles, his enemies were clearly a much more diverse lot. For rather than being revolutionaries, Besenval's enemies "in the house of the King" were, in all likelihood, influential courtiers who, fortified by years of resentment over past inter-court battles, succeeded in making him the scapegoat for the failures of July 12–14.[6] As we can now see, it was not at all accidental that it was Besenval who would eventually fall into the trap of the revolutionary "chasseurs."

On July 28, Besenval arrived in the village of Villegruis, about 100 km. east of Versailles. Not being a very experienced fugitive, he actually seems to have inquired how he could reach Vitry-le-François, 75 km. further east, "without passing through any towns where there were bourgeois militias." Not surprisingly, this question led directly to the appearance of one of these militias, that of the nearby town of Villenauxe, and Besenval soon found himself under arrest. However, he was not without influential local support. For the mayor of this small town in Champagne turned out to be a young officer with whom he was acquainted. After failing to persuade the Villenauxe militia to release the prisoner, this young man, the Marquis de Saint-Chamant, tried to convince the town's municipal council to send for royal troops to effect a rescue. But the local burghers rejected this idea, pointing out "the very great inconveniences" that could result. Instead, they decided to write to Paris for instructions.[7]

The message about Besenval's arrest reached the capital on July 29, at a time when municipal authority was in the process of being transferred from the Assembly of Electors to the Assemblée des Représentants. During this period, police matters were being handled by a Comité Provisoire de Police that included appointees from both municipal bodies, and this committee quickly decided to send two of its members and a small National Guard contingent to Villenauxe to bring Besenval back to Paris.[8] However, no trace of this crucial decision or even of Besenval's arrest itself can be found in the July 29 records of either municipal assembly, an absence explained by Bailly, who had participated in the Police Committee deliberations: "Fearing that [Besenval] would suffer the fate of MM. Foulon and Berthier [massacred on July 22] ... nothing was communicated to the two assemblies. We kept this secret so the People would not be warned of his arrival, thereby allowing the prisoner to be brought in safely."[9]

If there is any truth to this explanation, we can again note the enormous cultural gap separating the early revolutionary authorities from the revolutionary crowd and from the revolutionary popular movement in general. For in unilaterally ordering Besenval's transfer to Paris and in thereby seeking to bypass the National Assembly (which had just ordered the release of Maury and Calonne), the Police Committee had formulated a policy that was actually quite severe. Indeed if we can imagine an attorney for Besenval being present at the Police Committee meeting, ordering the immediate transfer of his client to the Parisian tinder-box would certainly have been the last course of action he would have suggested. Yet, even while issuing such a rigorous order, this committee felt compelled to rely on secrecy and subterfuge to avoid the possibly dangerous consequences of its own decision.[10] While such

precautionary action may seem only reasonable under the circumstances, the distrust of the People and the lack of commitment to the
principle of public accountability exhibited by the members of this
committee would in and of themselves eventually become grounds
for suspicion.

In any event, the two police commissioners arrived in Villenauxe
on the afternoon of July 30. Though the week which had passed since
the deaths of Berthier and Foulon had given Lafayette and his aides
time to organize further the Paris National Guard and thus increase
its chances of protecting Besenval from a vengeful crowd, these
traumatic popular executions were still weighing heavily on
everyone's mind. In Villenauxe, Besenval was told of the fate of
Foulon and Berthier, giving him "a preview of the destiny which
awaited me."[11] With the sounding of this ominous note, the old
general and his guards left for the capital that night.

NECKER AND THE MOVE FOR AMNESTY

In the mean time, the mayor of Villenauxe had continued his efforts
to help Besenval. During the evening of July 28, he learned that
Necker, in the midst of a triumphal return from a short-lived Swiss
exile, was in nearby Nogent-sur-Seine. Informed of Besenval's
plight, the Minister promptly sent a message to Villenauxe asking
for the old general's release. "All the motives which affect a sensitive
soul," he declared, "impel me make this request." But the town
officials replied that they preferred to wait for instructions from
Paris, thus forcing Necker to postpone his interest in Besenval until
his arrival in the capital.[12]

It would not be a long postponement. To "the sounds of military
music, augmented by cries of joy and universal acclaim," the "libér-
ateur de la France" entered the Hôtel-de-Ville on the morning of
July 30.[13] Hoping to take advantage of the enormous popularity
which he enjoyed at that moment, he immediately proceeded to
devote an entire speech to the issue of political crime and punishment. As he later wrote:

I profited from these magnificent circumstances by taking up the cause of
the oppressed and by trying to rekindle interest in the ideas of peace, justice,
and humanity ... [I tried] to soften the irritation and the animosities of the

People ... and to steer it away from the impulses of vengeance and ferocity to which it had just succumbed.[14]

As we will soon see, Necker's tear-bespattered speech, which was delivered first to the Représentants and then to the Electors, was indeed permeated with sentimental appeals to the kinds of emotion that had helped fuel the pre-revolutionary judicial reform movement. Yet he began with some words of sober encouragement for a business community which had hungered for his return, words which bring to mind the complaints about commercial interruption made by postal director Ogny two weeks earlier:

I come to entreat you to take the steps necessary to the establishment of that perfect and durable order ... [without which] confidence will be uncertain and a general uneasiness will trouble public well-being, thereby turning a large number of rich customers away from Paris and discouraging foreigners from coming here to spend their money.[15]

Having thereby outlined the economic reasons for curbing revolutionary excess, Necker turned to "a greater concern which is weighing on my heart and oppressing it." Asking his listeners to "consult nothing but your hearts" and to respect "this quality of kindness, justice, and mildness which distinguishes the French Nation," he called on them to "make the day of indulgence and forgiveness arrive as soon as possible." "In the name of God, gentlemen," he cried, "no more proscriptions, no more bloody scenes."[16]

Necker went on to describe his attempt to persuade the Villenauxe authorities to release Besenval, whom he praised for helping to assure public order during May, June, and early July. And in a burst of what could only have been feigned ignorance, Necker declared that "I don't know what he could be accused of." Perhaps realizing, however, that such a statement was carrying him dangerously close to an anti-revolutionary stance, the Minister then fell back on the legalistic argument used by the National Assembly three days earlier in ordering Calonne's release: in the absence of a formal accusation, Besenval should also be freed.[17]

But as Necker surely recognized, the most pressing need at the moment was to keep the old general away from Paris and the Parisians. Thus, his next line of defense was to put aside temporarily his demand for Besenval's release and to propose instead that proceedings be instituted in Champagne. "Could you," he asked the

Représentants, "limit yourselves to asking him the questions you believe need to be asked at Villenauxe?" Such a course of action, he argued, would allow Besenval to benefit from "mankind's most fundamental right," that of "not being condemned and punished without having had the opportunity to be heard and examined by honest and impartial judges."[18]

Having thus touched base with the rationalistic and legalistic currents that had also contributed to the movement for judicial reform, Necker followed with another appeal to humanitarian sentiment. "I prostrate myself, I throw myself on my knees," he proclaimed, "in order to ask that no one treat M. de Besenval or anyone else in a manner in any way comparable to the scenes which have apparently been recently enacted." He then concluded with these words:

> In fixing my attention on a single individual, M. de Besenval, I would be happy with this one favor of his pardon. But I would be much happier still if this one example would become the signal of a general amnesty that would bring calm to France and allow citizens ... to fix their attention on the future.[19]

Now before turning to the striking series of events touched off by this speech, let us first examine Necker's motives for delivering it. As already indicated, many contemporaries felt that Necker's solicitude for Besenval proved the two men were accomplices. One anonymous royalist, for example, charged that:

> M. de Besenval was in league with his friend Necker, the secret agent of insurrections ... It was to aid this minister's designs that the Baron knowingly neglected to fulfill the wishes of the General [Broglie]. And that is the reason for the extraordinary zeal with which, upon his return to Paris, M. Necker defended this fugitive, whose escape would have kept the lid on all the intrigue.[20]

Moreover, many "advanced patriots" also assumed that Necker and Besenval were partners in intrigue. Thus, one of Necker's most persistent radical critics, the Chevalier de Rutledge, wrote that "the fear of being implicated in the depositions of this aristocrat [Besenval] led him to this act of so-called generosity which was actually one of terror."[21]

These accusations, however, seem to have been fueled by little more than the instinctive suspiciousness which often led French revolutionary participants to assume that hidden personal connections were determining events. Hence, the early twentieth-century historian Eugène Lavaquery, who inherited this suspicion and who made a determined effort to find evidence to support it, could not unearth anything more compromising than a letter in which Besenval asked Necker for a bonus for 800 soldiers who were to serve at the Estates-General opening ceremonies. According to Lavaquery, this letter "pushes regard for the well-being of the Swiss Guards to the point of warning that this service will tire them out. This kind of prudence, frequent in the machination of plots, would assuredly be unique in the annals of an ordinary army doing its duty."[22] Besides this masterpiece of conspiratorial thinking, in which an officer's concern for his troops is somehow translated into evidence of plotting, Lavaquery also asserted that the two men had intrigued together during Necker's first ministry in 1780.[23] But if politics makes strange bedfellows, it is also true that political lovers are notoriously fickle. Even if the Swiss Protestant banker and the Swiss Catholic courtier had indeed been temporarily allied a decade earlier, there is little reason to believe they were still closely linked in 1789. Instead, we are, I feel, on much firmer ground if we take Necker at his word when he described himself as "he who consecrated the first moments of his return, the first test of his strength, to defending against a rigorous oppression the same party which had sent him away from the kingdom."[24]

In thereby defending his erstwhile enemies, Necker, it can be suggested, was actually acting in accordance with his own self-defined role as the Great Reconciliator of the Revolution, the one individual in French politics who could "inspire a common wish for peace and conciliation" and who could institute and administer "the mutual arrangements [*ménagements mutuels*] which must be established ... between particular interests." In other words, as one who considered himself uniquely qualified to create political as well as economic confidence, Necker felt that he would be able to "retain amongst us" those who were contemplating emigration and to facilitate a "reunion" with those who had already fled. Often derided as a financial "juggler," he saw himself as a kind of "political juggler" whose mission was to establish and maintain a balance of political forces, a balance which would permit as wide a definition of the political community as possible. Thus, the same search for political balance that had dictated Necker's defense of Third Estate "rebels" before July 14 now led him to take up the cause of counter-revolutionary "conspirators."[25]

But the problem with Necker's vision of balance and conciliation, which would be largely inherited by Lafayette once the Finance Minister's own political star had begun to fade, was that Necker himself had to be at the very center, impartially balancing all the forces. He could not, that is, accept the fact that he too was just one of the forces. Thus, for example, he was never able to overcome his antagonism towards another major early revolutionary moderate, Mirabeau. In late May 1789, Mirabeau, who had viciously attacked Necker in several pre-revolutionary pamphlets but who essentially shared his political principles, attempted to forge an alliance with him.[26] A meeting was set up, but Necker, always willing to preach "reconciliation" and "forgiveness" to others, rudely rebuffed and insulted his old enemy, leaving Mirabeau to tell Necker's friend Malouet: "Your man is a fool; he will hear from me." Sadly reflecting on Necker's failure to co-opt Mirabeau's talents and popularity, Malouet later wrote, with what was apparently unintentional irony: "In these times of political disagreements and civil troubles, one must leave a door open to *rapprochements* and conciliation, not believe too much in one's own enlightenment, and be indulgent towards the errors and passions of others."[27]

In addition, Necker also seems to have had a strong tendency to underestimate the disparity of a given set of political forces and to overestimate his own ability to bring them together. Thus, Bailly reported that, on the morning of July 30, he warned the Minister, who had not seen the "new Paris," not to make any overtures in favor of Besenval: "This move [for amnesty] was very dangerous. If he did not succeed, he risked losing popular favor. And if he did obtain what he asked, things could become very dangerous for those who gave it to him."[28] And Alexandre Lameth stated that "several of the people who were then the most closely attached to this Minister explained to him the inconveniences associated with seeking this kind of triumph in the capital." But Necker, his "very exaggerated opinion of his powers of influence" only further inflated by the cheering he had heard throughout his triumphant return journey, brushed aside these warnings and "his vanity carried the day."[29] In 1776, Necker had written that "reason and wisdom joined to sensitivity and to frank manners which announce the purity of the soul cannot be resisted. My entire life has proven this."[30] Entering the

Paris City Hall on July 30, 1789, this virtuous egoist must have felt that he would indeed be irresistible.

And sure enough he was, at least for those present in the Hôtel-de-Ville. According to the Représentants' minutes, when Necker finished his speech that morning, "an ardent and profound sensibility seized every soul . . . and the call for grace, escaping from every heart, was repeated a hundred times by every mouth." Somehow making himself heard "in the midst of this ecstasy," the Monarchien Clermont-Tonnerre, who had accompanied the Minister to Paris and who was then his closest ally in the National Assembly, declared: "Let us pardon the vanquished as we have fought those who have been brave . . . Will we stoop so low as to hate our enemies when we no longer have reason to fear them?" At these words, "a general eagerness led a crowd of people towards the bureau. Each man wanted to be the one to draw up the order that would set M. de Besenval free." With only one apparent objection and with Necker's own compromise proposal that Besenval be kept under arrest in Villenauxe long forgotten, an order for the old general's release was quickly signed. Accompanied by an aide-de-camp of Lafayette and by two other National Guard officers, two Représentants headed for Champagne early that afternoon with instructions to find Besenval and escort him to the Swiss border.[31]

Following this striking success, Necker went before the Electors, who proved to be especially responsive to his conciliatory message. According to their minutes, "the presence of M. Necker and his sweet and penetrating words won over every heart through an impulse which was, so to speak, involuntary. Every eye was bathed in tears." After Clermont again invoked Roman maxims about pardoning the vanquished, a decree was unanimously passed that was far more wide-ranging than the one just passed by the Représentants. This decree declared that the Assembly of Electors "pardons all its enemies . . . and now considers the only enemies of the Nation to be those who would trouble public tranquillity by engaging in any kind of violent excess."[32]

With this proclamation of a general amnesty, Necker had apparently achieved more than even he could have hoped. "This honorable result," he later wrote, "was the price of my tears." "Ah! How happy I was that day," he added, "each of its instants is engraved in my memory." With the Electors proclaiming that their general amnesty would be "posted to the sound of the trumpet in every street and square and sent to all the municipalities of the kingdom," one might have thought that the humanitarian and indulgent principles of the pre-revolutionary judicial reform movement had been transferred whole into the revolutionary arena and that an epoch of peace and forgiveness was really at hand. One might even have thought, as Clermont put it in his account of the day's events, that "the Revolution was over."[33]

THE FAILURE OF THE MOVE FOR AMNESTY

But, of course, it was not. Opposition to the decrees passed by the two municipal assemblies began to develop almost immediately, first manifesting itself among a large crowd gathered on the Place de Grève. According to some sources, this crowd cheered Necker when he left the Hôtel-de-Ville, but turned hostile as soon as it realized what had been done.[34] Lameth, however, attributed this hostility to a misunderstanding which, if accurately described, provides another striking illustration of the profound alienation and distrust which contaminated relations between the revolutionary crowd and the municipal authorities:

[The people in the crowd] deluded themselves into thinking they were the ones being pardoned. At that point, a sense of universal discontent and irritation developed. "What," they cried. "They think we are guilty! We should ask those who wanted to slit our throats to pardon us!" Cries and clamors now came from all over, and the most violent proposals followed.[35]

Whatever the source of this initial opposition, protest against the indulgent decrees rapidly became more extended and more serious, and, as one district leader put it, a day in which it had seemed as if "calm was going to be established forever" soon became "one of those in which spirits were most agitated."[36] Within three hours, "the entire capital had risen, the multitude had assembled, and the placards announcing a general amnesty had been torn down."[37] At the Palais-Royal, threats to burn down the Hôtel-de-Ville were shouted until early morning.[38] And in the sixty districts, the decision of the two municipal assemblies quickly become subject to a form of democratic scrutiny and accountability.

Taking the lead was the district which included the Palais-Royal within its boundaries, the Oratoire. Asserting that neither municipal assembly had the right to pardon the Nation's enemies and that the order to release Besenval was therefore illegal, the Oratoire declared this order "revoked." In addition, this district sent two commissioners, accompanied, it appears, by a part of its National Guard battalion, to make sure Besenval did not go free.[39] Though the Représentants immediately sent a delegation to the Oratoire to protest this action, this delegation was shouted down amidst demands for the arrest of Necker himself. Returning to the Hôtel-de-Ville, the delegates had to report that the Oratoire commissioners had already started on the by now well-travelled road to Villenauxe.[40]

In the mean time, many other districts were registering formal disapproval of the two indulgent decrees. At the Hôtel-de-Ville, the Représentants reported that "the protests are multiplying from moment to moment," while in the press, Brissot and the *Journal de Paris* spoke of protests passed by "several" districts, Loustalot referred to "a majority," and Gorsas' *Courrier de Versailles* indicated that "all the Paris districts hurried to disavow the decree of the Electors." And even the royalist writer Droz acknowledged that almost a third of the districts protested that day.[41] Moreover, there was apparently a good deal of "fermentation" in almost all districts, whether formal decrees were passed or not.[42]

There was, however, a certain degree of ambiguity in these district protests. On the one hand, popular opposition to the indulgent decrees was, in all likelihood, encouraged and exploited by largely bourgeois local politicians who were attempting to carve out an independent sphere of action in what was to become a long struggle with the Hôtel-de-Ville. On the other hand, several district leaders claimed, perhaps not entirely disingenuously, that they were only trying to appease their constituents. As a spokesman for the Blancs-Manteaux District put it, the protest against the indulgent decrees was designed "to disarm the People ... [by] making it see that it had defenders and thus did not have to defend itself."[43] Following this line of thought, Gorsas reported that "the most vigorous protests were precisely the ones that most contributed to the re-establishment of calm."[44]

Yet, whatever its dynamics, district opposition clearly contributed to the extremely difficult position in which the municipal authorities soon found themselves. With the city-wide explosion of protest continuing into the night, the Représentants declared at 10 p.m. that "prudence" required that they revoke their order for

Besenval's release. At the same time, they announced that they would take "the most prompt measures to insure that this officer remained in custody until the National Assembly states what should be done with him." Then, one hour later, in what bears the obvious imprint of a hastily arranged compromise with the Oratoire and a last effort to keep Besenval away from Paris, the Représentants sent off yet another commissioner on the road to Villenauxe accompanied by an Oratoire official. These two men had orders to arrest Besenval and hold him "in the place where they find him." Almost simultaneously, the Oratoire declared it "consented" to this arrangement.[45]

Meanwhile, the Electors were scrambling to retract their declaration of general amnesty. In what was to be the last official act of a body that had, in any case, already been almost totally eclipsed by the Représentants, the Assembly of Electors tried to save face by issuing an "explanation" of its earlier decree. "Upon hearing the protests of some districts," it declared that: "In expressing a sentiment of pardon and indulgence towards its enemies, it should not be understood as having declared amnesty for those who might be suspected, accused, and convicted of *lèse-nation*, but rather only to have announced that citizens will now only want to act and to punish through the Laws."[46]

As for Necker, he never recovered from the rapid reversal of fortune suffered that day. In fact, the "journée du 30 juillet" clearly marks the beginning of his downfall as a revolutionary politician, "the first blow," as his daughter Mme de Staël put it, "to his popularity." As he himself later wrote: "It is the day at the Hôtel-de-Ville ... to which I must trace the beginning of the intrigue and hostility from which I have suffered so much and of which I remain the victim." Or as the essayist Beaulieu stated: "From that moment on, it was as if he had been struck by lightning. All his power disappeared and his credit was exhausted."[47]

Seeking to explain the series of events just described, many contemporary observers stressed the importance of personal rivalries and connections. Thus, the "Deux Amis de la Liberté" stated that Necker's enemies "avidly seized this occasion as a means of slandering him and making him lose his popularity." More specifically, Ferrières presented Mirabeau as the moving spirit behind the crucial Oratoire District decree, while Necker himself attributed an even larger role to his old enemy:

On the evening of this happy day, he was seen agitating in all the clubs where the most violent men met. He painted the Hôtel-de-Ville's action and the speech which provoked it as collaboration with the aristocracy. He disparaged clemency, insulted kindness, threw suspicion upon all partisans of conciliation, and reawakened ideas of severity and vengeance ... Without perhaps realizing it, he laid the foundations for the terrible system which became synonymous with the French Revolution itself.[48]

Certainly it would have been only "poetic justice" if Mirabeau, left free to play the role of Popular Tribune because of Necker's inability to patch things up with him, had indeed almost single-handedly inflicted this serious political defeat on the Minister. Moreover, Mirabeau, who hoped to replace Bailly as Mayor, had actually been agitating against the municipality and making overtures to the districts even before Necker's arrival in the capital.[49] However, the protests of July 30 obviously had far deeper causes than Mirabeau's ambition. If he did play an influential role that evening, it was because his appeals to severity and vengeance had struck a responsive chord.

An alternative interpretation of Necker's reversal was provided by some apologists for the Minister who asserted that he was unaware of the local political situation and, in particular, was unaware of the weakened position of the Electors.[50] But this explanation is even less satisfying than the previous one since Necker spoke to the Représentants as well as to the Electors and the ensuing protest was directed against the work of *both* assemblies. Besides, the claim that a politician like Necker had approached the important political meetings of July 30 without the most elementary political "briefing" is hardly credible and we have already seen that several people had discussed the situation in the capital with him before he entered the Hôtel-de-Ville. Yet, the degree of political miscalculation taking place on that day seems so enormous that one cannot help wonder what might have happened if Necker had been satisfied with the Représentants' order for Besenval's release and had not pressed his advantage further with the already discredited Electors. At the very least, it is clear that the Electors' proclamation of a general amnesty left the Représentants' release order even more vulnerable to protest than it would otherwise have been.

A third explanation of the events of July 30 advanced by many contemporaries postulated a distinction between the spontaneous "enthusiasm" inspired by Necker and the "return to reason" that supposedly followed. Thus, Bailly described the Représentants as being "carried away by an irresistible impulse," while the embarrassed Electors from the hardline Oratoire District confessed to having "succumbed to the enthusiasm of our hearts." Along the same lines, an anonymous pamphleteer attacked Clermont for having "yielded to the impulses of his heart without consulting his reason." And the Petits-Pères District protested against an amnesty that had been "inspired by sensibility alone," and then praised the "wisdom" of the Représentants for retracting their pardon of Besenval.[51]

In thereby opposing judicial "wisdom" to a heartfelt but ultimately arbitrary and irregular granting of clemency, these comments reflect the tension between humanitarian and rationalistic currents within the pre-revolutionary judicial reform movement. On a more concrete level, however, the willingness to see judicial "reason" as furnishing a necessary corrective to spontaneous "sentiment" was especially favored by those attempting to reconcile perfunctory praise for Necker with criticism of his amnesty policy. As an anonymous spokesman for the Nation declared: "If the glory and generosity of a virtuous minister has led him to forgive the outrages perpetrated against him, justice and self-interest require that I not imitate him." And another critic gently lectured Necker: "It was only humanity towards a fellow human being that led you to seek clemency for M. de Besenval ... Reflection had not yet entered your mind."[52] But for an especially revealing example of this kind of effort to harmonize hymns to Necker with a more popular melody, let us turn to the coverage of these events provided by the future Girondin Gorsas.

On July 31, in an article evidently written before the outbreak of protest the previous evening, Gorsas presented a short and apparently sympathetic report on the passage of the Electors' general amnesty, a report which, at the very least, did not give any indication that the author might have any objection to it. On the next day, however, he was more ambivalent, combining praise for Necker's "touching words" with reminders of Besenval's "detestable" projects. And by August 3, though still polite to Necker, Gorsas' position on the amnesty had become clear:

You Aristocrats who have abused his kindness to get him to make an *indiscreet* request, know well this Nation that you have embittered and badly judged... M. Necker will obtain nothing contrary to justice ... and we do honor to him by resisting an unjust desire, the consequences of which he has not sensed clearly enough.[53]

Yet, though Gorsas' opposition to amnesty was now clear, his reasons for opposing it were not. Was the amnesty "unjust" or only "indiscreet"? Had it resulted from a lack of reflection concerning the true nature of justice or a lack of reflection as to what the People's response to a lenient policy would be? Had the sponsors of the amnesty failed to consider the real dangers still posed by the "conspirators" or had they failed to consider the popular fears concerning these dangers? In short, can we attribute Gorsas' shift in position to a change of opinion regarding proper judicial policy or to a deepening recognition of the imperatives of revolutionary politics? The answer seems to be indicated in a comment he made five days before Necker's return to Paris:

When the friend of man [Necker] is recalled, when every heart flies towards him, all hatred will cease and tumultuous passions will give way to the deliriousness of a sweet joy ... At last, the citizen–patriot who reports the events which pass before his eyes will happily have only peaceful pictures to paint instead of those bloody scenes which he could not depict without taking fright.[54]

Thus, rather than being caught up in a spontaneous outpouring of emotion, Gorsas had apparently been prepared to support Necker's amnesty policy well in advance of its public unveiling. As a "citizen-patriot" who had been appealing for "peace" and attacking "anarchy" ever since July 14, he was evidently looking forward to the moderating influence that Necker would presumably exert upon his return.[55]

On July 28, however, a strangely defensive tone crept into Gorsas' comments on the release of Maury and Calonne. "It is assuredly not suspect," he wrote, to favor these releases.[56] Could he have been responding to Robespierre's comments of the previous day on the treasonous implications of "ménagements pour les conspirateurs"? Might he have been beginning to think about the anti-popular implications of his opposition to "tumultuous passions"? Regardless of what may have prompted this defensive remark, the events of July 30 seem to have had a significant impact on Gorsas. For, as Bailly had predicted, Necker's move for amnesty had only resulted in the reanimation and further crystallization of the popular desire for vengeance. Suddenly what was "assuredly not suspect" on July 28 had become quite suspect indeed. As one anonymous pamphleteer put it: "Generosity in these circumstances comes too close to complicity."[57] Highly valuing his status as an "advanced patriot," Gorsas, who would later emerge as the Girondins' most consistent apologist of popular violence, moved swiftly to disassociate himself from Necker's judicial policies.[58]

In a similar vein, the bourgeois notables who were responsible for the passage of the two lenient decrees of July 30 also appear to have been acting in accordance with well-established pre-existing ideological tendencies towards punitive restraint, tendencies which the Electors had already exhibited at the height of the crisis two weeks earlier. As for their quick about-face that evening, while most of these municipal leaders were certainly not ready to go as far as Gorsas in cultivating a popular image, they were, after all, responsible for maintaining order and they obviously felt they had to adjust to the popular tide to meet this responsibility. Although such a reaction can and has been termed "fear,"[59] it can also be seen as a kind of *de facto* recognition of the democratic process!

Be that as it may, there was one Représentant who seems to have been particularly attuned to the political significance of the antiamnesty protests: Gorsas' future cell-mate Brissot. On July 31, the *Patriote français* carried a report on the events of the previous morning that generally paralleled the report in the July 31 issue of Gorsas' journal: praise for Necker, lots of applause and tears, and not a hint of opposition to Besenval's release. By August 1790, Brissot would be attacking Clermont for participating in the "tearful comedy" performed at the Hôtel-de-Ville a year earlier.[60] But on July 31, 1789, he wrote that "this humane sentiment [the call for clemency] redoubled when M. de Clermont-Tonnerre, with an eloquence that is so well known, supported M. Necker's request."[61] At that point, Brissot appears to have been quite willing to go along with Necker's indulgent policies. In fact, it will be recalled, he too had pointed out the merits of having the "generosity to pardon everything" barely a week earlier.

By the next day, however, the lack of political viability of Necker's amnesty had become painfully obvious, and Brissot clearly felt compelled to back away from it. Yet he did so reluctantly, proposing a dose of judicial rigor as a means of coping with a dangerous situation:

Considering how easy it is for a People which always believes itself to be on the edge of a precipice to become frightened, one would think it was imprudent to accord grace to M. de Besenval. But there was a way to reconcile respect for legal forms with the fears of the People: it was to keep this officer in prison without bringing him to Paris, where his life would be exposed, while also pressing for the creation of a Tribunal of Jurors... It is evident there was a conspiracy. Thus, a judgment is necessary. Pardons, whether partial or general, can only excite indignation.[62]

In this key passage, keeping Besenval in prison and creating a *lèse-nation* tribunal are presented as "prudent" rather than as inherently just measures. And while the existence of a conspiracy is acknowledged, there is no indication of a "punitive will," no suggestion that Besenval *deserved* to be punished. In his pre-revolutionary work, Brissot was, as we have seen, inclined to be quite tolerant of certain types of conspiracy, and he seems more interested here in protecting Besenval from vigilante justice than in expressing any moral indignation with respect to his alleged crimes.

Indeed Brissot did not even insist at this point on Besenval's guilt. For the need for a "judgment" is framed here as a means of containing popular anger, thereby implying that, while issuing a pardon was a mistake, it might be possible to dispose of this anger through the long drawn-out process of a public trial. In addition, Brissot's apparent reluctance to take a position on the question of Besenval's guilt is further indicated by his inclusion of a rumor that, on July 12, the old general had disobeyed orders from Broglie to put the royal troops into action, a rumor which, "if true, speaks in this officer's favor." Moreover, the long article on Besenval in the August 1 *Patriote français* also contained a dispassionate discussion of the vital question of whether a military officer could be charged with a crime if he had only been following orders. With its careful phrasing and its effort to acknowledge the value of a variety of positions at the same time, this article represents one of Brissot's earliest and most poignant efforts to play with revolutionary fire while maintaining contact with his "philosophic" principles.

In the next few days, Brissot continued to present himself as the advocate of a "justice impartiale" in which popular desires and fears would somehow be "reconciled" with the rights of the accused. Promoting his pet project of a "Tribunal of Jurors" on August 4,

Brissot stated that: "Two conditions must be religiously observed if the National Tribunal is to be reputable: (1) It must be constructed in such a way as to obtain the confidence of the People, who demand vengeance; and (2) it must be constructed in such a way that accuser and accused will each have an equal chance."[63]

But as if suddenly realizing that a program which combined a condescending tolerance of the People's childish fears with a pedantic concern for "forms" had little chance of winning popular confidence, Brissot switched gears again on the very next day. It was on August 5 that he presented his cleverly arranged report on the Court's plan to attack Paris, a report designed to fix the equation Besenval = July Conspiracy firmly in the minds of his readers. It was on that day, moreover, that he suggested Besenval was a "monster" for whom "no punishment would be sufficient to expiate [his] crime," though this suggestion was accompanied, it will be recalled, by a string of "woulds," "coulds," and "maybes."[64]

By August 10, Brissot's move away from Necker's amnesty policy was complete. Abandoning his relative neutrality of August 1, he now argued unequivocally that "the natural laws which constitute society" superseded any orders Besenval and his accomplices may have had. And jettisoning his epistemological qualifications of August 5, he now declared that:

Their crime is one of treason against the entire Nation. They have urged or wanted to help the King make war on his People ... Are these not crimes worthy of the most severe punishment? Do we need an explicit law before we can declare that an arsonist is a criminal or that a man who advises a King to make war against his People is an enemy of the People?

Having at last begun to pick up the spirit of vintage French revolutionary rhetoric, Brissot next recalled how the People, seen for the moment as a useful source of energy to be praised and perhaps even encouraged rather than as a panic-prone mass that had to be "calmed" and "appeased," had forced Lord Strafford's execution during the Puritan Revolution: "This People, eternally slandered, was responsible for those acts of justice which alone were effective in frightening ministerial despotism. Yet, after his execution, Strafford was an object of pity for those who saw only the pain endured by the guilty man and forgot the bloodshed he had caused."[65] From this point on, there would be no more pro-Besenval rumors appearing in the *Patriote français*.

However, though Brissot would remain in the forefront of the campaign against Besenval, the implicit incitement of the People contained in the above passage was actually something of an aberration for him. Inhibited by his conception of himself as an *esprit éclairé*, he would never be able to commit himself wholeheartedly to the role of Popular Tribune. Thus, on the very day he praised the People for its devotion to punitive justice, he also exhibited a paternalistic urge to enlighten and guide it: "This People is essentially good, but it is anxious and unstable, and not yet accustomed to reasoning. By reasoning with it, one gets its confidence, and it listens and obeys. Above all, it obeys when it is addressed by wise men who speak well and with moderation."[66]

In this connection, Brissot's response to an early critic of the Comité des Recherches is also instructive. Asked how "the People's suspicions could dissipate when it sees its administrators sharing them," he did not proclaim, as revolutionary radicals usually did, that there was good reason to be suspicious. Instead, he insisted that the Comité "has calmed fears," and that "the decrease in unrest among the People that we have noticed lately is due in part to the work of this Comité and to the confidence that the People have in it."[67] With Brissot, however, the balance struck between trying to calm the People and trying to excite them to further action is never quite clear, though I would stress the former. In the chapters that follow, we will see Brissot make many efforts to embrace the People's desires and concerns. Yet, by the end of this work, we will also have a clearer idea of why he and his party were ultimately rejected by them.[68]

One of the principal aims of this chapter has been to highlight the importance of popular pressure in generating the about-face performed by the municipal authorities on July 30. As the July Revolution had vividly demonstrated and as the protest against amnesty had again shown, "the People" had become a political force which could not be ignored, and this was a lesson that was being absorbed by those municipal notables who were primarily interested in maintaining order as well as by those who were beginning to think about future revolutionary career possibilities. But while it is clear that "the People" had suddenly become a powerful political force and equally clear that "the People" were consistently inclined to favor a punitive approach to revolutionary justice, it might be helpful at this point to look a little more deeply into some of the problems involved in defining this slippery concept.[69] Can "the People" indeed be identified, as has essentially been the case thus far in this study, with an uneducated and uncultivated populace or *menu peuple* largely untouched by the humanitarian assumptions of late eighteenth-century judicial thought? Or is it more meaningful to see a statement like "the People demand vengeance" as a cleverly manipulated slogan used by some members of the revolutionary elite to legitimize demands for judicial severity that were actually rooted in their own ideological and/or temperamental make-up? And if the latter is true, would it not follow that the quasi-unanimous support among the "enlightened elite" for the liberal and humanitarian ideals of the pre-revolutionary judicial reform movement was little more than an illusion and that a significant number of future revolutionaries were only superficially committed to these ideals?

Now it would certainly be foolish to insist that every member of the revolutionary elite was a Beccaria clone and that the uncultivated *menu peuple* was the only political force favoring judicial severity in the early Revolution. Moreover, it can certainly be assumed that those members of the elite who were personally disposed towards a more punitive style of justice engaged in two distinct activities which together can be termed "manipulation of the People": (a) mobilization of members of the *menu peuple* through the use of the rhetoric of vengeance and just punishment; and (b) promotion of the idea that those who are mobilized *are* (or at least represent) "the People." In addition, it can probably also be assumed that such "manipulation of the People" was also practiced by a different group of individuals, those who, without necessarily being personally disposed towards punitive justice, saw the support of punitive demands as a way of furthering their own goals and ambitions. (Those district politicians who, as indicated above, seem to have embraced the cause of judicial severity on July 30 as a means of mobilizing popular support in their struggle against the Hôtel-de-Ville would fall into this category.) Having thus recognized the diversity of motives and techniques involved in the "manipulation of the People," we obviously must concede that "encouragement of popular unrest" was often camouflaged and presented as "response to popular unrest."

However, just as a match cannot ignite a fire in the absence of firewood or other flammable material, successful manipulation of "the People" on behalf of punitive demands could never have occurred without a strong inclination towards support for these demands among the *menu peuple*. Thus, it was the presence of this revolutionary firewood that lent political viability to what was decidedly a minority tendency among the elite and that enabled the question of revolutionary justice to develop rapidly into a major political issue. With the enormous importance that "the People" seemed to attach to the need to punish its enemies, a politician's position on matters relating to revolutionary justice quickly became perhaps the most closely watched "litmus test" of his loyalty to "the People." Though largely ignored by historians, the "journée du 30 juillet" was an important crystallization point in the process by which support for punitive justice came to be seen as proof of patriotism.

INTERLUDE AT BRIE-COMTE-ROBERT

But let us now return to Besenval. With the Représentants and the Oratoire District having finally agreed on the night of July 30 that the old general's status would be determined by the National Assembly, all eyes turned to the Representatives of the Nation, who promptly took up the matter the next morning. Though the Assembly had ordered the release of Maury and Calonne just four days earlier and would probably have liked to do the same for Besenval, it should be clear by now why it did not. As Prieur put it: "The People seeks to avenge itself when it doubts that the Law will avenge it. This doubt has brought new unrest to the capital. Let us assure the People that it will have its revenge and it will await that revenge calmly and quietly."[70]

However, though the decision that Besenval would be kept under arrest was probably a foregone conclusion, this did not prevent a string of deputies from extolling the virtues of Necker's amnesty policy. Moreover, in a clear demonstration of the close ties between Necker and the Monarchiens, Lally-Tolendal argued that support for amnesty would constitute a vote of confidence in the Minister.[71] Recognizing the political significance of the Assembly's rejection of amnesty, Necker later wrote that "I should perhaps have turned in my resignation at that instant."[72]

Besides attempting to invoke Necker's already waning prestige, those who favored Besenval's release repeated one of the themes of the Castelnau debate by maintaining that the "conspirators" could be pardoned because they were no longer dangerous. In addition, it was also pointed out that, like Calonne, Besenval had not been formally accused or taken *en flagrant délit*, but had only been arrested on the basis of "simple suspicion" or "public rumor."[73] However, the most interesting statement in favor of amnesty that day was made by Garat, whose remarks aptly captured the idea that many enlightened intellectuals must have had of the way that a revolution was supposed to proceed in the "advanced" eighteenth century:

> I am far from wanting to justify the crimes of our persecutors. But our progress has been so rapid, we have moved so swiftly towards liberty that one would think centuries had elapsed since we began. Yet, some have not learned to follow you in this sudden march. We must leave them behind and pardon them, as one pardons madness and lunacy, for remaining in the centuries of barbarism and ignorance. Let us mark our own happy epoch by branding our justice with the sentiments of generosity and moderation which do honor to our century.[74]

As for those deputies ready to depart from Garat's "generosity" and "moderation," their task was made easier by what Robespierre called the "insurrection" of the previous day.[75] During the Castelnau debate, the proponents of vigilance had focused on the threats posed by the "conspirators." But this time it was not necessary to claim that real dangers existed. Instead, it was sufficient to invoke the problems created by popular fear that such dangers existed. Hence, in the manner of Brissot and Gorsas, vigilance could be justified as a prudent way of calming fears rather than as a means of protection against the "conspirators" themselves.[76] Moreover, the tense atmosphere generated by the anti-amnesty protest movement also seems to have induced the Assembly to put aside its ideas about what constituted a legal arrest. Thus, Volny declared that "we do not have to be constrained by the slowness of ordinary procedures ... This is a denunciation being made by the entire Nation."[77]

With other influential deputies like Mirabeau, Camus, and the respected jurist Target also agreeing that the Assembly had to show that its July 13 declaration of ministerial responsibility was more than empty rhetoric, there was little chance it would free Besenval. Yet, the decree finally passed still reveals a certain hesitancy about actually ordering an arrest: "The Baron de Besenval, if still detained, should be confined in a safe place and under sufficient guard in the closest town to the place where he will have been arrested. No one may harm the Baron de Besenval, who is under the safeguard of the Law."[78]

Thus, rather than explicitly commanding Besenval's arrest, the Assembly only ordered that he be kept under arrest if he were "still detained." By the time this decree was passed (somewhere around four in the afternoon), some of the deputies had probably received word that Besenval was in custody at Brie-Comte-Robert, 25 km. east of Paris.[79] If this was indeed known, then the tortured wording of the Assembly's decree might be regarded as a kind of polite but moot concession to the defenders of legal formalities and the doctrine of separation of powers. On the other hand, if the Assembly acted without any information as to Besenval's whereabouts, the decree passed can be seen as a genuine compromise that would have left his status to chance. In either case, the decree's wording seems to reflect at least some degree of reluctance on the part of the Assembly to become too actively involved in the legal pursuit of the Nation's enemies.

However, there can be no uncertainty concerning the meaning of the provision that Besenval be kept "in the closest town to the place where he will have been arrested." For under no circumstances did the Assembly want the prisoner to be brought to Paris. As DuQuesnoy put it, though he and his colleagues wanted "to make the people of Paris see that the guilty ... *could* be punished, it was above all necessary to keep the Baron de Besenval away from the unbridled populace which would have torn him to pieces."[80]

So once again, a messenger was sent off to find Besenval, who, as we have seen, had left Villenauxe for Paris on the night of July 30, just as anti-amnesty protest was reaching its height. Only a few hours after this departure, the prisoner and his guards were met by the "amnesty delegation" that had left the capital that afternoon with orders to escort him to Switzerland. But the temporarily pardoned Besenval and his rescuers did not get very far. Although the exact circumstances of his re-arrest are unclear and although the various armed groups claiming jurisdiction over him seem to have come close to blows, by morning Besenval was a prisoner once again, this time in the Hôtel-de-Ville in Brie-Comte-Robert.[81]

For the next three months, the old general remained at Brie-Comte-Robert while the revolutionary authorities wrestled with the problem of what to do with him. Though the National Assembly, it will be recalled, had promised on July 23 that a *lèse-nation* tribunal would soon be instituted, its July 31 decree did not give any indication as to how Besenval would be tried. Fearing that this void would impede the process of calming popular unrest, the Paris Représentants informed the Assembly that the immediate creation of a *lèse-nation* court was required "so that, the punishment of the guilty furnishing a necessary lesson, public tranquillity can be restored." No doubt hoping to show that they had themselves learned a "necessary lesson" from the events of July 30, the Représentants also had placards carrying the text of their demand posted all around the city. However, the Assembly ignored this demand, and its Comité des Recherches quickly ordered the removal of the placards, declaring that their message was "contrary to the Constitution and to the principles of the Assembly."[82]

Despite this rebuff, the Représentants continued, as we have seen, to demand a *lèse-nation* tribunal, and on September 3, they also requested Besenval's transfer to Paris "where we will know how to protect him from popular attack."[83] But while the National Guard had undoubtedly become a more reliable police force by early September, the main reason for increased confidence in Besenval's potential safety in Paris was that his case had lost the urgency it had possessed earlier. With public attention largely turning to the Assembly's constitutional debates and with popular "effervescence" settling down to a relatively manageable level, Besenval was almost totally ignored by the revolutionary press in August and September. Indeed, in the absence of significant radical and popular pressure, the Représentants' request for Besenval's transfer might be regarded as more of a ritual demand than a serious one.

Even Marat, who had emerged in the early autumn as a major spokesman for a punitive approach to revolutionary justice, displayed little interest during this period in seeing Besenval brought to trial. For Marat, the failure of the July "chasse aux bêtes" to register any significant results was one of the key mistakes of the early Revolution. "The People," he declared, "has stupidly missed its chance to get rid of the enemies of the State ... who have now resumed their machinations." And why was this chance missed? In Marat's view, it was because of the People's misguided confidence in the new regime: "Instead of relentlessly pursuing the punishment of public enemies, you were taken in by the maneuvers of feeble or corrupt men who did their best to save your enemies from your just vengeance." With Artois, Condé, and all the other top conspirators free to resume their plotting, the municipality's campaign to make a "necessary example" of Besenval held little appeal for Marat. Besides, given the policies already implemented by the revolutionary authorities, he foresaw only further equivocation. With a characteristic blend of cynicism and prophetic clarity, he was able to predict the final outcome of the Besenval case and all the other major counter-revolutionary cases of 1789–90 a full month before the designation of the Châtelet as *lèse-nation* court: "If the Chiefs of the Conspiracy ever fall into their hands, far from inflicting the least punishment upon them, they will hasten to whitewash their acts. And the Judges named by the government will make sure that these traitors get passed off as good patriots."[84]

As for Besenval himself, his stay at Brie-Comte-Robert was hardly a rigorous one. He had, in fact, no fewer than three servants to take care of him, and he later wrote: "My days were not very disagreeable. I read, I was amused by the mischievousness of my young Guards, and I played trictrac."[85] But this relative idyll, which, in some respects, does not seem so very different from his life as a member of Marie-Antoinette's circle, would last only until the next major explosion of revolutionary energy. As the National Assembly prepared, in the wake of the October Days, to place Besenval and all other *lèse-nation* suspects under the jurisdiction of the Châtelet, Reubell reminded the deputies that there were still many people not yet prepared to forget the "crimes of July": "There is no middle ground . . . It is necessary to try either M. de Besenval or the city of Paris."[86]

With judges finally assigned to the case, Lafayette went before the Représentants on October 24 to ask for and immediately receive an order to transfer Besenval to the Châtelet prison. Thus, as if to underscore the largely ritualistic nature of the Représentants' earlier demand for this transfer, when the municipal authorities were really ready to bring Besenval to Paris, they did not even bother to ask for authorization from the National Assembly. Instead, they simply went ahead and did it. On November 6, Besenval was, at last, brought to the capital, and on November 18, he was formally denounced by the Paris Comité des Recherches. Three days later, his trial began.[87]

4

Lafayette, Orléans, and the October Days

In authorizing the arrest and trial of Besenval, the National Assembly had, however reluctantly, set into motion a procedure which has been repeated countless times in countless revolutions in the past two centuries, the prosecution of a representative of a defeated regime by a group of victorious revolutionaries.[1] However, the judicial aftermath of the October Days followed an entirely different pattern. For, in direct contrast to the defeated military commander Besenval, the principal target of the revolutionary regime's investigation of the October Insurrection was one of the leading heroes of the seemingly victorious insurgents.

When the people of Paris marched to Versailles on October 5, 1789 to fetch "the baker, the baker's wife, and the little baker boy," Louis-Philippe-Joseph Duc d'Orléans (1744–94) was being hailed by many of the marchers as "notre père" and even as "roi."[2] And when the marchers returned the next day, in an "indescribable procession" which included a captured king and the severed heads of two of his bodyguards, this "Red Prince" was still the object of great acclaim.[3] Yet, within ten days, Orléans would be informally exiled from France, and, soon afterwards, legally pursued as the principal suspect in a Châtelet probe into the "crimes of October," a probe which formed part of a general post-October Days judicial campaign against the revolutionary left. Postponing my account of the outcome of the Besenval case to a later chapter, I will spend the next two chapters examining this campaign, an undertaking which, in addition to shedding some light on the nature of revolutionary justice in 1789–90, will also help clarify the nature and significance of the October Days themselves.

The idea of using a march on Versailles as a means of speeding up revolutionary momentum was actually first attempted in late

August, at a point when the primary objective of most "advanced patriots" was to prevent a royal veto from being included in the Constitution being prepared by the National Assembly. On August 30, some 1,500 unarmed opponents of "Monsieur Veto" left the Palais-Royal for Versailles, only to have their path blocked on the outskirts of Paris by Lafayette's National Guard. Seven of the presumed leaders of this march were subsequently arrested, including the Marquis de Saint-Huruge, a picturesque *déclassé* noble who was thought to be an Orleanist agent.[4] The agitation leading up to this march had been especially directed against the Monarchien deputies, and on August 31 two threatening letters sent to Clermont-Tonnerre from "La Société Patriotique du Palais-Royal" were read to the Assembly. Seeking to mock the "enlightened" values of the wealthy liberal nobles who dominated the Monarchien faction, one of these letters notified Clermont that the writers were eager to "éclairer vos châteaux et vos maisons." In response, Clermont declared that if Lafayette and Bailly could not guarantee order in Paris, the Assembly should move to a safer place, further away from the capital.[5]

By the first week of October, however, Monarchien support for the veto was no longer an issue. The rejection of an absolute veto and, more importantly, the rejection of the "English" system of two legislative chambers had sealed the definitive parliamentary defeat of the "Anglomane" Monarchiens, who had envisioned themselves as the natural leaders of a French House of Lords. This defeat was reflected, moreover, in the resignation of the Monarchien-dominated Constitutional Committee on September 12. By early October, the basic "program" of the revolutionary left now consisted of the following: (1) royal approval of the Assembly's Declaration of Rights and its "anti-feudalism" decrees; (2) vigorous action against new conspiracies supposedly being hatched at Versailles; (3) more substantial efforts to ease the continuing bread crisis; and (4) transfer of the King and the Assembly to Paris.[6]

Besides having different immediate goals from the August march, the October march to Versailles also, of course, had a totally different magnitude. For in place of 1,500 Palais-Royal regulars, it was a large chunk of Paris itself, including a contingent of perhaps 7,000 women, which went to Versailles in October. And most importantly, led (or followed) by Lafayette himself, the Paris National Guard, which had routed the August march, joined the October one! In all, there were probably some 30,000–35,000 Parisians who converged on Versailles on the evening of October 5.[7]

In the face of this mass of quite well-armed humanity, the options of the Court were extremely limited. With Louis XVI no more disposed to the use of force than he had been earlier and with most of the hardliners who had advocated force during the previous summer now gone, the King's rejection of the advice of the few remaining counselors inclined to military resistance is hardly surprising.[8] In fact, his own bodyguards were instructed "not to oppose force with force, but rather to expose themselves to the greater dangers," a remarkable order which recalls our earlier discussion of Louis as a "pacifist-king."[9] And lest it be thought that this supposed order is only royalist legend, when the Château itself was attacked on October 6, even the Gardes-des-Corps who were massacred by the invaders do not seem to have fired a shot in their own defense.

On the other hand, Louis does seem to have given serious consideration to a proposal by Interior Minister Saint-Priest that he withdraw to Rambouillet. About one month earlier, the Monarchiens (with the possible support of Necker) had proposed that the King adopt an "appeal to the provinces" strategy by taking steps to move the government from the Versailles–Paris area.[10] With the marchers from Paris bearing down upon him on October 5, the King apparently did agree to a version of such a strategy, actually sending Saint-Priest to Rambouillet to make the necessary preparations for his reception, only to change his mind and decide to stay.[11] One story pictures the eternally indecisive Louis XVI (who was said to have had "a kind of passive courage and to have found a sort of shame in the idea of running away") pacing up and down, sadly repeating to himself: "Un roi fugitif, un roi fugitif!"[12]

With military confrontation and flight ruled out, the only alternative left was a familiar one: capitulation. On the evening of October 5, the King accepted all the Assembly decrees, signed some orders that would supposedly help in the provisioning of Paris, and dismissed the notorious Flanders regiment, the recent arrival of which had seemed to confirm rumors of new aristocratic plotting. While he continued to resist the key demand that he come to Paris, this opposition crumbled the next morning after an invasion of the Château by some of the more radical and adventurous of the marchers, an invasion that was quickly subdued by the Paris National Guard and that would later become the focus of the Châtelet's

October Days investigation. It was this invasion, this "irruption soudaine" of "bandits," that capped the royal capitulation and set in motion the celebrated return march to Paris.[13] But though the events of the morning of October 6 had clearly convinced the King that he had to come to Paris, the political significance of these events remains unclear. Did Louis' final concession result from another demonstration of the power of the revolutionary crowd, or did it result from a demonstration of the enormous extent to which the security of the royal family now depended on the protection of Lafayette and the National Guard? Or to put it another way: who was really victorious in the October Days? Was it the People of Paris or was it Lafayette?

With the King now installed in the Louvre "under the watchful eye," as George Rudé put it, "of the majority in the National Assembly, the Paris city government, and Districts," and with the Assembly itself now "under the equally watchful eye of the Parisian *menu peuple*," it certainly seemed as if what I have loosely termed "the left" had been successful.[14] Here, for example, is Albert Mathiez's analysis of the position of "the patriots" after the October Days:

> Their desires are gratified and their victory is complete. They are now protected from a counter-revolution and all State powers are at their disposal. The King, the Court, and the Assembly still have the power to do good, that is, to enact popular measures. But from now on, they will no longer be able to do harm, that is, to resist the will of the Nation.[15]

But if the October Days are usually presented as a triumph for "the left" or "the patriots," they are also generally presented, sometimes by the same author, as a victory for Lafayette. Thus, Rudé stated that this episode "established the ascendancy of the constitutional monarchists which, in Paris, found its reflection in the long rule of Bailly as mayor and Lafayette as commander-in-chief of the National Guard."[16] Or as George A. Kelly wrote:

> The reluctant Lafayette was the apparent victor of the day. He rode like a constable of France beside the vehicle that returned Louis XVI to Paris. He had marched his troops in response to the will of the people. He had perhaps saved the king's life and certainly his popularity. And Lafayette still ruled Paris: while the capital was his, the king was his.[17]

In order to evaluate the extent to which the view that the Parisian General was the victor of October is consistent with the view that the "patriots" had triumphed, it will be necessary to say something about Lafayette's political status in the autumn of 1789, both as a national political figure and as the *de facto* leader of the Parisian municipal regime.

On what might be called the national political level, if the Monarchiens had by this time essentially passed out of the orbit of the *parti patriotique* and into the ranks of the *parti aristocratique*, Lafayette and his network of supporters in the Assembly and the capital should still be regarded at this point as moderate patriots who subscribed, at least to a certain degree, to the "program of the left" described above. Thus, Mathiez presented the Lafayette of late September as a "patriot" who "saw only one solution to all the problems: the King must be made to understand that coming to Paris would be in his own interest, that by doing so he ... would above all convince Lafayette that he was not supporting the counter-revolutionary projects being ascribed to him."[18] It is true that the Parisian General continued to negotiate with the Monarchiens, even after October, and that he continued to envision himself as the architect and centerpiece of a grand reconciliation of all the original supporters of the Third Estate. However, as Louis Gottschalk and Margaret Maddox have clearly shown, the more Lafayette and his closest political friends talked with the Monarchiens, the more the two groups realized how far apart they were.[19] On the level of national politics, then, it may be possible to reconcile a view of the left as the victor of October with a view of Lafayette as the victor. In any case, quite apart from the question of ideological affinity, Lafayette and the Parisian popular movement each had reason to believe that their own influence would be separately enhanced by the transfer of the King and the Assembly to the capital.

But if, on the national level, Lafayette largely shared the principles or at least the tactical goals of the left, the situation was quite different with respect to local Parisian politics. Here, it was already clear that the "Hero of Two Worlds" was no friend of the popular movement. For Lafayette's suppression of the August 30 march on Versailles was only the most visible of a series of incidents that had exacerbated relations between Paris radicals and a National Guard which day after day broke up demonstrations in the Palais-Royal and in the faubourgs.[20] Thus, though careful not to attack Lafayette directly, Loustalot complained in early October about "harassments against citizens a thousand times worse" than those practiced by the royal police.[21] And Marat, who blamed the Représentants on September 28 for ordering a crack-down on popular protest, came closer to the real target the next day in an open letter to the National Guard:

You used to be citizens, but now, through the orders of a chief, you have been transformed and may soon become the blind instruments of oppression. I want to believe that the heart of your general will always be in accord with his duty and that concern for personal glory will never let him forget his country. But in your current position, blind confidence is unpardonable and is even becoming criminal.[22]

Another radical paper, the *Fouet national*, went even further, asserting that the "ferocious beasts" of the National Guard were "only the vile executors of the despotism of their chief," while an anonymous supporter of Saint-Huruge explicitly demanded that Lafayette be declared a "criminel de lèse-nation."[23] But the contemporary source which perhaps best illustrates the growing gap between Lafayette and the Parisian popular movement was a widely circulated engraving which showed a National Guard patrol breaking up a demonstration: "Le Patrouillotisme Chasse le Patriotisme du Palais-Royal."[24]

As the most powerful municipal official as well as the leading "patrol-ist," Lafayette was also the implicit target of many of the other attacks on the Hôtel-de-Ville in late September and early October. Thus, when Marat denounced Bailly as "this royal pensioner who slyly seeks to monopolize authority," he was denouncing one of Lafayette's principal political associates.[25] And when Loustalot accused the Assemblée des Représentants of wanting "to substitute an aristocracy of wealth for an aristocracy of nobility," he was targeting a body that was largely under the thumb of the Parisian General.[26] And when the municipal constitution being considered by the Représentants was condemned as a plan for "municipal aristocracy," the object of this attack was another leading Lafayette ally, Brissot, who, as the plan's author, had quickly become one of the most visible municipal notables.[27] Moreover, at least one anonymous author did not mince any words in trying to explain the source of the most important problem faced by Parisians: "Citizens, why have Lafayette, Bailly, and the leaders of the Commune let you go without bread? So that they can fatten themselves up at your expense!"[28]

In short, the mounting tide of popular and radical agitation and protest of late September and early October was directed, in large part, against Lafayette's municipal regime. In fact, without perhaps giving it proper emphasis or drawing the proper conclusions from it, virtually all contemporary and historical accounts of the October Days note that the *journée* of October 5 actually began with a serious attack upon the Hôtel-de-Ville itself. On that morning, a huge crowd, largely composed of women, invaded the building, seized arms and money, burned papers, and almost hanged a well-known municipal official, the abbé LeFebvre.[29] Indeed the long-standing threat by "the People" to burn down the Hôtel-de-Ville might finally have been carried out that day, but, according to the Représentants' minutes, "some individuals were arrested at the moment that, torch in hand, they were going to ignite this building's most combustible spot."[30] Conveniently arriving at the City Hall on some unrelated business, the judicial clerk Maillard was told by a crowd of women that "the entire Commune was composed of bad citizens who all deserved to be hanged, beginning with M. Bailly and M. de Lafayette." To a certain extent, moreover, the very idea of going to Versailles seems to have been something of a diversionary move to take the heat (both literally and figuratively) off the Hôtel-de-Ville. At least the enigmatic Maillard, who played a major role in leading the women to Versailles, would testify that he had seen the march as "the only way to clear the crowd out of the Hôtel-de-Ville and the capital."[31]

Later that day, the Parisian General himself would have to deal with the energy and power of a revolutionary crowd. Though unusual oratorical or other charismatic qualities are not usually attributed to the rather bland Lafayette, he did, at least in the Revolution's early months, have a certain knack for charming a hostile crowd with the right words or gestures. At one point, in a kind of "delirium" of his own, he informed his mistress that "the People, in the delirium of its enthusiasm, can be restrained only by me . . . 40,000 souls assemble, the unrest is at its height, I appear, and one word from me disperses them."[32] But the several thousand mutinous National Guardsmen who wanted to leave for Versailles on the afternoon of October 5 constituted one crowd that he was unable to disperse. As some of his men pointed their guns at him and others prepared a noose on the Place de Grève's famous *lanterne*, Lafayette's efforts to dissuade the mutineers were futile.[33] With a large part of the Guard ready to leave with or without him, his only choice, short of provoking a local civil war, was to try to contain or, as Mathiez put it, to "dam up" the rebellion.[34] As Lafayette himself later explained: "The only thing left for me to do was to seize the movement. And so I asked for an order from the Hôtel-de-Ville ... and, with several battalions, I marched on Versailles."[35] Or as Brissot loyally wrote: "Our Commandant-General, whose prudence was equal to his courage, seeing it would be impossible to stop these impetuous troops, thought it was his duty to march at their head."[36]

Now given the puzzling nature of an insurrection that resulted in increased power for the very individual against whom it was ostensibly directed, some historians have insinuated, without ever furnishing any satisfying evidence, that Lafayette must have instigated the October Days.[37] But there is another way to resolve the October Days puzzle, and that is to see this episode as a failed rebellion that strengthened the hand of the authorities who were able to master it. Thus, it can be suggested that the October Days began as a revolt against the Fayettist municipal regime, but that the regime was somehow able to "co-opt" or, in Lafayette's words, "seize" the movement and re-focus its energies onto national rather than local issues, that is to say, to direct attention towards the enemies at Versailles rather than the enemies at the Hôtel-de-Ville. Having managed to make use of the movement for its own purposes and having thereby successfully arranged for the entire national government to operate under its auspices, Lafayette's regime then began a process of rewriting history, of transforming an essentially unsuccessful revolt into a "second dose of revolution" led by "this young hero who seems born for revolutions."[38] By turning what amounted to a defeat for the Parisian popular movement into another glorious victory over the Court, one almost worthy of equal billing with the fourteenth of July itself, this rewriting of history has bequeathed to us the October Days with which we are familiar, the episode which is inevitably described as having "consolidated" or "completed the Paris Revolution of July."[39]

One of the first of the "revisionist" historians of the October Days was Brissot. On October 8, the *Patriote français* tried to put a lid on the notion that tension between the popular movement and the Fayettist municipality had been in any way responsible for the just-concluded events. "The People," wrote Brissot, "was unhappy. But it was not its leaders, either military or civil, whom it accused. The sole object

of its hatred and its protest was the aristocratic party at Versailles."
Yet, if Brissot was able, through this recourse to what might eu-
phemistically be called "selective recall," to sustain his patriotic
credentials by presenting himself as generally sympathetic to the
recent revolutionary action, he certainly did not want to see a
repetition of it:

> What will be the consequences of this memorable day? They can be only
> happy ... if the Court is finally convinced that its interest cannot be
> detached from that of the People, and if the People, now satisfied, is willing
> to restrain itself ... if it is careful not to listen to the insinuations of turbulent
> men who incite revolt for their own private interest, and if it is willing to
> accept these principles: that a free People must be a reasonable People, that
> a reasonable People does not hang or exterminate before discussing and
> judging, and that, incapable of judging when it is too numerous, it must
> entrust this difficult mission to others.[40]

In the mean time, an alternative "authorized interpretation" of
the October Days was being advanced by the less philosophic Gorsas. In this version, a classic "center-left" attempt to discredit more
radical opponents, the revolt against the municipality was acknowledged, but attributed to counter-revolutionaries who were able to
create an artificial bread shortage and then persuade the People that
"this shortage had been brought about by the very same men to
whom Liberty has bestowed a civic crown." Among the worst of
these "pretended friends of the People" was Marat, "a vile and
corrupt man" whose "criminal goal was to set citizen against citizen
and whose bloodthirsty voice calls down the axe upon the most
respectable heads." But, said Gorsas, without going into any details
as to how this had occurred, the counter-revolutionary plot had
somehow backfired: "Yes, a guardian angel watches over my country! For yesterday we saw the most deadly of revolutions give way to
the most glorious of them!"[41]

THE OCTOBER DAYS AND THE HALTING OF REVOLUTIONARY
MOMENTUM

Although historians have always tended to view the October Days
as a successful insurrectionary episode, this interpretation is difficult
to reconcile with its judicial aftermath. For given the simple but

relentlessly accurate rule that, in political justice, it is the winners who prosecute and the losers who are prosecuted (a rule which leaves the question of the degree of severity of prosecution entirely open), the multi-faceted prosecution of the left that we are about to examine is only comprehensible if we can assume that the left had indeed been defeated. While such deductive logic may strike the reader as somewhat schematic, there are additional signals lending credence to the idea that this episode should be seen as an unsuccessful revolt.

For one thing, the national government itself did not change after the October Days. Despite numerous conferences on the subject of a new ministry and despite the further discrediting of the Monarchien faction that was their main base of support within the National Assembly, Necker, Saint-Priest, and the rest of the ministers were able to hang on to their portfolios for another entire year.[42] While this inertia can undoubtedly be partially attributed to the growing irrelevance of the royal government as Assembly committees increasingly assumed the actual tasks of government, the fact remains that an intact ministry is not something normally associated with a successful insurrection.

Secondly, there is the curious but apparently very real increase in the royal family's popularity among the Parisian *menu peuple* immediately after the October Days. As Mathiez wrote, "it may seem paradoxical, but the King and Queen were never more popular," a phenomenon which probably helps account for the noticeable inability of the popular movement to maintain revolutionary momentum in the post-October Days period.[43] While historians usually ascribe this slowing of momentum to an easing of the bread crisis, an independent surge of popular royalism might be seen as a contributing factor in generating what Rudé called the "remarkable period of social calm" which followed the October Days.[44]

In this connection, the popular "excess" of October seems to have produced a sense of revulsion and apprehension among "respectable" patriots that had been conspicuously absent or at least not publicly expressed in July. Thus, for example, after having been relatively submerged through the summer months, the moderate strains in Brissot's temperament were given much freer rein in the post-October Days period. Confining himself to occasional remarks about the need for reason and reflection, Brissot had been unwilling to condemn explicitly the popular violence of July. In fact, he had praised "the courage of this People who, in exercising prompt justice on some agents of despotism, have frightened others and forced them to abandon their posts," a comment that contrasts sharply with his just-cited comment of October 8 that a reasonable People "does not exterminate before discussing and judging."[45] Moreover, the October Days seem to have helped crystallize a new awareness among bourgeois revolutionaries regarding the potentially dangerous social consequences of the Revolution. Hence, on October 21, the deputy DuQuesnoy wrote: "It is being said everywhere that there will be no end to the disorder. And it is only too true that it is becoming a war of those who have enough money to eat against those who do not, a war of property-owners against those without property."[46]

In short, with a revival of royal popularity and with new misgivings about revolutionary "excess," the post-October Days period appears to have been one in which the Monarchy had a real opportunity to renew itself by forging a meaningful and lasting alliance with Lafayette and his allies. As the royalist pamphleteer Jean Pelletier remarked, in a tract that drew a great deal of attention in October and November, "the result [of the recent events] has been entirely admirable." Assuring his readers that Lafayette and Necker would protect the King and affecting a proper revolutionary hatred of "aristocrats," Pelletier declared: "With a vigorous arm, you have already repelled all the aristocracies, and they have dispersed into the emptiness of the air. *You have just trampled down the serpents of democracy, and they have returned to the mud.* Now preserve a *just milieu.*"[47]

Finally, another important symptom of the post-October Days loss of revolutionary momentum can be found in the crucial decision to delegate authority over political justice to the Châtelet. It is true that, after three months of parliamentary delay, the move to finally name a *lèse-nation* tribunal must, to some degree, be seen as a response to the new manifestations of popular violence that appeared in October and therefore as something of a concession to "the People." Yet, by putting political justice in the hands of this ancient royal court, the National Assembly was also, of course, going a long way towards insuring indulgent treatment of the People's enemies, and, at the same time, providing Lafayette with a judicial mechanism through which radical revolutionaries could be harassed and threatened. For in the two-month period following the October Days, the Parisian General would prove to be particularly interested in deploying his enhanced authority against his enemies on the left.

THE EXILE OF ORLÉANS

The idea that the Orleanist faction could be held responsible for inciting "seditious" popular activity had been in the back of Lafayette's mind since at least early June. "I am keeping an eye on M. le Duc d'Orléans," he wrote to his mistress on July 11, "and perhaps I will be in a position to denounce at one and the same time both M. le Comte d'Artois as a seditious aristocrat and M. le Duc d'Orléans as seditious through the use of more popular means."[48] However, regardless of what the Orleanists may have done during the summer of 1789, the same political climate which had largely precluded public criticism of popular violence in July also precluded taking any action at that time against what the bookseller Hardy called the "extreme revolutionary party."[49] Such action would only be feasible in the wake of the defeat suffered by this party in October.

According to Lafayette's account of the October Days, it did not take him long to conclude that blame for provoking the October "troubles" should be placed squarely on the shoulders of the Orleanists. Thus, when the soon-to-be-exiled Orléans told Lafayette that "when he got to London he would try to discover the authors of the troubles," the Parisian General replied: "That question concerns you more than anyone else, for no one is as compromised in them as you." Moreover, Lafayette, convinced that the true aim of the October uprising had been the establishment of an Orleanist dynasty, also reported that he told Orléans: "I have contributed more than anyone to upsetting the workings of the throne. Still, the Nation has placed the King there. I will defend him against you, and before you take his place, you will have to go over my dead body. And that will not be easy."[50]

But whatever Lafayette believed or said he believed concerning the role played by the Orleanists in October (and, for that matter, whatever their actual role may have been), the Parisian General clearly had a very strong personal interest in accusing this faction.[51] For despite the modern tendency not to take the indolent and frivolous Orléans too seriously (he often appears as a rakish version of his hapless royal cousin), the fact is that in using his newly acquired strength to banish this Prince, Lafayette was getting rid of his principal competitor for power. As Orléans' erstwhile ally Mirabeau told the National Assembly a year later, Orléans' departure "above all left without a rival the man to whom chance and the course of events had just given a new dictatorship."[52] Moreover, Orléans was not only a viable alternative to Lafayette, he was a "left" alternative. For regardless of whether the radical and popular movement is viewed as using Orléans or vice versa, it is clear that the influence of this "Red Prince" largely derived from his links with radical politicians and journalists and his popularity among the *menu peuple*.

During the second week of October, Lafayette met with Orléans three times, finally persuading him to leave for London with "a sort of mission that could justify his departure."[53] At one of these meetings, he told Orléans that "if I could produce proofs against you, I would already have had you arrested." Or as he wrote to the Monarchien leader Mounier: "Three days after the King's arrival, I explained myself clearly to M. le Duc d'Orléans. The result was his departure for England. Not that I had any proof against him. If I did, I would have denounced him. But getting him worried was enough to encourage his natural taste for travel."[54]

But what did "proofs" really have to do with Lafayette's handling of this situation? Even with all the evidence in the world, would the Parisian General really have attempted to arrest Orléans and put him on trial? Surely Lafayette knew that any such attempt would only have provoked the very unrest and protest that Orléans' removal from the scene was supposed to dampen.[55] In addition, despite Mirabeau's reference to a "new dictatorship," there were limits to Lafayette's authority. Is it likely, for example, that the National Assembly (which, as we have seen, had already shown itself to be reluctant to authorize political arrests even in the face of popular pressure) would have authorized the arrest of a popular hero, especially one who, as a deputy, had been declared inviolable? Proofs or no proofs, from Lafayette's point of view, Orléans' banishment was clearly preferable to his arrest. Moreover, it seems doubtful that the Parisian General would have pushed the matter much further if Orléans had refused to leave. Rather, it appears as if Lafayette managed to "bluff" the diffident Orléans into thinking he would be arrested if more evidence were uncovered.

In discussing the departure of Orléans a year later, Mirabeau described Lafayette as:

the man who at that moment controlled, in the midst of Liberty, a police more active than that of the Old Regime; who, through this police, had just gathered a body of accusatory information without accusing; and who, in imposing the law on M. de Orléans and forcing him to leave instead of having him judged and condemned if he was guilty, overtly eluded the inviolability of the members of the Assembly.[56]

As exaggerated and self-interested as these remarks were, they do point to an important characteristic of the Orléans exile: it represented a continuation of a well-established eighteenth-century practice, the imposition of exile on defeated political figures. Compared to the seventeenth-century tendency to execute opponents after a perfunctory trial, such a practice might be considered rather "civilized" and quite in keeping with the punitive mildness recommended by pre-revolutionary reformers. For with exile, particularly the luxurious exile to which Orléans and many of his eighteenth-century predecessors were subjected, the vengeance and moralistic harshness associated with the rendering of a "judgment" and with "justice" itself are largely put aside and the victim is treated as more of a "nuisance" than a "criminal."

On the other hand, Lafayette's handling of the Orléans matter was a clear violation of the reform movement's insistence on uniform, regular, and public procedures. Moreover, ironically enough, at virtually the same moment that the Parisian General was "imposing the law" on Orléans, the National Assembly was passing a Lafayette-sponsored decree establishing judicial publicity and the right to legal counsel.[57] Though an Assembly committee had just praised the "enlightenment" of the "soldier-philosopher" who had asked for these reforms, Lafayette certainly seems to have put aside many of his philosophic pretensions when it came to dealing with Orléans.[58]

Still, the fact remains that the procedural irregularity or even illegality of the Orléans exile occurred within the framework of an affair in which the "victim" was actually treated quite leniently, a pattern which was quite typical of revolutionary justice in 1789–90. While the Fayettist regime's willingness to use such blatantly "political" procedures would probably have made some of the pre-revolutionary judicial reformers wince, the ultimate result of these sometimes arbitrary methods was a punitive indulgence which was essentially consistent with the humanitarian inclinations of most of the reformers. By contrast, procedural irregularities would be utilized to quite different ends by later revolutionary regimes.

In any event, Lafayette's manner of handling the Orléans situation proved effective. Though Orléans' leading advisers (Mirabeau, Choderlos de Laclos, and the Duc de Biron) tried to convince the Prince to ignore the Parisian General and take his case to the Assembly, their efforts were ultimately futile. Each time Orléans met with Lafayette, he promised he would leave, only to be persuaded by his advisers to change his mind. On October 13, he promised Mirabeau that he would be at the Assembly the next day to support a denunciation of "the authority which takes the place of the laws," but then changed his mind again and finally left Paris. It was upon hearing this news that Mirabeau let slip his best known assessment of Orléans: "They claim I am in his party, but I wouldn't want to have him as my valet."[59]

The exile of Orléans and the Prince's willingness to submit to it also did not please the Parisian patriotic press. "Your mission is being represented as flight," scolded Loustalot, who urged Orléans to "come back and confound the liars by demanding a judgment, and console the good citizens by proving your innocence." And in what was a rare display of independence for this period, even Brissot hinted that he did not approve of Lafayette's course of action, commenting that "the true friends of this Prince and of Liberty strongly desire to see him descend into the arena to refute the slanderers."[60] But Orléans, kept busy at the racecourses and salons of London, did not return to France until July 1790, and, in the mean time, the Châtelet's investigation of the October Days served to further encourage his "taste for travel." By the time he returned, his political influence had virtually disappeared. Though there would be intermittent flurries of interest in Orléans as an alternative to the ruling branch until the establishment of the Republic (notably during the Varennes crisis of summer 1791), the banishment of the Prince in October 1789 effectively signalled the end of Orleanism as an important political force for the remainder of the Revolution. Lafayette's "surgical strike" had been right on the mark. But his campaign against the revolutionary left was only getting under way.[61]

5

The post-October Days campaign against the left

The exile of Orléans was only one dimension of a comprehensive campaign against the left undertaken in the post-October Days period. Seeking to hamper the ability of the popular movement to mobilize opposition against it, the newly strengthened Fayettist regime employed the judicial system to pursue radical journalists, popular rioters and agitators, recalcitrant district leaders, and troublesome deputies. The two years of relative calm which followed the October Days can be seen, at least in part, as a reflection of the success of these efforts.

MARAT AND THE ATTACK ON PRESS FREEDOMS

One of the main objectives of the Fayettist regime after the October Days was to shut down the incendiary journal of Marat, who had already attracted official displeasure in late September. On September 25, the self-proclaimed Friend of the People, who had just denounced the municipality and Necker for working together on a "plan de trahison," was summoned before the Assemblée des Représentants.[1] Marat, however, was not nearly as easily intimidated as Orléans, and he immediately announced that "the hard truths" contained in his journal were "too important to public security for me to be able to retract a single one of them." "I am the eye of the People," he told the Représentants, "while you are nothing more than its little finger." On October 2, he warned the authorities that "if they continue to sacrifice the Public to their own petty passions, I will pursue them relentlessly ... I am the Attorney of the Nation and I will never retreat." And in keeping with this mission, he next declared that Necker's crimes were "more than sufficient to brand him as a corrupt administrator and to make him carry his guilty head to the scaffold."[2]

With informal censorship having had no effect on Marat, the authorities turned to more formal methods. On October 3, the Représentants officially denounced him to the Châtelet in its capacity as ordinary criminal court for Paris, and on the following day, Châtelet prosecutor Flandre de Brunville filed an indictment accusing him of having written "slanderous and insulting articles." On October 8, an arrest warrant was issued and Marat went into hiding. Though he was not apprehended, his journal did not appear between October 9 and November 4.[3]

This first episode of what was to become an ongoing war between Marat and the authorities would probably have ended in much the same way even if the October Days had not occurred. In the period of heightened tension preceding October 5, the municipality had obviously decided to make an example of an author who signed his own name to his denunciations and whose perverted brilliance had already attracted a wide following.[4] However, the events of October 5 and 6 may well have accelerated the process, perhaps by triggering a direct "request" for an immediate arrest warrant from Lafayette and the Hôtel-de-Ville. In any event, the October 8 warrant against Marat must be seen in the context of a post-October Days environment in which the fear of another popular uprising took at least temporary precedence over philosophic assumptions about the importance of press freedoms. Thus, when Brissot, particularly squeamish about actions taken against fellow journalists, gently criticized the pursuit of Marat by reiterating his pre-revolutionary position that "scorn" was "the only weapon needed against libels," the Représentants noted that "the scorn in which we have held the slanderer and his slanders was not sufficient to avoid the suspicions that uneducated persons could conceive."[5]

Now the conflict between the National Assembly's official policy of virtually unlimited press freedoms and the efforts of local officials to protect both public order and their own reputations by imposing some meaningful restrictions on these freedoms was a chronic one in the early Revolution.[6] However, the Paris municipality seems to have been particularly anxious about the potentially dangerous effects of radical publications in the period immediately following the October Days. For the action taken against Marat was only part of what seems to have been a general campaign to harass the revolutionary press.

On October 8, the Représentants attempted to ban the press' major form of advertising by decreeing that public shouting by newsvendors would be limited to the contents of official documents. While this decree was only a reaffirmation of an almost identical but largely unenforced decree of September 1, the enlistment of the services of a group of well-known market-women for the specific purpose of policing the activities of newsvendors suggests that the municipality was now more serious about its enforcement.[7] Moreover, National Guard patrols appear to have been particularly active against newsvendors during October. According to Loustalot, who reported he had personally seen the arrest of several newsvendors who had not violated the ordinance against public shouting, the Guard had orders to apprehend any *colporteur* selling any paper that seemed dangerous.[8] It was, in all likelihood, this campaign against newsvendors that led Garran de Coulon, another municipal politician who always tried to maintain good relations with the popular movement, to complain in mid-October about "very dangerous attacks" against press freedoms.[9]

Yet, if there was a kind of *première pousse* of press repression after the October Days, its magnitude should not be exaggerated. The harassment of newsvendors plus one arrest warrant issued against an inflammatory journalist who himself confessed to having "carried the love of truth, justice, and humanity to the point of delirium" does not add up to what Loustalot called "a censorship a thousand times more repressive than that of the old police." While many of Marat's accusations may well have been true, there has probably never been a government in history (let alone a revolutionary one) that would not have taken some action against a journal like *Ami du Peuple*. Defending Marat, Loustalot argued that English newspapers were permitted to make scathing anti-government attacks, and he published excerpts of an article from the *Morning Post* lambasting Pitt, "the Necker of Great Britain." But the worst thing this paper said about Pitt, at least in the excerpt Loustalot published, was that he had "enriched his family and placed his creatures on the payroll," a somewhat less explosive statement than Marat's declaration that Necker was a traitor who should be executed.[10]

Hiding out somewhere near Versailles, even Marat seems to have recognized the need for a change in strategy. In an unusually docile "open letter" published clandestinely in mid-October, he conceded that some of his information had been incorrect and sheepishly

claimed he was not good at remembering names and dates, a start-
ling admission coming from a man who had been specializing in
denouncing public officials.[11] Through this virtual apology, Marat
seems to have persuaded the authorities that he could be tolerated,
at least unofficially. Though its author remained hidden, *Ami du
Peuple* began to appear again on November 5, with noticeably muf-
fled tones.

In mid-December, however, Marat's hiding place was discovered
and he was taken to the Hôtel-de-Ville, where he was questioned by
Lafayette and the Comité des Recherches. Yet, although the Châtelet's case against him was still pending, he was released and even
allowed to reclaim his printing presses which had been seized in
October, a decision that can be attributed to a combination of
Marat's tactical retreat and a generally less dangerous political
situation. Commenting on the methods of his interrogators, an
amazingly compliant Marat wrote that "I compared them in silence
to those that would have been used in a parallel case by Royal
Commissioners. I sensed the extreme difference between the old and
the new regime and a delicious emotion penetrated my soul." His
conflicts with the municipality, he stated, were only "petty disagreements regarding details of the passage from servitude to
liberty."[12]

But Marat's relatively moderate tone did not last for long. In late
December, he resumed his violent attacks on the municipality and
on Necker, and, on January 4, he suggested that Brissot and the
Comité des Recherches might be "sold to the enemies of the
State."[13] Some of his heaviest artillery was reserved for the Châtelet
and, in particular, for Boucher d'Argis, who quickly became one of
his favorite targets.[14] Though his journalistic work of late December
and early January lacks the hysterical brilliance of late September
and early October, it was bothersome enough to end the policy of
unofficial toleration that the authorities had been pursuing. In early
January, the October 8 warrant against Marat was taken out of
dry-dock and several unsuccessful attempts were made to arrest
him. Finally, on January 22, soon after the publication of especially
fierce personal attacks on Necker and Boucher d'Argis, Lafayette
sent several hundred National Guardsmen to try to take him into
custody.[15]

Three days earlier, however, Danton and the Cordeliers District,
further cementing the close ties which had developed between

opposition districts and radical journalists, had moved to protect Marat by declaring that no citizen could be arrested on its territory without the consent of five specially elected officials. This challenge to the authority of the Hôtel-de-Ville resulted in an extremely tense situation which featured the threat of a confrontation between Lafayette's troops and the Cordeliers' own National Guard battalion, and in the midst of all the confusion, Marat somehow managed to escape again. This time he fled to England and his journal did not appear for four months.[16] Shortly after his return, his "petty disagreements" with the municipality led him, as we will see in chapter 10 below, to issue a chilling call for the removal of "five to six hundred heads," including, of course, those of the members of the Comité des Recherches.[17]

REPRESSION OF POPULAR RIOTS

In banishing an opposition prince and in temporarily silencing a dissident writer, the Fayettist authorities had acted with a degree of restraint that seems essentially consistent with the punitive mildness advocated by pre-revolutionary judicial reformers. Rather than being interested in punishing Orléans and Marat, the authorities appear to have been primarily interested in removing them from the political scene and, in the case of the latter, were apparently even prepared to tolerate a semi-housebroken Friend of the People. But these same authorities would act in a much less "civilized" manner towards two individuals from the *menu peuple* who were arrested during the first serious post-October Days popular disturbances in Paris.

Though the October Days produced a temporary easing of the bread crisis, it would be a while before the capital's new provisioning system began to function at maximum efficiency. By the third week of October, long lines had reappeared in front of Parisian bakeries, creating new apprehensions about the possibility of another popular explosion.[18] On the morning of October 21, two days after the arrival of the National Assembly, a baker named François, whose shop was located near the Assembly's meeting place, was found to have hidden some freshly baked bread in his cellar. A furious crowd seized François and took him to the Hôtel-de-Ville, where Garran and other municipal officials promised he would be put on trial.[19] But the impatient crowd dragged the baker out of the building and hanged him. Repeating the ritual established in July, his head was then cut off, attached to a pike, and paraded triumphantly around the city.[20] Fittingly enough for a society in which the age-old "petites corruptions" of everyday life were coming to be seen as treason, the bread that François had hidden seems to have been set aside for the National Assembly itself.[21]

The reaction of the Fayettist regime to the François killing was swift and decisive. The entire National Guard was immediately mobilized to break up the parading of François' head and to disperse some accompanying disturbances in various parts of town, and cannon were even wheeled out on the Place de Grève to clear the area around the Hôtel-de-Ville.[22] Within twenty-four hours, two men had been publicly executed on the same spot where the unfortunate baker had been killed. One of them, a dock porter named Blin, had apparently lowered the rope used to hang François and thus had at least been accused of participating in a homicide.[23] In contrast, the charge levelled against the second condemned man, a 25-year-old day-laborer named Michel Adrien, was a far less serious one. Here is Lafayette's account:

During the disturbance stirred up against the baker François, another one broke out in the Faubourg Saint-Antoine, the object of which was to unite with the Faubourg Saint-Marcel for purposes of reducing the price of bread, and for getting into the convents under the pretext of taking the muskets stored there. The National Guard, in breaking up these seditions, arrested the assassin of the banker [Blin] and the principal instigator of the faubourg [Adrien]. Both were judged and hanged the next day.[24]

Perhaps sensing that a more dramatic rendition might help justify the precipitous nature of the Adrien execution, Louis Gottschalk and Margaret Maddox added to this rather matter-of-fact account by speaking of a "dangerous crowd" and the need to use "considerable force" to disperse it.[25] However, the Châtelet dossier on the Adrien case actually furnishes a quite different impression as to the magnitude of this incident from that provided by either Lafayette or his biographers. Thus, the arrest report on Adrien says nothing about breaking up a disturbance. On the contrary, the patrol that arrested Adrien found him "surrounded by a number of persons who were complaining about him and who had witnessed the riot he had *tried* to provoke."[26] In other words, the disturbance of that afternoon appears to have been so minor as to have already been over before the arrival of the Guard, and it was probably not very different from countless other disturbances in the explosive Faubourg Saint-Antoine. Moreover, at Adrien's trial the next day, the charge against him was not that he had, in fact, incited a seditious riot but rather that he had merely attempted to incite one.[27]

In addition, there is also the matter of Adrien's intentions and responsibility. According to the arrest report, he had been circulating a handbill which stated: "The Bastille workers, the Faubourg Saint-Antoine, and the Faubourg Saint-Marcel should come to the Gros Raisin, rue Saint-Paul. We must try to get them to provide food for us. We must have bread." At his trial, five witnesses testified that Adrien had shown them this flyer while shouting that they should go to the Gros Raisin, a local tavern, and to the Filles-Saint-Marie convent to get the arms kept there. Adrien replied that he had been drunk and that, not being able to read or write, he didn't know what the handbill said. Yet he acknowledged that what the witnesses had said was essentially correct. The handbill, he claimed, was given to him by a fellow-worker named Pierre Bourguignon whose instructions he had followed.[28]

From the limited amount of information available, it is impossible to determine the degree of political awareness of Adrien, who obviously would have tried to appear as ignorant as possible. But Presiding Judge Boucher d'Argis and his colleagues do not seem to have had a great deal of interest in answering this question. Though they did issue an arrest warrant for Pierre Bourguignon, they were in far too much of a hurry to wait and see if he could have furnished some information to clarify Adrien's motivations or to indicate to what extent Adrien may have participated in other political actions in the Faubourg Saint-Antoine.[29] Nor did they wait to see whether an in-court confrontation between Adrien and Bourguignon might have provided some useful general information about the popular movement in this district. Instead, it is clear that the main priority of the authorities was to display a swift and terrible "example" to the residents of the Faubourg Saint-Antoine and the other popular districts.[30] Given this concern, considerations of "justice" and "fair play" or even information-gathering had to take a back seat.

In a bizarre twist to a procedure which bore such a strong resemblance to the traditional practice of hanging rebellious peasants, Adrien was one of the first defendants tried by the Châtelet under the provisions of the new criminal law reform decree passed by the National Assembly on October 8.[31] However, the use of these new regulations as a means of lending legitimacy to what amounted to classic "summary justice" does not seem to have aroused any protest by pre-revolutionary critics of Old Regime "barbarisms." The only comment made by Brissot, for example, was that the executions of Adrien and Blin "were carried out quietly due to the precautions taken."[32] And even Loustalot, who, in the absence of Marat, was the revolutionary authorities' most dependable and most persistent radical critic, asked only that a counter-revolutionary bishop in Brittany be treated with equal rigor.[33] It would not be until early March that an explicit attack on the class-based nature of the Adrien execution finally appeared in the revolutionary press. Comparing Adrien with the recently executed Marquis de Favras, Camille Desmoulins wrote:

> When one recalls that the day-laborer Adrien was judged and hanged in twenty-four hours for circulating a seditious flyer, although he didn't know how to read, it is strange to see some people complain about the fate of Favras, who was convicted of a multitude of much more serious charges. This shows how difficult it is to uproot certain aristocratic prejudices, such as the one which assigns a day-laborer and a marquis different weights on the scales of justice.[34]

Reporting on the National Guard's dispersal of Palais-Royal protesters in the pre-October Days period, Lafayette had proudly written to Latour-Maubourg that "all this was done with politeness and respect for the rights of decent citizens," thereby implying, whether consciously or not, that less respectable elements could not count on such restrained treatment.[35] Yet, if the Adrien execution provides a striking demonstration that the inclination of the early revolutionary authorities to treat political offenders in a civilized manner did not necessarily extend across the social spectrum, this execution was not at all typical of the kind of punishment meted out to rioters in Paris during the early Revolution. On the contrary, Adrien seems to have been the only *émeutier* executed in the capital throughout the entire period of the Constitutional Monarchy.[36] More typical was the three-month sentence given on September 11, 1789 by the Châtelet's *prévôtal* court to Antoine Revel, a laborer also charged with attempting to incite a riot. Almost exactly three months later, Revel reappeared before the same court. Charged this time with "uttering seditious words," he was released and told to be more discreet. Included among several other relatively lenient judgments rendered by this court in cases involving seditious rioters are decisions in the cases of six other members of the *menu peuple* arrested on the day of the François killing. One man apprehended during a disturbance at the Pont Notre-Dame was sentenced to six months in prison. And of five persons arrested on the Place de Grève, three were sentenced to a few hours in the stocks (certainly a "barbaric" punishment but hardly fatal) and two were released.[37]

Why, then, was Adrien treated so harshly? Since he had apparently tried to direct attention towards the arms in the Filles-Saint-Marie convent, it might be argued that he was the only rioter arrested on October 21 who was involved in an organized attempt to provoke an armed revolt. (The paucity of available information makes it impossible to determine if any of the others arrested that day were involved in anything comparable, though the Pont Notre-Dame disturbance actually appears to have been more serious than the one which led to Adrien's arrest.)[38] However, rather than being based on something distinctive about his actions, it seems more likely that the most important factor determining Adrien's fate was that he had been arrested in the Faubourg Saint-Antoine, the universally acknowledged heart of the revolutionary popular movement. In their fear of another explosion, the municipal authorities were always most anxious about this faubourg, which had furnished most of the shock troops for all the major revolutionary *journées*, from the Réveillon Riots to the fourteenth of July to the fifth of October. With the general nervousness that accompanied the transfer of the National Assembly to Paris augmented by the burst of violence of October 21, it appears that the authorities wanted to intimidate and overawe the people of the Faubourg Saint-Antoine by engaging in some "pre-emptive" violence of their own.

But if the Adrien execution was an attempt to send a message to potential trouble-makers in the Faubourg Saint-Antoine and other popular districts, there was also a message in it for the newly arrived National Assembly. As the Fayettist regime was moving to consolidate its police and judicial powers through the creation of the Comité des Recherches and the designation of the Châtelet as *lèse-nation* tribunal, the François killing and the subsequent executions of Adrien and Blin provided a convenient opportunity for it to show the deputies that it was prepared to take rigorous action to maintain order. Along the same lines, the disturbances of October 21 also furnished an excellent pretext for the municipal authorities to demand the passage of a measure which would allow them, under certain circumstances, to declare martial law. Moreover, the National Assembly's immediate passage of such a measure generated a district protest movement which, in its turn, led directly to the next phase of the post-October Days judicial offensive against the revolutionary left.[39]

CONTAINMENT OF DISTRICT PROTESTS

On the evening of October 23, Jean-Marie Martin, a notary, and Pierre Duval, a master craftsman, denounced the Saint-Martin des Champs District National Guard Battalion for having indicated its intention to co-operate in the enforcement of the just-enacted Loi Martiale (Riot Act). Duval reportedly declared that any Guardsman found in uniform should be disrobed and insulted, and, according to some sources, even shot. In the mean time, Martin proposed that the district announce the new law would not be enforced, and that it proclaim that each district "has the right to refuse to enforce police laws within its own territory."[40]

Although the Saint-Martin des Champs District Assembly was not prepared to issue such a direct challenge to the authority of the Hôtel-de-Ville, a decree was passed demanding that the Représentants ask the National Assembly to revoke the Loi Martiale. Moreover, at least two other districts quickly registered formal protests against the new law.[41] However, shortly after the stormy meeting at Saint-Martin des Champs finally broke up near midnight, thirty-four members of the district battalion sent a report on the meeting to Lafayette and the municipal Comité de Police. Within hours, Martin and Duval had been arrested and imprisoned.[42]

Slipping easily into a professorial mode, Brissot attempted to justify these arrests by suggesting that the problem was "the ignorance of men regarding their rights": "A Citizen or a District certainly has the right to think and even announce that a law passed by the National Assembly is bad and dangerous. But while thinking this, they must comply with it. They can demand its revocation, but it must be enforced provisionally."[43] However, as eminently sensible as this distinction may appear, it is doubtful that Lafayette and the Comité de Police were thinking about political theory when they ordered Martin and Duval's arrest. Backing up a loyal National Guard unit which felt physically threatened, nipping in the bud what might have appeared to be the beginning of another grass-roots revolt against the Hôtel-de-Ville, signalling that a certain tone of protest (threats and violent insults) would not be tolerated: each of these considerations almost certainly outweighed the fact that Martin and Duval seem to have strayed beyond the ultimately murky line that separates protest from the advocacy of disobedience.

Besides, though Martin and Duval were attacking a law passed by the National Assembly, the proper context for examining their case is actually the continual early revolutionary struggle between the districts and the municipality. On July 30, 1789, the cause embraced by the districts (opposition to Necker's amnesty) had such widespread support and centralized control of the newly established National Guard was so tenuous that the Hôtel-de-Ville could do nothing more than negotiate a hasty compromise with the rebellious districts. For given the political climate of summer 1789, there was clearly no possibility of taking judicial action against the leaders of the Oratoire District or the officers of its mutinous battalion, just as there was no possibility of prosecuting the Orleanists during that period, or, for that matter, of prosecuting those involved in the massacres of July 14 and 22. Similarly, on January 22, 1790, an independent Cordeliers battalion protected Marat from arrest, and, as will be seen in chapter 9 below, the same protection would be extended to Danton in March 1790.

However, the threat posed to the municipality by the martial law protest was much less formidable than the challenge that had been mounted by the Oratoire or the one that would be mounted by the Cordeliers. With the Saint-Martin des Champs battalion loyal to Lafayette, with the overwhelming majority of the districts apparently willing to accept the Loi Martiale, and with significant segments of public opinion reacting in a particularly unfavorable manner to recent outbursts of popular violence, it was easy for the municipality to exercise judicial muscle against Martin and Duval. Thus, though tension between the Hôtel-de-Ville and the Paris districts and sections was continuous throughout the early years of the Revolution,[44] these two men were, so far as I can determine, the only local militants prosecuted until the Varennes-Champ de Mars crisis of summer 1791, a period which, in some respects, resembles that of October 1789. For in both these periods, the judicial pursuit of the left followed in the wake of a failed radical offensive. Or, to consider it from another angle, in both periods, the capture of the King resulted, paradoxically, in a swing to the right.

In any event, Martin and Duval's arrest effectively blunted any possibility of a general district revolt against the municipality. Only hours after the two men were seized, the officers of the Trinité repudiated the anti-martial law resolution passed by that district the previous day, and two days later, the officers of Martin and Duval's own district did the same. Within days, at least fifteen districts had expressed formal approval of the Loi Martiale, and there is no indication of any further district opposition to the new law.[45] As for Martin and Duval, they remained in custody while the Châtelet held several hearings in an ostensible effort to determine exactly what had been said on October 23. On February 22, they were finally convicted of "having uttered imprudent and indiscreet words" and then released and told to be more "circumspect" in the future. Their real sentence, of course, was the four months they had already spent in prison.[46]

THE CASE OF THE CHEVALIER DE RUTLEDGE AND THE BAKERS

The Chevalier de Rutledge, who would become the next victim of the post-October Days conservative reaction, was one of the more colorful though largely forgotten figures of the early French Revolution. A good candidate for Robert Darnton's "Grub Street," Rutledge combined a mediocre pre-revolutionary literary career with a part-time position as a government informer providing information to Necker on the machinations of Parisian grain monopolists.[47] In January 1789, he was approached by the master bakers of Paris and asked "to use his pen to defend this community," and the result was a violent and hysterical pamphlet which created a sensation by publicly exposing much of the information he had been privately passing along to Necker.[48] However, though Rutledge was undoubtedly already convinced that the "monopolists" depended on government protection, this work did not contain any criticism of Necker himself. Moreover, Rutledge continued to defend Necker publicly even after the government suppressed his pamphlet in March.[49]

Yet, even as he was defending Necker publicly, Rutledge was privately warning the Minister that "I will become your enemy the moment I come to believe you are separating your cause from that of the public good." On October 7, encouraged in all likelihood by the general excitement of the October Days, he notified Mme Necker that he was ready to publicly accuse her husband. Declaring that

Necker had displayed a "haughty ingratitude towards me," he gave the Minister a choice between denouncing the "monopolists" or being denounced himself.[50] But instead of taking Rutledge's apocalyptic tone seriously, the advocate of "ménagements mutuels" responded by offering his potential denunciator a job, proposing that he take charge of a new government program to provide large interest-free loans to Parisian bakers. Rutledge accepted and immediately began to survey the needs of the bakers.[51]

However, this arrangement quickly came unglued. In late October, Necker's aide Valdec de Lessart told Rutledge to suspend operations because it had been decided that the municipality would handle all loans for the bakers.[52] But Rutledge ignored this directive and continued to meet with his clients. On November 2, he was arrested by order of the Paris Comité de Police for falsely representing himself as a government official and for having thereby "interfered without mission" in the system for the provisioning of Paris.[53]

Had Rutledge really acted "without mission"? De Lessart later testified that he had notified Rutledge "in general" that the municipality would take over the new program, whereupon Rutledge pounced upon the phrase "in general" and forced the witness to admit there had been no "formal counter-order."[54] Yet, regardless of whether or not Rutledge had been formally relieved of his mission, it is clear that the legal charge against him was little more than a pretext to take him out of circulation. But why were the revolutionary authorities so anxious to remove him from the scene? What had happened to upset his agreement with Necker?

By providing Rutledge with a new position, Necker must have thought that he had sufficiently demonstrated his "gratitude" so as to be able to expect no further criticism of government grain policies and, above all, no further personal attacks. Rutledge, however, seems to have been too caught up in his exciting new revolutionary identity of unmasker of corruption and defender of oppressed humanity to be held to such a vulgar arrangement. For rather than being a calculated invitation to negotiate, his threats and his references to "ingratitude" appear to have resulted from a sense of genuine and bitter disappointment that his muck-raking efforts had been ignored. Hence, instead of seeing Necker's offer as a "deal" that carried an implicit price tag, he probably saw it as proof that the Minister had been forced to institute a major change in his policies.

Like many apparent compromises between pragmatic moderates and exalted ideologues, this arrangement may have been doomed from the start because Necker's concession would only have served to stimulate Rutledge's appetite.

With this in mind, we can probably assume that Rutledge had used his official access to the bakers to propagate further his ideas on grain supply corruption, ideas that could only have generated more anger and resentment among his clients towards a government that would not act against the "monopolists" and towards a Minister whom he would later describe as "the secret and cowardly abettor and accomplice of the hideous monopoly."[55] Though an accusation of sedition was not pursued at Rutledge's trial, the reason is clear. In charging him with acting "without mission" rather than with some form of seditious activity, the authorities were obviously hoping to avoid providing Rutledge with a public forum for airing his views.[56]

Yet, despite the narrowness with which the case against him was framed, Rutledge did manage to find several opportunities to express his opinions about his former patron, though none of these remarks found their way into the trial transcript. "Let this Minister appear," one journal quoted him as declaring, "so I can make the public see who is the criminal." And in an even more sensational statement, he reportedly proclaimed: "M. Necker is a crook ... If he is not a traitor, he is at least a coward ... Yes, gentlemen, it is either M. Necker's head or my own."[57]

Certainly having no desire to expose himself to Rutledge's questioning, Necker never did appear before the Châtelet. On January 2, Rutledge was released on his own recognizance, and the proceedings in the case were simply allowed to lapse.[58] With the goal of cutting off Rutledge's access to the bakers at a dangerous moment already met, it must have been felt that continuation of his circus-like trial could only be counter-productive. Moreover, it may also have been felt that two months in prison had helped the defendant to develop sufficient respect for the authorities. However, Rutledge's imprisonment only inflamed him further. Undaunted by the Cordeliers District's refusal to grant him the same protection it had given Marat or by the failure of the radical press to take up his cause, he continued to insist that either Necker's head or his own had to fall, and he soon began to publish a series of violent personal attacks on the Minister.[59] But unlike Marat, Rutledge was never able to parlay his penchant for denunciation and for exposing corruption into a position as a recognized spokesman for popular interests. Though he remained active as a journalist and a Parisian sectional militant, he never achieved any degree of revolutionary prominence.[60]

To what extent can the Rutledge case be considered part of the post-October Days campaign against the left? While Rutledge's generally isolated position can partially be attributed to the eccentric and even comic aspects of his personality,[61] his efforts to be accepted by the revolutionary left were also undermined by his links to the master bakers. For if bread was not available to the People, it was always the bakers who were the first to come under suspicion. By comparison, the major suppliers that Rutledge railed against were faceless and far-away abstractions. The authorities, moreover, tried to take advantage of these suspicions by charging that Rutledge's bakers had tried to stop other bakers from buying flour, thereby implying that his arrest was part of the municipality's campaign to insure a plentiful bread supply.[62] Thus, the National Guardsmen who arrested Rutledge declared that he was "an aristocrat, a grain monopolist, and a man who paid the bakers not to bake," words which "so infuriated the People that M. le Chevalier de Rutledge thought he would have to submit to the fate of the unfortunate François."[63] On the other hand, it does not seem unreasonable to consider bakers as part of the "popular classes," or to consider an attempt to mobilize them against giant wholesalers and their governmental protectors as part of the "popular movement." As artisans and tradesmen, bakers would certainly seem to have some claim to being regarded as members of Albert Soboul's "sans-culotterie."

But a more significant reason for seeing Rutledge as a revolutionary radical can be found in his exalted and eschatological style. In moralistically insisting that there was no intermediate zone between virtue and crime (it's either Necker's head or mine), in relentlessly exposing the hidden mechanisms by which powerful and wealthy men maintained their positions, in quixotically refusing to grant any legitimacy to the day-to-day compromises which lubricate the gears of all societies, and in dramatically bestowing the status of major evil on the petty corruption and dishonesty of ordinary life, Rutledge was expressing themes which would become increasingly dominant as the Revolution proceeded. It was, therefore, no accident that he, too, was prosecuted in the post-October Days period, a period when those who felt the Revolution had gone far enough were temporarily able to curtail its momentum. Though Necker was too politically crippled by that point to be able to take advantage of this turn of events, the generally restrained and pragmatic manner in which Lafayette and his allies pursued opponents on both the left and the right can be seen as a continuation of Necker's own inclination towards accommodation and *ménagement*. Supported and sustained by the popular desire for a more punitive style of justice, the left would handle things quite differently when it came to power.

THE PROSECUTION OF ORLÉANS AND MIRABEAU

As if to provide a capstone to its post-October Days efforts to harass the revolutionary left, the Fayettist regime waited until late November to open an official investigation of the October Days episode itself. But the prosecution of the presumed instigators of the "crimes of October" would proceed much less smoothly than the other cases described in this chapter. An examination of some of the problems which this case posed for the regime will help demonstrate the limits of the post-October Days turn to the right and, at the same time, shed some light on the inherent instability of Lafayette's coalition.

Denunciation by the Comité des Recherches

The October Days Inquest was triggered on November 23, 1789 when the Paris Comité des Recherches issued a formal denunciation of the "authors, abettors, and accomplices" of the "disgraceful crime which defiled the Château of Versailles on the morning of Tuesday, October 6." According to the Comité, the attack on the Château was carried out by "bandits who were incited by clandestine maneuvers and who had mingled among and been confounded with citizens." This attack, moreover, had interrupted the "harmony" and "fraternity" that had been established after the events of October 5:

All appeared calm thanks to the zeal of [the Paris National Guard] and the wise arrangements of its Commander. Trust and harmony reigned everywhere, and thankfulness, love, and fraternity were the only things being talked about when, between 5 and 6 a.m., a troop of these armed bandits . . . suddenly invaded the Château, attacked the bodyguards on duty inside, broke down the doors, rushed towards the Queen's apartment, and massacred some of the guards.[64]

Thus, the Comité sought to make it absolutely clear from the start that its denunciation only applied to the "bandits" (and those who had incited them) who were responsible for the "excess" of October 6 and not to the "citizens" who had marched to Versailles the previous day.[65] This sharp distinction between "citizens" and "bandits" and between October 5 and 6 reflects the delicate problem which the October Days affair created for Brissot and his "left Fayettist" colleagues on the Comité. On the one hand, as revolutionary politicians who were anxious to maintain good relations with the radical and popular movement, these men certainly did not want to denounce a popular uprising which had, as Brissot himself put it, "caused a general sense of joy" by enabling Paris to obtain "that which it most fervently desired, the presence of its King."[66] And as Comité member Agier indicated, the last thing they wanted to do was implicate the people of Paris in their *recherches*: "We must learn who was behind the attacks committed at Versailles on the morning of October 6, and we must learn the purpose of these attacks. But, above all, we must learn how much these attacks were not the work of the good inhabitants of this city."[67]

On the other hand, the members of the Comité were important municipal officials responsible for maintaining order. Though they were careful not to denounce the events of October 5, it was their job to see to it that these events did not recur. "The People, now satisfied," as Brissot had put it in his "revisionist" account of the October Days, must be "careful not to listen to the insinuations of turbulent men who incite revolt for their own private interest."[68] With the Comité having been assigned the task of "discovering the odious maneuvers used by evil individuals ... to excite the French people to actions which go against its own interests,"[69] it would seem that it had been given a mandate to pursue some of these "turbulent men."

But let us look a little deeper into the context of the November 23 denunciation. Five days earlier, after hearing Garran's report on the July Conspiracy, the Comité had formally denounced Besenval and his accomplices, and it was already clear that the Comité intended to devote the bulk of its energies to this key case.[70] In addition, by the middle of November, the Comité had also denounced two counter-revolutionary plots linked to the October Days, though, as will be seen shortly, these cases were much less important to the Comité than the Besenval case.[71] Thus, despite the fact it had been created in the midst of the post-October Days reaction against the left, the Comité had quickly shown that its real interest was pursuing conspirators of the right, an attitude that naturally aroused considerable uneasiness in certain quarters. As Mallet du Pan wrote on November 21 in the prestigious *Mercure de France*: "Everyone is astonished that no judicial proceedings or even investigations have yet been opened concerning the plots which, after the events of October 5, had led the municipality ... to institute a Comité des Recherches." And the departed Monarchien leader Mounier complained in mid-November that both the municipality and the National Assembly appeared content "to accord the rewards of virtue to crime, to celebrate the attacks of October 5 and 6 as heroic actions, and to consider the most cowardly assassinations as courageous."[72]

In addition, Lafayette himself could not have been very happy with the Comite's conduct during the first month of its existence. Always eager to present himself as the middle ground between the quarreling factions of a once united patriot party, he needed a viable political force on his right to balance the never-ending pressure on his left. Hence, one of his main objectives during this period was to convince the Monarchiens to reverse their slide into the counter-revolutionary camp, and, in particular, to convince Mounier to retract his post-October Days resignation from the National Assembly. Pleading for the Monarchien leader's return, Lafayette envisioned another Orleanist offensive and asked if "my eyes would search in vain for Mounier to defend me."[73] Whether responding directly to Monarchien demands or acting in accordance with a general need to bolster his right flank, the Parisian General probably insisted that the Comité des Recherches do something to satisfy moderate and conservative opinion. Indeed he came close to acknowledging such a scenario in his *Mémoires*: "It suited the purposes of Lafayette, Bailly, and the municipality to provoke an investigation that would give everyone the right to state what he had seen and that would prevent anyone from saying we had suppressed evidence." Moreover, Brissot later claimed that the Comité had been "taken in" by Lafayette's "intrigues" with respect to this case. However, since this comment was made in October 1793, at a point when the imprisoned Girondin leader was desperately trying to re-interpret his past associations with the Parisian General, a more accurate rendition of it might be that the Comité had been "willing to be taken in" by Lafayette's "intrigues."[74]

In any event, it seems clear that the Comité's November 23 denunciation of the "crimes of October" should be seen as an effort to project a more moderate image by presenting itself as the enemy of conspirators of the left as well as the right. In fact, the opening lines of the denunciation were explicitly framed in such terms:

Since its creation, the Comité has devoted itself with indefatigable zeal to discovering the authors of last July's conspiracy against the National Assembly and the city of Paris . . . Today, the Comité proposes to denounce another crime, the investigation of which has kept it equally occupied since its establishment, a crime which appears to have derived from a different source, and which has excited indignation and pain among all good citizens.[75]

Yet, the release of this denunciation by no means indicates that the Comité had a serious interest in co-operating with the October Days proceedings which would soon be opened by the Châtelet. By December 10, in a preview of the rupture in the Fayettist coalition which this affair would help produce, charges were already being made that the Comité had "engineered the disappearance of many pieces of evidence pertaining to the horrors," and, as Brissot later wrote, he and his colleagues did "whatever we could to block the prosecution."[76] However, since the Châtelet's inquest did not really get into high gear until spring 1790, let us postpone our account of these efforts until chapters 9 and 10 below. For now let it just be noted that the Comité's future role in this case is suggested by the fact that, in contrast to every other major denunciation it issued, its October Days accusation was the only one that contained no names and that did not follow an actual arrest. No one, of course, could have expected that the Comité would be as enthusiastic about the October Days case as the Châtelet, which responded to the Comité's denunciation by officially opening proceedings against Orléans on December 5.[77] But the Comité could have signalled a reasonable degree of interest in the case without going so far as to target Orléans or any of his top lieutenants. It would not, for example, have been hard for it to learn the identities of some of the "bandits" who had attacked the Château and then order some arrests or at least name some suspects. The absence of names in the Comité's denunciation is a reflection of its essentially empty nature. Though this denunciation did lend a certain legitimacy to their subsequent activities, the Châtelet judges could and probably would have proceeded in much the same manner if it had never been issued.

Investigation by the Châtelet

Although the Châtelet's October Days probe would drag on for seven and a half months and eventually encompass 394 witnesses, the guiding principles behind it can be easily discerned in the testimony of the very first witness, the journalist Pelletier, whom, we can be sure, was quite carefully chosen. In his widely circulated *Domine salvum fac regem*, which had been published in the wake of Orléans' exile, Pelletier had explained how the "cowardly regicide" and "vile conspirator" had "fallen at the feet of the Monarch he wanted to replace" and how "the King's mercy saved him from the fate that awaited him."[78] Appearing as a star witness in a proceeding that could potentially have ended with a public execution on the Place de Grève, Pelletier showed little inclination to emulate the forgiving attitude that he attributed to the man whose cause he was defending.

Setting the tone for the kind of hearsay testimony that would dominate the Châtelet's inquest, Pelletier began by stating that he had come to relate "various events and anecdotes relative to the disastrous scenes of October 5 and 6, information which, without him being able to recall the exact sources, was gathered from rumors in cafés, clubs, and other public meeting places."[79] Having thereby immediately discarded the careful distinction the Comité had tried to draw between October 5 and 6, the witness then described how Mirabeau, identified as one of Orléans' principal agents, had plotted to create an artificial bread shortage; how Orleanist operatives had spread malicious rumors about the Flanders Regiment among the Parisian populace; how Orleanist agents had instigated the October 5 National Guard mutiny; how Orléans himself had directed the October 5 marchers from a command post in the Bois de Boulogne; and, finally, how Laclos had personally directed the October 6 invasion of the Château.[80]

But beyond the detailed attention to Orleanist plotting in October, Pelletier's testimony also touched on two other issues worth discussing at this point. The first is his attempt to link the Duport–Barnave–Lameth Triumvirate to the alleged Orleanist conspiracy. Thus, interspersed among his string of *bruits publics* was the rumor that Duport and Barnave had personally attempted to incite the *menu peuple* of Versailles against the hated Flanders Regiment. Moreover, Pelletier also claimed that a certain Mme de Tesse had complained to Barnave about his desertion of his former close associate Mounier and had been told: "What can I do, Madame? I am pledged to someone else." The significance of these otherwise silly rumors is that they signal the role that the Châtelet inquest would play as a potential threat to the Triumvirate, an aspect of it generally overlooked by historians.[81]

Though the bulk of the testimony in the October Days case was directed against Orléans and Mirabeau, the undercurrent of testimony against the Duport faction that was also present may have had greater political significance.[82] For the exile of Orléans had already effectively crippled the Orleanists as a political force, thereby leaving the "advanced patriots" of the Duport faction as the strongest remaining challengers to Lafayette for national supremacy. Thus, it is hardly surprising that the period during which the Châtelet conducted its probe was also the period of fiercest competition between Lafayette and the Triumvirate. It was during this time that Lafayette created a split in the Triumvirate-dominated Jacobin Club by founding the Society of 1789, and it was also during this time that the Parisian General was beset by fears that either Alexandre or Charles Lameth was plotting to replace him as Paris National Guard Commander.[83]

Now there was probably never any real chance that any deputy associated with the Duport faction would actually be indicted. Even if Lafayette would have liked to indict some of them and even if there had been a more substantial case against them, they were clearly too influential in the Assembly and in Paris for this to have been a realistic possibility. Yet, the prospect, the threat, the rumor that some members of this faction would be indicted was always there and may have served as a restraining force on the Triumvirate as it battled with the Fayettists. Moreover, since the Châtelet probe was technically only an investigatory procedure, it could be and, in fact, was held secretly, in spite of the new criminal law regulations.[84] Thus, no one knew what the witnesses were saying, and rumors abounded. In mid-April, for example, one generally sober journal reported that seventeen deputies might be indicted, and one not very sober one put the number at 200.[85] As many political activists of our own time have discovered, threats and rumors of prosecution are often as effective in restraining and discouraging opposition as prosecution itself.

A second issue touched on by Pelletier was his mention of rumors about Orleanist plotting in July and even earlier, rumors which were to be repeated and expanded upon by several other witnesses.[86] Although ostensibly limited to the October Days, the Châtelet probe would also become a vehicle for an investigation of all Orleanist political activity since the beginning of the Revolution, thus providing another indication of how much the political climate had changed since the summer. Thus, it is hard to imagine the question of who arranged for the manufacture of several hundred pikes on July 14 being made part of a criminal proceeding before the October Days. But in early 1790, the Châtelet summoned two workers who had helped make these weapons in an attempt to answer this very question.[87] That a Parisian court could have dared to suggest that there might have been something criminal about making pikes for the People of Paris on July 14 is a striking indication that there had indeed been a conservative reaction in the post-October Days period.

But this trend, of course, was only temporary. In the final section of this study, we will see how the wave of reaction triggered by the October Days began to recede in spring 1790, and, in particular, we will see how protest against the Châtelet's probe led the "left Fayettists" of the Comité des Recherches to abandon Lafayette's governing coalition. Although the Châtelet's October Days investigation continued to hang like a "sword of Damocles" over the revolutionary left until October 1790, it would soon become obvious that this sword lacked effective cutting power.

POSTCRIPT:

PROSECUTION OF THE RIGHT AFTER THE OCTOBER DAYS

Although this study has been emphasizing the extent to which the October Days should be seen as a serious defeat for the revolutionary left, the traditional conception of this episode as another defeat for the right is not entirely without foundation. Nor were the prosecutions of the left that we have been considering the only political prosecutions to emerge in its wake. On the contrary, Lafayette, whose political credibility largely rested on his ability to present himself as an impartial centrist, attempted to balance his post-October Days campaign against the left with a certain degree of judicial action against the right. However, in contrast to the comprehensive and broad-ranging offensive undertaken against the left, the post-October Days pursuit of the right seems to have been little more than a token effort.

In the period preceding the October Days, Paris had been flooded with rumors that the "aristocrats" were plotting to take the King to the safety of the royal garrison at Metz.[88] While these rumors certainly played a large part in intensifying popular unrest and in thereby provoking the October Days episode itself, their significance for us at this point is that Lafayette also took them very seriously, as demonstrated by a September 14 letter from Versailles National Guard Commander d'Estaing to Marie-Antoinette:

> It is said that enrollments are being taken among the nobles and the clergy
> ... and that the King will withdraw or be carried off to Metz. M. de Bouillé
> [Metz commander] is named and by who? By M. de Lafayette, who
> whispered it to me as we dined together ... I beg Her Majesty to use all her
> wisdom to calculate all that could happen through such a mistaken move.[89]

But despite Lafayette's apparent conviction that some very high-level supporters of the traditional Monarchy, including perhaps the Queen herself, were implicated in the Metz conspiracy,[90] the only trace of this plot in the judicial records of 1789–90 is in the prosecution of a group of recruiters for a shadowy organization known as the Gardes de la Régénération Française.[91]

Arrested on October 6 after an enrollment list was found in his room, the best known of those prosecuted was the abbé Douglas, a reactionary agitator who had been frequenting the Palais-Royal. Douglas and three friends arrested with him would spend almost six months in prison, eventually being released by the Châtelet on March 30, 1790, though no final judgment in their case was ever rendered. There were also two other arrests in this case, with one of those arrested being held for four months and the other for a week. In addition, charges were filed against two other men who seem to have been connected to the Gardes de la Régénération Française, but neither of these men was ever arrested and the case against them was barely pursued.[92] All in all, a rather meager display of judicial muscle, especially considering the parallel procedure being conducted at the very highest level against Orléans and Mirabeau.

Besides the Douglas case, there was one other prosecution which can also be considered as part of the post-October Days campaign against the right. On October 24, Jacques Augeard, a farmer-general who was one of the Queen's leading financial officers, composed a memorandum which seemed to contain a new plan for the royal family's escape. Denounced immediately to the municipality by his secretary, Augeard was arrested that same day. Though the Comité des Recherches left no stone unturned in an attempt to establish that he had taken steps to implement his plan, his written memorandum was the only solid piece of evidence it was able to uncover. After four months in prison, Augeard was released by the Châtelet in early March 1790, and officially acquitted later that month. Although Augeard was certainly a more significant target than the defendants in the Douglas case and although his arrest can be considered as a kind of warning to the Queen herself, taking action against him and his embryonic "conspiracy" was a rather poor substitute for taking vigorous action against the apparently very real Metz conspiracy.[93]

Finally, the token nature of the post-October Days campaign against the right is also indicated by the absence of any judicial action against the defeated Monarchien deputies. As we have seen, the Monarchiens had urged the King during the pre-October Days period to try to effectuate the removal of the National Assembly and the royal government from the Paris–Versailles area, a suggestion which could hardly have been accomplished without the use (or at least the threatened use) of military force. It is highly unlikely that Lafayette was unaware of this proposal, and, if he had been so inclined, he certainly could have construed it as a "conspiratorial" or "seditious" maneuver. But he was more interested, as we have seen, in trying to persuade Mounier and the Monarchiens to rejoin a broad-based patriotic coalition than in initiating any kind of action against them. The possibility of proceeding against the Monarchiens would only arise with the resumption of revolutionary momentum in the spring of 1790.[94]

Apart from the executions which followed the outburst of popular unrest of October 21, the Fayettist regime's post-October Days pursuit of opponents on both the left and the right was marked by the general absence of punitive severity that we are coming to see as characteristic of political justice in the early Revolution. Though the regime was certainly not above using the judicial process to intimidate and discourage political opposition, its behavior was still subject to a sense of restraint that can be seen as a reflection of the humanitarian assumptions of pre-revolutionary judicial thought. However, the strategic imperatives of the post-October Days period, in which Lafayette was particularly inclined towards seeking some kind of accommodation and reconciliation with the enemies of the Revolution, led the regime to pursue especially lax policies towards counter-revolutionary opponents. Moreover, the period following the October Days was, as we have seen, one in which the prospects for successful conciliation with supporters of the traditional Monarchy were, in many ways, much brighter than they had been before. These prospects, however, would soon be threatened by the Favras affair which would present a complex challenge to the Fayettist regime and its indulgent and accommodationist policies.

6

The Favras conspiracy

Thomas de Mahy, Marquis de Favras (1744–90) occupies a unique place in the history of early French revolutionary justice. For surprising as it may seem considering the degree of vindictive emotion aroused from the very beginning, this obscure ex-military officer and adventurer who "had more titles than assets" was the only counterrevolutionary conspirator legally executed until after the fall of the Monarchy, "the only individual," as Lafayette put it, "who, amongst so many parties, conspiracies, and intrigues, was made to pay the supreme penalty for crimes against the state during the first three years of the French Revolution."[1]

Yet, though the final outcome of the Favras case was very different from that of all the other major cases of 1789–90, the manner in which it was handled was quite similar. The exercise of restraint in the prosecution of political opponents, the absence of investigatory rigor, the tendency towards pragmatic and secret judicial arrangements, and the promotion of conciliation and forgiveness: all these previously encountered themes will remain prominently featured in our account of the Favras affair.

In addition, our account of this affair will demonstrate how the Favras case became deeply intertwined with the as yet unresolved Besenval case and how Favras' execution served, in effect, as Besenval's ticket to freedom. In exploring the complex interplay between these two cases, we will find further evidence of the internal tension embedded in the pre-revolutionary judicial reform movement's call for the system of justice which would be both more "humane" and more "rational." For the complicated *ménagements* of the Fayettist authorities with respect to these two cases ultimately resulted in a degree of punitive leniency which was quite in keeping with the reform movement's humanitarian tendencies. At the same time, this leniency was achieved through a procedural irregularity

124

which was hardly compatible with the movement's rationalistic currents.

Finally, our examination of the Favras affair will also reveal how a strengthened Fayettist regime made use of its control of the judicial process to deal with a serious threat to its post-October Days ability to maintain a tenuous check on both revolutionary and counter-revolutionary momentum. For by all appearances, Favras was indeed quite guilty of the serious crimes of which he was accused. But he was no guiltier than any number of other real conspirators, including, most notably, his own accomplices. A careful analysis of how Favras became the only one of these conspirators to wind up in front of a cheering crowd at the Place de Grève should, then, go a long way towards exposing the true nature of revolutionary justice in 1789–90.

THE "MONSIEUR CONNECTION"

On September 21, 1789, with Paris inundated by rumors of a projected royal flight, a veteran recruiting sergeant named Jean-Philippe Morel informed Lafayette about a new version of the Metz plot. Loyalist troops would be assembled for an attack upon Paris and Versailles, Lafayette and Bailly would be assassinated, the National Assembly dissolved, and the King seized and brought to Metz.[2] Nine days later, Morel reported that "he had seen a man in the rue Royale ... who told him that the plot was still on, that the Queen, M. d'Estaing, and M. de Saint-Priest are in on it, and that they hope to lure the King into it."[3] At this point, Lafayette gave Morel an official commission in the National Guard, with orders to find out as much as possible about this supposed conspiracy.[4]

Morel, however, seems to have invented this meeting in the rue Royale. For he later testified at Favras' trial that everything he had known about the supposed plot when he spoke to Lafayette had come from a fellow recruiting sergeant named Tourcaty, who, in turn, had learned about it from "a man named the marquis de Favras."[5] As Tourcaty testified: "Around July 17 or 18, M. de Favras approached me and said ... he needed a large number of men of good will and good breeding" to form the loyalist force described above. But, continued Tourcaty, Favras informed him at some unspecified point during "this period" (presumably sometime close to mid-July) that "this operation had failed ... because M. de

Saint-Priest could not furnish the required horses." According to
Tourcaty, he did not see Favras again until early November, and it
was only then that he arranged for Morel to meet Favras.[6]

Besides trying to create the impression that he had more direct
knowledge than he actually did, Morel may also have been trying to
feed the Parisian General information about a conspiracy that was
no longer operational. Given the vagueness of Tourcaty's testimony
concerning the point at which Favras told him the plot had fallen
through, it is possible that the project was still viable when Morel
approached Lafayette in September.[7] However, with rumors about
Metz circulating freely, it would seem more reasonable to suggest
that what Morel did in September was to dust off an already defunct
conspiracy and sell it to Lafayette as a current one. Considering the
difficulties that a recruiting sergeant for the royal army would have
had finding clients in the fall of 1789, it is easy to see how Morel could
have contrived to create a new post for himself as National Guard
officer and spy by exaggerating and distorting some hearsay and
outdated information.

In any event, regardless of the status of this early version of his plot,
the Marquis de Favras had a much more public role to play during
the unfolding of the October Days. Ostensibly seeking support for
various financial and diplomatic schemes, Favras was in Versailles
on October 5.[8] "Trembling for the life of the King" as he saw the
arrival of the first groups of marchers from Paris, he ran to the
Château and quickly made contact with a number of other ex-
military officers who were prepared to make an attempt "to get rid of
this rabble." Selected as the spokesman for this group of hard-liners,
Favras went to see Interior Minister Saint-Priest to request a contingent of horses from the royal stables. But given the unwillingness
of the Court to attempt any resistance that day, it is hardly surprising that this hare-brained scheme was flatly rejected.[9]

Could Tourcaty have been referring to this quasi-public and
seemingly spontaneous incident when he testified that Favras' first
plot had failed because Saint-Priest "could not furnish the required
horses"? If so, our suggestion that this plot had fallen through before
the October Days would have to be discarded. But then so too would
Tourcaty's portrait of Favras as a classic conspirator who had
designed an elaborate, well-planned, and, above all, totally secret
operation. Moreover, even if Tourcaty was referring to the October 5

Favras–Saint-Priest encounter, the possibility remains that Favras and the Interior Minister had other considerably less public dealings with each other in the pre-October Days period. (Morel, it will be recalled, had implicated Saint-Priest in the Favras plot in his report to Lafayette.) We can certainly understand why a seriously compromised Saint-Priest flew to the Châtelet almost immediately after Tourcaty's appearance at Favras' trial to insist that he had never had any contact with the accused before October 5.[10] But why were both the revolutionary authorities and the radical press so willing to refrain from questioning his story? Already under suspicion, as we have seen, in late July and eventually formally indicted by the Comité des Recherches in connection with the Maillebois affair, Saint-Priest was one of the most prominent beneficiaries of the consistent pattern of *ménagement* that would characterize the entire Favras affair. In fact, no one seems to have ever publicly raised any questions regarding the Saint-Priest–Favras connection, even after the Interior Minister's own nephew, the Comte d'Antraigues, fled the country shortly after being accused of involvement in Favras' plot.[11]

In any case, Favras' activities at the Château on October 5 did not go unnoticed among certain defenders of the Monarchy. For it was in the immediate aftermath of the October Days that he assumed a new position under the direction of an unidentified high-ranking Court noble: "Hoping to calm the royal family, I sought to become informed about all the popular movements. I observed their aims, calculated their importance, and reported to a person who was well placed to give wide circulation to the information I gathered."[12] Though Favras never named him, all the sources agree that the person to whom Favras was referring here was the Comte de Luxembourg, one of the commanders of the now disbanded Royal Bodyguards.[13] Moreover, it is clear that the purpose of the Favras–Luxembourg connection went well beyond the purely defensive one of intelligence gathering. According to Augeard, who was imprisoned in the Abbaye with Favras and his wife, Mme de Favras named Luxembourg as a leading figure in the plot for which her husband had been arrested and stated that the young Count had demanded Lafayette's job as Paris National Guard Commander as reward for his participation.[14] And Gouverneur Morris, who frequently saw both Lafayette and Luxembourg socially, reported that the latter had been dropping "dark hints" since the beginning of November about his desire "to meddle with State Affairs."[15] Lafayette, however, seems to have convinced Luxembourg to withdraw from the plot:

Sensing perfectly well the unhappy consequences this affair could have for M. de Luxembourg, who was a member of their circle, [Morris] asked M. de Lafayette to warn him to stay away from such a plot and such company. As a result, M. de Lafayette spoke to M. de Luxembourg, who at first denied everything, but when M. de Lafayette gave him the names of all the plotters and all the details of the plot ... M. de Luxembourg promised he would stay out of it.[16]

If there is any truth to this story, here is another example of the pattern of laxity that would dominate the Favras affair. And in this particular case, the oil that lubricated the gears of *ménagement* was social familiarity among a select group of aristocrats. Because Luxembourg and Lafayette, conspirator and target, moved in the same social circles, it was possible delicately to derail them from a collision course with one another.

Be that as it may, the period following the October Days also seems to have been the time when Favras forged a conspiratorial link with his most important accomplice, the future Louis XVIII, known then as the Comte de Provence or simply as Monsieur. Although the two men had known each other for years, Favras having served as an officer in one of Monsieur's personal regiments during the 1770s,[17] I have not found any evidence linking Monsieur to Favras' pre-October Days plotting. In comparison to his reactionary brother Atrois, the Comte de Provence enjoyed a reputation as something of a liberal, largely based on his having been the only Prince of the Blood besides Orléans to support the Doubling of the Third Estate at the Second Assembly of Notables.[18] But whatever inclination he might have had to play a moderating role in the Revolution was apparently extinguished by the time the Court's melancholy October 6 journey to Paris had ended. It was soon after settling into his own gilded prison in the capital that Monsieur seems to have entered the counter-revolutionary camp.

As will be seen shortly, Monsieur's involvement in the Favras plot was widely known, though not publicly acknowledged, throughout the unfolding of the judicial phase of the Favras affair. But any possible lingering doubt about it was put to rest in 1910 with the publication of this apparently authentic "confession": "I shouldn't have listened to Favras' projects and I shouldn't have disavowed them either . . . But I must say that if there were assassination plans, I didn't know anything about them. The only thing I knew about was an escape plan."[19] The disavowal of Favras and the question of assassination plans will be taken up later in this chapter. However, Monsieur's interest in an "escape plan" can be traced to his establishment of political relations with another possible Favras accomplice, Mirabeau.

Having hastily severed his ties with the suddenly moribund Orleanists, Mirabeau spent much of October, as we saw in chapter 1 above, trying to forge an alliance with Lafayette. But driven by what seems to have been a compulsion to seek power via any potential source, this "only man of genius to emerge from the Revolution of 1789" was also cultivating Monsieur.[20] In fact, the versatile Mirabeau was already reserving a place for himself in the counter-revolution even as he was urging Orléans to resist banishment by Lafayette. As LaMarck explained:

Mirabeau visited me on the morning after the King was conducted or, better yet, dragged to the Tuileries. "If you have a way," he said, "of being heard by the King and the Queen, convince them that they and France itself are lost if the royal family does not leave Paris. I am working on a plan for their departure."[21]

On October 15, LaMarck presented Mirabeau's plan to Monsieur. Explicitly ruling out the more extreme counter-revolutionary step of an escape to Metz or some other frontier city where the King would be "reduced to begging foreigners for assistance," it called for Louis XVI to withdraw to Normandy and appeal for provincial support against Parisian dominance. After perusing the plan, Monsieur, who evidently saw himself as the power behind the reconstituted monarchy it envisioned, told LaMarck that while he favored it, his hapless brother would never agree: "The King's weakness and indecision are beyond belief. To get an idea of his character, you must imagine a pack of greased balls of ivory that you vainly try to hold together."[22]

Apparently nothing was ever done to implement Mirabeau's "Normandy plan," and Monsieur would soon move on to embrace the hardline "eastern frontier option" embedded in the Favras plot. But Mirabeau does not seem to have followed him along this path. For despite Albert Mathiez's assertion that Mirabeau had an important role in the Favras plot, there is no satisfactory evidence to

support such a claim.[23] In late November, Lafayette warned Mirabeau to avoid "other political liaisons," which, according to La-
Marck, meant his relations with Monsieur. Like the one given to
Luxembourg, this warning might have helped dissuade Mirabeau
from dabbling in the Favras plot, and, in any case, Lafayette later
wrote that Mirabeau had "withdrawn" from the Favras plot "very
early."[24] Moreover, Mirabeau's lack of involvement in this affair is
also indicated by a letter in which he seems to be advising Monsieur
to stay clear of the extreme measures being envisioned by the Favras
plotters: "Do calm down an impatience that will wreck everything . . . We are neither in the Orient nor in Russia to be able to take
things so lightly. Nobody in France would submit to a palace
revolution."[25]

But let us now leave Mirabeau and return to Monsieur. We have
seen that he would later confess that "I shouldn't have *listened* to
Favras' projects," (my emphasis) thereby implying a rather passive
sponsorship of the post-October Days version of the Favras plot.
However, several sources assign him a much more active role.
According to Châtelet head Talon's friend Sémonville, Favras
drafted a declaration shortly before his execution in which he insisted that it was Monsieur who had enlisted him in the plot.
Moreover, Monsieur had only been able to entice him into participating, Favras stated, by convincing him that the Queen was also
involved. "I don't want to die," he supposedly told Talon, "or at
least I don't want to die alone if I am not pardoned in exchange for
my revelations."[26]

Though Favras wanted his statement released publicly, Talon
somehow managed to persuade the condemned man to entrust him
with the explosive document. As a masterpiece of cynicism spoken in
the name of honor, the Châtelet leader's argument deserves to be
quoted at length:

You fight against death and yet run towards it. But with this difference:
death on the scaffold, with this document in my hands, will be glorious for
you and certainly useful to your family. But the other death, infamous and
perhaps cruel and certainly as inevitable as the first, will dishonor the last of
your descendants. Don't you realize that a thousand avenging arms will
arise all over Europe to punish you for directing the sword which menaces
you onto the heads of Monsieur and the Queen . . . You are pious, M. de
Favras, accept the martyr's crown, heaven will be open to you. The burdens
of the earth . . . will be light for your children. Monsieur will owe his life to

your silence, and if, in the future, he hesitates to fulfill his duty towards your family, I have his honor in my hands.[27]

As it turned out, however, it would largely be Talon's family which would profit from the non-publication of the Favras declaration. While Favras' widow and children received only modest pensions from Monsieur, Talon's daughter, Mme du Cayla, would reap millions as the final "favorite" of Louis XVIII.[28]

In any case, Monsieur's recruitment of Favras was independently affirmed by the Napoleonic general Thiébault, whose source was a certain abbé LeDuc, a confidant and perhaps even an "uncle" of Monsieur. (He was reputed to have been an illegitimate son of Louis XV.) As Thiébault explained:

[Monsieur] was becoming frightened by the course of events. In order to stop them or change them to his liking, the means that appeared most certain was getting the royal family to leave Paris and getting rid of M. Necker and M. de Lafayette. Thus, he resolved to have these two assassinated and to have the King carried off. But, struck with the idea that no one was better equipped than M. de Favras to be charged with the execution of this double project, he approached M. de Favras and got him to accept this mission.[29]

A similar conclusion was provided, moreover, by the Comte de Bouillé, who discussed the Favras case in 1797 with Monsieur's long-time mistress, Mme de Balbi. According to Bouillé, Favras "acted under the prompting of Monsieur, and with the funds provided him by Monsieur."[30]

THE "COVER-UP"

Talon's suppression of Favras' declaration was only one of a number of actions taken by the Fayettist regime to protect the King's brother from being implicated in the Favras affair. Let us now examine this "cover-up" in more detail.

Lafayette

For some three weeks before his arrest on Christmas Eve 1789, Favras had been attempting to negotiate a large loan from a group of Dutch bankers.[31] The main thing holding up this loan had been Monsieur's reluctance to sign a document identifying him as its ultimate guarantor. However, on December 23, the Prince finally signed. On the next evening, this document was given to the banker Chomel, who then went to pick up the first installment of the loan while Favras waited at the home of Monsieur's Treasurer.[32] But there was not going to be any money paid out that night. For the prospective lenders had informed Lafayette and the Comité des Recherches about the entire business and only been engaged in trying to get Monsieur's signature on a compromising document.[33] With that document now safely in Chomel's pocket, Favras was promptly arrested by a Comité agent named Geoffrey who had been maintaining surveillance on him for two months.[34]

But Lafayette would soon find additional evidence against Monsieur. According to Morris' diary entry for December 27:

For a long Time he [Lafayette] had had Information of a Plot. That he has followed the Track and at length took up M. de Favras. That on M. de Favras was found a letter from Monsieur which seemed to shew that he was but too deeply concerned in it. That he had immediately waited upon him with that Letter, which he delivered, telling Monsieur that it was known only to him and to M. Bailly; consequently that he was not compromised.[35]

At first glance, it might be thought that the "letter" mentioned here was Monsieur's promissory note or perhaps some other document relating to the Chomel loan. However, when Morris made his diary entry, Monsieur had already publicly acknowledged his connection to this loan at a well-publicized December 26 meeting of the Assemblée des Représentants.[36] Therefore, it seems reasonable to assume that the document mentioned by Morris went beyond the loan and instead contained some compromising information about the plot itself.

On the other hand, it is unlikely that this document was a much-discussed note supposedly written by Monsieur to Favras, a note which included the following:

I have often stated and written that we will not be able to get rid of Bailly and Lafayette with libels and bribes to a few deputies and discontented groups... It will take an insurrection to overthrow them and make sure they never come back. This plan, moreover, has the advantage of intimidating the new Court and forcing the departure of the nonentity (*le soliveau*). Once he is at Metz, he will have to resign himself to the situation.[37]

But the problem with this apparent "smoking gun" is its highly questionable authenticity. According to one expert, the handwriting of the original is a very amateurish imitation of Monsieur's writing. Moreover, it is generally agreed that the usually circumspect Monsieur would never have compromised himself so thoroughly on paper, especially concerning his true feelings about his royal brother. This document was probably a Bonapartist forgery designed to embarrass and discredit the would-be Louis XVIII.[38]

But regardless of the contents of the letter found on Favras, we can now see that Lafayette was well aware of Monsieur's involvement in the Favras plot, quite apart from anything he might later have learned from Talon. In fact, the Parisian General revealed in his *Mémoires* that he sent an aide to warn Monsieur that Favras was about to be arrested, thereby giving the Prince the opportunity to destroy evidence or otherwise disengage himself from the affair. Yet, according to Augeard, Favras and his wife were both offered pardons and 48,000 *livres* if they would provide information implicating Monsieur. Thus, Lafayette seems to have been playing a kind of "double game," trying to gather as much information as possible so as to have the man he would later describe as Favras' "august accomplice" at his mercy, while ostentatiously demonstrating his willingness to be merciful. But it is the second part of this strategy that is of more significance to us here. For Lafayette's overall guiding principle in this case was clearly to limit prosecution as much as possible. Of course, the arrest and/or public investigation of the King's brother would have been all but unthinkable at this point in the Revolution. It would have meant cutting away the very ground upon which defenders of the ruling dynasty like Lafayette stood. However, the Parisian General surely could have ordered the arrest or at least the investigation of more than one subordinate plotter. Thinking perhaps of Saint-Priest, Luxembourg, and some of Monsieur's top personal aides, Lafayette would later write that "five or six men, of whom two or three are still alive, took part in this mischief." But it was Favras who took the fall for all of them.[39]

In this affair, Lafayette appears to have operated in accordance with a by now familiar pattern of behavior, the pattern of "ménagements pour les conspirateurs" through which the early revolutionary authorities, prompted by a combination of an ideological inclination towards leniency and a strategic desire to counter-balance continuous pressure from the left, attempted to foster conciliation and inclusion rather than punishment and exclusion. Quite logically, however, the ultimate result of all these *ménagements* would be a fatal erosion of popular support for the defenders of the Constitutional Monarchy. The notion that Lafayette fell because he lost popular support is, of course, part of standard French revolutionary historiography. However, the mechanisms which generated this loss of support have never been adequately explored and too much emphasis is usually given to spectacular events like the military mutiny at Nancy and the Champ-de-Mars massacre. A generally consistent policy of *ménagements* for the earliest counter-revolutionary conspirators can now be seen as one of the mechanisms through which a more gradual loss of support took place.

The Comité des Recherches

In carrying out the Favras "cover-up," Lafayette and the "right Fayettists" of the Châtelet had the full co-operation of the Paris Comité des Recherches. Up to now, we have seen Brissot and his "left Fayettist" colleagues struggling to work out a balance between their moderate instincts and their desire to accommodate themselves to the democratic imperatives of the revolutionary process, the result being the staking out of a position slightly to the left of the Constitutional Monarchist mainstream. But it is impossible to detect any such nuance in the Comité's handling of the Favras case. Instead, it functioned in this affair in exactly the manner in which it was designed to function, as an administrative instrument of the Fayettist municipal regime. In the Besenval, Augeard, and Maillebois affairs, the Comité published detailed prosecutory briefs intended, at least in part, to disassociate itself from the lack of vigilance being displayed by Lafayette and the Châtelet.[40] And, as will be seen in the final section of this study, it even sent Oudart before the National Assembly in August 1790 to attack publicly the Châtelet's handling of the October Days case. But in the Favras affair, there were no public briefs and no public appearances. Instead, the Comité acted almost exclusively behind the scenes, co-ordinating and directing the intelligence work of operatives like Geoffrey and Chomel. The only materials released by the Comité in this affair, its formal denunciation of Favras and two other documents which related to peripheral aspects of the case, were nothing more than official police documents which were not in any way designed to stimulate public discussion.[41]

Furthermore, though he had recently warned that the "sinister plots being fomented" must be publicized lest the People "drop its guard," Brissot's own newspaper barely made any mention of the Favras case. Always ready with an explanation, he tried to excuse this lack of coverage by claiming that "the delicacy of my position" required that he remain silent.[42] But, while the *Patriote français* actually did have less coverage of most of the other cases handled by the Comité than many other journals, the "delicacy" of Brissot's position never prevented him from making editorial comments on these cases or from reprinting long extracts from almost all published Comité reports.[43] However, in the Favras case, a partial eclipse of information became an almost total eclipse, and the would-be revolutionary journalist who had paid homage to the "precious publicity that is the only means by which the Nation can identify its defenders and stop the treason of its enemies" was himself eclipsed by the discreet municipal official.[44]

In addition, one of the clearest indications of the Comité's role in the Favras case is the temporary reappearance in its ranks of its most conservative member, Lacretelle. This pre-revolutionary notable's disenchantment with the Comité's "left Fayettist" slant had been signalled by his failure to endorse its autumn 1789 decisions in the Besenval, Augeard, and October Days cases, and was then reaffirmed by his lack of participation in its spring 1790 activities. However, Lacretelle suddenly joined his colleagues for their deliberations in the Favras case, the one case in which their position most closely corresponded to that of the Châtelet and the Fayettist mainstream and the one case in which they did not actively seek popular approval.[45]

Certainly one reason the Comité did not "go public" in the Favras case was that to do so was unnecessary. As will be seen in the next chapter, no major political faction had any real interest in saving Favras, and his conviction was therefore almost a foregone conclusion. But it is equally certain that another reason for the Comité's silence was that it knew too many things it did not want the public to know. As Peuchet, a member of the Paris Comité de Police, recalled:

Among the activities of the Commune's Comité des Recherches, we must mention the discovery and denunciation of the Favras conspiracy... Among those participating in this project, but with a cowardice that is well known, were persons that an important consideration prevented from naming at the time... A vague rumor designated Monsieur, brother of the King, as the head of this plot. The people who were well-informed about the intrigues and secret doings of the discontented royalists had information which left them no doubt that this Prince was prudently engaged in facilitating its execution.[46]

With an "haute considération" preventing the revelation of the truth and with near-certain conviction removing the need to create a tissue of lies, the Comité simply retreated into a position of official silence.

By its eagerness to join the Favras "cover-up," the Comité des Recherches may have been helping to sow the seeds of the bitter conflict that would erupt between Paris radicals and the Girondins of 1792–3. For it was in this affair that the Comité's members acted most clearly as the "tools" or "spies" of Lafayette that they would soon be accused of being.[47] Beginning in spring 1790, as will be seen below, Brissot and his "left Fayettist" friends would do their best to distance themselves from an already faltering Lafayette. Indeed they would gradually outflank the Duport–Barnave–Lameth group and, in the critical summer of 1791, hesitantly emerge as republicans. But they would never be able to erase completely the memory of their old ties to the "Hero of Two Worlds" and their past collaboration with Fayettist *ménagement*.

The radical press

On the morning after Favras' arrest, a sensation was created in Paris by a placard posted all over the city. The source of the rumor mentioned by Peuchet, this placard, signed by a certain "Barauz," proclaimed that Monsieur was the director of the Favras plot. Naturally quite alarmed by this charge, Monsieur decided to approach the problem head-on through an immediate appearance before the Paris Représentants. In a masterfully cynical speech partially composed by Mirabeau, he declared that he would not even bother to comment on Barauz's "atrocious slander." "You surely do not expect me," he said, "to lower myself to the point of discussing such a vile crime," though, as we have seen, he did acknowledge his connection to the Chomel loan. Reminding his listeners of his progressive reputation, he assured them that he still believed that "a great revolution is brewing" and that "royal authority must be the rampart of national liberty, and national liberty the base of royal authority."[48]

Considering the lengths to which Lafayette, Talon, and the Comité des Recherches were willing to go to protect him, the eagerness of the Représentants to exonerate Monsieur is hardly surprising. Cheering the Prince wildly, they unanimously demanded that "Barauz" be brought to justice.[49] Similarly, the response of pro-regime journalists like Gorsas, who wrote that "this accusation of a Prince has been painfully received by friends of peace and conciliation," is also rather predictable.[50] However, the complacent reaction of the radical press to the comedy that had been played at the Hôtel-de-Ville may raise some eyebrows.[51] "Monsieur's declaration has destroyed this miserable placard," declared Loustalot, "his reputation is beyond attack." And Audouin of the *Journal universel* asserted that the Prince, "so greatly admired by the French people," had been "accused by wicked men," while Louise Keralio was horrified that "they have dared to link" Monsieur to Favras. Furthermore, Desmoulins stated that "the Comité des Recherches must award its robe of innocence to Monsieur."[52]

Although he censured the Représentants for having fallen all over themselves to flatter Monsieur, even Marat never lent any credence to the charge that the Prince was involved in Favras' plot. Instead, he suggested that the authorities were exaggerating the dangers posed by this plot for their own purposes and speculated that the supposed conspiracy to assassinate Lafayette and other government leaders was nothing more than a "clever ruse imagined by an administration which is able to derive profit from everything." "There is no trap," he warned, "in which our enemies will not try to catch us, and of which we should not be suspicious."[53]

Thus, the entire radical press seems to have been just as determined as the revolutionary authorities to avoid implicating the King's brother in the Favras plot. Moreover, just as Monsieur's name did not even appear in the Favras trial transcript (except in connection with the Chomel loan), so too, once the excitement created by the Barauz placard had died down, was his name almost totally absent from subsequent reports on the case in the radical press. Shortly before Favras was executed, Audouin praised the "patriotic operations" conducted by the Comité des Recherches in the case and lauded Monsieur as "le premier citoyen français." Desmoulins also praised the Comité's handling of the case and invited Monsieur to join the Jacobin Club.[54] Meanwhile, Keralio's journal made no subsequent mention of the Favras case, while Marat, almost totally preoccupied with his own legal problems, also continued to show little interest in it.

Of the major radical journalists, only Loustalot offered any meaningful criticism of the official handling of the Favras affair. But other than a hesitant statement that some people would have liked to have seen the Châtelet investigate the case more carefully, his critique did not focus on the authorities' lack of investigatory or prosecutory vigor. On the contrary, Loustalot insisted that Favras had not been given a fair trial, arguing that, although he was "an enraged aristocrat who wanted a counter-revolution," there was no convincing evidence that he had actually done anything. Moreover, Loustalot also attacked the authorities from a more socially oriented angle. The People, he said, can easily see that "les seigneurs patriotes" (i.e., Lafayette and his friends) were not demonstrating the same "criminal complacency" for an obscure adventurer like Favras that they were exhibiting on behalf of a high-ranking courtier like Besenval.[55]

In short, the Barauz placard's denunciation of Monsieur was promptly and effectively buried by revolutionary authorities and radical journalists alike, and it is only in some obscure and isolated pamphlets that even a trace can be found of what had been so boldly proclaimed on the morning after Favras' arrest.[56] As for "Barauz" himself, a tailor and a Palais-Royal valet were soon arrested and charged with composing the offending placard. The two men claimed they had heard rumors and had only written the placard as a joke. After perfunctory efforts by the Comité des Recherches and the Châtelet to track down the source of these rumors, the two were simply released.[57] Could the Barauz incident have been a trial balloon sent up by remnants of the Orleanist faction, which would still have had an obvious interest in attacking the ruling branch of the Bourbon family? (With a Palais-Royal servant involved, one's first instinct is always to look to the Orleanists.) Or could it have been the work, as Gérard Walter has suggested, of agents of Lafayette attempting to tighten the screws on Monsieur, thereby making the Prince even more dependent on the Parisian General's "generosity"?[58] Whoever "Barauz" was, the authorities were as little disposed to uncover his identity as to expose the truth about the Favras plot itself.

In any event, the ability of the Fayettist regime to obtain the implicit collaboration of the radical press in carrying out the Favras cover-up provides another impressive indication of the strengthened position of moderate and conservative elements in the post-October

Days period. For this implicit collaboration should be attributed, at least in part, to simple prudence, to the recognition, that is, that the authorities were in a particularly favorable position during this period to make trouble for anyone who raised embarrassing questions. Yet, it would be a mistake not to see a certain measure of sincerity in the radical press' willingness to accept Monsieur's story. The eagerness of the French to retain their faith in the ruling dynasty during the early stages of the Revolution is another historiographical commonplace, and the lengths to which even radical journalists sometimes went to confirm this faith is shown by Loustalot's use of a version of the hallowed "good king–bad advisers" formula to explain how Monsieur may have innocently stumbled into the Favras affair. Thus, even as he suggested that Favras must have been part of a wider conspiracy, Loustalot speculated that "an aristocratic intrigue ... pushed Favras in Monsieur's direction, so as to envelop this Prince in some sort of trap." In recommending Favras as a go-between for a loan, the Comte de la Châtre, Monsieur's Premier Gentilhomme, had "voluntarily or involuntarily compromised this Prince's name."[59]

But if all segments of political opinion still retained some sense of loyalty to the royal family, how could a policy of protecting that family have, as asserted above, eventually helped to undermine the political credit of people like Lafayette and Brissot? With everyone so willing to collaborate in the Favras cover-up, how could that cover-up later return to haunt its original sponsors? One way of dissolving this apparent contradiction is to take proper account of the concept of psychological ambivalence by suggesting that public expressions of faith and trust in the ruling dynasty by radical journalists coexisted with unacknowledged and, at times, unconscious feelings of disbelief and suspicion. Though these journalists may have wanted to believe Monsieur's claim that he was not plotting to destroy the Revolution, the decades-long process that Dale Van Kley has called the "de-sacralization of the monarchy" had insured that, in the deeper recesses of their psyches, their longing to believe would be accompanied by a persistent sense of doubt.[60]

However, whatever combination of trust and distrust of the ruling family may have prevailed through the first two years of the Revolution, the tenuous coexistence of these two feelings would have been effectively shattered by the attempted flight of Louis XVI in June

1791 and by the successful escape of Monsieur himself at the same time. But with the truth about the loyalty of the ruling family to the Revolution now finally known, the embarrassment of having been duped for so long would have created an intense need to blame all those who had been responsible for protecting the reputation of that family. The failure of the radical press to criticize the official handling of the Favras affair while it unfolded may well have been at least partially rooted in a profound desire to trust the King and his family. But with the definitive exposure of the royal family's disloyalty, the revolutionary authorities who had been actively engaged in covering up that disloyalty would now be regarded as traitors themselves.

THE EVIDENCE

Favras' execution might itself be seen as an extension of the cover-up that dominated the official handling of his case, for, to put it bluntly, his death guaranteed that he would remain silent.[61] But though there is probably some truth to this, we can obtain a more complete understanding of why Favras was executed by looking into what he actually *did*.

On February 18, 1790, the Châtelet convicted Favras of:

having formed, communicated to military officers, bankers and others, and attempted to implement a plan for counter-revolution in France which was to have been carried out by assembling the malcontents of several different provinces, allowing foreign troops to enter the kingdom, winning over some of the former French Guards, creating division within the National Guard, assassinating three main government leaders, seizing the King and the royal family and taking them to Peronne, dissolving the National Assembly, and attacking the city of Paris.[62]

However, one of Favras' more unlikely defenders painted a very different picture of the case against him. Upset over the release of the farmer-general Augeard only two weeks after the execution of the "poor devil" Favras, Loustalot pointed to some "frightening parallels" between the two cases:

The Marquis de Favras planned to take the King to Peronne, while Augeard planned to make him go to Metz. Favras wanted to have 1,200 cavalry and 20,000 malcontents ready to follow the King, while Augeard wanted to assemble the nobility to form an army of 40,000 men. Favras was accused of wanting to dissolve the National Assembly by setting off a civil war. Augeard favored the same plan.[63]

For Loustalot, the differing fates of Favras and Augeard demonstrated the truth of the maxim that "the judgment of the Tribunal will depend on whether or not you are powerful." But while this factor can hardly be entirely discounted, the two cases were not nearly as similar as he claimed. Although Loustalot used the word "voulait" several times in hopes of convincing his readers that both men had only *wanted* a counter-revolution, Favras seems to have actually done a great deal more.[64] For even though much of what had been discovered about his plot could not be publicly revealed in the interest of protecting all the other potential defendants in the case, the evidence presented at Favras' trial still provides us with a good idea of why his activities were considered to be so dangerous.

The idea that military power is the ultimate guarantor of political authority may be only a truism, but it is one which can never be far from the minds of the actors in a revolutionary situation. And in 1789–90, the ultimate line of revolutionary defense was, of course, the Paris National Guard. Thus, the charge that Favras had sought to compromise the loyalty of this extremely sensitive institution can probably be regarded as the most serious of those lodged against him. Though Favras may have had contact with other Guardsmen, the only one who spoke to this accusation in court was Lieutenant Jean-Philippe Marquié, an officer in the old Gardes-Françaises who had attracted some public attention by crying profusely as the royal family was being brought back to Paris on October 6. Seeing a certain potential for counter-revolutionary activity in this gesture, Favras soon made contact with Marquié and met with him four times in November.[65]

According to Marquié, Favras' main aim in these meetings seemed to be to promote dissatisfaction among the former Gardes-Françaises, who now formed the core of the National Guard. In particular, Favras insinuated that Lafayette was showing favoritism towards volunteer bourgeois companies and a newly formed cavalry unit. The Gardes-Françaises, suggested Favras, should not allow themselves to be subsumed under the direct authority of the Parisian General, for "it would be a real shame if such a beautiful regiment were to lose its identity."[66]

After several weeks of such rhetoric, Favras apparently decided it was time to up the ante. At his fourth meeting with Marquié, he brought a copy of the counter-revolutionary pamphlet *Ouvrez donc les yeux* with some specifically marked passages:

The Gardes-Françaises have been deceived and they know it. They exhibit their repentance every day. They are ready to return to their duty and never stray from it again. All they lack is a man who knows how to bring them back to the path they used to follow. A thousand can be found to lead them astray. Only one man presents himself who has enough courage to show them their error. *Yes, soldiers, it is to you, the Gardes-Françaises, that I speak. You will find this man, it is me.*[67]

Upon reading these words, Marquié must have felt that he was getting in too deep. After this meeting, he decided that "he should no longer return to see this Marquis de Favras."[68]

Responding to Marquié's testimony, Favras claimed he had only posed questions and had not expressed any opinions concerning the Gardes-Françaises. He maintained that his only motive for meeting with Marquié had been to learn whether the Lieutenant's troops were prepared to defend the King in the event of a new insurrection. However, just before his execution, Favras revealed that the "grand seigneur" to whom he was reporting (Luxembourg) had told him that the authority of the Monarchy could only be recovered by "establishing a Supreme General and by naming a new commander of the Paris militia," a sensational revelation which amounted to an admission that the task of properly "defending" the King entailed the overthrow of the existing government. "Was it possible," asked the *Chronique de Paris*, "to name a commandant-general without getting rid of M. de Lafayette? Could a Supreme General be appointed without destroying the Constitution, dissolving the National Assembly, and establishing a military government?"[69]

Thus, it seems evident that Favras hoped to employ Marquié's troops to generate some kind of rebellion in the National Guard. Though he insisted that he had not given "any advice which would turn them [Marquié's men] away . . . from their duty," it is clear that the "duty" Favras had in mind was not their duty as defined by Lafayette, but rather their duty as described in *Ouvrez donc les yeux*. While Alexis de Valon's suggestion that Favras himself may have been the author of this anonymous pamphlet must remain unproven, there can be little doubt that, in his own mind, he had come to think of himself as that "one man" who would be able to get the

Gardes-Françaises "to return to their duty" and "to bring them back to the path they used to follow."[70]

The spectre of National Guard disloyalty raised by Marquié's testimony was underlined and reinforced by an event that occurred exactly one week after his appearance at Favras' trial. On January 12, a gathering of some 200 mutinous National Guardsmen on the Champs-Elysées was broken up by about 1,700 loyal troops led by Lafayette. Though this incident was probably rooted in little more than a demand for higher pay, the widely circulated rumor that one of the real aims had been to free the imprisoned Favras could only have served to make the prosecution's case against him seem more credible. The mutiny of January 12 was, in fact, the most concrete display of dissatisfaction within the National Guard seen thus far in the Revolution, and its outbreak undoubtedly further undermined Favras' already precarious position.[71]

In addition to Marquié's charges regarding efforts to subvert the National Guard, we must also consider allegations made by the recruiters Morel and Tourcaty that Favras had taken steps to implement more spectacular counter-revolutionary projects: the assembling of a strike force that would make a direct attack upon Paris, the assassination of Lafayette, Bailly, and Necker, the dissolution of the Assembly, and the "carrying-off" of the King. However, before proceeding to the substance of Morel and Tourcaty's charges, we might briefly examine a controversy which arose concerning their right to testify.

Citing a long legal tradition, Favras' attorneys contended that the two recruiters should not be admitted as witnesses because they were the denunciators in the case. Although even Favras' brother later conceded that this practice had not usually been followed in political cases,[72] the defense was able to create a momentary flurry of interest around the question of whether the defendant was being treated fairly. Thus, on January 28, Lafayette, Bailly, and the Comité des Recherches issued a carefully worded statement that Morel was "the first person to reveal the activities attributed to the Marquis de Favras," a statement which did not quite satisfy Favras' insistence that Morel be explicitly identified as his denunciator.[73] In any case, the Châtelet had already ruled that Favras' legal denunciator was the Commune's Procureur-Syndic, and the wishy-washy statement from the Hôtel-de-Ville did not induce a change in this ruling.[74]

While anxious to avoid the appearance of arbitrariness, the municipal and judicial authorities were obviously not going to allow either of their star witnesses to be disqualified on a technicality.

Now in evaluating the significance and impact of Morel and Tourcaty's testimony, it should be stressed that, as professional military recruiters, these men were precisely the kind of individuals one would approach if one wanted to assemble a counter-revolutionary force. Thus, their very involvement in the case provides a good indication that, in contrast to Augeard, Favras had indeed crossed the sometimes ambiguous line which separates "thought" from "action." Furthermore, though the actual implementation of Favras' plan was clearly still a long way off when he was arrested, both Morel and Tourcaty asserted that concrete steps had already been taken to help bring the plot to fruition. According to Morel, Favras stated: "We have 1,200 horses, mostly at Versailles. We need enough sure men to mount these horses. I am counting on you, M. Tourcaty, and some others to get these men for us." And Tourcaty testified that Favras told him and Morel: "You two must send as many known and sure men as you can ... I have the horses ready, and if we can get 1,200 men together, there will be nothing to worry about."[75]

According to the two witnesses, Favras then described how his 1,200 troops would gain control of the main entry points to the capital, and how, aided by whatever detachments of Paris National Guards and Swiss Guards that could be won over, they would proceed to assassinate Lafayette and his colleagues, dissolve the Assembly, and seize the King. He also described how steps were being taken to insure that vast numbers of loyal French and foreign troops would be ready to support these actions. According to Morel, 22,000 men would be available to escort the royal family to Peronne, and as many as 150,000 would eventually be available to guarantee that the King would be able to reassert his authority once he reached Peronne.[76]

How much of this testimony can be taken seriously? Though many historians who have written on this case stress the unreliability of the witnesses, the fact is that if any of it were true, that in itself would have been enough to justify Favras' conviction. Moreover, the defense's continual demand that the witnesses' allegations be backed up by supporting evidence can be answered by again noting the overarching priority given to the cover-up in this affair.[77] All of

which is not to deny the likelihood that the two witnesses exaggerated and even invented some details. In particular, it is difficult to
have much faith in the reputed assassination plans which attracted
so much public attention. Monsieur, it will be recalled, insisted that
"if there were assassination plans, I didn't know anything about
them. The only thing I knew about was an escape plan." And the
banker Chomel, who claimed that Favras had disclosed all his plans
to him, declared that "I have no knowledge of the plan for three
assassinations or of the plan to invade Paris."[78] In a strange twist,
Morel stated that he had personally volunteered to kill Lafayette:
"Afraid that someone less sure than he would be assigned this
assassination, and wanting to make sure it didn't take place, he
asked to be chosen ... and the Marquis de Favras acceded to this
request."[79] While there is nothing inherently unbelievable in this
claim, it somehow lacks the ring of truth and leaves this researcher
more inclined to believe that the threat of assassination actually
originated in Morel's imagination.

In fact, taking Monsieur at his word, it seems reasonable to
suggest that the real aim of the Favras plot was not a mad-cap
assault on the capital, but rather the formation of a military force
that, aided by some friendly National and Swiss Guards, was ex-
pressly designed to escort the royal family to the safety of Peronne.
Such a plan could not have succeeded, moreover, without the co-
operation of large numbers of provincial troops, though the numbers
mentioned by Morel were probably exaggerated. Once the King was
safely among loyal forces, the Monarchy would then have been free
to resume its struggle with the Revolution from a position of
strength. And as the mastermind of the entire operation, Monsieur
could then have had himself declared Regent of the Kingdom.[80]

If this indeed approximates the scenario envisioned by Monsieur
and Favras, their plan can be seen as one of a host of schemes to
extract Louis XVI from the dominance of Paris and to seek political
and military support from loyal forces in the provinces. Beginning
with the King's own inclination to flee to Metz on July 15, 1789 and
the Monarchien proposal discussed earlier and ranging all the way
to the ill-fated Varennes affair and beyond, the "conspiracy of
flight/abduction" recurs again and again in the first stages of the
Revolution.[81] But if the Favras plot was only one of countless such
plans and if all of these plans would ultimately have required some
form of military support, Favras was the only conspirator captured

behind enemy lines, so to speak, with his weapons virtually in his hands. He was, that is, the one conspirator caught in Paris during the early Revolution who had most clearly crossed the line which separates political strategy from military action.

Yet, there were many other conspirators captured under somewhat similar conditions in other parts of France during the first two years of the Revolution, conspirators who, largely due to the indulgent tendencies of the National Assembly, were able to escape Favras' fate. Though none of these cases can be discussed in detail, let us at least mention the following: (1) Comte de Toulouse-Lautrec, career military officer and Assembly deputy: arrested in June 1790 for trying to recruit a counter-revolutionary militia in Toulouse; released almost immediately by order of the Assembly on grounds of parliamentary immunity;[82] (2) leaders of the counter-revolutionary Catholic militia at Nîmes which engaged in a bloody battle with Protestant National Guards in May 1790: amnestied by the Assembly in February 1791;[83] (3) Comte de Bussy, career military officer: charged with organizing a counter-revolutionary force in the Beaujolais and arrested by the Mâcon National Guard in October 1790 after a virtual siege at his own château; ordered to be released by the Assembly in accordance with the recommendation of its Comité des Recherches in January 1791;[84] (4) Camp de Jalès: an August 1790 gathering of 25,000 National Guardsmen from all over the south-east which took on a vaguely counter-revolutionary tinge; though its directing committee was formally dissolved by the Assembly, the prosecution of its leaders was quickly abandoned; moreover, the leaders of a second more blatantly counter-revolutionary Camp de Jalès in February 1791 were arrested but eventually released under a general amnesty declared by the Assembly in September 1791;[85] and (5) three agents of Artois, who had been preparing a long-awaited royalist uprising in Lyon: arrested in December 1790, but also released under the terms of the September 1791 amnesty.[86]

Unlike Favras, none of these conspirators, all of whom appear to have been prepared to undertake a military assault upon the revolutionary regime, were captured in the capital; that is to say, none of them had been operating in a place where the authorities had to reckon with a sustained, organized, and powerful popular movement which had already established judicial rigor as one of the central items of its political program. Thus, the case against the organizers of the first Camp de Jalès was dropped after the National Assembly received a petition requesting dismissal of the charges from the Directory of the Department of the Ardèche.[87] But having already been burned by the popular movement on the Besenval amnesty issue the previous July, the local authorities in Paris were in no position even to think about making such a request on Favras' behalf. Nor, for that matter, did the Assembly itself dare to intervene in Favras' favor, making it quite clear, in quickly brushing aside the defense's request that the Châtelet be forced to name his denunciators, that it had no desire to get involved in this affair.[88] To round out our examination of the factors which combined to put Favras' neck in a noose, we must, therefore, look more deeply into the local context in which his affair was played out.

7

The Favras–Besenval judicial transaction

As the year 1789 drew to a close, the cast in the revolutionary drama could not have known that a temporary breathing spell was about to be written into the script.[1] With the October Days having erupted approximately three months after the July Revolution, many Parisians were quite prepared to believe that another major outburst was going to occur sometime around the beginning of the new year. In mid-December, tensions rose as the capital was engulfed by a new wave of rumors of aristocratic plotting. And since the connection between aristocratic plotting and pre-emptive popular action against such plotting had already become firmly imprinted in public consciousness by the events of July and October, this new rash of rumors was itself probably taken as a signal that the revolutionary thermometer was about to jump again.

The rumors of mid-December focused on Christmas as the day on which a great counter-revolutionary uprising was to be launched. As Desmoulins reported: "Rumor generally had it that on the day and night of the Nativity, our venerable Clergy and Aristocracy would be reborn out of their ashes." Or as Loustalot more matter-of-factly stated: "Christmas night was designated for the execution of their horrible schemes." Meanwhile, Gorsas revealed on December 26 that he hadn't published these rumors for fear of creating too much popular excitement. Furthermore, all the Parisian rumors were accompanied by reports from Dauphiné that a plot hatched by Artois and the *émigrés* would be carried out on Christmas Day.[2]

Coming as it did in the wake of all these rumors, the Christmas Eve arrest of Favras seems to have reinforced and intensified popular fears by giving a measure of concreteness and credibility to what had hitherto been only rumor. As the *Annales patriotiques et littéraires* reported:

Even the most suspicious and the quickest to flare up appeared calm until the idea of a new conspiracy and the arrest of M. de Favras have once again generated unrest and mistrust among Parisians. People are especially fearful for the leaders, and it is thought that M. de Lafayette is in more danger than ever.[3]

For some relentlessly conspiratorial minds, moreover, Favras' arrest had itself been engineered in order to conceal the source of the real danger. As the *Journal général de la cour et de la ville* stated on December 30: "Rumor has it that the conspiracy on everyone's mind at this moment is actually only a maneuver arranged by an adroit political strategy which, to hide its projects from us and thwart the efforts of our generous defenders, has thrown this decoy to the People."[4]

Fears for Lafayette's safety were further reinforced on December 28 when a sentry named Trudon was found stabbed in front of a National Guard barrack with an alarming message resting nearby: "It's your turn now, but Lafayette will be next."[5] This new indication of what one district called "the dangers which threaten the hero-protector of our new-born liberty" produced a flurry of expressions of concern for the physical well-being of the Parisian General and his associates and a number of offers to provide them special protection.[6] Many people breathed easier when it became apparent that Trudon, who had begun to exhibit "all the symptoms of complete madness," had probably stabbed himself.[7] Yet, the day after announcing that the Trudon incident was a hoax, Gorsas reported that someone had fired an errant shot at Lafayette. And one week later, a rumor circulated that his house had been mined.[8]

THE DISTURBANCES OF JANUARY 1790

As fears and rumors of new aristocratic intrigues intensified, so too did the rhythm of popular unrest. Though given little if any attention by most historians, the disturbances that took place in and around Paris during the second week of January were easily the most severe since the October Days and, for that matter, the most severe that would occur in the capital for at least another year. I have already mentioned the January 12 National Guard mutiny, and we will now see that it was by no means an isolated incident.

On January 7, a serious bread riot broke out in nearby Versailles, with martial law being declared and order only being restored by summoning the Paris National Guard.[9] This event generated concern within the Paris municipality that chronic grumbling among unemployed and otherwise disgruntled workers would solidify into something more substantial and that "the People [would be] led to some form of excess." But while some protesters from the Faubourgs Saint-Antoine and Saint-Marceau actually did begin to march on the Hôtel-de-Ville on January 10, Lafayette was able to disperse them with a patriotic speech. "The words of this hero," it was reported, "immediately calmed this potential insurrection, and the malcontents went home filled with admiration for this great man."[10] Economic discontent seems to have generated only "an undercurrent of unrest" in the faubourgs at this time.[11]

However, there was an issue around which very large numbers of people would be mobilized in the capital that week and it was not an economic one. For several days prior to January 11, tumultuous scenes had been enacted inside the Châtelet courtroom where Besenval was being tried. (The Besenval trial, it will be recalled, had begun in mid-November, and was now proceeding concurrently with the Favras trial, which had begun only days after Favras' arrest.) The reason for this uproar was that the judges were making it increasingly clear how favorably disposed they were to the defendant. As Loustalot reported, angry spectators were becoming more and more impatient with "judges who . . . smile at the accused."[12] And matters were not helped by the condescending lectures of Presiding Judge Boucher d'Argis, who asked the audience how they would like it if they were on trial and heard themselves reviled by the public. "Why treat another more severely than you would want to be treated yourselves," he innocently wondered, as the hated Besenval sat and confidently awaited his apparently imminent release.[13]

As tensions rose inside the Besenval courtroom, protesters began to gather outside. In addition, the public interrogation of Favras, which began on January 9, also attracted many demonstrators. On January 11, the Châtelet was besieged by perhaps 10,000 people screaming death threats against Besenval, Favras, and the judges themselves, and the National Guard once again had to wheel out cannon to scatter a dangerous crowd.[14] One side-effect of the day's events was the suspension of all judicial proceedings. "All this activity," reported the *Moniteur*, "chased away the judges and witnesses," including Boucher d'Argis, who might well have been reflecting at that moment on his pre-revolutionary prediction that public trials would create a "murderous arena, with the Magistrates themselves forced to descend from their Tribunal in order to defend their lives and their edicts."[15]

With a measure of calm settling on the capital by the next evening, a consensus quickly developed among radical and "left Fayettist" journalists alike regarding the origins of all the disturbances of the past week. As Audouin explained:

All the unrest we have witnessed is an aristocratic maneuver. The aristocracy is sending scoundrels among the People, paid scoundrels who are seducing it and making it turn its arms against itself. The enemies of the Revolution wanted to induce the multitude to commit excesses which could only be repressed by force, thereby leading to discord between the People and the National Guard.[16]

The idea that the unrest had been instigated by counter-revolutionary agents was echoed by Gorsas, who, as he had done after the October Days, again attributed enormous influence to the inflammatory pen of his favorite counter-revolutionary agent, Marat.[17] And Brissot also blamed the "aristocrats":

Reader, bring together all these events: Favras plot–discontent–sedition by some of the paid troops in Paris–bread riots at Versailles–an undercurrent of unrest in the Faubourgs Saint-Antoine and Saint-Marceau–atrocious libels multiplying and circulating without limit–and finally open insurrection by the Parlement in Brittany. And our enemies swear to us they are not doing anything![18]

Yet, even as we hear him sound an alarmist note here, we must again recall the great difficulty Brissot always had in comfortably adapting to the central role of the revolutionary journalist, that of focusing on the frightful dangers posed by the machinations of the enemies of the Revolution. For he had seemed much less concerned about the recent profusion of counter-revolutionary pamphlets only one day earlier:

Good citizens are becoming too frightened by the abundance of these pamphlets. They will not excite the unrest that is expected from them. To the extent that a People marches towards Liberty, it marches towards Reason, and a People that reasons sees it has everything to gain under the new regime, and everything to lose under the old.[19]

Reading these words, we are reminded of the young judicial reformer who had written ten years earlier that libels should be scorned, pitied, or pardoned. However, it may have been exactly this kind of complacent language that would eventually get Brissot into trouble with the Parisian *sans-culottes*, who would prove to have little patience for the enlightened rhetoric that he and his Girondin friends would seek to dispense.

But let us temporarily take leave of Brissot and his touching if pedantic little lessons and return to the explanation of the January disturbances being disseminated by so many patriotic journalists. "It was in Versailles," reported Loustalot, "that the signal for insurrection was first given" by an "aristocratic faction" that had "stirred up" the "poor classes" through bribery and promises of lower bread prices. Next, he stated, the aristocrats had fomented the mutiny on the Champs-Elysées by making "seductive offers" to disgruntled National Guardsmen. And finally, they had used similar methods to instigate the riots at the Châtelet: "The hordes of un-employed, bribed by the aristocracy in Paris, assembled again at the Châtelet in order to divide our attention and our forces. Their example carried along some honest citizens," who had been in-flamed by a rumor "spread by the faction that Favras would be released." Moreover, the organizers combined rumors about Favras with rumors about Besenval, thereby "further animating the People, already very irritated with the evident partiality with which the Besenval trial is being conducted." According to Loustalot, the goal of all this activity was to secure the escape of both Favras and Besenval, presumably through the creation of mass confusion.[20]

The intermingling here of allegations of prison escape plots with popular riots and demands for justice and vengeance brings to mind the atmosphere which produced the September Prison Massacres of 1792. In this connection, a rumor printed in Audouin's journal on January 9, two days before the most serious Châtelet disorder, is especially striking. According to this rumor, the aristocrats were arranging for large crowds to "assemble chaotically at the Châtelet during the night, and in the midst of this uproar, all the criminals and suspects could escape, spread out all over town, and replace the calm we enjoy with the horrors of a counter-revolution."[21] Thus, the fantasy of escaped prisoners serving as the central actors in a counter-revolutionary conspiracy was present in the revolution-ary imagination long before the dangers of war would sharpen and intensify it and turn it into a very real motive for actual behavior.

Commenting on patriotic press coverage of the Châtelet protests, the early nineteenth-century historians Buchez and Roux noted that "although these journalists attributed these demonstrations to the maneuvers of the opposing party, they themselves had not abstained from any of the words which might have angered the People against the Châtelet."[22] And indeed, just days before January 11, Loustalot had observed that "the People are the only ones not in on the secret of the comedy" then being enacted in the Besenval courtroom, while Audouin had recently stated that he was afraid the Châtelet would allow Besenval to emerge "as white as snow" from his affair.[23] And Carra had just declared:

The Châtelet is really embarrassed. It has never judged *lèse-nation* crimes, and it doesn't know what one is, though thousands of them have been committed in the past 500 years... [But] the failure to punish *lèse-nation* crimes will only regenerate and multiply their occurrence; and we will be justly punished by those that our cowardly indulgence will have spared.[24]

Why, then, with the notable exception of Marat, were all the leading patriotic journalists so quick to disown the protests at the Châtelet and, for that matter, all the other disturbances of the second week of January?[25] While the evidence which would be necessary to determine exactly who or what was really "behind" these events has probably been lost forever, the idea that they were primarily fomented by counter-revolutionaries is, at best, an extremely dubious one. Rather, it would seem more reasonable to ascribe them to some combination of spontaneous popular protest and organized radical agitation, much in the manner of my previous discussion of the anti-amnesty protests of July 30. Yet, the eagerness of patriotic journalists to blame them on the "aristocrats" will perhaps appear more comprehensible after we have approached the political situation of January 1790 from another angle.

To begin, let us note one significant difference between the events of January and the October Days. Whereas it may still be possible to debate the question of who emerged victorious from the October Days, there can be no doubt that the only political winner of January was the commander of the Paris National Guard. Lafayette's Guard had repressed the unrest at Versailles, it had stood firm against a serious challenge to its unity on the Champs-Elysées, and it had prevented the Châtelet riots from turning into something more dangerous. But if January was a period which confirmed and reinforced Lafayette's political dominance, it was also a period during which the remnants of the discredited Monarchien faction were making what would amount to a final effort to avoid total isolation by seeking an alliance with the Fayettists. On December 29, hoping to drive a wedge between Lafayette and the left, the Monarchien leader Malouet invited the Parisian General "to put yourself at the head of all moderate men who want liberty, peace, and justice for everyone."[26] While the Monarchiens were simply too closely associated with the *parti aristocratique* at this point for there to be much chance that the Fayettists would give any kind of serious consideration to Malouet's proposal, Lafayette and his closest associates in the National Assembly did hold two well-publicized conferences with Malouet's group during the first week of January. And though nothing substantial resulted from these meetings, patriotic journalists who would have been anxiously watching these developments could not have known that at the time. How, moreover, could they be sure that Lafayette would continue to reject Malouet's overtures?[27]

Fearful of the possibility of a Fayettist–Monarchien *rapprochement* and all too aware of the fact that Lafayette was now less subject to popular pressure, the patriot press, it can now be suggested, may have seen the foisting of responsibility for all the January disturbances onto the "aristocratic faction" as a means of further discrediting and compromising the Monarchiens. In thus seeking to torpedo any chance of a Lafayette–Monarchien alliance, both "left Fayettist" and radical journalists would have been attempting to prevent Lafayette's post-October Days drift to the right from proceeding any further than it already had.

In this connection, the renewed political threat being posed by the Monarchiens during this period is especially indicated by an escalation of patriotic attacks upon this group and, in particular, by an attempt to blur the difference between the Monarchiens and the "hard right," thereby connecting the Monarchiens to all the accusations then being made against the "aristocratic faction." Thus, Brissot charged that the self-declared "Impartials" who "want to bring all parties together into a single one and who say they are the moderate defenders of the People ... are actually part of the

Aristocratic Party," while Loustalot stated that the followers of "Malouétisme" were nothing but "conspiring and disorderly aristocrats." In the mean time, Desmoulins imagined a speech by Malouet in which the Monarchien leader bemoaned the increased effectiveness of the National Guard, complained that "Lafayette is upsetting all our plans," and invented the label "moderate" as a clever ruse through which his group could "rid ourselves of this name 'aristocrats'."[28]

But let us now return to Favras. For whatever considerations may have been involved in the disowning of the January Châtelet protests by the patriotic press, these protests, which marked the re-emergence of the revolutionary crowd as a key actor in the judicial process, served, in my view, as the final nail in Favras' coffin. Though Lafayette joined the patriotic press in publicly attributing these protests to aristocratic maneuvers,[29] the authorities were certainly well aware that they had actually been largely fueled by the popular desire for justice and vengeance. We have already seen how that desire had ignited a wave of protest that forced a frightened municipality to rescind its endorsement of Necker's amnesty policy the previous summer. While the January protests were certainly not as extensive as those of July 30, they were a reminder that further violent action could always be centered around this extremely sensitive issue. Moreover, paradoxically enough, the allegation that the aristocrats had manipulated popular anger in an effort to free Favras and Besenval could itself have helped intensify that anger, thereby further increasing the possibility of another explosion.

In trying to defuse this possibility, one strategy adopted by the authorities was, as we have already seen, to make a temporarily successful effort on January 22 to silence once again the one influential journalist who had openly welcomed the Châtelet riots. "Already the indignant public ... is murmuring loudly," Marat had written on January 11, "it fears, and with good reason, that its guilty enemies will escape the sword of justice, that the scoundrels who have machinated its ruin will be absolved and whitewashed." For Marat, of course, the only solution was a new insurrection:

The black plots of our enemies are going to produce a horrible storm. Already it rumbles near our heads. Oh, my fellow citizens! Redouble your vigilance, be on your guard: and if some unexpected event brings a new general insurrection, make use of this turn of events to finally expel the

priests and the nobles from the National Assembly ... Purge the municipality ... Arrest all public officials who have expressed anti-patriotic
sentiments.[30]

But if acting against Marat was one way that the Fayettist authorities sought to head off the possibility of a new uprising, another
way they pursued the same goal was to demonstrate to "the People"
that they were prepared to deliver at least one of its "guilty enemies"
to "the sword of justice." Yet, though the execution of Favras must
be seen, at least in part, as a concession to popular demands for
justice and vengeance, we must look further into the context in which
this concession was made. In particular, we must look more deeply
into the relationship between the Favras case and the Besenval case.

THE TRIAL OF BESENVAL

In contrast to the Favras trial, which had begun only five days after
his arrest (itself an indication of the heated atmosphere in which this
affair was played out), Besenval's trial had been proceeding at a
rather leisurely pace since mid-November. With the events of the
previous summer perhaps already seeming like ancient history to
many, this trial did not attract a great deal of public attention or
protest during its early stages. Thus, the *Moniteur*, already in the
process of establishing itself as a semi-official governmental organ,
reported that a mood of "great respect" prevailed in the courtroom
when the "distinguished" general was publicly interrogated on November 21, and even Loustalot, who had quickly denounced the
Châtelet's evident bias in favor of the defendant, made no reference
to any public disturbances during the trial's early weeks.[31] Moreover, one especially striking indication of the relatively relaxed
atmosphere which marked this period was provided by a leading
gossip sheet: "This illustrious prisoner, detained for so long, has
permission to receive friends of both sexes, and even has permission
to serve them dinner. One is astonished to hear the ladies of the
Court say to each other in their little circles: 'I am going to dine at the
Châtelet.'"[32]

This eminently civilized ambience was shattered, however, by the
arrest of Favras and the increased tension generated by his arrest. As
we have seen, large crowds began to gather at the Châtelet in early
January, and this development was accompanied by a noticeable
expansion of Besenval press coverage. Gorsas' journal, for example,

which had barely mentioned the Besenval trial through its first seven weeks, suddenly began extensive and almost daily coverage on January 11.

From the very beginning of the Besenval trial, it had been clear that it was going to be difficult for the Comité des Recherches to find satisfactory evidence linking the defendant to "the conspiracy formed against the National Assembly and the City of Paris between the month of May and July 15."[33] In part, this difficulty was a reflection of the same problem that two centuries of historians have faced in trying to determine the Monarchy's intentions during this period. Obviously Besenval's troops had been summoned to do more than simply protect grain convoys, but, as we saw in chapter 2, it is unlikely that anyone will ever be able to discover exactly what.[34] As Garran put it in his second report on the July Conspiracy: "Plotters seldom put their plans down on paper, and it is especially hard to find the Plans that ambitious ministers well-versed in insidious Court Politics form against the Liberty of Peoples."[35] In addition, it was also clear that it was going to be especially difficult for the Comité to properly vilify a general who was more noted for his exploits in the boudoir than on the battlefield,[36] and who, as we have seen, had been an essentially passive observer of the crucial events of July 12–14.

Furthermore, another problem faced by the Comité was that Besenval, as the only "July conspirator" being held in custody, had to serve as a kind of "proxy" for three fugitive "co-conspirators" (the ex-ministers Broglie and Barentin and Condé's military attaché, the Maréchal d'Autichamp) who were being tried *in absentia* along with him.[37] Indeed it would not be inaccurate to say that the Besenval trial had to serve as a vehicle for a general indictment of the entire July Conspiracy. Especially keen on having the trial fulfill this educational and propagandistic function, the Comité sent witness after witness to the Châtelet to recite testimony which, while implicating some of the missing defendants, had painfully little to do with Besenval himself. Thus, for example, six deputies were assigned the task of presenting detailed accounts of late June efforts by the royal government to prevent the Third Estate from constituting itself as the National Assembly.[38]

With compliant judges and a co-operative press, such testimony could easily have become a central feature of a classic political trial in which the outgoing regime's attempts to retain its power are defined as "criminal."[39] But in the France of 1789–90, with an unsympathetic tribunal and, as we shall soon see, a largely un-cooperative press, the Comité's attempts to generalize the Besenval trial produced a certain backlash effect. Thus, the *Journal général de la cour et de la ville* reported that the six deputies "told everything they knew, and all of it exonerates this general, thereby irrefutably prov-ing the iniquity of the accusation against him."[40] Moreover, the total absence of any mention of the testimony of these deputies in Gorsas' *Courrier de Paris* and a simple one-sentence report in the *Chronique de Paris* indicate that even these two "left Fayettist" papers, which usually expressed views very close to those of Brissot's journal, were not very much in tune with the Comité's vision of a trial that would help educate the public about "the final battles between Despotism and Liberty."[41]

Yet, despite all the problems in constructing a solid case against him, Besenval could easily have been convicted, if the judges had been so inclined, on the simple basis of having ordered the Governor of the Bastille to "defend himself until the last extremity." But the judges, of course, were not so inclined. For it is clear that the outcome of the Besenval case was actually decided on the day that the National Assembly decreed that loyal agents of the Old Regime would be judged by a judicial remnant of that regime, a decision which reflected both the Assembly's essential lack of interest in inflicting punishment on its enemies and its desire to discourage further emigration and thereby construct a political community with as wide a base of support as possible. With ideological and strategic considerations dovetailing in this manner, it is difficult to evaluate and weigh the relative causative impact of one or the other, though, as already indicated, an ideological inclination towards leniency may have helped to shape a conciliatory strategy. In addition, the primacy of ideology as a determinant of Assembly judicial policy is also suggested by the apparent dominance of ideology over strategy in other policy areas. On religious matters, for example, ideological anti-clericalism seems to have dictated policies which clearly under-mined a strategy of inclusion and accommodation.[42]

In any event, whatever relative weight should be assigned to ideological and strategic factors, the willingness of the National Assembly to forgive the commander of the troops which had been on the verge of attacking it the previous summer should be seen as the centerpiece of its remarkably lenient judicial record. Forced by popular pressure to repudiate the amnesty of July 30 and to order that Besenval remain under arrest, the Assembly was, as we have seen, careful to keep him at a safe distance from Paris. Then, after more than two months of inaction, when pressed by a new wave of popular violence to name judges for Besenval, the Assembly selected a tribunal which was hardly likely to convict him. Surely, the intended scenario now called for the old general's release after a decent interval and, to use Loustalot's term, a well-played judicial "comedy."

Moreover, several important patriotic journals, though not the most radical ones, were developing a willingness to go along with this script. Perhaps most significant in this respect was the sudden change in attitude of the influential *Chronique de Paris*. On November 24, the *Chronique* had called Besenval's claim that he had not given an order to the Bastille Governor but had instead been asked for one "a miserable equivocation," and on December 12, it had argued that natural law superseded any orders he may have received.[43] Yet, within a week of Favras' arrest, the *Chronique* was reporting that the depositions were "all to the advantage of M. de Besenval." And on January 14, the same day on which it stated that "the case against M. de Favras is very strong," it declared that: "[The People] must ultimately recognize that since all the legal aspects of the case are favorable to [Besenval], it cannot be more barbarous than the law. It can refuse him its friendship, its esteem, and his salary of 70,000 *livres*. But it cannot refuse him his liberty, and the pity owed the unfortunate."[44]

In the same vein, Gorsas, who never questioned the prosecution of Favras, was also unveiling a softer line towards Besenval. Though he had been, as we have seen, particularly harsh towards the July conspirators in the aftermath of Necker's amnesty defeat, Gorsas was sounding a very different note by early January: "Everyone has heard about the great *lèse-nation* crimes of which such and such great persons appeared already convicted. Little by little, the trace of these great crimes disappeared. Soon, it was only a question of ordinary sins, then peccadilloes, then almost nothing, and then nothing at all."[45]

In addition, several other moderately patriotic journals also showed themselves to be much more favorably disposed to Besenval than to Favras. Thus, the *Moniteur* reported that one of Besenval's attorneys, Bruges, had "distinguished himself by his zeal, his firmness, and his attachment to the interest of his client." Favras' attorney Thilorier, on the other hand, was said to have shown an "inconsiderate zeal" in an "unpardonable" speech filled with "antipatriotic outbursts."[46] Similarly, the *Journal général de la cour et de la ville* stated that there was no evidence against Besenval on the same day it reported that the case against Favras was "terribly convincing" and his defense "quite feeble."[47]

With a large portion of the moderately patriotic press now sympathetic to Besenval, there seems, by the beginning of the new year, to have been a significant shift in public opinion in his favor. On January 1, Gouverneur Morris told Lafayette that "the People begins to take his Part."[48] And while Morris, who regarded himself as a friend of the old general, may only have been whistling in the dark, Garran certainly knew what he was talking about when he later lamented that Besenval's defenders were "even able to persuade a part of the Public, not that the conspiracy did not exist, but that there was no legal proof of it." Garran blamed this public fastidiousness on "old prejudices only too justified in the past because of the barbarism of our criminal laws."[49] Thus, at least according to a disappointed Garran, pre-revolutionary liberal "prejudices" in favor of criminal defendants had been inappropriately carried over into the revolutionary arena and, as a result, a guilty conspirator had been allowed to escape.

But through its own insistence on adhering to legal forms and, in fact, through its very participation in the "judicial comedy" that was the Besenval trial, the Comité des Recherches was itself helping to perpetuate these legalistic "prejudices" and, at the same time, helping to legitimize the ultimate decision to release Besenval. Hence, in a report published just after Besenval's January 29 release, Garran carefully avoided any criticism of the Châtelet. Instead, his main concern was to rebut charges that he and the Comité had incited popular hatred against the defendant. Commenting on his own initial report on the July Conspiracy, Garran presented himself as a responsible participant in a fundamentally legitimate judicial system:

In place of the rantings one employs when one wants to incite the People, the author devoted himself to assembling all possible details. He continually cited documents, and no one has pointed out even a single error in these citations. He was content to use the words *it is said* and *we have been assured* while speaking about testimony by witnesses. He discussed questions of public law, and has produced a long and scholarly work. And that is not the kind of work that appeals to the People.[50]

Indeed, when one recalls that Brissot's journalistic allies at the *Chronique de Paris* and the *Courrier de Paris* had recently abandoned their earlier hostility to Besenval, it seems appropriate to wonder whether the members of the Comité might also have moved in this direction had they not already been assigned the prosecutorial role in the "judicial comedy" being produced by the Fayettist regime.

On the other hand, some observers of the Besenval trial took Garran's warnings about Enlightenment "prejudices" more seriously than he appears to have taken them himself. Audouin, for example, totally frustrated by the direction the proceedings were taking, seems to have been looking for a new form of jurisprudence in which those whose guilt is self-evident could be condemned without the bothersome necessity of finding witnesses to testify against them. For Audouin, the very presence of royal troops was sufficient to convict their commander of having conspired against the capital:

Witnesses have been heard, but it is just as if they had said nothing. We will produce witnesses who will testify eloquently against this M. de Besenval. Who are these witnesses? The cannon brought to Paris, the cannon-balls, the grills to heat these balls, the formidable military camp at the Champ-de-Mars. These are our witnesses, they are credible, and if they are admitted, M. de Besenval will not be able to emerge from his affair as white as snow.[51]

Along the same lines, Desmoulins imagined a kind of popular tribunal in which witnesses would sometimes not be required: "If witnesses must appear in front of a tribunal before a death sentence can be passed and a man subtracted from among the living, such witnesses are not necessary for the People to cut a man off from society and condemn him to exile. What need do we have for witnesses?"[52] In thereby reacting against a legalism which seemed to be blocking the rendering of true justice, what Audouin and Desmoulins were groping towards, of course, was the judicial system of the year II.

For Loustalot, however, rather than being too legalistic, the Besenval trial had not been legalistic enough. Instead of denying the need for witnesses, he insisted that the most important witness had not been called:

Do you want the truth? The King should have been summoned as a witness. Yes, the King! For *to testify truthfully* is a citizen's duty, and the King is only the first citizen ... Only the King knows and can say who deceived him, who made the treacherous reports upon which the decision to surround a starving city with troops was based ... The King owes the Nation a detailed deposition concerning everything that happened ... He must testify in this *lèse-nation* case. A witness who knows and does not name the author of a crime must himself necessarily be presumed to be guilty.[53]

In daring to suggest at the beginning of 1790 that the principle of equality before the law could be pushed to the point of implicating Louis XVI, Loustalot was implicitly invoking one of the primary tenets of the pre-revolutionary judicial reform movement: its call for uniform and non-arbitrary judicial proceedings. But before the Revolution, rather than being perceived as allowing the guilty to escape, arbitrary proceedings were usually regarded as a means by which innocent victims were unjustly condemned. In this way, the reform movement's twin ideals of "humanitarianism" and "rationality" could be seen as complementing each other in the pursuit of a system that would be more humane *and* more rational. However, from the moment one tends to see criminal defendants as guilty conspirators rather than as innocent victims, the convergence of these two ideals breaks down and policies which, from one angle, appear as compassionate and tolerant efforts to give the benefit of the doubt to potential victims begin to look, from another angle, like the granting of arbitrary privileges to dangerous suspects.

THE JUDICIAL COMPROMISE OF JANUARY–FEBRUARY 1790

In any event, let us now return to the status of the Besenval case at the beginning of the new year. With the National Assembly, the Hôtel-de-Ville, the Châtelet, and a large segment of the patriotic press and of public opinion itself all favorably disposed to lenient treatment, the only factor which might conceivably have left Besenval in danger was the reawakening of popular interest in his fate exhibited in the Châtelet protests of early January. But to counter this reawakened interest, the revolutionary authorities had one more card to play in what amounted to a long and elaborate campaign to protect the old general while, at the same time, attempting to create the appearance of being responsive to popular demands for justice and vengeance. In July, Besenval had been kept in detention, but also kept at a distance from the vigilante justice of the Parisian crowd. In October, he had finally been assigned judges, but hardly the kind of judges likely to condemn him. Now, in late January, Lafayette and Talon prepared to play the final card in this long campaign, and that card was named Favras.

With Favras and Besenval being tried concurrently, their fate was being discussed in the same breath by several observers. Thus, the English traveler Arthur Young noted on January 13 that: "The Current Discourse is that Favras ... must be hanged to satisfy the People; for as to Besenval ... they will not dare to execute him." And a visiting Breton nobleman wrote to a friend on January 20 that "M. de Favras, accused of wanting to bribe soldiers to make a counter-revolution, is at the Châtelet, and everyone says they are going to hang him within a week. [Besenval's] trial is still dragging on. If he was guilty, he would have been executed long ago." But the most prophetic comment linking the two defendants was made on January 23 by the anonymous but generally well-informed author of the *Correspondance secrète*: "It is believed M. de Favras' affair will save M. de Besenval. A victim must be provided to the People and M. de Favras can serve as one. Besides, the reality of his criminal projects is no longer in doubt."[54]

Now the most effective way in which Favras could have been used to "save" Besenval was for the execution of the former to have been timed in such a way as to create the maximum possible distraction from the release of the latter. But while Lafayette and Talon would almost certainly have preferred a Favras condemnation to precede or coincide with a Besenval release, the implementation of such a plan seems to have been precluded by the stubborn independence of a number of Châtelet judges. For here is how things actually unfolded:

On the night of January 29, Besenval was finally released through a unanimous decision of thirty-three judges.[55] In the mean time, Favras' case was scheduled for judgment on the next day, only thirty-seven days after his arrest. While this was already a deviation from the preferred course of events described above, the rapid winding-down of the Favras trial and the preparations made for the judging of the two cases on two consecutive days could hardly, it seems, have been coincidental. Perhaps realizing they did not yet have enough votes to condemn Favras and feeling themselves unable to delay Besenval's release any further, Lafayette and Talon may have thought that the next best thing was to try to forestall protest by attempting to create the impression that Favras was about to be condemned. As Loustalot wrote:

The Châtelet judges arranged to provide the People's hatred of the conspirators with an aliment at the very moment the news broke that Besenval had been released. Besenval was let out of the Châtelet during the night of the twenty-ninth. And that morning it was announced everywhere that they were assembling to judge Favras, who would certainly be condemned to lose his head.

Loustalot then turned to the January 30 proceedings in the Favras case:

The session lasted well into the night: At 11 p.m. the rumor was spread that judgment had been pronounced. And on the next day, the government-certified newsvendors spoke so mournfully about the *great judgment* condemning Favras to death that we could scarcely think about the release of Besenval that *they announced at the same time.*[56]

But Loustalot was not the only journalist to furnish an account which points towards the existence of an organized effort to manipulate information coming out of the Favras courtroom on January 30. For essentially the same story was related by the Fayettist loyalist Gorsas, who found himself forced to explain why he had mistakenly reported on January 31 that Favras had been condemned. According to Gorsas, a flood of false rumors began circulating immediately after Châtelet prosecutor Flandre de Brunville recommended that Favras be executed:

As soon as the recommendation of M. le Procureur du Roi was announced, and while the judges were deliberating, a hundred people ran out and spread the rumor at the Palais-Royal and in all the cafés of Paris that the Marquis de Favras had been definitively judged. Yesterday morning, all the streets and intersections of our capital reverberated with this cry: THE MARQUIS DE FAVRAS CONDEMNED TO BE HANGED.[57]

In reality, however, with the votes of four-fifths of the judges present needed to pass a death sentence, the Châtelet was not yet ready to accept Flandre's recommendation. With either forty or forty-one judges attending, reports on the number favoring death ranged from twenty-one to twenty-nine, and instead of a final ruling, the judgment finally released late that night called only for more witnesses to be heard. Since none of these witnesses added anything at all to the case against Favras, it seems clear that the call for new witnesses was actually little more than a device to give Talon time to round up the missing votes.[58]

Meanwhile, Paris was remarkably quiet in the days following Besenval's release, and in the absence of protests, several journals featured reports of the old general being joyfully received at the Tuileries.[59] Had the authorities managed to generate just enough belief in the impending execution of Favras to head off the development of protest at the critical moment when popular anger over the release of Marie-Antoinette's old friend would have been most raw? Had the collaboration of several major daily newspapers contributed to this "disinformation" campaign? (It seems hardly accidental that the most radical daily then publishing, Audouin's *Journal universel*, was, so far as I can determine, the only one that was somehow able to hold off its January 31 deadline long enough to include the news that the Favras trial was not yet over.)[60] Had the presence of a better organized National Guard, which had just demonstrated its effectiveness in containing the disturbances of early January, also helped discourage protest? Whatever the reasons, it is a curious fact that, although the fear that Besenval was going to be freed had triggered a great deal of popular unrest since July 1789, his actual release was effected amidst what appears to have been almost perfect calm.

As for Favras, while a parade of meaningless witnesses testified in the courtroom, the real action was taking place in the *couloirs*. By February 14, two Châtelet judges, who had complained a week earlier that the Assembly "had made it impossible for us to hang anyone," were assuring the deputy Thomas Lindet that there were now enough votes to condemn Favras.[61] And as if to underscore the extent to which judicial institutions were used for political purposes in this affair, the process by which this result was obtained may not have been unlike the kind of maneuvering that often occurs in parliamentary bodies. For the final condemnation of Favras on February 18 was decided, at least according to some of the sources, by a vote of twenty-eight to seven (that is, exactly four-fifths), with three judges disqualifying themselves. However, since twenty-eight judges may also have voted for death on January 30, it seems entirely possible that the same twenty-eight men voted for death on both ballots, with just enough judges staying away or disqualifying themselves on the second ballot to turn these twenty-eight votes into the necessary four-fifths majority.[62] Some support for this hypothesis is provided, moreover, by one historian who had access to the papers of a young Châtelet magistrate: "On February 18, the number of votes for death did not increase, but two judges didn't come and three disqualified themselves."[63]

Like a seemingly haphazard set of movements which is actually precisely choreographed, this dance of absences and self-disqualifications may therefore have come to a halt at exactly the required number. However, such dances are often choreographed by parliamentary tacticians to work around legislators who do not want to be recorded as voting for a measure but who are willing to acquiesce in its passage. With a significant number of Old Regime judges hesitant to condemn a man who wanted to restore the Old Regime, one can only imagine what kind of inducements or other forms of arm-twisting Talon may have employed to finally secure Favras' condemnation.

In any event, if we can believe Lindet, Favras' fate was already sealed by the time the judges assembled for the trial's final session on February 18. But if any further reinforcement of the decision to condemn the defendant was still needed, it was furnished by the appearance that morning of a huge crowd intent on making sure that Favras did not go free. As one journal put it: "It remembered Besenval's release ... and it shouted promises to invade and even burn down the prison if this criminal was not punished."[64]

With this crowd in mind, some royalist writers later charged that Lafayette "seized this moment to let it be known to the Châtelet that the People needed a victim, and that, if Favras were acquitted, he would not be the master of either the People or the Guard and could not answer for the safety of the judges." The Parisian General, of course, denied this and insisted he had told the judges that "your judgment will be carried out, whatever it is."[65] Moreover, with Favras' fate apparently already settled before the appearance of this crowd, there would have been no need for such a warning anyway. Yet, the general spirit of this reported warning seems entirely consistent with the message that Lafayette and Talon had probably been conveying to the Châtelet magistrates, albeit in a more discreet manner, since the beginning of the trial. For while it may not have had any practical effect on the decision announced that day, the crowd at the Châtelet on February 18 represented a not very discreet reminder of the potential political danger of being too firmly committed to judicial indulgence, even during the Revolution's first year.

When the announcement was finally made that Favras would be executed the next day, a packed courtroom burst into applause, prompting Gorsas to bemoan "these cannibals who savored in advance the detestable pleasure of seeing the scaffold erected." "Nature always suffers," he lectured, "when a death sentence is pronounced against a fellow human being, even if he is a criminal."[66] But Desmoulins had a very different view of this applause. Comparing the cheers in the Favras courtroom to the cries for mercy recently voiced for two condemned counterfeiters, he was able to detect an instinctive understanding of Beccarian proportionality:

The Marquis de Beccaria, with his trained sense of reason, was not any better equipped than the People, with its natural instinct, to recognize the barbarity and absurdity of laws that apply the supreme penalty to that which is not the worst of crimes. The People sensed there was a great difference between these two crimes that were punished with the same penalty, that of the Agasse brothers, of wanting to take some money away from citizens, and that of Favras, of wanting to take Liberty away from a Nation.[67]

In contrast to future Girondins like Gorsas and Brissot, who were always prepared to provide lessons to an unenlightened People, Desmoulins was more inclined, from the very beginning, to defend and even glorify the People's "natural instinct." However, reference to the language of Beccaria and the pre-revolutionary judicial reform movement would soon be discarded by Defenders of the People, and as if in anticipation of this development, Desmoulins' rhetoric quickly took a more ominous turn. For he followed his discussion of proportionality with an argument for the usefulness of vengeance and hatred:

There is nothing in all that [the joy exhibited at the condemnation and execution of Favras] which dishonors the People. It only proves its hatred against the nobility and the ancient inequalities, and how difficult it will be to take away its liberties... We would be lost if the People could contemplate the suffering of the Launays, the Berthiers, and the Favrases with indifference.[68]

Meanwhile, Favras was only informed about the verdict the next morning, at which time, in a widely reported remark, the Presiding Judge Quatremère told him that "your life is a sacrifice which you owe to public security and tranquillity." Though Quatremère would insist that he had only uttered a judicial "platitude," his phrase actually served, however unintentionally, as a particularly fitting commentary on the Favras condemnation.[69] For in addition to functioning as a commonplace warning to future conspirators, the dispatching of Favras was designed to help insure public tranquillity in two other ways: as a concession to popular demands for punishment, and as a protective seal for the massive cover-up that had been engineered in the case.

And appropriately enough, Quatremère's words took on a special poignancy that very afternoon, as he officiated at the dictation of Favras' last statement. As already noted, this statement contained the revelation that Favras' *grand seigneur* had spoken of the need for a "supreme general" and a new Paris National Guard Commander. But Favras also revealed that afternoon that the *grand seigneur* had named the two people who had been designated to fill these positions. Certainly realizing that a public disclosure of these names could only reopen the immense can of worms which the revolutionary authorities had been so diligently trying to keep closed since Favras' arrest, Quatremère made what can only be termed a pro forma request for them: pro forma because he made absolutely no effort to pursue the matter any further after Favras answered that "it would be useless to name them."[70]

But the condemned man was not yet ready to drop the matter. Just moments earlier, he had declared that "at the moment of losing my life ignominiously, I can, by my silence, lose it, in at least some fashion, gloriously." At the very end, however, the "fermeté" he had been displaying since his arrest melted away:

I will allow myself before closing to ask M. Quatremère ... if he thinks revealing the names he asked of me could change the sentence which I face... If so, I beg him to tell the Court which has judged me that one of its victims must bring before it a delicate matter that will make it hesitate to pronounce a death sentence... I pray, and, if necessary, I summon, if I may, M. Quatremère, this worthy jurist, to follow his conscience and respond to my interpellations.[71]

Here is a man clearly bargaining for his life, a man who could probably have been persuaded at that point to reveal far more than the two names ostensibly at issue. But such revelations would hardly have contributed anything to "public tranquillity." With the large crowd at the Place de Grève growing increasingly restive (Favras had been speaking for more than three hours), with Monsieur waiting impatiently for word that he could dine in peace, and with Talon, "spurred boots under his judicial robes ... ready to jump upon a racehorse" in case Favras said too much, the "worthy jurist" did not answer the condemned man's anguished "interpellations." According to Desmoulins, after repeating himself three times, Favras "paused to see if the judge would reverse ... his refusal to respond to his questions. The judge persisted, and Favras, no longer being able to doubt he had understood the true meaning of this silence, finally resigned himself to drinking the poison."[72]

Before that day, a condemned noble had enjoyed the legal "privilege" of being beheaded instead of being hanged. But on December 1, 1789, the Assembly had decreed that "all crimes of the same type will be punished by the same penalty, regardless of the culprit's rank and estate,"[73] and as a result, Favras was led to the gallows rather than to the chopping-block. (The guillotine was not introduced until 1792.) Whether "detestable pleasure" or useful hatred of the "ancient inequalities," there can be little doubt that many in the huge crowd of perhaps 50,000 gathered at the place of execution were particularly excited about the novel opportunity to view the hanging of a noble, or, as some in the crowd put it, to see Favras "dance on nothing." Just before the end, there were numerous shouts of "Saute, marquis, saute marquis," a *double entendre* which referred to the abrupt loss of status the condemned man was about to suffer as well as to the "jump" produced by the actual hanging. Then, when it was all over, there were cries of "Bis, bis." While those who had called for an encore would have to wait two and a half years, they would eventually be rewarded with many somewhat similar performances.[74]

It may, at first glance, seem paradoxical to present the most important political execution of the period during which Lafayette dominated French political life as a key example of Fayettist compromise and conciliation. Nevertheless, as a measure which sought to provide "something for everyone," the Favras execution can be seen as a politically astute effort to hold together a patchwork and amorphous political coalition. On the one hand, the execution was obviously designed to help secure the Fayettist regime's left flank by furnishing what Loustalot had called an "aliment" for the People.[75] With the regime unable or unwilling to do very much about satisfying popular needs for true nourishment, Favras' execution was an attempt to respond to an important non-economic popular demand. Or, to put it another way, if the regime could not or would not provide bread, it could at least deliver circuses. On the other hand, the main thrust of Fayettist policy in the Favras affair was clearly directed towards securing the regime's right flank, and the execution served this policy in two important ways: (a) it protected the cover-up which had been devised to accommodate and forgive Favras' powerful accomplices, and (b) it provided political cover for the decision to exonerate Besenval, a decision which signalled the regime's willingness to accommodate and forgive those who had opposed its coming to power. Finally, for loyal adherents of the regime who liked to think of themselves as "sensitive souls," the execution provided assurance that dangerous enemies would be treated fairly but firmly. The sense of reluctant satisfaction that the execution brought to many supporters who had been willing to forgive Besenval was perhaps best expressed by the *Chronique de Paris*:

The men of the party for which M. de Favras has perished on the scaffold want to make his judgment seem unjust. However, one must reflect upon the fact that this judgment was rendered by honest and enlightened judges, and that the votes of four-fifths of them were required for him to lose his life... Moreover, the proof of his crime can even be found in his published defense... But now we need to see this condemned criminal as an unfortunate soul who has given a great example to society through his suffering, and whom sensitive men should pity, though the Law is obliged to strike him down.[76]

Although generally absent from contemporary commentary, there is one further sense in which the execution of Favras illuminates and underscores the restrained and conciliatory nature of Fayettist policies, and here again we must return to the complex relationship between Favras and Besenval. In his final statement before the Châtelet, Besenval's attorney de Sèze argued that the events for which his client was being held accountable had occurred when "the Revolution had not yet taken place" and that Besenval had therefore acted lawfully as an agent of a regime which was still in place. In contrast, de Sèze continued, those who tried to undo the "magnificent harmony" that now existed "would be worthy of all the vengeance of the laws."[77] By suggesting, in effect, that there was a difference between conspiring to maintain a regime in power and conspiring to overthrow a new one, de Sèze had pointed to an important distinction between the Besenval case and the Favras case.

As Michael Walzer has written, a revolution always brings with it a need for "the leaders of the new regime to settle with the leaders of the old."[78] But does "settlement" necessarily mean punishment? Though it is certainly now standard operating procedure for incoming revolutionary regimes to define the agents and activities of outgoing regimes as criminal, there are a number of overlapping and interconnected reasons why it is not surprising that the "settlement" attempted during the first phase of the French Revolution was one that emphasized forgiveness and reconciliation: (1) the general tendency towards punitive mildness in late eighteenth-century judicial thought and practice, especially with respect to political offenses; (2) the hybrid nature of the incoming regime, as best illustrated by the delegation of responsibility for administering the "settlement" to an Old Regime court like the Châtelet; (3) the fact that, in comparison to the modern state of "permanent revolution" in which political officials are well aware that they are always subject to reversal and subsequent criminal prosecution, there was a certain element of unexpectedness associated with the coming of the French Revolution, an unexpectedness which may have engendered a feeling that prosecution of people like Besenval was, in a real sense, simply "not fair"; and (4) the fact that, on the level of individual moral responsibility, it was difficult to charge people like Besenval and Broglie with blatantly horrendous actions analogous, let us say, to those of any number of bloodsoaked twentieth-century regimes.

Yet, as admirable and, dare it be said, as civilized as the idea of a non-punitive settling of accounts may appear to battered late twentieth-century sensibilities, the failure to impose a more punitive settlement on the agents of the regime it replaced may well have contributed to the ultimate failure of the Fayettist regime to generate a sufficiently powerful belief that it was legitimate, i.e., morally entitled to rule. For the crafting of a coherent and comprehensive definition of political wrongdoing may be seen as a key factor in the development of a regime's belief in its own rectitude and in its ability to transmit that belief to its citizenry. And while it is difficult enough to establish legitimacy in a revolutionary situation, the incoherence reflected in the prosecution of Besenval by one Fayettist institution (the Comité des Recherches) followed by his exoneration by another Fayettist institution (the Châtelet) could hardly have helped. Though the compromise and balance of Fayettist judicial policies may, in the short run, have secured a fair amount of acceptance and support for the regime, legitimacy is a much more profound and elusive phenomenon than mere acceptance.

But if the new regime's non-punitive settling of accounts with its predecessor may ultimately have adversely affected perceptions regarding its right to rule, it was by no means suicidal and it was not about to extend its non-punitive policies to those who, like Favras, would plot its overthrow. This, at least, seems to be the underlying message of the Besenval–Favras judicial transaction of January–February 1790, a message of reconciliation and forgiveness combined with a warning that this message only applied to past and not to present and future behavior. Certainly it was easier to condemn a "poor devil" like Favras than a high-ranking courtier like Besenval. And certainly too the relative absence of direct evidence against Besenval compared favorably with the detailed evidence against Favras provided by Moral, Tourcaty, and Marquié. But the different fates of these two defendants may ultimately have depended less on who they were or on what they did than on when they did it.

As symbolized by Louis XVI's celebrated visit to the National Assembly on February 4,[79] the beginning of 1790 was precisely the period in which Lafayette's attempt to weave a workable compromise between the Revolution and the Old Regime appeared most promising. And with the Parisian General having demonstrated his control of the political–military situation through his ability to contain and neutralize the aristocratic plotters of December and the various popular disturbances of January, the Besenval–Favras judicial transaction can be seen as an effort by the new regime to close the books on this most recent series of challenges to its authority. Moreover, the willingness of some of the hitherto most vehement proponents of punishment for the July conspirators to accept this transaction is a particularly telling indicator of the seemingly favorable prospects for Fayettist success at this time. Thus, Desmoulins, who had been ready to dispense with the need for witnesses in the Besenval case, had a surprisingly mild reaction to the news that the old general had been released. "I can't entirely blame them," he said of the Châtelet magistrates, "for having absolved as judges, he whom, as men, they all condemned." At the same time, Camille served notice that he would not be so complacent if Favras was also exonerated, for that would signify "there is no longer any risk of being hanged, unless one is a friend of the Revolution and an honest man." But when the Châtelet upheld its end of the implicit bargain, Desmoulins appeared satisfied. "It can be presumed," he wrote after Favras' execution, "that his punishment will satisfy the Nation's need for a great example. It can be said that all the aristocrats have been hanged through him."[80]

Similarly, Audouin, another radical journalist who had resisted the general shift of opinion in Besenval's favor, also refrained from criticizing the decision to release him. Like Desmoulins, he replaced his disdain for legal forms with praise for the Châtelet's professionalism: "[Favras] was condemned by thirty-eight judges, but it is said these judges were afraid of the People. This is a frivolous pretext. Were they afraid of the People when they absolved M. de Besenval, whose head the People was also demanding?" And like Desmoulins, Audouin also expressed confidence that Favras' execution would send the proper message to future conspirators: "Tremble, enemies of the Nation, there is a system of justice that knows how to punish you." Moreover, Audouin appeared particularly willing to accept the policy of forgiveness and conciliation inherent in the Besenval–Favras transaction. One of the leading July fugitives, the Prince de Conti, had supposedly been considering a return to France, and Audouin approvingly reported a rumor that Lafayette had let Conti know such a return was perfectly safe. Lafayette, added Audouin, "knows the Parisians and he knows how much they are being slandered when they are insolently called frenzied tigers or cannibals thirsting for blood."[81]

With Marat in flight, the only major radical journalist unwilling to accept the conciliatory atmosphere of early 1790 was Loustalot. He alone attacked both the Châtelet and the Comité des Recherches for conducting a "simulated procedure" against Besenval; and he alone suggested, however hesitantly, that the Châtelet had been derelict in tracking down Favras' accomplices. And in early March, he came close to denouncing Lafayette himself: "Who is it that negotiates between the Court and the Châtelet to have the weak punished though they are innocent ... and to have the powerful exonerated though they are guilty? . . . Citizens, if you do not see who I mean, there is no point in naming him."[82]

But Loustalot's criticism of the political justice of 1789–90 did not find an echo among other influential journalists during this period. Moreover, though Loustalot followed his veiled attack on Lafayette by reporting the rumor that he too would soon become a victim of "the claws of the Châtelet,"[83] the apparent absence of any attempt to silence him may itself be an indication of a new-found sense of confidence on the part of the revolutionary authorities. Yet, despite the seemingly strengthened position of the Fayettist regime, rumors and fears of aristocratic plotting continued. And despite the hope that Favras' "example" would be sufficient "to contain the evil-doers,"[84] actual plotting continued also. Just days after the Favras execution, a pamphlet was circulated in Paris announcing the *Nouvelle trahison de Monsieur le Baron de Besenval.* "Following the example of the Marquis de Favras," it declared, "this enemy of the public interest will finally pay with his head for the hideous projects he has contrived against public tranquillity."[85] And though the information contained in this pamphlet was completely fanciful and Besenval would live quietly in Paris until his death in July 1791,[86] there were, at that very moment, other "enemies of the public interest" who were not hesitating to contrive other "hideous projects." As we shall see in the chapters which follow, the Fayettist regime, which had been so successful in meeting the threat posed by the Favras plot and in garnering a wide range of support for its methods of dealing with that threat, would be much less successful in dealing with the challenges posed by the next round of counter-revolutionary plotting.

8

The Maillebois conspiracy

On February 21, 1790, two days after Favras' execution, an aide-de-camp of the Comte de Maillebois named Bertrand de Bonne-Savardin left for Turin, where the Comte d'Artois presided over a kind of "High Council of the Emigration." According to one Comité des Recherches informer, Bonne, who would soon be described as a possible "second Favras," was sent to Turin to present a plan which was designed to allow Artois to return to France "in a manner suitable to his dignity." Or as another Comité source put it, Bonne "offered a plan for counter-revolution in France to the Comte d'Artois, a plan devised by the Comte de Maillebois, who would also direct its execution." Maillebois' plan supposedly called for an invasion of France by troops from Sardinia, Naples, Spain, and several German states to be combined with various internal uprisings and the escape of the royal family from Paris.[1]

But as appealing as a project of that nature might have been to Artois, the Turin Council was hardly in a position to be very receptive to Maillebois' plan. For months prior to Bonne's arrival, the *émigré* Princes had been sounding out various European monarchs on the possibility of launching a military assault on the revolutionary regime and the responses had been uniformly negative.[2] In addition, though a defiant Prince de Condé was insisting that "we must save them [the royal family] in spite of themselves," the counter-revolutionary efforts of the Princes were severely inhibited during this period by Louis XVI's lack of co-operation. As Artois' closest friend Vaudreuil put it: "No matter what you fellows say, you can't do anything. To serve them in spite of themselves is impossible." Moreover, Vaudreuil also recognized that there was too much general support for the new regime at that moment to count on the internal rebellions called for in the Maillebois plan: "Our best people in Paris fear any premature attempts... The intoxication still endures, and we will need to wait until the situation ripens."[3]

In addition, even if his plan had been seen as a practical option, it is unlikely that Maillebois himself would have been chosen to help execute it. Although Yves-Marie Desmarets, Comte de Maillebois (1715–91) was certainly considered a man of great military talent and although he came from one of the most powerful and distinguished families in France, his career had been under a cloud since 1758, when he became embroiled in a bitter controversy regarding French strategy in the Seven Years War. Having had the effrontery to publicly accuse the Maréchal d'Estrées of "irresolution," Maillebois was convicted of slander by a military court, retired from active duty, and imprisoned for several years in the citadel of Doullens.[4] And while the fact that Vergennes had sent him to take command of the Dutch army in 1784 indicates that he had been at least partially rehabilitated, he still had many enemies among high-ranking French officers, including Broglie, who had been a protégé of d'Estrées.[5]

With so many obstacles facing him, it is hardly surprising that Bonne was given what amounted to little more than a polite brush-off at Turin. According to one report, the Princes told him that "circumstances were not yet favorable enough" and that "for the present all means should be employed in Paris to bring M. de Maillebois into the King's Council so he could little by little reduce His Majesty's confidence in M. de Lafayette and M. de Liancourt."[6] However, even as his aide prepared to leave Turin, any remaining possibility that Maillebois would ever play a role in carrying out his plan had been shattered by his sudden flight from France. For by the time that Bonne left Italy on March 23, the Maillebois conspiracy, if that term can be used for such an embryonic scheme, was already turning into the Maillebois affair.

While Bonne was making his ineffectual rounds in Turin, Maillebois' secretary, Thomas-Jean Grandmaison, was thinking about denouncing his employer. Grandmaison had been asked to transcribe a copy of Maillebois' plan and had been, he later claimed, "horrified" by the ideas contained in it. Moreover, this horror was intensified when he realized that he too could be implicated in the plot, since, in an amateurish attempt to evade surveillance, Bonne

was addressing letters from abroad to "mon cher Grandmaison."
On March 20, Grandmaison left the provincial château which Maillebois was visiting and headed for Paris.[7]

Alarmed by Grandmaison's disappearance, Maillebois found a
hidden summary of his plan in a satchel that belonged to the secretary. Declaring that Grandmaison "has done a terrible thing to
me," Maillebois hastily gathered his belongings and fled to Holland.[8] Two days later, Grandmaison denounced him to the Paris
Comité des Recherches. Almost simultaneously, the Comité received reports from two anonymous French patriots in Turin,
reports which essentially corroborated Grandmaison's accusation.[9]
On March 28, the first fragmentary accounts concerning the Maillebois conspiracy appeared in the Parisian press, and by the time
Bonne arrived back in Paris on April 1, the police were already
looking for him and the new plot was one of the leading topics of
conversation in town.[10] Indeed, if we are to believe Louis Gottschalk
and Margaret Maddox, one would think that the atmosphere surrounding the emergence of the Maillebois affair paralleled the feverish atmosphere associated with the late December surfacing of
the Favras affair:

The Comte de Maillebois was denounced as a counter-revolutionary by one
of his servants and took flight on March 22. Reports about the *émigrés* in
Turin soon lent plausibility to the fear that he was fomenting an uprising in
southern France . . . The date anticipated by most Parisians for the uprising
was Easter Sunday, which would fall on April 4. In the closing days of
March, Paris journals were filled with frightening accounts of the plans of
the Turin *émigrés* under Maillebois' leadership . . . In the uneasy atmosphere created by the alleged Maillebois conspiracy any combination of
circumstances might have triggered an outbreak.[11]

However, though reports about the new plot certainly created
something of a stir in the capital, neither the sources cited by
Gottschalk and Maddox nor any other sources I have seen provide
any evidence of belief in imminent counter-revolution, or, for that
matter, even the presence of rumors about imminent counter-revolution. On the contrary, the initial reports on the Maillebois plot
appearing in the Parisian press during this period made it perfectly
clear that the plot was only in its formative stages. Thus, the "left
Fayettist" *Chronique de Paris*, which had probably been given its
information by the Comité des Recherches, was the first major
newspaper to break the Maillebois story. But the *Chronique*'s March

28 "scoop," reprinted by several other papers the next day, only reported that Maillebois "has taken steps to have his plan *delivered* to M. le Comte d'Artois." And three days later, the *Chronique* reported that Artois "has refused to adopt this plan."[12]

Of course, many people reading or only hearing about such reports might not have paid much attention to these reassuring details. Moreover, it is certainly possible that some news-sheets distributed in the Paris area during the last week of March did proclaim the imminent execution of the Maillebois plan. Still, it seems clear that the level of tension and fear in the capital was not nearly as high in late March and early April as it had been in the period immediately following the arrest of Favras. Thus, registering its satisfaction with the relative absence of popular response to news about the new plot, the by now resoundingly right-wing *Journal général de la cour et de la ville* declared on April 3 that "it is becoming harder to rouse the People each day ... It is tired of hearing about plots, conspiracies, counter-revolutionary projects, etc. It is even beginning to laugh at this word 'aristocrat' that it could not pronounce without rage only three or four months ago."[13]

Now the difference in mood between late March–early April and late December–early January is of great significance for this study because it was, I believe, this difference which largely determined the differing outcomes of the Maillebois and Favras affairs. At first glance, one might be inclined to think that the different outcome in the Maillebois affair was produced by a combination of Maillebois' successful escape from France and Bonne's avoidance of arrest until the end of April. In other words, one might argue that a quick arrest of Maillebois and/or Bonne would have allowed some of the emotion which crystallized around Favras to crystallize around one or both of these men, and that if this had occurred, events in the Maillebois affair would probably have more closely followed those of the Favras affair. However, it could just as easily be argued that if the atmosphere of late March had been as charged with emotion as that of late December, the failure to arrest Maillebois and Bonne would have led to just as much, if not more, commotion than their hypothetical capture. In any case, the crucial differentiating factor about the Favras arrest is that it intensified emotions *already* charged by a wave of rumors regarding an impending Christmas Day aristocratic uprising. On the other hand, it seems to have been the surfacing of the Maillebois story itself that largely triggered the relatively limited flurry of counter-revolutionary rumors which developed in late March and early April.

Emerging into public consciousness approximately ten weeks after the October Insurrection (which itself had taken place approximately ten weeks after the July Revolution), the Favras affair surfaced at a moment when the rhythm of events seemed to portend another major revolutionary explosion. In contrast, the Maillebois affair came into public view at a moment when things genuinely appeared to be "settling down" and at a point when the Fayettist regime was in a particularly strong position. Though the breaking of the Maillebois story itself generated a certain increase in tension, the already superheated atmosphere of the Favras affair was decidedly absent.

This difference in revolutionary "barometric pressure" at the beginning of these two affairs was undoubtedly a major cause of the radical difference in pace that marked their unfolding. In the highly charged atmosphere of the earlier affair, we saw Favras denounced by the Comité des Recherches within forty-eight hours of his arrest, put on trial three days after that, and executed seven weeks later. On the other hand, the Maillebois affair unfolded, as we will see, at a much more leisurely pace, with the Comité only issuing an official denunciation on July 9; that is to say, three and a half months after Maillebois' flight and two and a half months after Bonne's arrest. Moreover, the judicial phase of the affair dragged on for so long that the National Assembly's September 1791 declaration of a general amnesty for all crimes relating to the Revolution took effect before the case was ever judged.

Closely linked to these differences in atmosphere and pace was another important variable, the respective presence or absence of the revolutionary crowd. In contrast to the intense public interest and massive popular demonstrations that marked the Favras case, the proceedings in the Maillebois affair attracted, as we will see, remarkably little public attention, a lack of attention that should be seen as largely responsible for another characteristic which differentiates this case from the Favras case. While the judicial proceedings in the Favras affair (and, for that matter, the Besenval affair) revolved around and, to a certain degree, attempted to come to grips with such basic moral issues as justice, punishment, and revenge, these issues, which were capable of mobilizing popular energy throughout the Revolution, faded into the background during the unfolding of the Maillebois affair. For rather than serving as a vehicle for the ritualistic working-out of the emotions attached to these issues, the case against the Maillebois plotters took on an almost exclusively "political" complexion, essentially resolving itself into an effort to bring down a governmental ministry and to discredit the supporters of that ministry. Or, to be more precise, the Maillebois case soon became little more than a device to get rid of the minister who, in early 1790, was seen as the most formidable bastion of what remained of royal authority, the Comte de Saint-Priest.[14]

THE CAMPAIGN AGAINST SAINT-PRIEST

Although direct evidence of Saint-Priest's connection to the Maillebois plotters would only become available after Bonne's late April arrest, a wave of suspicion enveloped the Interior Minister and his colleagues from the moment news about the new plot first became public. "All the journals are talking about the Maillebois conspiracy," wrote Tournon, "yet everyone knows nothing is ever done in France without the ministers knowing about it and even consenting to it." Meanwhile, Desmoulins was suggesting that the new counter-revolutionary scheme might be connected to some suspicious gatherings of the newly baptized "Austrian committee" that were taking place in the Queen's apartments at the Tuileries. According to Camille, Saint-Priest was "the soul of the Austrian party" and was "hoping that this party will provide him a means to recover his power and even overturn the Constitution." And a similar theme was being sounded at this time by Loustalot who declared that the ministers "are working with all their energy for a counter-revolution, for it has reached the point where they must ruin the patriots to avoid being ruined themselves."[15]

But the concerted attack on the ministers which began to emerge in late March and early April was not confined to the radical press. "The discovery of the Maillebois conspiracy has produced uneasiness in the Austrian committee of the Tuileries," noted the "left Fayettist" *Chronique de Paris*, which, in an especially significant twist, also reported that "the Austrian cabal and M. de Saint-Priest are using all kinds of flattery to get M. de Lafayette on their side ... If he is not careful, M. de Lafayette will find himself greatly embarrassed and will lose much of the confidence we have in him."[16] In thereby warning Lafayette that its support was not unconditional, the

Chronique was displaying a new-found independence that will become increasingly evident as we follow developments in this affair. For the period during which the Maillebois affair unfolded was precisely the period during which Brissot and his friends began the long process of detaching themselves from the Fayettist coalition.

In the mean time, other "left Fayettist" journalists were also joining the campaign against the ministers. According to Carra, "the adored ministers, the patriot ministers, the citizen ministers could easily and very sweetly restore the yoke and the gag." And in an interesting foreshadowing of Brissot's December 1791 call for war as a means of unmasking traitors, Carra greeted the news of the Maillebois plot by predicting that a foreign invasion would "tear the masks off certain people." (Was he already thinking of Lafayette?) As for Brissot himself, his contribution to the new campaign took the form of another civics lesson. Responding to Saint-Priest's contention that the growing mistrust of the ministers was politically unhealthy, Brissot stated that "to advise free men to give up the spirit of distrust is to give them bad advice. Ministers should always be distrusted, even in a state which has enjoyed liberty for centuries, let alone one in which it has existed for only six months."[17]

While Brissot reflected on the conditions necessary for the preservation of French liberty, a fugitive Bonne-Savardin was still managing to enjoy his own liberty. Though agents of Lafayette and both Comités des Recherches were looking for him, Bonne was able to do a good deal of travelling in April, and the ease with which he moved around can itself be taken as indicative of the relative inefficiency of early revolutionary surveillance. Leaving Paris on the third, he went straight to Maillebois' refuge in Holland and then turned around and came back to the French capital on April 24. Three days later, he took off again, this time in the direction of Turin. However, on April 30, he was finally arrested at the Savoyard border, and Lafayette and Bailly quickly arranged for his transfer to Paris. Though Bonne expressed fears for his personal safety, there is no evidence that his arrival in the capital aroused any significant degree of popular emotion.[18]

It was, as already indicated, Bonne's arrest which directly linked Saint-Priest to the Maillebois plotters. But in order to explain this connection, we must briefly return to the summer of 1789, a period during which Bonne, who had been a close aide of Maillebois for years, was temporarily attached to the staff of his patron's bitter enemy, the War Minister Broglie. As a man who had held an important military post during the July crisis, Bonne was questioned on December 5 by the Paris Comité des Recherches, and although he soon boasted that he had easily convinced the Comité that he didn't know anything, his interrogators apparently decided to keep an eye on him. For, in some unexplained manner, the Comité was able to get its hands on Bonne's written account of a meeting held just before his interrogation, a meeting with an individual designated as "Farcy."[19]

In Bonne's account, Farcy emerges as the organizer and director of certain unspecified but clearly compromising "projects." "There must be an end to all this," Farcy is quoted as saying, "and if this hope did not sustain us, we might as well put the key under the door and wait for them to come and slit out throats." "But," asked Bonne, "aren't you afraid that this militia [the Paris National Guard] will impede you, that it will keep its eyes on you and render your projects useless?" And, he continued, "how will you get rid of Betville [Lafayette]?" "We will find the means," answered Farcy, and with a touch of saltiness that reminds us of the French nobility's general familiarity with military life, he added that "once our asses are in the saddle, we'll see what happens then." "But you will need a general," said Bonne, who then proceeded, as he would do with Artois in Turin three months later, to try to persuade Farcy that Maillebois was the man for the job. "You preach to a convert," answered Farcy; "I know he's our man, but it's not my decision to make." Farcy then asked Bonne to report back to him after seeing the Comité des Recherches, and Bonne ended his account by noting that he had indeed gone back to see Farcy the next morning.[20]

Now one obvious question raised by this conversation is the identity of Farcy's superior. If Farcy did not have the authority to decide whether to employ Maillebois, who did? Was it Artois? Or did Maillebois only offer his services to Artois in March after having first been rebuffed by Farcy's superior? If so, could Farcy's superior have been Monsieur, who, as we have seen, was busily involved in early December with his own project for "getting rid of" Lafayette? These are questions to which we will return shortly. But first let us identify Farcy, a problem that was effectively resolved when the Comité des Recherches examined a *livre de raison* found in Bonne's possession at the time of his arrest. For while, as one contemporary commentary noted, "it is hardly the practice of conspirators to keep a register of their activities," Bonne was hardly the most prudent of conspirators, and his aptly misnamed *livre de raison* contained a detailed accounting of all his movements, visits, and expenditures. And when the members of the Comité opened this book and looked at the entries for early December 1789, they were undoubtedly, as Farcy himself would later put it, "charmed" to discover that the only person whom Bonne was listed as having seen on both December 5 and 6 was the Comte de Saint-Priest![21]

As he would later acknowledge in his *Mémoires*, Saint-Priest was indeed Farcy.[22] But the matter was not settled so easily during the actual unfolding of the Maillebois affair, at which time the minister naturally denied having any idea who Farcy was. "I cannot know what documents have been used to link this name to mine," he first declared, "but I certify them in advance as false and illusory."[23] Then, after Bonne's account of the Farcy conversation was published by the Comité, Saint-Priest and his lawyers claimed that Bonne must have seen someone else on December 5 and 6 without having noted it. In fact, they contended, the relations between Bonne and Farcy seemed to have been of just such a nature as to make it extremely unlikely that Farcy's real name would be listed in Bonne's journal.[24]

Anticipating these arguments, the Comité tried to get Bonne to identify Farcy as Saint-Priest, and it almost succeeded. Though Bonne doggedly denied he had ever engaged in any compromising activities,[25] he seems to have been susceptible to some of the tricks often used by enterprising interrogators. Thus, before making any mention of Farcy, the Comité asked Bonne about his early December movements, obviously hoping he would not connect this question to his written account of his meeting with Farcy:

He was asked if on the morning of the day he came to the Comité des Recherches on our invitation, he went to see *one person* whom he told about our invitation, and if he returned the next day to tell this person what had happened there; he was also asked to identify this person. He responded YES, and said this person was the Comte de SAINT-PRIEST.[26]

With this cat already out of the bag, Bonne was confronted with his account of the Farcy conversation. But by then he seems to have realized what the Comité was up to and he retreated into denial, claiming he didn't remember who Farcy was. However, the Comité pointed out that he had just admitted that Saint-Priest was the "one person" with whom he had discussed his Comité visit on both December 5 and 6, while his written account indicated he had discussed this visit with Farcy on both those days. At this point, Bonne could only reply that "it appears it was he [Saint-Priest] whom I meant to indicate ... but I cannot risk affirming something about which I am not certain."[27]

Since the Châtelet never gave any serious consideration to the Comité's official indictment of the Interior Minister, the legal validity or persuasiveness of the Comité's argument that Saint-Priest was Farcy was never formally addressed. However, the Comité was actually more interested in obtaining a verdict from the tribunal of public opinion than in securing a judicial verdict against the minister. That is to say, it was not the conviction and punishment of Saint-Priest that the Comité was seeking so much as his political demise. And for that purpose, the Farcy revelations were absolutely capital. For whatever ingredients of proof might be considered necessary for conviction in a court of law, the requirements for generating loss of confidence in a public official are clearly much less stringent. And even if one argues that the Comité had not quite "proven" that Saint-Priest was Farcy, it had certainly created a strong presumption against him. From the moment the Comité published the text of the Farcy conversation, it became extremely difficult for even the most moderate and conciliatory patriot to feel comfortable about the possibility that this Farcy was in charge of the sensitive Interior Ministry. Even putting aside the likelihood that Farcy was an active conspirator against the new regime, it would clearly have been disastrous, in patriot eyes, to have allowed a man with such blatantly anti-revolutionary opinions to continue in office. As Garran observed: "The ministers exercise so much power that their personal sentiments greatly advance or retard the progress of the Constitution. And when they are the enemies of this progress, they multiply the obstacles that can be placed in its path."[28]

For an already embattled Saint-Priest, the publication of the Farcy conversation was only the latest in a series of problems. Although he had been dismissed along with Necker on July 11, 1789 and subsequently welcomed back as one of the "patriot ministers,"[29] Saint-Priest quickly became viewed as a much firmer supporter of royal authority than Necker and thereby found himself an object of great mistrust almost immediately. Having aroused the suspicions of the Saint-Séverin District in late July in an incident discussed in chapter 2 above, the Interior Minister's next scrape with revolutionary militants came when he was denounced at the Saint-Philippe du Roule District in September. Although the precise nature of this denunciation remains unknown (Saint-Priest claimed he was accused of having "suspect opinions"), it may well have had something to do with the Favras conspiracy. Morel, it will be recalled, had informed Lafayette on September 30 that Saint-Priest was "in on" this plot, and someone in the Saint-Philippe du Roule District could have had similar information.[30]

But regardless of whether or not the Saint-Philippe du Roule accusation had anything to do with Favras, the entire subject of Saint-Priest's connection to the Favras affair is one that has been generally overlooked by historians. In particular, the possibility that the December 5 Bonne–Farcy meeting could have been linked in some way to the Favras plot has apparently never even been considered. Yet, it makes more sense to think about this meeting in the context of the Favras case than it does to connect it to the plan Bonne presented to Artois in Turin in March. Although the Comité des Recherches made its accusations against Farcy-Saint-Priest within the framework of Garran's first report on the Maillebois plot and although many contemporary observers accepted this implied connection and routinely identified the Interior Minister as the "director-general" of this plot,[31] neither the Comité nor anyone else ever produced any evidence linking Saint-Priest to the Maillebois–Turin plan. Nor, for that matter, did the Comité ever directly assert the existence of such a connection. In fact, its official denunciation in the Maillebois affair scrupulously separated the accusations made against Saint-Priest from those relating to the Turin plan. Thus, the Comité declared that "[Maillebois and Bonne] offered their plan and their services to M. d'Artois and the Court at Turin," and then went on to charge that "M. Bonne-Savardin *also* offered M. Desmarets-Maillebois' treacherous services to a person designated by the name of Farcy, whom the documents proclaim to be M. Guignard Saint-Priest."[32] While the Comité des Recherches, which had played an important role in the Favras cover-up, certainly had its own reasons for wanting to imply that Saint-Priest was an agent of the *émigré* Princes, it seems more likely that he was really an agent of Monsieur, for whom he would become a kind of "Prime Minister" during the late 1790s.[33] As for Maillebois and Bonne, these two gentlemen seem to have been prepared to join any counter-revolutionary network that would have had them.

At any rate, whatever the exact nature of Saint-Priest's secret activities, an indiscreet remark made during the October Days created additional public disapproval. On October 10, Mirabeau, whose obsessive desire to become a minister made him a natural enemy of every standing ministry, denounced Saint-Priest for having told a group of Parisian market-women: "When you had one king, you had bread. Today you have 1,200 of them [i.e., 1,200 Assembly deputies]. Go ask them for bread."[34] Though Mirabeau's denunciation had no official ramifications, this well-publicized incident could only have added to the growing mistrust of the Interior Minister. Moreover, if Saint-Priest's October 5 attempt to get the King to flee to Rambouillet had been known, we can be quite sure that the controversy surrounding him in the immediate post-October Days period would have been, to put it mildly, even more intense.

After the market-women episode, Saint-Priest managed to avoid further public suspicion for the next five months as the post-October Days conservative reaction and the conciliatory mood of early 1790 created a kind of "grace period" for him. However, beginning in late March and early April, the anti-Saint-Priest drums began to beat again, this time, as we have seen, in the form of a campaign against the machinations of the "Austrian committee." In the next chapter, we will explore the question of why this campaign happened to materialize at this particular time, but for now let us note that Saint-Priest's enemies soon found a new grievance against the minister who was seen as "the most odious to enlightened patriots."[35]

On April 30, the same day Bonne was arrested, an insurrection broke out at Marseilles which resulted in the local National Guard taking control of that city's military fortresses from the royal army.[36] When Saint-Priest emerged as the leading spokesman of those who were trying to reassert royal authority, he became the target of a new round of patriotic attacks and denunciations. And when Lafayette mounted the tribune at the National Assembly to support the minister's unsuccessful demand that the deputies order the removal of the insurrectionary Guardsmen from the Marseilles forts, even Brissot had to wince. Hence, in an early expression of disenchantment with Fayettist policies, Brissot first registered "surprise" at the strong backing that Saint-Priest received from "the wise and popular" LaRochefoucauld. Not yet ready to acknowledge that

LaRochefoucauld was expressing what amounted to official Fayettist policy, Brissot then noted that LaRochefoucauld's speech had "won over M. de Lafayette," as if the Parisian General had only been carried away by his friend's eloquence.[37]

For Saint-Priest, however, the patriotic reaction to his role in the Marseilles episode was part of an already well-established pattern and we can now understand why his official denunciation by the Comité des Recherches on July 9, 1790 should be seen as a response to a series of grievances that had been accumulating for almost a year. At the same time, this denunciation of a minister who was being publicly supported by Lafayette and whom the Parisian General clearly had no intention of pursuing judicially constituted a significant departure from the Comité's customary willingness to make at least some effort to co-operate with Fayettist *ménagements*. In view of the stress which this study has placed on popular opposition to judicial indulgence, the fact that the Comité's movement away from the Fayettist mainstream occurred in the context of an affair that was marked by a relative absence of popular emotion and pressure may seem paradoxical. Yet, the Comité's shift away from *ménagement* in its handling of the Maillebois affair should not necessarily be equated with a new emphasis on judicial severity and punishment. In a delicate balancing act, the Comité appears to have been interested in mobilizing only enough public indignation to nudge Saint-Priest out of office and to advance some other "left Fayettist" objectives that were emerging in conjunction with the campaign against the ministers. But in order to fully appreciate the nature of the "left Fayettist" political agenda during the crucial spring and summer of 1790, it will be necessary to reconsider another important judicial affair that was also unfolding during this period. For just as the Favras and Besenval affairs became inextricably intertwined with each other, so too was the Maillebois affair played out in tandem with another affair with which we are already acquainted, the Châtelet's ongoing investigation of the "crimes of October."

9

The October Days affair and the radicalization of the Comité des Recherches

The Châtelet October Days Inquest had opened, it will be recalled, in December 1789 with a long deposition in which the journalist Pelletier previewed most of the charges that would eventually be made against Orléans, Mirabeau, and the Duport faction. However, Pelletier was only the first of almost 400 witnesses in an investigation that would grind on for seven and a half months. Thus, at the same time the Châtelet was listlessly pursuing counter-revolutionaries like Besenval, Favras, Augeard, and Saint-Priest, it was also investigating some of the most prominent leaders of the Revolution. Barring a dramatic shift in the balance of power within a National Assembly that always insisted on having final jurisdiction over its own members, there was probably never any real possibility that the Châtelet would actually be able to punish or even arrest any of these leaders. But until the Assembly finally took action to definitively quash the Châtelet's pretensions in October 1790, the October Days Inquest was always hovering in the background, posing a certain threat, and serving, as we will see, as a kind of bargaining chip that would ultimately be handed over in return for lenient treatment for those implicated in the Maillebois case.

Although its denunciation of the October 6 attack on the Versailles Château had officially triggered the Châtelet probe, the Comité des Recherches was, as we have seen, never very enthusiastic about this investigation. However, the Comité's efforts to impede it were confined to behind-the-scenes maneuvering until April 1790, when, for the first time, it publicly attacked the Châtelet. In the Favras affair, Comité "left Fayettists" and Châtelet "right Fayettists" had worked together to convict one conspirator and cover up the activities of his accomplices. And in the Besenval affair, despite the strong public position it had taken against the defendant, the Comité had swallowed hard and refrained from public criticism of

188

the Châtelet's decision to release him.[1] But by the end of April, the Comité had decided that its position as a responsible organ of the Fayettist municipal regime could only be maintained at the expense of its image as a group of advanced patriots. In choosing to protect its patriotic credentials and in thereby propelling itself into the bitter struggle with the Châtelet described below, the Comité was reflecting a general evolution in "left Fayettist" political thinking.

THE DANTON AFFAIR AND THE "LEFT FAYETTISTS"

With Brissot still taking refuge in the "delicacy" of his position as a member of the Comité, the *Patriote français* will be of little help to us in probing the timing and motivation behind the critical shift in "left Fayettist" strategy that occurred in spring 1790. However, this shift can be followed with some precision in the pages of the influential *Chronique de Paris*. Throughout January and February, the *Chronique* had featured a quite moderate line on judicial issues, arguing that there was insufficient evidence to convict Besenval and then describing Favras as "an unfortunate soul ... whom sensitive men should pity, though the Law is obliged to strike him down." This conciliatory stance was reinforced on March 4 when the *Chronique* complimented Besenval's lawyer de Sèze for the "new republican ideas" contained in his final plea for his client, and even printed the text of some of de Sèze's criticism of the Comité des Recherches. Two days later, another Besenval attorney, Bruges, was praised for his "zeal" and "sensitivity," and on the following day, this string of laudatory comments about conservative jurists reached a climax with a defense of Châtelet head Talon, who had been accused of financial irregularity: "A patriotic journal is a sentinel which must keep a constant vigil for the People and against abuse. But men who are pure, such as M. Talon, have little to fear from this surveillance, since they can always easily cleanse themselves of the accusations lodged against them."[2]

In the next ten days, the *Chronique*'s moderate line continued with the printing of neutral reports on three new Châtelet decisions that could hardly have been very pleasing to vigilant patriots: on March 11, a report on Augeard's release; on March 13, a report on the release of a royalist journalist, the Chevalier de Laizer; and on March 17, a report on a life sentence in the galleys being given to Pierre Curé, a suspected Orleanist agent.[3] But March 17 was also the day on which the Châtelet, which had been operating for months with only a minimal degree of opposition, appears to have tried to push its luck too far. For it was on this day that it issued an arrest warrant against the most popular radical politician in Paris, Georges Danton.[4]

It is difficult to understand exactly what the Châtelet and Lafayette (who at the very least must have authorized the decision) were hoping to accomplish with this warrant, issued almost two months after an allegedly seditious speech made by Danton in defense of Marat at a Cordeliers District meeting. Surely they knew that any attempt to arrest the Cordeliers' "illustrious president" would meet stiff resistance from the district's National Guard battalion, which had shielded Marat on January 22. Perhaps the authorities were hoping that a vague threat of arrest would induce Danton to flee, a tactic that had worked with Orléans the previous autumn. (According to Gorsas, Lafayette warned Danton of the impending warrant and "invited him to seek safety.") Or perhaps Talon and Lafayette thought that the stigma of an arrest warrant would somehow help to discredit the Cordeliers leader. But whatever they may have had in mind, they never did try to arrest him. As Babut put it, "the Châtelet did not dare risk sending its bailiffs in front of Danton's door."[5]

Yet, while the Danton warrant had no legal repercussions, it seems to have been crucial in triggering an abrupt "left Fayettist" political about-face.[6] On March 19, a Cordeliers delegation sought support from within the Hôtel-de-Ville for its demand that the National Assembly annul the Danton warrant. Though the Assemblée des Représentants refused to endorse the Cordeliers' demand, this meeting marked an important step in the political odyssey of the "left Fayettists." For it was at this meeting that, in the course of a speech supporting Danton, the influential abbé Fauchet became the first of Brissot's close political friends to denounce the Châtelet's acquittal of Besenval and to call for its replacement by a "truly national tribunal." In a tantalizing phrase, Fauchet added that "it is suspected that [the Châtelet] has let itself be directed by powerful men who are seeking arbitrary authority. This idea is false, or at least I would like to think it is."[7] Who were these "powerful men"? The ministers? Lafayette? And just how false did Fauchet really think this idea was? In leaving his audience to ponder these questions, Fauchet, known to that point as one of the Parisian

General's most obsequious admirers, seemed to be backing away from the unrestricted loyalty implied in his proposal of six weeks earlier that Lafayette be named "First Brother-in-Arms" of all the National Guards in France.[8]

It was in its report of this Assemblée des Représentants meeting that the *Chronique de Paris* first began to display a strikingly new attitude towards Fayettist judicial policies. Although not yet ready explicitly to attack the Châtelet or endorse Fauchet's demand for a "national" tribunal, the *Chronique* declared that the Cordeliers had "proven" that Danton could not be prosecuted for a speech made at a district meeting, and, in what appears to be a veiled criticism of Lafayette, stated that Danton's refusal to listen to "those who told him to leave Paris" would be favorably received by the public. Moreover, the *Chronique* also reported in the same article that Oudart had complained about Châtelet procrastination in the *absentia* trial of Lambesc, the first time, so far as I can determine, that a Comité des Recherches member had attacked the Châtelet at a public meeting.[9]

While all this does not add up to a ringing indictment of the Châtelet, it did mark a significant departure from the *Chronique*'s attitude of the previous three months, and there would certainly be no further praise of Châtelet judges or counter-revolutionary defense attorneys appearing in its pages. By April 4, as we have seen, the *Chronique* had begun to wonder aloud about possible ties between Lafayette and the "Austrian committee," and by April 22, it had embraced Fauchet's position on the need for a new *lèse-nation* tribunal: "The Châtelet is clearly one of the Revolution's greatest enemies... How can we not suspect it, considering the zeal with which it receives denunciations against patriots and the fervor with which it absolves aristocrats?"[10]

To what extent can the rapid left turn taken by Fauchet and the *Chronique* be attributed to the Danton arrest warrant? As unenforceable as it was, the symbolic importance of this warrant should not be underestimated. For the willingness of patriotic opinion to tolerate the Châtelet as France's *lèse-nation* tribunal was predicated on the assumption that this court would be able to present itself convincingly as an impartial dispenser of justice, magnanimously presiding over the epoch of peace and forgiveness that the King had alluded to in his February 4 National Assembly appearance.[11] The release of Besenval and Augeard and the Favras cover-up might be accepted as the price of peace and reconciliation, but only, of course, if patriotic "excess" was also seen in such a forgiving light. With this in mind, consider the possible impact of an arrest warrant issued against a popular radical leader for a public speech made two weeks before the King's Assembly appearance. Coming on the heels of a series of indulgent decisions concerning secret counter-revolutionary activity and in the midst of the prevailing emphasis on conciliation, this warrant, which must have seemed comparable to an enemy counter-attack prepared and launched under cover of an uneasy truce, could only have served to compromise severely both the Châtelet's ability to claim impartiality and the always tenuous "spirit of February 4" itself.[12]

Such, at any rate, was the "spin" on the Danton affair being offered by Gorsas, another prominent "left Fayettist" who used this affair as a vehicle with which to negotiate a sharp left turn. Contrasting the unforgiving aggressiveness of one side with the sincere desire of the other to keep the peace, Gorsas focused on the efforts Danton had been making to tone down his behavior since his unfortunate defense of Marat: "He has been conducting himself in a conciliatory manner . . . and has made us forget the reproaches he seemed to have earned in the Marat affair . . . [But] while M. Danton participated in municipal affairs by discussing issues of public interest, the Châtelet was secretly investigating him . . . and has now issued a warrant against him."[13]

Following this opening gambit, Gorsas, who had never before written a word of criticism of the Châtelet and who as recently as March 11 had applauded Augeard's release, quickly became an enthusiastic and habitual contributor to what was rapidly developing into a vigorous and well-orchestrated anti-Châtelet campaign. On April 17, for example, he joined several other journalists in printing the following epigram:

> O vous qui lavez Broglie, Augeard
> Qui lavez Besenval, qui laveriez la peste,
> Vous êtes le papier brouilliard,
> Vous enlevez la tache, et la tache vous reste.[14]

In suddenly turning against the Châtelet during this period, journalists and politicians like Gorsas and Fauchet were undoubtedly moved, to at least some degree, by a genuine feeling that the Danton arrest warrant had violated "the spirit of tolerance, indulgence, concern for individual liberty, and forgiveness of temporary faults" that this tribunal had ostensibly been upholding in its treatment of counter-revolutionaries.[15] However, there was a more overtly politicial dimension to the about-face performed by the "left Fayettists" during this period. For the Danton affair had, in fact, surfaced at a key moment in the ongoing struggle between the Parisian districts and the Fayettist municipality.

In the weeks preceding the issuing of the warrant against him, Danton had been the most visible leader of an alternative municipal assembly that had been challenging the authority of the "soi-disant Représentants."[16] While the Représentants attempted to cripple the districts as a vital political force by proposing a new municipal constitution that put severe limitations on their right to meet, Danton's assembly was invoking the virtues of "direct democracy" by insisting that the districts be permitted to meet whenever they chose. A formal demand for such "permanence" was adopted by the alternative assembly on March 16, and it seems hardly coincidental that the judicial arm of the Fayettist municipality issued the Danton arrest warrant on the very next day. Certainly the sponsors of district permanence did not regard the Châtelet's timing as accidental, and the Danton warrant was greeted by a strong wave of grass-roots protest. Within days, forty of the sixty Parisian districts had petitioned the National Assembly for its annulment.[17]

For the "left Fayettists," who were in total agreement with the more conservative Représentants in opposing district permanence (both Brissot and Fauchet had major roles in formulating the Hôtel-de-Ville's proposed municipal constitution) but who were also eager to project a more radical image, the Danton affair was an opportunity to express solidarity with the districts and "the People" on an issue which did not involve a direct challenge to their own prerogatives. Consequently, Brissot was able to defend Danton's rights to free speech and to praise the "famous Cordeliers District" for being "always animated by the same fervor for defending principle" on the very day after he had written that district permanence would "exclude harmony and lead to a monstrous anarchy."[18] Thus, it appears that it was far easier for Brissot and his friends to take a popularly oriented position on a glamour issue which possessed something of the emotional resonance of contemporary campaigns to free imprisoned radical leaders than to support local democrats on the crucial "nuts-and-bolts" issue of municipal organization. At any rate, the new attitude of the "left Fayettists" towards the Châtelet must be seen, at least in part, as a response to the grass-roots pressures generated by the Danton warrant.

THE CAMPAIGN AGAINST THE CHÂTELET

Although our examination of the Danton affair has helped us locate the precise moment when a number of "left Fayettist" journalists and politicians began expressing public opposition to the "right Fayettists" of the Châtelet, this affair was only the most visible component of a vast judicial counter-offensive. For if the Danton warrant was a kind of "tip of the iceberg" of a conservative effort to take advantage of a late 1789–early 1790 lull in revolutionary momentum, the bulk of that iceberg was the Châtelet's secret investigation of the "crimes of October." And if the revolutionary left had been able to avoid the iceberg's tip by mobilizing enough support for Danton to further insure that no attempt would be made to arrest him, the rest of this glacier was still lurking in the background. The Danton case and the October Days case were, in fact, components of one fundamental *procès* being conducted during this period. "What is the Châtelet up to," asked Carra on April 22, "does it want to put the Revolution itself on trial?"[19]

But if the Danton affair was only part of one much larger case, were the "left Fayettists" then responding to developments in the October Days probe as well as to the Danton warrant? While the precise timing of threat and response is harder to establish for the October Days case than for the Danton case, it is certain that at some unspecified point "a few months after" the Comité des Recherches issued its November 23 denunciation of the attack on the Versailles Château, the Châtelet asked the Comité to add some "additional articles" to that denunciation. According to the Comité, Talon and Procureur du Roi Flandre de Brunville wanted it to "adopt a set of articles which would have led to nothing less than an indictment of ... a plan for a Regency Council and other maneuvers designed to corrupt the Gardes-Françaises from the beginning of the Revolution." In other words, the Comité was being asked to denounce an Orleanist conspiracy dating back to summer 1789 or even earlier.[20]

Responding to the Comité's negative reaction to this proposal, Flandre insisted, with an air of feigned innocence, that the proposed

additions were based on the language of the Comité's own denunciation: "It is impossible to find anything in them [the proposed
articles] not relevant to discovering the authors, abettors, and accomplices of the crimes which defiled the Versailles Château on the
morning of October 6, or those who by promises, bribes, and other
maneuvers excited or provoked these crimes."[21] The key word here,
however, is "relevant," for in the investigation of a conspiracy, any
kind of information *might* turn out to be "relevant" to uncovering its
origins. In effect, Flandre was arguing that an investigation of the
Orleanist conspiracy of July 1789 was "relevant" to an investigation
of the Orleanist conspiracy of October 1789.

But let us put these verbal gymnastics aside. Whatever their exact
content, we can be quite sure that the proposed additions to the
Comité denunciation were designed to make it easier for the Châtelet
to gather as much compromising information as possible against
Orléans, Mirabeau, and other left-leaning deputies. In all Châtelet
cases, the Procureur du Roi's indictment was read to a witness, and
it was then up to the witness to decide what evidence he or she could
provide that related to it. However, Flandre's indictment in this case
was an exact reproduction of the Comité's original denunciation,
which had, of course, been carefully limited to the events of October
6.[22] While this restriction did not prevent several witnesses from
providing an abundance of detail on Orleanist maneuvering in
July,[23] other witnesses were careful to avoid mentioning even the
events of October 5 or were at least uncertain about what they
should or should not say. According to Flandre, it was "this uncertainty, this impediment, this variety among the witnesses as to
what they believed they should depose" that led the Châtelet leaders
to propose "an addition to the complaint which would have removed
all the difficulties," all the difficulties, that is, that were preventing
the Châtelet from finding out as much as possible about the activities
of Lafayette's political enemies.[24] Since the Châtelet could have
supplemented its indictment unilaterally, Comité approval was not
a legal necessity. However, Lafayette and Talon obviously felt that
the credibility of the October Days probe depended on its being seen
as a co-operative enterprise involving all elements of the Fayettist
coalition.

Given the Comité's lack of enthusiasm for the October Days probe
from the start, it is hard to believe that the Châtelet really thought
that the Comité might go along with its proposed additions. But as

difficult as it would have been to be very hopeful about Comité co-operation before mid-March, it would have been impossible to entertain any such hope after the Danton arrest warrant had exposed the Châtelet to a torrent of public criticism. Thus, we can probably assume that the Châtelet's additions were proposed before the issuing of the Danton warrant, most likely in late February or early March. If so, the post-March 17 explosion of "left Fayettist" anti-Châtelet sentiment can now be more easily understood. While the Châtelet probe had been posing a certain threat to leading patriotic deputies since it had opened in December, the proposed additions amounted to a significant escalation of that threat. Yet, the attempted expansion of the October Days probe was still not a public issue, and whatever animosities and tensions this attempted expansion produced were consequently not expressed publicly. By contrast, the Danton affair was played out entirely in public, allowing it to become a vehicle for the expression of grievances that should more properly be seen as being attached to the October Days case.

In any event, whatever the timing and content of the Châtelet's proposed additions, the Comité flatly refused to have anything to do with them. Moreover, the Comité told the Châtelet leaders (or at least later claimed to have told them) that, rather than serving as the object of a criminal investigation, some of the activities they wanted to denounce "were worthy of the gratitude of all friends of the Nation."[25] There the matter rested until early April when the October Days Inquest, which had been proceeding for months without attracting a great deal of public attention, suddenly became the subject of a flood of alarming rumors. As Comité member Oudart later put it: "Rumors were rampant that the Châtelet was proceeding without limits, and, under the pretext of avenging the crimes of October 6, was trying the Revolution itself and the People of Paris."[26]

Confirmation of Oudart's statement can be found in journals of the left and the right. Thus, the *Annales patriotiques et littéraires* noted that "it is being said all over Paris at this moment that the Châtelet is secretly investigating the best patriots and the bravest defenders of the People's rights and liberties in the National Assembly," a claim that was echoed in Tournon's report that ten deputies were included on a list of forty-four indictments that were about to be handed down.[27] Meanwhile, the increasingly anti-revolutionary *Journal général de la cour et de la ville* praised the Châtelet's "courageous activity" and announced that this tribunal had obtained evidence "so grave as to be truly frightening," while the Monarchien-oriented *Gazette universelle* was pleased to report that seventeen deputies might soon be indicted.[28] In addition to Orléans and Mirabeau, who were certain to be charged, some of the names being bandied about as possible Châtelet victims were Barnave, the Lameth brothers, Chapelier, Pétion, Robespierre, and Aiguillon.[29]

Although rumors about the Châtelet probe appeared in journals from across the political spectrum, the timing of this new wave of rumors suggests it may initially have been set off by "leaks" from the Comité des Recherches. With the Danton arrest warrant having just generated the first public "left Fayettist" criticism of the Châtelet, the release of previously withheld information about Châtelet designs in the October Days case could easily have followed as the next step in the nascent campaign against the old royal court. But if early April marks a significant deterioration in relations between the Châtelet and the Comité, this period was also marked, as we have seen, by the surfacing of news about the Maillebois plot and the emergence of a new campaign against the ministers. Thus, in the newly polarized climate taking hold in the wake of the Danton warrant, it is hardly surprising that the Châtelet's efforts to "try the Revolution" were soon seen as part of a comprehensive counter-revolutionary scheme. Do the Châtelet judges think, asked Carra, that "they will be able to accomplish that which the Parlements, the nobles, the clergy, and Maillebois could not accomplish between them?" Or as the *Chronique* explained: "If the patriots protest against the [October Days] proceedings ... it is because they sense how closely these proceedings are linked to all the plans of the aristocrats."[30]

One journalist particularly worried about the counter-revolutionary *conjoncture* of April was Loustalot, who saw a parallel between the threat to the patriotic deputies posed by the Châtelet, which he called "a sword in the hands of the ministers," and the threat to the National Assembly posed by the royal army in July 1789. "The death of Flesselles and de Launay," he wrote, "saved the lives of 100,000 citizens who would have perished in a civil war. Has not this example taught the French what they must do when the life of the legislative body is endangered?" And sounding the alarm even more loudly was an anonymous "counterfeit Marat," who attacked the Châtelet judges as "vile slaves in the pay of the Court and the ministers" while announcing that 200 deputies were about to be indicted: "Frenchmen! Compatriots!... In ten days you will be slaughtered or put back in irons if you do not arm yourselves with a new courage ... and force the National Assembly to emerge from its lethargy and immediately dismiss the corrupt Châtelet judges who are secretly plotting your ruin."[31]

One important consequence of the surge of publicity given to the Châtelet's aggressive designs was the rapid development of a powerful grass-roots anti-Châtelet campaign. Thus, when the Cordeliers District (which had received no support from the other districts two months earlier in a call for the creation of a "special" *lèse-nation* tribunal) renewed its demand for Châtelet disinvestiture on April 20, it immediately found a ready audience.[32] As the Carmelites District proclaimed: "The alarm is general... Even the august Assembly is thought to be in danger."[33] By May 10, more than two-thirds of the districts had formally adhered, with varying degrees of enthusiasm, to the Cordeliers' insistence that "responsibility for avenging the People cannot be left in the hands of a tribunal that the People designates as its enemy."[34] Only two districts explicitly refused to accept the Cordeliers' contention that the Châtelet had "lost the confidence of citizens," and at least one district called for the prosecution of the Châtelet's leaders.[35]

The National Assembly, however, did not share the alarm of the districts. Since March 24, it had been devoting a great deal of attention to the construction of a new nation-wide system of elected courts, and these efforts were about to culminate in a comprehensive law that would be passed on August 16.[36] Thus, by the time the anti-Châtelet district petitions arrived, it was evident that the long-awaited disappearance of venal tribunals would soon become a reality. With the Châtelet living on borrowed time anyway, the Assembly, which, as we have seen throughout this study, was fundamentally sympathetic to the Châtelet's lenient treatment of counter-revolutionaries, was not yet ready to deal it an immediate death-blow or even to take the less drastic step of annulling the October Days proceedings.

While it is true that the Assembly had felt obliged to take account of district protests against the Necker amnesty the previous July, those protests had been accompanied by massive and potentially violent popular demonstrations. In contrast, judicial issues never captured the attention of the revolutionary crowd in spring 1790 and the district anti-Châtelet campaign proceeded in an essentially peaceful and legalistic manner. Besides, if the Châtelet Inquest did turn out to present a threat to any patriotic deputies, the Assembly certainly reserved the right to intervene, and, as we will see shortly, it eventually did quash indictments against Orléans and Mirabeau. But what the Assembly was not prepared to do in May 1790 was to take any step that might hasten the creation of any kind of "special" or "national" *lèse-nation* tribunal. For while the protests against the Châtelet had ostensibly been motivated by the desire to protect threatened patriots and to promote the concepts of "amnesty" and "forgiveness,"[37] it was quite clear that the radical politicians behind these protests were not terribly interested in seeing these concepts applied to their opponents, and equally clear that their intention in proposing a "special" tribunal was to create a court that would be a great deal harder on such opponents than the Châtelet had been.

Although the anti-Châtelet campaign of spring 1790 did not elicit an immediate response from the Assembly, there can be little doubt that it caused considerable damage to the reputation of the tribunal that was now rapidly becoming known as "the Queen's wash-house."[38] While the October Days Inquest would continue until the last of its 394 witnesses were heard, it is hard to observe this affair's concluding stages without sensing that the Châtelet was, by that point, merely going through the motions. Talon, who had been seated in the National Assembly since December 1789, was certainly capable of recognizing a sinking ship, and on June 24, he suddenly discovered that he had to resign from the Châtelet "in order to devote himself more assiduously to his duties as deputy."[39] And Boucher d'Argis, who became acting Châtelet head when Talon left, was careful not to assume the title of lieutenant-civil, apparently judging that such a step would only further compromise his political future.[40] But the best indication that the Châtelet had indeed "lost the confidence of citizens" can be found in the results of the judicial elections held at the end of 1790. For only one Châtelet magistrate was elected to the new tribunals created by the Assembly, and Boucher d'Argis did not receive a single vote.[41]

It was, however, public repudiation by the Comité des Recherches which probably constituted the *coup de grâce* to the Châtelet's credibility. Although the Comité and the Châtelet had been quarreling privately about the October Days probe for months, in early April the Comité was still being viewed by a significant portion of the public as a vital cog in the Fayettist judicial system. Thus, some of the rumors about the October Days Inquest circulating at that time indicated that the Comité was co-operating with the Châtelet. Noting this supposed co-operation, the *Modérateur* appeared ready to grant the Comité a form of "forgiveness" it most assuredly was not seeking: "By avenging royal majesty, [the Comité] will obtain forgiveness in the eyes of good citizens, and in that way truly avenge the rights of the People."[42]

With the Comité thus running the risk of being confounded with the "accursed shysters" and "wolves" of the tribunal that was now being routinely referred to as "this nest of all crimes,"[43] Brissot and his colleagues evidently decided the time had come to "go public." Or as Oudart later explained: "We felt ourselves obliged to push away the reproaches we shared with the Châtelet."[44] On April 24, the Comité formally disassociated itself from any attempt to "try the Revolution" by issuing a statement which, as the *Mercure de France* put it, officially "united it with the Châtelet's enemies":

Seeing that our denunciation of the attack on the Versailles Château on the morning of October 6 is being distorted, and, in fact, extended to cover events that occurred the day before and even earlier ... [and] considering that, if we continued to keep silent, doubts could be thrown upon our patriotism through the imputation that we wanted to pursue those who have participated in the Revolution's most important events, we therefore feel obliged to declare that our denunciation of November 23 only concerns the attack that occurred on the morning of October 6 ... and any pursuit and investigation that goes beyond ... this single point will not be recognized by us.[45]

In abandoning its silence for fear that "doubts could be thrown upon our patriotism," the Comité had come close to acknowledging that it was a group of revolutionary politicians who valued popular approval. Yet, Brissot immediately attempted to back away from such an acknowledgment by explaining that the Comité's venture into the public arena on this issue had been a reluctant one, that its declaration had been "required" for purposes of "maintaining tranquillity in this capital," a tranquillity endangered by "fermentation in the districts."[46] However, this effort to portray the Comité as a group of harried administrators primarily interested in calming unrest and preserving order must be viewed in a wider perspective. As the probable source of many of the October Days probe rumors then circulating, the Comité had, in all likelihood, consciously contributed to the creation of the very "fermentation" it was now supposedly trying to pacify. It must, therefore, be seen, at least in this case, as attempting to shape as well as to respond to public opinion.

Moreover, Brissot's unwillingness to admit that the Comité had chosen sides in a political struggle can itself be seen as part of his political strategy. By presenting himself, at the very moment he moved to the left, as having been "required" or "forced" to take that step, he seems to have been seeking to retain as much credibility as possible on his right. But while this habitual strategy of "reluctant radicalism" helped Brissot achieve an ever increasing degree of political influence over the next two years, the revolutionary engine, partially stoked by Brissot himself, continued relentlessly to grind potential moderate supporters into political oblivion or to thrust them into the arms of the counter-revolution. Thus, when Brissot looked to his right after August 10, 1792, there was nobody there.

In addition, the hesitation with which Brissot and his Comité colleagues negotiated their turn to the left in spring 1790 left them vulnerable to criticism from radical journalists who were by no means won over by the anti-Châtelet declaration of April 24. Thus, Loustalot sarcastically noted that the Comité "has congratulated itself in *one* public statement for having only denounced the invasion of the morning of October 6." But, argued Loustalot, even this event and the massacre of the bodyguards which followed could have been acts of "legitimate defense" since a demonstrator had been killed by a bodyguard just before the Château was invaded. "Is it really astonishing," he declared, "that the People entered the Château to search for the guilty bodyguard, and that the resistance of his comrades precipitated the unfortunate death of several of them?"[47] For Loustalot, the Comité's continued willingness to see the events of October 6 as criminal was itself unacceptable.

Other radical journalists simply paid no attention to the Comité's anti-Châtelet declaration. According to the newly-returned Marat, the Comité was "composed of jurists who are devoted to the Court and who have given themselves over to the views of the ministers and to the solicitations of the aristocratic faction." Meanwhile, the *Observateur* was proclaiming that "this detestable Comité" was "united [with the Châtelet] in a coalition that was seeking to crush the party devoted to the People... They are sold to the Court and to the

Ministers and are working with them in a counter-revolutionary plot."[48]

Like the Girondins of 1792–3, the Comité des Recherches of 1789–90 was never able to overcome the suspicions of the most "advanced" elements of patriotic opinion. Though the declaration of April 24 constituted a kind of repudiation of the Fayettist regime, the "reluctant radicalism" of Brissot and his colleagues would never be taken seriously by the revolutionary vanguard. Beyond this, the fact that the Comité's withdrawal from the Fayettist coalition had occurred during a period of relative popular quiescence is itself suggestive of future Girondin problems. In the absence of the massive popular gatherings which had dominated earlier revolutionary events, Brissot and his friends may have felt that they could safely break with Lafayette and the mainstream Constitutional Monarchists without becoming unduly vulnerable to overwhelming pressure from the left, that it might be possible for them to move the Revolution along in the direction they desired without losing control of it. However, the impending reappearance of the revolutionary crowd as a major player on the political scene would have a fatal effect upon this calculation.

In any event, whatever clues to the future can be mined from the Comité's April 24 declaration, there can be little doubt that this statement served as a severe blow to the viability of the Châtelet's October Days Inquest. In fact, the final stages of this proceeding were, in essence, anti-climactic. Once the Comité had openly repudiated the Châtelet probe, it was only natural for it to make a great public show of refusing to give up some evidence relating to Orléans that it had in its possession.[49] Ostensibly responding to bitter complaints from Boucher d'Argis about this lack of co-operation, the National Assembly ordered the Comité on August 7 to hand over all evidence "relevant to ... the Châtelet's proceedings on the events of October 6."[50] However, this decree was carefully worded to allow the Comité to take refuge in another round of verbal gymnastics concerning the meaning of the phrase "relevant to October 6." Rather than turn over its evidence, the Comité coyly announced that it did not have "any piece that appears to us to be relevant to October 6."[51]

Now if the Assembly had really wanted the Châtelet to obtain the evidence in question, it could have threatened the Comité with some form of punishment or it could have passed a decree specifying the pieces it wanted handed over. (Some members of the Assembly's Comité des Recherches had already given the Châtelet detailed information on the evidence being held by the municipal Comité.)[52] Or, at the very least, the Assembly could have signalled its seriousness by ordering its own Comité des Recherches to examine the disputed evidence and report back to the full Assembly. But though outwardly respectful towards the Châtelet, the Assembly was actually little more disposed to co-operate with the October Days probe than the Comité. Knowing the Assembly would not press it any further, the Comité simply continued to hold on to the evidence it had.

And just as the Comité's stonewalling on evidence flowed naturally from its April 24 repudiation of the Châtelet probe, so the Assembly's final decision on October 2, 1790 to quash the indictment of Orléans and Mirabeau flowed naturally from its failure to take meaningful steps to provide the Châtelet with all the available evidence in the case. Yet, despite the sense of inevitability that pervades the closing stages of this affair, the question still remains as to why the Châtelet Inquest was allowed to linger for so long on what amounted to an artificial respirator. As already indicated, the Assembly's failure to pull the plug on the probe after the eruption of the anti-Châtelet campaign of April and May was ultimately rooted in its approval of the lenient treatment that the Châtelet had been dispensing to enemies of the Revolution and its fear that any overt repudiation of the Châtelet would only stimulate more insistent demands that it create a "special" *lèse-nation* court. But for a more precise understanding of what was at stake in the Assembly's unwillingness to abandon the Châtelet, it will be necessary to look more closely into the relationship between the October Days Inquest and the case against those enemies of the Revolution who had been implicated in the Maillebois affair, a relationship which crystallized just as Lafayette's coalition was beginning to disintegrate.

10

The Maillebois and October Days affairs: mutual amnesty and the breakup of the Fayettist coalition

With their eyes on the spectacular but fundamentally superficial display of national unity that unfolded at the Fête de la Fédération of July 14, 1790, historians have traditionally described Lafayette as being at "the zenith of his influence" during the summer of 1790.[1] However, in direct contrast to January–February 1790, when an intact Fayettist coalition was able to secure a wide range of support for the Favras–Besenval judicial compromise, the summer of 1790 was actually marked by a clear deterioration of the Parisian General's ability to serve as the centerpiece of a broad revolutionary coalition.

As Brissot, in his turn, would discover in 1792–3, it is very difficult to present oneself as a centrist without being solidly anchored by viable political forces on both left and right. With this in mind, the Châtelet's aggressiveness in the October Days affair might be seen as an attempt by the Fayettist regime to prop up and accommodate a Monarchien faction which could not be allowed to continue its relentless slide into political oblivion and counter-revolution.[2] Along the same lines, Lafayette's support for Saint-Priest in the Marseilles affair, which was only one of a series of incidents in spring–summer 1790 in which the Parisian General defended beleaguered royal army officers and officials, can also be regarded as an effort to preserve a viable anchor on the right.[3] But unlike the turn to the right which Lafayette undertook in the aftermath of the October Days, the accentuated move to the right of spring–summer 1790 was not dutifully accepted by the most advanced elements of the Fayettist coalition. Instead, it produced, as we have seen, the first signs of "left Fayettist" disaffection. Like Necker the previous summer, Lafayette was finding it increasingly difficult to sustain the juggling act upon which his authority largely rested.

Given this situation, the reciprocal threats posed by the October

Days Inquest and the Maillebois case can now be seen as signals of the Fayettist coalition's impending breakup. Whereas Comité des Recherches "left Fayettists" and Châtelet "right Fayettists" had been able to work together during the Favras affair and at least keep their differences under wraps during the Besenval affair, all pretense of co-operation or even respectful disagreement disappeared during the unfolding of these two cases, each of which served as a means for one wing of a disintegrating coalition to threaten the natural allies of the other. In the October Days probe, Lafayette and the Châtelet were investigating the very people whom the "left Fayettist" press and the Comité itself were praising as the "best patriots," while in the Maillebois case, the Comité was denouncing the same ministerial and Monarchien elements towards whom Lafayette was reaching out. This early willingness of center-rightists like Lafayette and center-leftists like Brissot to use their control of judicial mechanisms to threaten non-extremist opponents bears watching. Although each side seems to have been more interested in discrediting those implicated in these two cases than in actually punishing them and although power was simply too dispersed during this period for either side to have much chance of obtaining convictions, the inclination to see even mainstream opponents as criminals would have deadly consequences when the ideological and political restraints of 1789–90 would no longer be operative.

THE MONARCHIENS AND THE MAILLEBOIS PLOT

Let us begin an analysis of the reciprocal threats in these two cases with an examination of the Monarchien angle. As we have seen, Monarchien pressure had been instrumental in provoking the October Days probe. Moreover, some of the key depositions in the investigation were being furnished by Monarchien leaders.[4] In fact, the entire Châtelet Inquest might be regarded as a joint "right-Fayettist"–Monarchien project. But at the same time as the Monarchiens were levelling accusations in the October Days case, some of their leaders were being considered as potential defendants in the Maillebois case.

The issue of Monarchien complicity in the Maillebois conspiracy had first arisen in March, when the Comité des Recherches was informed that Mounier and Lally-Tolendal, who had both resigned from the National Assembly after the October Days, had been asked to draft a manifesto for the Maillebois plotters.[5] However, the names of the two Monarchien leaders were absent from all the early newspaper accounts of the Maillebois plan, and as the probable source of the information contained in these accounts, the Comité seems to have decided to suppress any mention of the Mounier–Lally connection. While this discretion may have had something to do with the inherent unlikelihood that Mounier and Lally would actually have agreed to write such a manifesto,[6] a more compelling explanation can be found in timing. If the Maillebois plot had surfaced after the Comité's April 24 public repudiation of the Châtelet, Brissot and his colleagues would almost certainly have been less hesitant about embarrassing the Châtelet's Monarchien collaborators. But the Comité had learned about the Maillebois plot a full month before completing its decisive turn to the left, and, as a still loyal component of the Fayettist regime, it might well have been reluctant to release negative information about a faction the Parisian General was seeking to mollify.

On the other hand, by the time that Garran published his first report on the Maillebois affair in July, the Comité would no longer have had any interest in protecting the Monarchien leaders. Thus, the proposed Mounier–Lally manifesto was prominently featured in this report, as was a note from the Comte de la Châtre, Monsieur's Premier Gentilhomme, which had been found in Bonne-Savardin's possession on April 30. Addressed to Mounier in Grenoble, this note contained little more than the cryptic phrase "I have spoken in great detail to the person who will deliver this to you."[7] Nevertheless, the mere fact that Bonne was carrying a message for Mounier was itself sufficient, at least in the eyes of the newly radicalized Comité, to justify the presumption that the Monarchien leader was involved in the Maillebois plot. Knitting together the La Châtre note, the proposed Mounier–Lally manifesto, and Bonne's admission that he had met with Mounier in Grenoble in March, Garran wove a tissue of innuendo:

It is remarkable that among the documents we found a note from M. de La Châtre to M. Mounier that M. Bonne-Savardin was supposed to deliver. In it, M. de la Châtre mentioned a very detailed conversation with M. Bonne-Savardin. In his interrogation, M. Bonne-Savardin admitted he had seen M. Mounier at the time of his previous trip to Turin... But it was MM. Mounier and Lally-Tolendal who were supposed to be entrusted with writing the manifesto of the Turin rebels.[8]

However, though the Comité was not adverse to drawing political capital from such logic, it was not prepared to institute formal judicial proceedings without something more substantial. Recognizing that there was no real case against him, the Comité did not include Mounier in its official denunciation of Maillebois, Bonne, and Saint-Priest. Instead, Garran noted only that "the documents necessarily have led to suspicions about some other persons against whom we do not have sufficient evidence to include in the denunciation. It is our duty to maintain surveillance upon them without interruption, and we will do so rigorously."[9]

But Mounier had already acted to elude the Comité's continued surveillance well before this report was issued. With publicity about the La Châtre note undoubtedly adding to the mistrust that had been accumulating around him since the October Days, the Monarchien leader fled France on May 20. Whether provoked by fear that more concrete evidence against him might surface or, as he and his friends claimed, by ominous threats from Grenoble radicals, Mounier's flight could only have served to further embarrass the remaining Monarchiens in Paris at a moment when controversy about the October Days Inquest was still raging.[10] Though Mounier was never officially charged, the suspicion that he was involved in the Maillebois plot helped contribute to the discrediting of both the Monarchiens and the Inquest they were co-sponsoring.

SAINT-PRIEST AND THE COUNTER-OCTOBER DAYS INQUEST

Another aspect of the connection between the Maillebois affair and the October Days probe can be explored through further consideration of the proceedings against Saint-Priest. Although the Interior Minister had almost persuaded the King to flee to Rambouillet on October 5, this had remained generally unknown through the autumn and winter of 1789–90. However, by the time the Châtelet's Inquest had emerged as a major public issue in spring 1790, the belief that Saint-Priest had been involved in some kind of attempt to help the royal family escape from Versailles had become fairly widespread, largely due to the extensive publicity given to the testimony of a Versailles National Guard officer named Lecointre. According to Lecointre, five of Marie-Antoinette's carriages were prevented from leaving the Château that day. Then, he continued, "another carriage, loaded with trunks . . . was brought to the sentry-post by a patrol which had stopped it. I tried to find out whose carriage it was, and learned it belonged to the Interior Minister, the Comte de Saint-Priest. I confirmed the order that this carriage stay put."[11]

In the anti-Châtelet campaign of April and May 1790, one of the main themes of the patriotic press was that, rather than pursue the heroes of those who had marched to Versailles, the authorities should have been investigating those who had either provoked or tried to counteract the march. As the *Chronique de Paris* put it:

Why have proceedings not been opened against those who incited the Royal Bodyguards and those who distributed [royalist] cockades? ... Why has no action been taken against the person ... who pretended to be the Queen when five carriages were stopped at the Dragon's Gate, the person who dressed the servants in bourgeois costumes, and the person who prepared the carriages? ... These are the outrages which must be punished first.[12]

And while the *Chronique* spoke only of "the person" who had disguised the servants and prepared the carriages, and, in effect, organized an attempted escape, Desmoulins was less discreet. In a passage which neatly parallels the one just cited, he named this person:

Everyone is asking why the Châtelet has not proceeded against those who incited the Royal Bodyguards, against those who distributed anti-national cockades ... and against the individual who was in the carriage of the wife of the king ... which was forced to turn back by the sentry at the gate. And why has it not proceeded against Saint-Priest, whose carriage filled with trunks ... was also stopped at the gate?[13]

Thus, in addition to the litany of complaints against him discussed earlier, Saint-Priest had, by the spring of 1790, again come under fire for his activities during the October Days, this time for something far more serious than making sarcastic comments to Parisian market-women. With this in mind, we can now see his denunciation by the Comité des Recherches as a response to patriotic demands for the opening of what could be called a "counter-October Days Inquest." Moreover, the Comité was able to follow up on this opening of a "counter-Inquest" by uncovering further evidence linking the Interior Minister to an attempted escape from Versailles. For Mme de Saint-Priest had actually been sent to Rambouillet on October 5 to prepare for the arrival of the King and Queen, and the son of the Rambouillet concierge soon revealed to the Comité that he had seen her on that day.[14]

In denouncing the would-be engineer of the royal family's escape, the Comité was taking another step to disassociate itself from the Châtelet's October Days probe, a process which would be completed in October 1790 when Brissot admitted that the Comité's original denunciation of the attack on the Versailles Château had been a mistake. In the Comité's denunciation, the invaders of the Château had been described as "bandits." By October 1790, they had become "the People":

A furious and distracted People, whose patience had been exhausted by long suffering, was looking for bread rather than victims... It wanted its King to come to the capital because it knew the famine which had been creating martyrs every day for four months would end when he arrived, and it was right.[15]

Reflecting the increasingly radical line being taken by the erstwhile "left Fayettists," Brissot's comments on the massacres of October 6 now echoed those expressed by Loustalot during the previous spring: "This crime, if it can even be called that, was one of those chance occurrences that upset all calculations. It was not premeditated. And if, as cannot be doubted, ... the sacrifice of the two bodyguards was only an offering to the soul of a murdered citizen, how can it be called a terrible crime?"[16]

In January 1790, Agier had maintained that the Comité des Recherches sought to please neither "aristocrats" nor "democrats" but only "honest men" and "true friends of the public good."[17] While this effort to describe a centrist institution which "indiscriminately and without respite strikes at all seditious factions" was somewhat disingenuous, it was true that, until spring 1790, the Comité formed part of a governing coalition which, as a whole, could claim to be equally active against both right and left. Moreover, the Comité's willingness to refrain from public criticism of Lafayette's pursuit of the left after the October Days can be considered as part of the "dues" it had to pay to remain as a member in good standing of this coalition. But by withdrawing from the Fayettist coalition in April, Brissot and his colleagues had, in effect, freed themselves to follow their natural inclination to regard the activities of the right as the true "crimes of October."

Thus, the breakup of the Fayettist coalition produced two competing October Days Inquests, the official one still being pursued by the Châtelet and the counter-Inquest now being pursued, in the form of the Saint-Priest prosecution, by the Comité. Or, to put it another way, the Comité's withdrawal from the governing coalition left it free to attack a ministry that was being propped up by Lafayette. In this respect, the Saint-Priest denunciation can be considered as a dress rehearsal for Brissot's March 1792 denunciation of de Lessart, another minister who found himself tarred with the "Austrian committee" brush.[18]

THE ABBÉ DE BARMOND AND MUTUAL AMNESTY

On July 13, 1790, just four days after the Comité formally denounced Maillebois, Bonne-Savardin, and Saint-Priest, two impostors posing as National Guardsmen and carrying a forged transfer order were able to spirit Bonne out of the Abbaye Prison.[19] Considering the level of popular emotion generated in January 1790 by rumors that Besenval and Favras would escape from prison, to say nothing of the impact of similar rumors prior to the September Massacres of 1792, Bonne's very real escape attracted remarkably little public attention, a development which reflected the absence of the revolutionary crowd throughout the Maillebois affair. However, this escape did elicit one notable outburst. In his July 26 pamphlet *C'en est fait de nous*, Marat accused Lafayette and Bailly of having "engineered the escape of the traitor Bonne from the prisons" and, at the same time, denounced the "traitors" of the Comité des Recherches for complacency in their investigation of the Maillebois plot. "Five to six hundred fallen heads are necessary," he proclaimed, "to assure peace, liberty, and happiness. It is a false humanity which has held back your arms and suspended your blows."[20]

But Marat's accusations found no echo in the rest of the radical press. "He will compromise all of us with his intemperate patriotism," declared Desmoulins. And even Loustalot, who had been mercilessly attacking the Comité des Recherches since its creation and who now openly accused Lafayette of being "pledged to the ministerial party," did not attribute Bonne's escape to anything more sinister than negligence.[21] Without support from his fellow radical journalists, Marat's impassioned plea that the People "take to arms and again find that heroic valor which saved France on July 14 and October 5" had no apparent effect on the actual course of events.[22] Rather than generating any significant level of patriotic indignation, the most important result of Bonne's escape was to bring to the surface the involvement in the Maillebois affair of a new figure, the abbé Perrotin de Barmond. For on July 28, this obscure right-wing deputy and Parlement de Paris magistrate found himself in the embarrassing position of being forced to explain why he had been caught riding in his own carriage with Bonne as a passenger.[23]

Arrested at Châlons-sur-Marne and quickly hustled back to Paris, Barmond appeared before the bar of the National Assembly on August 18 and admitted that he had sheltered Bonne in his home. Moreover, he also admitted that he had agreed to help Bonne flee France. However, he insisted that he had been moved by purely humanitarian considerations and that Bonne, with whom he claimed to have been totally unacquainted until July 16, had sought refuge with him because of his reputation as an *homme sensible*:

> You will see from all my correspondence that I am always busily searching for misfortune in order to console it; that I have traversed all the state prisons; that I have descended into all the dungeons; that an unfortunate has never shed tears in my presence in vain... My house is the temple of misfortune. It is my religion.[24]

But even if we accept Barmond's description of himself as a well-known humanitarian, how can his melodramatic defense be taken seriously? Descending into all the dungeons to console misfortune is one thing, but harboring an escaped prisoner is quite another. And though Barmond attempted to slide over this distinction by presenting Bonne as just another "unfortunate" whose tears he could not resist, his interest in this particular "unfortunate" was almost certainly primarily political rather than humanitarian. If Barmond was not deeply implicated in the Bonne escape and/or the Maillebois plot itself, he must at least have been known to be extremely sympathetic to the counter-revolutionary cause. And while his defense may have been exactly the kind of justification we might expect to find enunciated in the "age of sensibility," it must still be regarded as little more than an effort to put the best possible face on an inherently bad situation.

Having been taken *en flagrant délit* and having confessed to harboring a fugitive, one would think that Barmond was in an extremely vulnerable position. In addition, another deputy, Barmond's friend Foucault, also admitted sheltering Bonne at *his* home, and he too would seem to have been an easy target for a successful prosecution.[25] The fact that two individuals so obviously guilty of such a

serious crime would be able to emerge unscathed from their predica-
ment is yet another indication of the indulgent if not almost impotent
nature of revolutionary justice in 1789–90. More specifically, as we
will now see, Barmond and Foucault's avoidance of punishment can
be attributed to an implicit mutual amnesty granted to right-wing
defendants in the Maillebois case and left-wing defendants in the
October Days case. As Ferrières predicted on August 8: "The Châtelet's [October Days] denunciation and the affair of the abbé de
Barmond and Bonne-Savardin will perhaps be resolved reciproc-
ally. Those concerned would rather pardon each other than mutually avenge themselves through punishments that would fall upon
the chiefs of their parties."[26]

On June 26, the National Assembly had ordered the release of the
right-wing deputy Lautrec and, undoubtedly thinking about the
indictments being prepared by the Châtelet, it had decreed at that
time that an arrest warrant could not be issued against a deputy by
any court unless the Assembly itself had explicitly ruled that there
were grounds for an accusation.[27] Hence, when Boucher d'Argis
announced on August 7 that the Châtelet was ready to issue warrants against Orléans and Mirabeau, this decree was invoked and it
was decided that the Comité des Rapports would examine the
charges against them. Knowing that this committee would almost
certainly recommend the dismissal of these charges, the leaders of
the extreme right, Cazalès and Maury, contended that the June 26
decree only applied to Lautrec. But this argument was quickly
brushed aside, and even the Monarchiens, who failed to support
Cazalès and Maury, seem to have been resigned to the fact that the
Assembly was not about to allow the Châtelet to arrest the two
patriot deputies.[28]

On September 30, the Comité des Rapports' long-awaited report
was finally presented. Written by Charles Chabroud, a close associate of Barnave, this 116-page document amounted to little more
than a brief for Orléans and Mirabeau, "names that are dear to
citizens and odious to the enemies of the People." For Chabroud, the
notion that the march on Versailles had resulted from an Orleanist
conspiracy was "a dangerous slander." Echoing the claims of
patriotic journalists that the Châtelet and its allies were trying to
engineer a judicial counter-revolution, he charged that the real
conspirators were those who were seeking to undo the work of the
Revolution:

I see only one conspiracy, the one hatched against the Constitution. A league has been formed upon the debris of the old regime in order to try to reverse the new one... This league has instigated and nourished this monstrous proceeding, this, pardon the expression, judicial war, and the pretext for this proceeding cannot hide its secret pretension from our eyes.[29]

In conclusion, Chabroud recommended that the Assembly declare that there were no grounds for the accusation against either Orléans or Mirabeau, a recommendation which was officially accepted two days later by what the *Moniteur* called "a very large majority."[30] Thus, the Châtelet's attempt to "put the Revolution itself on trial" had finally been put to rest.

As for those implicated in the Maillebois plot, their "pardons" were arranged in a somewhat different manner. On August 23, the Assembly declared that there *were* grounds for an accusation against Barmond and ordered that he be kept under house arrest.[31] But while this decision certainly indicates that the deputies were not persuaded by Barmond's dramatic justificatory speech, it by no means implies that they wanted him punished. For the Assembly's unwillingness to dismiss the charges against him meant only that his fate would be left in the hands of the Châtelet, and there could have been few deputies who would not have realized by then that this old royal court was hardly likely to convict him. If the Assembly was really interested in seeing Barmond punished, it would have taken action at that point to relieve the Châtelet of its authority over *lèse-nation* cases. As Robespierre put it:

You certainly realize that you are proposing to entrust an affair which ... could have an important effect on the public interest to a tribunal which has not until now earned public confidence. I know we need a tribunal to pursue *lèse-nation* crimes, but it is better not to have one than to have one which operates in a direction opposite to that of the Revolution. I therefore demand that M. Perrotin dit de Barmond remain under arrest ... and that the National Assembly devote all its energies to organizing a national tribunal.[32]

Once again, however, Robespierre had no support within the Assembly that day. Even Brissot's friend Pétion, generally regarded as the Incorruptible's closest parliamentary ally during this period, was still perfectly willing to turn Barmond over to the Châtelet, a step which, predictably enough, led directly to his release from house arrest on October 8.[33] In thereby formulating a policy in which apparent severity (declaring there were grounds to the accusation against Barmond) masked actual indulgence (sending the case to a court which was bound to be sympathetic to him), the Assembly had returned to a pattern from the previous summer, when its decision to keep Besenval under arrest camouflaged its unwillingness to order his immediate transfer to Paris. In both cases, the need to retain popular confidence appears to have led the Assembly to attempt to project an image of judicial rigor that went counter to its own ideological inclinations. As Barnave explained, the deputies could not order Barmond's release because such obvious complacency "would compromise him and compromise the Assembly itself."[34]

The Assembly's continued reluctance to repudiate the Châtelet also benefited the much-maligned Saint-Priest. Though he was officially listed as a defendant in two hearings held in the Maillebois case, no witnesses who might have said anything against him were called, and on October 7, the Châtelet's Procureur du Roi formally recommended his acquittal. Undoubtedly realizing, however, that endorsing this secret recommendation would only exacerbate patriotic sentiment against them, the judges opted to say nothing at all about Saint-Priest in the Maillebois affair judgment that they rendered the next day, and the minister's case was simply not pursued any further. With Saint-Priest finally resigning in December, his patriotic enemies, who had been primarily interested in his political demise all along, never attempted to revive this case, and he quietly emigrated the following spring.[35]

Thus, as Ferrières had predicted, the most prominent figures in the October Days and Maillebois affairs were the beneficiaries of a process of mutual amnesty, a process in which the Assembly and the Châtelet each exercised what amounted to a "veto" on behalf of their respective clients. Could this mutual amnesty have resulted from the creation of a legislative package in which retaining the Châtelet was linked to dismissal of the charges against Orléans and Mirabeau? According to LaMarck, Lafayette, who had originally provoked the Châtelet probe as a means of attacking his two most formidable political enemies, used his influence behind the scenes to urge approval of the conclusions in the Chabroud report.[36] Perhaps the Parisian General had agreed to this important shift in position in exchange for a commitment on the part of the powerful Duport–Barnave–Lameth faction not to press for immediate repudiation of the Châtelet.[37]

But even if there was no such explicit arrangement between Lafayette and the future Feuillants, the timing of the Châtelet's October 8 Maillebois judgment seems to indicate that we can at least speak about an implicit process of mutual amnesty. For it would hardly seem accidental that the Châtelet's move to quietly drop proceedings against Saint-Priest and to release Barmond occurred only six days after the Assembly's dismissal of the charges against Orléans and Mirabeau, at a moment when patriotic vindictiveness and vigilance could have been expected to be in a state of temporary relaxation. In this connection, the virtual absence of direct criticism of the October 8 judgment in the patriotic press and the apparent absence of popular protest against this judgment seems to indicate that the Châtelet had indeed picked a good moment to issue what would turn out to be its last "veto" against punitive revolutionary justice.[38]

However, the mutual amnesty of October 1790 did not apply to everyone involved in the October Days and Maillebois affairs. As if to signal to both left and right that there were limits to the indulgent tendencies of the new political order, two less prominent figures in the two affairs were not as lucky as the deputies and ministers implicated in them. In the October Days case, the Assembly's quashing of the indictment against Orléans and Mirabeau did not affect the Châtelet's efforts to prosecute some of the subordinate agents in the alleged Orleanist conspiracy of October 1789. Yet, of five individuals for whom arrest warrants were ultimately issued, only one was actually apprehended, a young market-woman named Reine Audu, who had apparently been one of the leading Palais-Royal orators in the days preceding October 5. After spending a year in prison during which the Assembly took no action on a series of petitions presented on her behalf, Audu was finally released under the terms of the general amnesty declared by the Assembly in September 1791.[39] In the mean time, with Maillebois, Saint-Priest, and Barmond all able, in one way or another, to extricate themselves from the perils of revolutionary justice, the hapless Bonne-Savardin was "left alone to pay the damages" in the Maillebois affair.[40] Like Audu, Bonne endured a relatively long prison stay without a final verdict ever being rendered in his case, and he too owed his ultimate release to the general amnesty of September 1791. Upon being released, he immediately joined the *émigrés* at Coblenz.[41]

The mutual amnesty of October 1790 was a typical early French revolutionary response to the ongoing problems posed by conspiratorial challenges to the new regime. As had occurred on so many other occasions during the period examined in this study, the Fayettist impulse to sweep these problems under the rug in hopes they would somehow disappear had once again led to a policy of "ménagements pour les conspirateurs," "ménagements" which, in this case, were even-handedly dispensed to conspirators of both right and left. Thus, the mutual amnesty of October 1790 appears as a suitable successor to the Besenval–Favras judicial compromise of February 1790. In fact, the Maillebois–October Days transaction, which did not, after all, produce a "second Favras," can be seen as a purer illustration of how humanitarian inclinations and strategic considerations dovetailed to create lenient judicial policies. In part, of course, the punitive mildness encompassed in the outcomes of the Maillebois and October Days cases can be attributed to the relative quiescence of the revolutionary crowd from the spring through the autumn of 1790. But beyond this, the ability of the "right Fayettists" and the Monarchiens to keep the October Days probe afloat for as long as they did meant that, with respect to this issue at least, the patriots would remain on the defensive. Hence, when the time came to "cut a deal," the concession offered to the left could consist of *ménagement* for its own people rather than, as in February, the execution of a token aristocrat.

However, if the mutual amnesty of October 1790 was indeed a characteristic example of Fayettist indulgence, the prospect that judicial *ménagements* could help effect a successful working compromise between the Revolution and the Old Regime had dimmed considerably since February. Coming on the heels of Lafayette's show of strength in January and the conciliatory "spirit of February 4," the Besenval–Favras transaction had been accepted by many influential radicals as an honest effort to cope with a difficult political situation. But the Maillebois–October Days transaction failed to evoke a similar reaction. Coming soon after the traumatic repression of the troop mutiny at Nancy and in the wake of the withdrawal of the "left Fayettists" from the municipal governing coalition, the Parisian General's efforts to accommodate the left in October 1790 seem to have done little to disperse the clouds of suspicion that had been gathering around his head since April. Consider, for example, Desmoulins' sarcastic comments of mid-October:

The ingenious patriotism of M. Motier [Lafayette's family name] should be blessed and adored more than ever. See how the purity of his conscience and motives defies your suspicions. Why is he so friendly with the ministers? To unravel their plots, so we can be protected from them! Why does he go to see Leopold's sister [Marie-Antoinette] so often? How ungrateful you are! He wants to serve us better by turning her away from all the dangerous proposals presented to her![42]

Meanwhile, another indication of Lafayette's eroded position was being provided by the erstwhile "left Fayettist" Carra, who reported that an unnamed municipal politician had wisely rejected an offer of free membership in Lafayette's 1789 Club. Acceptance of the offer, this politician feared, would have resulted in his "de-popularization," a reaction which shows that Lafayette's embrace was already being seen as something of a political kiss of death.[43]

Even Brissot came close to targeting his old friend at this time. On the very day after the Assembly exonerated Orléans and Mirabeau, Brissot devoted more than half of his journal to reprinting an attack on Lafayette's 1789 Club by an unnamed deputy, who may well have been Pétion. Included in this attack was the following commentary on the bankruptcy of early revolutionary justice:

Do you know what you [the members of the 1789 Club] have done? Our enemies were at our feet. We were their masters. We were strong enough to be neither unjust nor barbarous towards them, and they were too weak to revolt against the Law of the Victor. But endowed with a false compassion and a cruel pity, you could not let them go fast enough. And in your blindness, you have released tigers.[44]

By implying that the patriots were now no longer strong enough to avoid being "unjust" or "barbarous" (we *were* strong enough, but now there are tigers on the loose), this curious passage seems to point towards the policies of greater judicial severity that would be pursued by Brissot and the Girondins during the "intermediate" revolutionary period of 1791–2.[45] More immediately, however, the passage also points towards an important decision that would be made by the Assembly in late October 1790. Though his colleagues had paid no attention to Robespierre's August 23 attack on the Châtelet, their response was quite different when the Incorruptible rose to make one of his periodic denunciations of this tribunal on October 25. Following a bare minimum of debate and with no stated objection except that of the die-hard abbé Maury, the Assembly suddenly decreed that the Châtelet would no longer be responsible for *lèse-nation* cases.[46] From that point on, counter-revolutionary "tigers" would no longer be able to count on the protection of a royal court.

Yet this repudiation of the Châtelet, which does not seem to have been connected to any new mobilization of district or mass protest, should not be taken as indicative of a significant shift in Assembly judicial policy. Having sustained the Châtelet's *lèse-nation* authority for a full year in the face of often intense grass-roots pressure, the Assembly had finally withdrawn this authority, it appears, only because the Châtelet was now on the verge of expiring by "natural causes." By the end of October 1790, the new judicial system created in August was about to be activated, and preparations were being made for electing judges to the six Parisian tribunals slated to replace the Châtelet. By December 9, a provisional tribunal staffed by ten of the new judges (including Garran, Agier, and Oudart) was already operating, and by January 4, 1791, seals had been placed on all Châtelet records, thereby registering what Seligman called its "act of decease."[47]

Imprisoned, to some extent, by its own timetable for judicial reorganization, the Assembly may well have seen the voiding of the Châtelet's *lèse-nation* powers as a politically attractive move that would have little practical impact. For this step, which, it needs to be stressed, was only taken after the mutual amnesty of early October had been carried out, by no means signified that the Assembly was ready to create the kind of "national" tribunal long demanded by advanced patriots. On the contrary, the October 25 disinvestiture of the Châtelet left France without a *lèse-nation* court until March 5, 1791 when the Assembly established a Haute Cour Nationale Provisoire, a decision which itself seems to have been largely seen as a means of calming an outbreak of popular unrest triggered by the emigration of Louis XVI's two aunts.[48] Moreover, heeding the argument that the Haute Cour should be "protected from the power of popular opinion" (in other words, placed outside Paris), the deputies sought to make it easier for the new tribunal to act indulgently by providing that it would sit at Orléans and be staffed by judges from the Orléans area.[49] As a result, the Haute Cour Provisoire compiled a record of leniency in its handling of political justice essentially equivalent to that of the Châtelet. Furthermore, the "permanent" Haute Cour (also placed in Orléans), which succeeded it in September 1791 and which remained in place until the fall of the Monarchy, operated in a remarkably similar manner. In short, if early revolutionary political justice policies can be likened to the sweeping of problems under the proverbial rug, then the Haute Cour Provisoire of 1791 and the Haute Cour of 1791–2 were both little more than two rugs hastily patched together to replace a threadbare and worn-out Châtelet.[50]

Yet, though Assembly repudiation of the Châtelet did not significantly alter this court's indulgent policies, the decree of October 25 can still be taken as an important symbolic act which brings to a close the period examined in this work. For the Châtelet's career as the French Revolution's first "revolutionary tribunal" largely reflects the political vicissitudes of 1789–90. Thus, its original designation as *lèse-nation* tribunal resulted from Lafayette's strengthened position after the October Days. With revolutionary momentum temporarily halted through the Hero of Two Worlds' ability to "co-opt" the march to Versailles, the Châtelet's investiture was part of the general swing to the right that emerged in the final months of 1789. This conservative trend continued through the early months of 1790 as Lafayette further consolidated his authority through his capacity to control the popular unrest which emerged shortly after the beginning of the new year. And the Châtelet was able to profit from this development, with early 1790 being the period of its greatest influence and acceptance, the period in which it worked most smoothly with the "left Fayettists" of the Comité des Recherches and the period in which it even garnered some hesitant praise from the radical press.

But impelled perhaps by a kind of political hubris, the judges of the Châtelet tried to push the conservative reaction of late 1789 and early 1790 too far when they attempted to "faire le procès à la Révolution" in the spring of 1790, a move which quickly wiped out any credibility they may have accumulated. This effort to put the Revolution itself on trial was, moreover, the key factor in prompting the withdrawal of the "left Fayettists" from the Fayettist coalition, a withdrawal which, together with Lafayette's support of the military establishment and the royal government in various confrontations during the summer of 1790, was instrumental in launching the Parisian General down the slippery slope of "de-popularization." Lafayette appears to have sought to halt this slide by trying to reach a new accommodation with his critics on the left in October 1790, and his acquiescence in the disinvestiture of the Châtelet can be attributed to a willingness to jettison a thoroughly discredited ally in the interest of such an accommodation. But the gap between La-fayette and the advanced patriots was, by this point, too wide to be bridged, and the impending disasters of Saint-Cloud, Varennes, and the Champ-de-Mars would soon turn this gap into a chasm.

Thus, while devoid of any immediate impact on judicial policies, the Châtelet's disinvestiture marked an important stage in the disin-tegration of the broad-based Fayettist coalition that had adminis-tered and managed political justice during the first year of the Revolution. While the indulgent policies implemented during this first year would continue for almost two more years, the legitimacy of these policies would be fatally compromised by the breakup of a coalition that, for a brief period of time, appeared capable of main-taining a certain degree of political viability. With the "de-popu-larization" and eventual political ruin of the leader who seemed to have had the best chance of securing wide acceptance of the lenient policies described in this study, these policies themselves would eventually be cast aside in the face of overwhelming pressures and demands for a different kind of justice.

Conclusion

Whereas many nineteenth- and early twentieth-century French revolutionary historians tended to make a sharp distinction between
the liberal revolution of 1789 and the Jacobin Revolution of 1793–4,[1]
the trend among recent generations of revolutionary scholars has
been to view the Revolution as a self-contained process in which the
developments of the later stages can be seen as being foreshadowed
in the earlier or even pre-revolutionary stages. In recent years, this
trend has been especially evident in the assertion of many influential
revisionist scholars that the Jacobin dictatorship of 1793–4 and the
Terror that accompanied it were rooted in pre-revolutionary "Rousseauian" ideology. For if the events of 1793–4 reflected a mature
realization of pre-revolutionary ideology, then the events of the
Revolution's earlier stages would logically fall into place as reflecting
a less mature realization of the same ideology. As François Furet has
written: "From the meeting of the Estates General to the dictatorship of the Committee of Public Safety, the same dynamic was at
work; it was fully developed, though not yet supreme, as early as
1789." Thus, for Furet:

There is no difference in kind between Marat in 1789 and Marat in 1793.
Nor were the murders of Foulon and Berthier fundamentally different from
the massacres of September 1792, any more than Mirabeau's aborted trial
after the October Days of 1789 was different from the sentencing of the
Dantonists in the spring of 1794.[2]

But the eagerness to find prefigurations of the Terror in the events
of 1789 has not been confined to revisionists like Furet. For the same
inclination can also be found among some of the modern leaders of
the "classical" school. Georges Lefebvre, for example, endorsed
Clemenceau's aphorism that "the Revolution is a bloc" and discussed the events of July 1789 as "the first manifestations of the

221

Terror." For Lefebvre, the National Assembly's Comité des Recherches was "the prototype of the famous Committee of General
Security" while the Paris Comité des Recherches was "the prototype
of the local revolutionary surveillance committees." And in a similar
vein, Albert Soboul wrote that the Assembly's Comité was "a real
forerunner of the Committee of Public Safety," while the Paris
Comité "anticipated the Revolutionary Committees of
Surveillance."[3]

The tendency for recent generations of scholars to stress the
similarities and causal links between the earlier and later stages of a
revolutionary "process" may be rooted, to at least some degree, in
the unfolding of a seemingly endless procession of modern revolutions with dynamics which appear analogous to those of the Great
French Revolution itself. Or to put it another way, the cumulative
impact of the horrors of the twentieth century may have led to an
overwhelming though often unconscious inclination to highlight
those aspects of the early French Revolution which could help shed
some light on the origins of events closer to home. This study,
however, has attempted to demonstrate some of the pitfalls of this
type of analysis. For some of the curious statements that have just
been cited can perhaps only be explained by positing a fierce deter-
mination to squeeze the unique characteristics of historical events
into a preconceived historiographical scheme – the toothless and
lackadaisical Assembly Comité des Recherches, which almost
always recommended a suspect's release, as the "prototype" or
"forerunner" of the Great Committees of 1793–4, or, even more
revealingly, as the "first organ of a revolutionary police state"?[4] The
only marginally more vigilant Paris Comité, which operated within
the framework of a judicial system explicitly designed to exonerate
its potential victims, as the "prototype" or "anticipation" of the
deadly surveillance committees of the year II? The July 1789 murder
of two royal officials literally torn from the protective grasp of
shocked municipal officials as "fundamentally no different" from
twelve hundred murders carried out amidst the silence and perhaps
even the encouragement of the authorities? And most curious of all,
the Châtelet's pursuit of Orléans and Mirabeau, which did not even
result in an arrest, as "fundamentally no different" from the kan-
garoo court condemnations of the Dantonists? While some hints and
clues of what was to come can certainly be found in the events of

1789–90, an obsessive effort to track down and sniff out such hints and clues everywhere seems to have led, paradoxically enough, to a kind of "historiographical Jacobinism."

Through a detailed examination of a group of largely forgotten judicial affairs of 1789–90, this study has presented a very different perspective on revolutionary justice during the first year of the Revolution, one that stresses the great differences between 1789–90 and 1793–4. It is true that investigatory committees and political police agencies were created in 1789, and it is true that political opponents were judicially pursued. However, those responsible for administering and dispensing revolutionary justice in 1789–90 acted with a degree of self-restraint and within a context of built-in limitations upon their authority that together operated to insure lenient treatment for the early enemies of the Revolution. Thus, we have seen that only one counter-revolutionary conspirator was executed during the entire period covered by this study, while numerous other "enemies of the People" were able to avoid severe punishment through a wide variety of formal and informal mechanisms.

Instead of concentrating on uncovering links between the events of 1789–90 and those of the near future, this study has focused on the extent to which the judicial policies of 1789–90 were a logical outgrowth of earlier developments. Thus, the indulgent political justice of the first year of the Revolution has been presented as a product of the liberal and humanitarian ideological assumptions of the pre-revolutionary judicial reform movement, and, at the same time, as a continuation of the generally non-punitive political justice that marked the later years of the Old Regime itself. On the other hand, the lenient judicial policies of 1789–90 have also been presented as resulting from the efforts of the Fayettist authorities to attract moderate and conservative support and thereby to maintain as wide a definition of the political community as possible. However, the inclination to pursue a strategy of inclusion and compromise might itself be viewed as a product of the liberal and tolerant currents present in late eighteenth-century thought. Thus, it has been suggested that the willingness of the Fayettist regime to make use of cover-ups, judicial complacency, and other "corrupt" arrangements can be seen as a reflection of its commitment to ideological assumptions which were the antithesis of the moralistic assumptions that produced the purges and purification rituals of the year II.

In focusing on the liberal and indulgent nature of political justice in 1789–90 and in thereby turning away from the recent tendency to stress the extent to which this period can be seen as an embryonic representation of what was to come, am I suggesting that the events of 1793–4 could perhaps have been avoided? While such a question should be approached very gingerly and with a great deal of trepidation, this study has indeed placed an unusually heavy emphasis on the Fayettist regime's ability to temporarily halt revolutionary momentum in the post-October Days period. Moreover, in contrast to the contention of both Lefebvre and Furet that the Revolution did not have a workable government until the year II, this study has insisted that Lafayette was able to maintain a viable governing coalition, at least with respect to the administering of political justice, until the spring of 1790.[5] With the Besenval–Favras judicial compromise attracting a wide range of support from across the political spectrum, the early months of 1790 seem to have been a period in which the Parisian General may actually have had a decent chance to solve the fundamental problem of stopping the Revolution.

But was this apparent chance really nothing more than a mirage? We have seen that the decomposition of the Fayettist coalition was triggered by a "right Fayettist" attempt "to put the Revolution itself on trial," a move that impelled the "left Fayettists" to withdraw from the coalition for purposes of protecting their own patriotic credentials. Although such a rendering of historical reality certainly implies the possibility of alternative choices and alternative outcomes, might it be necessary to search for a deeper explanation of Fayettist failure? Why did the "right Fayettists" of the Châtelet try to push the post-October Days conservative reaction further than it could realistically have been pushed? Could they have been acting out a "counter-revolutionary dynamic" that paralleled and interacted with the more familiar "revolutionary dynamic"?[6] And even if the Châtelet had been less aggressive, could the "left Fayettists" of the Comité des Recherches have continued to maintain a precarious balance between their governmental responsibilities and their radical pretensions, between their humanitarian scruples and their efforts to present themselves as popular spokesmen? Or might some other precipitating event have eventually forced them out of the governing coalition? Were there, that is, factors inherent in the revolutionary process itself that would, sooner or later, have shattered an intrinsically unstable Fayettist coalition? And might these same factors have insured the failure of other compromise attempts to halt revolutionary momentum?

Questions like these cannot, of course, be answered within the scope of this study, if indeed such questions can ever really find a satisfactory "answer." However, even if the revolutionary dynamic was, in some sense, uncontrollable, this study has indicated that some of the recent efforts to search for the roots of this "uncontrollability" in the ideological assumptions of the early revolutionary authorities may be misdirected. It was not, that is, some "Rousseauian" urge towards "unanimity," "exclusion," or "undivided power" that was primarily responsible for those previews of the judicial practices of the year II that can be detected in the handling of political justice during 1789–90.[7] Or to put it another way, it was not some form of "incipient Jacobinism" lurking in their minds that led the revolutionary authorities of 1789–90 to depart occasionally from the indulgent and non-vigilant practices that generally characterized their treatment of the enemies of the Revolution. Instead, these occasional departures were largely prompted by what was seen as a need to respond to popular pressure and to retain popular confidence. As we have seen throughout this study, it was the knowledge that "the People" wanted its enemies to be punished that gave political viability to demands for judicial severity that could otherwise have been more easily ignored. Moreover, it was the increasing influence and pressure of the popular movement that made these demands more and more compelling as the Revolution proceeded.

Consequently, rather than focusing exclusively on the ideology of the revolutionary elite, efforts to understand the revolutionary dynamic should perhaps be directed towards exploring the interaction between one particular aspect of Rousseauian ideology and the development of the popular movement itself. While this study has found the early revolutionary authorities to have been far more liberal and tolerant than some recent historians have suggested, these men were also influenced, to at least some degree, by the Rousseauian emphasis on popular sovereignty. Although they certainly resisted the judicial and constitutional implications of a full commitment to democratic theory, their obsessive concern with retaining popular confidence and the very respect they accorded popular demands even while circumventing them constituted an

implicit acceptance of the notion that "the People" had indeed
become the only viable source of revolutionary legitimacy.[8] But how
did this partial acceptance of the ideas of popular sovereignty and
popular legitimacy arise and develop in the pre-revolutionary period
and how did it expand during the course of the Revolution itself?
And how might the development and expansion of these ideas have
facilitated the creation and growth of the popular movement? Cre-
ative investigation of these questions might help us reach a better
understanding of the precise way in which the revolutionary process
unfolded.

In this study, however, my primary concern, once again, has not
been to present the first year of the Revolution in terms of what was
to come later. As interesting and important as such an endeavor
might be, it is also subject to an unavoidable tendency to over-
emphasize those glimpses of future revolutionary events which may
be detected and, by the same token, to under-emphasize important
aspects of historical reality which were soon destined to fade out.
Instead, my primary aim has been to reconstruct a significant portion of historical reality that has been generally ignored by historians
whose vision has been focused on the events of the year II, to present
the political justice of 1789–90 "as it really was" rather than as if it
were a mere rehearsal for what was to come. In the first year of the
French Revolution, the revolutionary authorities made a genuine
effort to treat their political opponents in a relatively lenient and
even humane manner. Despite the blood and inhumanity that was to
follow, let it at least be remembered that this effort was made.

Notes

INTRODUCTION

1 M. Hillerin, preface to M. Pagano, *Considérations sur la procédure criminelle*, (Strasbourg, 1789), i, vii; A. Desjardins, *Les Cahiers des Etats-Généraux et la législation criminelle*, (Paris, 1883), xxviii; Boucher d'Argis, *Observations sur les lois criminelles*, (Amsterdam, 1781), 3; and *Arrêt de la Cour de Parlement*, (Paris, 1786), BN F 2376(713), 5.

2 J. V. Delacroix, *Réflexions philosophiques sur l'origine de la civilisation*, (Amsterdam, 1778), 5.

3 See J. Kaufmann, "The Critique of Criminal Justice in Late Eighteenth Century France: A Study of the Changing Social Ethics of Crime and Punishment," unpublished Ph.D. dissertation, Harvard University, 1976, esp. vii, xvii, 246; and Foucault, *Discipline and Punish*, 82. For examples of the more traditional approach to the judicial reform movement, see S. McCloy, *The Humanitarian Movement in Eighteenth-Century France*, (Lexington, Ky., 1957), 172–209; and M. Maestro, *Voltaire and Beccaria as Reformers of Criminal Law*, (New York, 1942), esp. 125–7. For a more recent study along the same lines, see G. Wright, *Between the Guillotine and Liberty*, (New York, 1983), 3–23.

4 See, for example, M. Servin, *De la législation criminelle*, (Basle, 1782), 37–42; M. Landreau de Maine-au-Picq, *Législation philosophique, politique et morale*, (Geneva, 1787), II: 378–90; P. L. Lacretelle, *Discours sur le préjugé des peines infamantes*, (Paris, 1784), 362–5; and Boucher d'Argis, *Observations*, 107–18.

5 Kaufmann, "Critique of Justice," 249–50, 253. For Delacroix's discussion of domestic theft, see *Observations sur la société*, (Paris, 1787), I: 178–90.

6 See, for example, J. P. Brissot, "Les moyens d'adoucir la rigueur des lois pénales en France," as found in *Les moyens d'adoucir la rigueur des lois pénales en France sans nuire à la sûreté publique*, (Châlons-sur-Marne, 1781), i; C. M. Dupaty, *Lettres sur la procédure criminelle de la France, dans lesquelles on montre sa conformité avec celle de l'Inquisition*, (n.p., 1788); M. Desgranges, *Essais sur le droit et le besoin d'être défendu quand on est accusé*, (Paris, 1785), 90; and Landreau de Maine-au-Piq, *Législation philosophique*, II: 283–4.

227

7 Kaufmann, "Critique of Justice," 192. The statements cited here are taken from Servin, *Législation criminelle*, 349; and Lacretelle, *Discours*, 295.

8 See "The Cunning of Imagery: Rhetoric and Ideology in Cesare Beccaria's Treatise 'On Crimes and Punishments'," *Begetting Images: Studies in the Art and Science of Symbol Production*, eds. M. Campbell and M. Rollins, (New York, 1989), 121–2. (For demands for more rapid judicial procedures, see Beccaria, *Traité des délits et des peines*, tr. A. Morellet, [Lausanne, 1766], 147–52; Brissot, "Les moyens," 98–100; Servin, *Législation criminelle*, 350–1; and J. M. Servan, *Discours sur l'administration de la justice criminelle*, [Geneva, 1767], 31.)

9 See Kaufmann's remarks on the reformers' "vision of an all-encompassing, inter-connected, controlling society," "Critique of Justice," 246.

10 See P. Gay, *The Enlightenment*, (London, 1973), II: 428.

11 J. P. Brissot, *Le sang innocent vengé*, (Paris, 1781), 2–3. For a contemporary reference to Brissot's prominence in the pre-revolutionary judicial reform movement, see Lacretelle, *Discours*, 338–40.

12 J. P. Brissot, *Théorie des lois criminelles*, (Paris, 1836), I: 1–2.

13 J. E. Bernardi, "Les moyens d'adoucir les lois pénales en France," v–vi. This essay and Brissot's essay with the same title were published together with separate pagination in the volume cited in note 6 above. The two essays shared honors in a competition sponsored by the Châlons Academy.

14 See S. Maza, "Le Tribunal de la nation: Les mémoires judiciaires et l'opinion publique à la fin de l'ancien régime," *Annales ESC*, (January–February 1987): 82. While Maza's comment specifically refers to the style used by many defense attorneys in published briefs, it could also easily be applied to the style of most judicial reformers. In fact, the main figure she discusses, Pierre-Louis Lacretelle, was a noted reformer as well as defense attorney. He was also, as we will see, a member, along with Brissot, of the Paris Comité des Recherches in 1789–90. (For other examples of judicial reformers presenting themselves as "sensitive souls," see Boucher d'Argis, *Observations*, 162; Servan, *Discours*, 149–50; Desgranges, *Essais*, 65; and C. E. Pastoret, *Des lois pénales*, [Paris, 1790], I: 7–8.)

15 N. Elias, *The Civilizing Process*, tr. E. Jephcott, (New York, 1978), 80.

16 Brissot, *Théorie*, I: 296. Montesquieu's maxim is from Book XII of *De l'esprit des lois*, as cited by Brissot, *Théorie*, I: 286.

17 Brissot, "Les moyens," 56. While the *Théorie des lois criminelles* was originally published in Berlin, it was certainly not accidental that this less anti-monarchical version of the passage just cited appeared in a work published within France itself. (For a close comparison of "Les moyens" with *Théorie*, see L. Loft, *"La théorie des lois criminelles*: Brissot and Legal Reform," *Australian Journal of French Studies* 26 [1989]: 242–59.)

18 See E. Ellery, *Brissot de Warville*, (Boston, 1915), 268–9, 421–2.

19 See *Théorie*, I: 153, 282, 299. He was much less generous to regicides and other traitors in "Les moyens," 55.

20 See *Théorie*, I: 307, 312.

21 G. Cavallaro, *J. P. Brissot Criminalista, al Tramonto dell' Ancien Régime*, (Ferrara, 1981), 148–9.

22 Bernardi, "Les moyens," 77–8; J. H. Roussel de la Bérardière, *Dissertation sur la composition des lois criminelles*, (Leyden, 1775), 101; and P. Chaussard, *Théorie des lois criminelles*, (Auxerre, 1789), 33. Also see Servin, *Législation criminelle*, 122; B. Carrard, *De la jurisprudence criminelle*, (Geneva, 1785), I: 286; and G. H. Mirabeau, *Essai sur le despotisme*, (London, 1775), 67–8.

23 See Montesquieu, *De l'esprit des lois*, (Paris, 1979), II: 329–40; and Voltaire, "Prix de la justice et de l'humanité," *Oeuvres complètes*, (Deux-Ponts, 1792), XXXIX: 275–322.

24 C. E. Valazé, *Lois pénales*, (Alençon, 1784), 35.

25 See, for example, F. Guizot, *De la peine de mort en matière politique*, (Paris, 1822), esp. 37–45.

26 *Observations*, II: 84. Also see Bernardi, "Les moyens," 79; Servin, *Législation criminelle*, 241–4; Carrard, *Jurisprudence criminelle*, I: 271–2; and Roussel de la Bérardière, *Dissertation*, 3–9.

27 See, for example, Marat's eloquent defense of individual political rights, originally composed in 1778, in *Plan de législation criminelle*, (Paris, 1790), 43–4; and Robespierre's Lockean-style critique of *lettres de cachet* in *Mémoire pour le sieur L. M. H. Dupond*, (Arras, 1789), 76–7.

28 For the exile of eighteenth-century ministers, see Doyle, *Origins*, 57; S. L. Kaplan, *The Famine Plot Persuasion in Eighteenth Century France*, (Philadelphia, 1982), 14–15, 60, 69; and *Mémoires authentiques du Maréchal de Richelieu*, (Paris, 1918), 145–6. For the more rigorous treatment of ministers in the past, see W. Church, *Richelieu and Reason of State*, (Princeton, 1972), 179–82, 234–65, 328–33.

29 This was the execution of General Lally-Tolendal, who lost the battle of Pondichéry in India in 1761. (See P. Perrod, *L'Affaire Lally-Tolendal: Une erreur judiciaire au XVIIIe siècle*, [Paris, 1972].)

30 For some seventeenth-century examples of executions and banishments of dissident intellectuals, see J. S. Spink, *French Free-Thought from Gassendi to Voltaire*, (London, 1960), 28–31, 42–5. For Brissot's imprisonment in the Bastille, see R. Darnton, "The Grub Street Style of Revolution: J. P. Brissot, Police Spy," *Journal of Modern History* 40 (1968): 319.

31 Historians who emphasize greater leniency include G. Aubry, "La Juridiction criminelle du Châtelet de Paris sous le règne de Louis XVI," Thèse pour le doctorat en droit (unpublished), Université de Paris, 1971, esp. 204; Langbein, *Torture and the Law of Proof*, 39; and D. L. Rader, "Beccarian Reform in France," *Proceedings of the Sixth Annual*

Meeting of the Western Society for French History (1979): 172–7. Those who question the argument for greater leniency include P. Petrovich, "Recherches sur la criminalité à Paris dans la seconde moitié du XVIIIe siècle," *Crime et criminalité en France: 17e–18e siècles*, ed. A. Abbiateci and F. Billacois, (Paris, 1971); A. Farge, *Délinquance et criminalité: Le vol d'aliments à Paris au XVIIIe siècle*, (Paris, 1974); and Kaufmann, "Critique of Justice," 215–42.

32　Chaussard, *Théorie*, 33–4.

33　Brissot, "Les moyens," 54–6; and Robespierre, *Oeuvres*, I: 41. For other references to such a "softening of manners," see Voltaire, "Prix de la justice," *Oeuvres*, XXXIX: 303; *Mémoires et journal inédit du Marquis d'Argenson*, (Paris, 1858), V: 307; and Servin, *Législation criminelle*, 369. Also see J. Carey, *Judicial Reform in France Before the Revolution of 1789*, (Cambridge, Mass., 1981), 63–4.

34　Lacretelle, *Discours*, 195.

35　*APL*, April 3, 1790 (supplement), 2.

36　*Dénonciation à la nation et à l'opinion publique de trois décrets de l'Assemblée Nationale*, (Paris, 1790), 18. The matter being debated here was the arrest of the abbé de Barmond, which will be discussed in chapter 10.

37　*AP*, VIII: 265.

38　For a recent effort to delineate the "radicalizing" and "self-accelerating" character of the Revolution's "political logic," see F. Fehér, *The Frozen Revolution: An Essay on Jacobinism*, (Cambridge, 1987), 15–22.

39　See Furet, *Interpreting the French Revolution*, 46–9.

40　See C. Lucas, "The Crowd and Politics," *The French Revolution and the Creation of Modern Political Culture: The Political Culture of the French Revolution*, ed. C. Lucas, (Oxford, 1987), 276.

41　Instead of resuming an old debate between "opportunism" and "bloodthirstyness," it might be more fruitful to see the abandonment of the pre-revolutionary "common faith" by figures like Robespierre and Marat as being rooted in a commitment to democratic ideology, a commitment which ultimately took priority over loyalty to humanitarian ideals. Along these lines, Edna Lemay sees Robespierre's consistent defense of what he perceived to be the interests of "the People," (i.e., "les pauvres") as the key to what is sometimes thought of as his inconsistency in the Constituent Assembly. Thus, Robespierre could immediately assume a harsh prosecutorial stance in order to demand the swift punishment of the People's enemies and, at the same time, insist that ordinary crimes, which were generally committed by the poor, should be treated more leniently. Moreover, as it was primarily the poor who normally faced the death penalty, he could oppose capital punishment in debates on a future Criminal Code and, at the same time, issue passionate calls for the vigorous pursuit of counter-revolutionary conspirators. (See Lemay, "Une Voix dissonante à l'Assemblée Consti-tuante: Le prosélytisme de Robespierre," *AHRF* 53 [1981]: 390–404.)

42 See *Interpreting the French Revolution*, 44–6.

43 See Bernardi, "Les moyens," 176–7; Delacroix, *Observations*, II: 30–51; Landreau de Maine-au-Piq, *Législation philosophique*, II: 283–99, 313–14; Carrard, *Jurisprudence criminelle*, I: 211; and A. F. Prost de Royer, *Diction-naire de jurisprudence et des arrêts*, (Lyon, 1782), II: 211–12.

44 *Théorie* II: 194, 196. Also see the comment of Brissot's future Comité des Recherches colleague Lacretelle: "Justice has nothing to hide, only crime needs secrecy." (As cited by Kaufmann, "Critique of Justice," 195.)

45 See Furet, *Interpreting the French Revolution*, 48; and L. Hunt, *Politics, Culture, and Class in the French Revolution*, (Berkeley, 1984), 43–6.

46 See LaCroix, I: 515–17; and L. Gottschalk and M. Maddox, *Lafayette in the French Revolution: Through the October Days*, (Chicago, 1969), 319–20.

47 Brissot, *Correspondance et papiers*, (Paris, 1912), 240–1; and *PF*, Novem-ber 21, 1789, 3.

48 See, for example, Brissot, *Lettres à M. le Chevalier de Panges* (Paris, 1790), 13–14.

49 Bernardi, "Les moyens," 172. Also see Brissot, *Théorie*, I: 178; Servin, *Législation criminelle*, 366–9; Carrard, *Jurisprudence criminelle*, II: 190–2; and Beccaria, *Traité*, 60.

50 P. L. Agier, *Compte-rendu à l'Assemblée des Représentants de la Commune*, (Paris, 1789), 5.

51 The assertion that the main impetus for judicial severity and punish-ment at the beginning of the Revolution came from an unenlightened populace largely untouched by the liberal and humanitarian currents of eighteenth-century thought may perhaps sound dangerously similar to the claims of generations of anti-revolutionary and anti-democratic historians that a savage, uncivilized, and scarcely human "mob" or *canaille* was responsible for all revolutionary horrors and atrocities. In opposing such a view, defenders of the People often cite Babeuf's maxim that "our masters have made us as cruel as them and have reaped what they have sown." However, in apparent response to François Furet's call for a de-politicization of the study of the Revolution, Michel Vovelle has recently suggested that the time has come to go beyond the in-stinctive defensiveness reflected in Babeuf's maxim. "Today," writes Vovelle, "we no longer have to search for such justificatory arguments." Thus, it may now be possible to recognize and stress the violence and even the cruelty of the People without being accused of slandering them. Furthermore, although the "uncivilized" character of various social and racial under-classes is often cited as a reason for the need to maintain an existing *status quo*, such an argument is logically defective. One can acknowledge the People's brutality and, at the same time, recognize the validity of their grievances and rights. (See M. Vovelle, *La*

Mentalité révolutionnaire, [Paris, 1985], 83–4; and Furet, *Interpreting the French Revolution*, 9–13.)

1 REVOLUTIONARY JUSTICE IN 1789–1790

1 *Lèse-nation* (literally harming or endangering the nation) was the post-1789 equivalent of *lèse-majesté*. (See G. Kelly, "From *lèse-majesté* to *lèse-nation*: Treason in Eighteenth-century France," *Journal of the History of Ideas* 42 [1981]: 268–86.)

2 Though it has been impossible to determine to what degree of detail the future operations of this system were consciously worked out in advance by Lafayette and his allies, there can be little doubt that those involved were quite capable of making the political calculations necessary to design at least the broad outlines of the "roles," "functions," and "assignments" to be described shortly.

3 Lefebvre, *The French Revolution From Its Origins to 1793*, tr. E. Evanson, (London, 1962), 136.

4 For a more complete analysis of Lafayette and the October Days, see chapter 4.

5 See LaCroix, II: 366; and *Moniteur*, October 20–22, 1789, 79.

6 For recent examples, see E. Taillemite, *La Fayette*, (Paris, 1989), esp. 8, and 525–7; and G. Chaussinard-Nogaret, *Mirabeau*, (Paris, 1984), 226–7. For an antidote to the usual emphasis on Lafayette's political naiveté, see his correspondence with Latour-Maubourg, in which he appears, as early as March 1789, as the self-conscious leader of a reasonably well-defined political network (referred to as "our friends," "our society," or, when speaking of Assembly matters, "our deputies"), issuing instructions and directives to a top lieutenant. (AN F7 4767; partially reprinted in L. Mortimer-Ternaux, *Histoire de la Terreur*, [Paris, 1862], I: 419–34; and *Le Curieux* I [1884]: 91–6, 123–6.)

7 Though the relationship is obviously not iron-clad, a tendency for those who operate according to a tolerant and non-punitive ideology to employ inclusive and conciliatory strategies can, as already indicated, at least be postulated.

8 See *RdP*, February 13–20, 1790, 22.

9 Although Lacretelle, as we will see, barely participated in the Comité's activities, he was never replaced. The other five members resigned together on December 18, 1790. (See LaCroix, ser. 2, I: 566–7.) For Brissot's contention that frequent changes in the national Comité's personnel were destroying its effectiveness, see *PF*, November 23, 1789, 3. For the discrediting of the Assemblée des Représentants, see LaCroix, IV: I–XV, and V: XVII–XIX.

10 LaCroix, II: 366, and I: 190; and *RdP*, November 7–14, 1789, 8–9.

11 For exceptions to this general rule, see *Expédition du général Lameth au*

couvent des Annonciades célestes, (n.p., n.d.); *J. P. Brissot à Stanislas Clermont,* (Paris, 1790), 3; and AN D XXIX bis, 10, 110, piece 11.

12 See F. de Pange, "Réflexions sur la délation et sur le comité des recherches," in *Oeuvres,* (Paris, 1832), 55–6, 62; S. Clermont-Tonnerre, *Oeuvres,* (Paris, an III), III: 315, 342–8; J. Necker, *Sur l'administration de M. Necker,* (Amsterdam, 1791), 91; R. de Sèze, *Plaidoyer pour le Baron de Besenval,* (Paris, 1790), 109; *Gazette de Paris,* January 11, 1790, 2; and *RdP,* November 7–14, 1789, 10–11.

13 *Biographie Universelle,* ed. Michaud, (Paris, 1854), xv: 603; and M. Lescure, Introduction to *Mémoires de Brissot,* (Paris, 1876), XLVIII. Also see G. Bord, *La Conspiration révolutionnaire,* (Paris, 1909), 387. Simon Schama has recently revived and modernized this line of thinking by referring to the national Comité des Recherches as "the first organ of a revolutionary police state." (*Citizens,* 448.) However, as Schama specifically attributes the power of arrest to this committee, he may have confused the national committee with the municipal one. In any event, this kind of hyperbolic and apocalyptic language is of little use in helping us reach an understanding of anything that either of these two committees actually did.

14 See G. Kates, *The Cercle Social, the Girondins, and the French Revolution,* (Princeton, 1985), 5–6, 36, 44.

15 For the former view, see A. de Lamartine, *Histoire des Girondins,* (Paris, 1871), III: 472; and M. J. Sydenham, *The Girondins,* (London, 1961), 210. For the latter, see Ellery, *Brissot,* 412; and T. Di Padova, "The Girondins and the Question of Revolutionary Government," *French Historical Studies* 9 (1976): 432–50.

16 See *Mémoires de J. P. Brissot,* ed. C. Perroud, (Paris, n.d.), II: 53–6, 76–8, 137; Brissot, *Correspondance et papiers,* 126, 169, 192; C. Perroud, "La société française des Amis des Noirs," *Révolution française* 69 (1916): 122–47; L. Gottschalk, *Lafayette Between the American and the French Revolution,* (Chicago, 1950), 247–8, 293–4, 370–1, 384–5; R. Darnton, *Mesmerism and the End of the Enlightenment in France,* (Cambridge, Mass., 1968), 78–80; L. A. Whaley, "The Emergence of the Brissotins During the French Revolution," unpublished D.Phil. dissertation, University of York, 1988, 61–70; and AN 446 AP 21 (Brissot Papers), letter of April 8, 1787, where Brissot thanks Lafayette for helping to subsidize the publication of *De la France et des Etats-unis.*

17 AN 446 AP 21, letter of April 30, 1787. For Brissot's claim that he had always attempted to push Lafayette "to elevate himself to the height of his destiny," see *PF,* February 2, 1792, 132.

18 *Examen critique des voyages dans l'Amérique septentrionale de M. le Marquis de Chatellux,* (London, 1786), 135. Also see Brissot and E. Clavière, *De la France et des Etats-unis,* (London, 1788), 188, where Lafayette is characterized as a "sensitive soul" who deserves "the homage of that peaceful

philosophy which ... favors liberty and the progress of light and reason."

19 See Gottschalk, *Lafayette Between the Revolutions*, 437.

20 AN w 292, as printed in A. Mathiez, "Brissot électeur de Lafayette," *Annales révolutionnaires* 14 (1922): 421.

21 Gottschalk and Maddox, *Lafayette: Through the October Days*, 111. A hint of dissatisfaction with Brissot's role in the election can be found in a letter to Lafayette from Monarchien leader and Necker friend Clermont-Tonnerre. (See C. DuBus, *Stanislas Clermont-Tonnerre et l'échec de la révolution monarchique*, [Paris, 1931], 107–8.) For the standard account of the spontaneous election of "the illustrious defender of the Liberty of the New World," see *PV*, 1: 422–3, 459–60.

22 See Lefebvre, *The French Revolution*, 137; and *PF*, September 1, 1789, 3. Also see *PF*, July 28, 1789, 4; August 10, 1789, 3; September 23, 1789, 2; and October 6, 1789, 2.

23 See *Mémoires, correspondance, et manuscrits du général Lafayette*, (Paris, 1837), II: 178–9, 294–5; and LaCroix, 1: 515–17. Also see M. Maestro, "Lafayette as a Reformer of Penal Laws," *Journal of the History of Ideas* 39 (1978): 503–10.

24 Brissot, *Discours prononcé au district des Filles-Saint-Thomas, le 21 juillet 1789*, (n.p., n.d.), 8; and Lafayette, *Mémoires*, II: 439.

25 In the immediate aftermath of the October Days, for example, Brissot was chosen to write and present an important address welcoming the National Assembly to Paris. (See LaCroix, 1: 245–8, 254–5.)

26 *PF*, February 2, 1792, 132.

27 See Darnton, "The Grub Street Style of Revolution," 326–7.

28 See, for example, "Liste des amis du peuple qui méritent de fixer le choix des Electeurs de Paris," as reprinted in C. Chassin, *Les Elections et les cahiers de Paris en 1789*, (Paris, 1888), II: 312–13. On this pre-election circular, Brissot is listed as the third (after Condorcet and Target and ahead of Sieyès) of twenty-one hardly obscure names and is described as being "long known for the energy with which he has defended the People and free Constitutions." Brissot, of course, did not win election to the Estates-General, and instead turned to the municipality as the next most attractive theatre of political operations.

29 *Biographie Universelle*, xv: 603. For general information on Garran, see *ibid.*, xv: 602–4; *Nouvelle biographie générale*, (Paris, 1862), xix: 536–8; and *Dictionnaire de biographie française*, (Paris, 1933), xviii: 548–50.

30 See "Papiers de Garran de Coulon (1756–1788)," *Revue d'archéologie poitevine* 3 (1900): 315–18. Garran did publish some technical articles in legal compendiums, but these give little indication of his pre-revolutionary views on criminal justice or on politics in general. Even an article on "Dénonciation" is purely descriptive. (See *Répertoire universel et raisonné de jurisprudence*, ed. Guyot, [Paris, 1784–5], v: 432.)

31 See "Les Grandes Journées de juin et de juillet 1789, d'après le 'journal'

inédit de Creuzé-Latouche," *Revue des questions historiques* (1935): 264; and Chassin, *Les Elections*, II: 357, III: 255.

32 Garran may have replaced one of his district's elected delegates, but it seems more likely that he was one of several supplemental delegates who also attended the Electors' meetings.

33 See Kates, *Cercle Social*, 21–9.

34 In addition to his friendship with Creuzé-Latouche, Garran's prominence within the developing "proto-Girondin" political network was also undoubtedly enhanced by his pre-1789 ties to three of Brissot's closest friends, Bancal and the Rolands. (See Whaley, "Emergence of the Brissotins," 81.)

35 See E. Charavay, *L'Assemblée électorale de Paris: 26 août 1791–12 août 1792*, (Paris, 1894), 138.

36 *Biographie Universelle*, XV: 604. For Garran as a member of the Mountain, see J. F. Robinet, *Dictionnaire et biographie de la Révolution et de l'Empire*, (Nendeln, 1975), II: 17; and *Dictionnaire de biographie française*, XVIII: 549. More plausible, however, is A. Patrick's placing of him in that part of the Plain which collaborated with the Mountain by serving on committees after the fall of the Gironde. (*The Men of the First French Republic*, [Baltimore, 1972], 321, 348.) For a similar view, see G. Kates, "Commentary to Lewis-Beck, *et al.*," *French Historical Studies* 15 (1988): 544–5.

37 For Lacretelle, see *Biographie Universelle*, XXII: 382–6; *Nouvelle biographie générale*, XXVIII: 567–71; J. Bénétruy, *L'Atelier de Mirabeau*, (Geneva, 1962), 229; and Maza, "Le tribunal de la nation."

38 See *Discours*, 238.

39 *Mélanges de jurisprudence*, (Paris, 1788), 291.

40 For Agier, see *Dictionnaire de biographie française*, I: 720–2; *Biographie Universelle*, I: 222–4; A. Mahul, *Annuaire nécrologique*, (Paris, 1824), 1–13; and A. Douarche, *Les Tribunaux civils de Paris pendant la Révolution*, (Paris, 1907), 854–5.

41 For Brissot's endorsement of Camus, see *PF*, July 31, 1790, 4. Also see Kates, *Cercle Social*, 66–7.

42 *Collection de décisions nouvelles et de notions relatives à la jurisprudence*, Camus and Bayard, eds., (Paris, 1783–8), I: LXXIV; and Agier, *Le Jurisconsulte national*, (n.p., 1788), sec. 3, 165.

43 See LaCroix, I: 537, and II: 292.

44 See P. Robiquet, *Le Personnel municipal de Paris pendant la Révolution: Période constitutionelle*, (Paris, 1890), 441.

45 See F. Braesch, *La Commune du dix août*, (Paris, 1911), 185; and P. Caron, *Les Massacres de septembre*, (Paris, 1935), 498.

46 See E. Charavay, *L'Assemblée électorale de Paris: 18 novembre 1790–15 juin 1791*, (Paris, 1894), 623.

47 *Ibid.*, 142, 166. Garran was also elected, but soon left to join the Legislative Assembly.

48 E. Charavay, *L'Assemblée électorale de Paris: 2 septembre 1792–17 frimaire an II*, (Paris, 1905), 321.

49 See AN f 7 4774 60; and M. Slavin, *The French Revolution in Miniature*, (Princeton, 1985), 197, 381–2.

50 See Décembre-Alonnier, *Dictionnaire de la Révolution française*, (Paris, 1866), ii: 502.

51 *Essai sur l'organisation du jury de jugement et sur l'instruction criminelle*, (Paris, 1819), 2, 56–68.

52 See C. Desmaze, *Le Châtelet de Paris*, (Paris, 1863); and A. Williams, *The Police of Paris: 1718–1789*, (Baton Rouge, 1979), 18.

53 J. S. Bailly, *Mémoires*, (Paris, 1821), ii: 128; and *PF*, August 7, 1789, 4.

54 See *PV*, ii: 288, 300–25. For an interesting analysis of the cultural gap faced by bourgeois revolutionary officials in attempting to deal with a violent crowd, see B. Conein, "Le Tribunal et la terreur du 14 juillet 1789 aux 'massacres de septembre'," *Révoltes logiques* no. 11 (1979–80): 2–42.

55 *Bulletin de l'Assemblée Nationale*, July 23, 1789, 7.

56 *Courrier français*, July 24, 1789, 1–2.

57 *Journal de Paris*, July 26, 1789, 927.

58 AN c 28, 220, piece 1. This speech is not mentioned in any of the newspapers I have seen. Perhaps it was prepared but not delivered.

59 *AP*, viii: 266–7; *Journal de Versailles*, July 25, 1789, 120; and *Courrier français*, July 24, 1789, 2. For Brissot's own similar proposal, see *PF*, August 4, 1789, 3–4; and August 7, 1789, 4.

60 AN c 28, 211, piece 8. Like Anthoine's speech, this motion does not appear in any of the newspapers. It too may not actually have been presented.

61 *AP*, viii: 267.

62 *PF*, August 4, 1789, 3.

63 See LaCroix, i: 61–2, 464; and ii: 123.

64 *Addresse de l'Assemblée Générale des Représentants*, (Paris, 1789), BN lb 40 28. For the general circumstances surrounding the transfer of the Assembly, see LaCroix, ii: 245–61; and Gottschalk and Maddox, *Lafayette in the French Revolution: From the October Days through the Federation*, (Chicago, 1973), 10–15.

65 See *Moniteur*, October 14–15, 1789, 63.

66 Mirabeau stated that the Assembly should not have been discussing either the creation of a *lèse-nation* tribunal or the enactment of a martial law decree (also passed that day), but instead should have been focusing on providing bread for the People. "If the assembled People cry 'the bakers have no bread'," he declared, "what monster would dare to fire upon them," thereby echoing a remark made that day by Robespierre. But unlike Robespierre, Mirabeau argued that the way to solve the economic crisis was to put more power in the hands of the King!

(*Moniteur*, October 20–22, 1789, 78–9.) Mirabeau's relations with Orléans and Provence will be discussed in chapters 4 and 6.

67 Remarks of "M. Robert-Pierre," *PdJ*, October 22, 1789, 400.

68 See *Journal d'Adrien DuQuesnoy*, ed. R. Crevecoeur, (Paris, 1894), 1: 459.

69 *Moniteur*, October 20–22, 1789, 79. On October 21, Lafayette's friend the Duc de LaRochefoucauld indicated that there were some questions about the Châtelet's ultimate right to judge *lèse-nation* cases. However, LaRochefoucauld seems to have been assuring the deputies that the Châtelet's assignment would only be temporary, and that the Assembly's Constitution Committee would soon fashion a permanent *lèse-nation* court. But it would, in fact, be sixteen months before the Constitution Committee made such a proposal. (See *ibid.*, October 20–22, 1789, 79.)

70 *APL*, October 31, 1789, 3; *RdP*, October 10–17, 1789, 15; and *AdP*, November 5, 1789, 5.

71 Garrigues, *Les Districts parisiens pendant la Révolution française*, (Paris, n.d.), 195. For evidence of the heavy participation of artisans and shopkeepers in district assemblies in 1789–90, see R. B. Rose, *The Making of the Sans-culottes*, (Manchester, 1983), 50–65.

72 See *Révolutions de Paris* (Tournon), no. 39 (mid-April 1790), 21. This journal was a rival of the original and better-known *Révolutions de Paris* which employed Loustalot.

73 *Avis aux bons citoyens touchant la grande conjuration des aristocrates*, (n.p., n.d.), BN LB 39 2399, 2.

74 See *PV*, 1: 200–1; and Bailly, *Mémoires*, 1: 349.

75 See royal letter of appointment in *Recueil de documents relatifs à la convocation des états généraux*, ed. A. Brette, (Paris, 1896), II: 311–12.

76 See *Moniteur*, July 3, 1790, 22; and AN BB 30 82.

77 See E. Seligman, "Le Dossier d'un magistrat au XVIIIe siècle," *Revue du palais* 2 (February 1898): 431–50. For the Talon family, see J. F. Bluche, *Les Origines des magistrats du Parlement de Paris (1715–91)*, (Nogent, 1956), 392.

78 Ministry of Justice Archives, as cited by Seligman, "Le Dossier," 448.

79 See A. Ferrand, *Mémoires*, (Paris, 1897), 34–5; and *Mémorial de J. de Norvins*, (Paris, 1896), 1: 231.

80 See *Correspondance entre le comte de Mirabeau et le comte de LaMarck pendant les années 1789, 1790, et 1791*, ed. A de Bacourt, (Paris, 1851), 1: 359–63, 384–8, 392–4, 401–2, 408, 413–16; E. Charavay, *Le Général Lafayette*, (Paris, 1898), 199; and A. Stern, *La Vie de Mirabeau*, tr. M. Busson, (Paris, 1896), II: 143–4. An important role in these negotiations, which revolved around an effort to put together a new governmental ministry acceptable to both Lafayette and Mirabeau, was also played by the Monarchien Justice Minister Champion de Cicé, with whom Talon was closely linked in the pre-October Days period. In fact, apparently fearing that Cicé (who had assumed his post after the fall of the Bastille)

might become too influential, Lafayette was initially hesitant about conferring the Châtelet leadership on Talon. (See undated letter to Latour-Maubourg, AN F7 4767, piece 26.) However, Talon was often quite adept in knowing exactly when to abandon a sinking political ship, and the crushing defeat suffered by the Monarchiens in the October Days seems to have impelled him into Lafayette's camp, though he also maintained nominally friendly relations with Cicé. Thus, those historians who have described him as Cicé's agent during the post-October Days period appear to have seriously underestimated the sensitivity of his political antennae. (See Gottschalk and Maddox, *Lafayette: Through the Federation*, 40; and L. de Loménie, *Les Mirabeau*, [Paris, 1891], v: 37–8)

81 *Correspondance entre Mirabeau et LaMarck*, I: 220–1; Also see *ibid.*, II: 64, 172; J. Droz, *Histoire du règne de Louis XVI*, (Paris, 1858), IV: 46; and H. de Sybel, *Histoire de l'Europe pendant la Révolution française*, tr. M. Bosquet, (Paris, 1869), I: 99–100.

82 See *Correspondance entre Mirabeau et LaMarck*, I: 221–2, and II: 472–3, 515-16.

83 "Pièces présentées à Louis XVI à la Convention," piece I, as cited by Seligman, *La Justice*, II: 14.

84 See *Nouvelle biographie générale*, XLIV: 866–7.

85 See *Dictionnaire de biographie française*, VI: 1214–15.

86 Only four of fifty-nine Conseillers au Châtelet in 1789 clearly belonged to one of the great Parlement de Paris families, and only five others had names which indicate they may have belonged to one of these families. (For the list of Châtelet judges, see *Almanach royal* [Paris, 1789], 388–90; for the Parlement de Paris families, see Bluche, *Les Origines des magist-rats*.) While some Châtelet judges undoubtedly came from the families that served the other Parisian Sovereign Courts or from provincial robe families, it appears likely that most came from recently ennobled or bourgeois families. As for Boucher d'Argis, he inherited noble status from his father who had attained hereditary nobility by serving more than twenty years as a Châtelet magistrate. (See J. de Sèze, *Le Châtelet de Paris à la fin de l'ancien régime*, D.E.S., Université de Paris, Faculté de Droit, 1971, 30.)

87 G. Sallier, *Annales françaises, mai 1789–mai 1790*, (Paris, 1832), II: 234.

88 See Boucher d'Argis, *De la bienfaisance dans l'ordre judiciaire*, (London, 1788); and Ferdinand-Dreyfus, "L'Association de Bienfaisance Judiciaire," *Révolution française* (January–June 1904): 385–411.

89 See Ferdinand-Dreyfus, "L'Association," 397. Lafayette had been a member of this organization since 1788. (See *Almanach national pour l'année 1790*, [Paris, n.d.], sec. 4, 77.)

90 See MM. Bretelle et Alletz, *Etrennes aux Parisiens patriotes, ou Almanach militaire national de Paris*, (Paris, 1790), sec. 1, 40.

91 Seligman, *La Justice*, I: 343–4.

92 Ferdinand-Dreyfus, "L'Association," 409–11.
93 See Boucher d'Argis, *Observations*, 17, 111–12, 162.
94 See Chassin, *Les Élections*, III: 281.
95 *Observations*, 63, 66.

2 THE JUDICIAL AFTERMATH OF THE JULY REVOLUTION

1 The most comprehensive study of the Court's behavior during this period places heavy emphasis on the significant role played by the Queen as a leader of this hardline faction. See P. Caron, "La Tentative de contre-révolution de juin–juillet 1789," *Revue d'histoire moderne et contemporaine* 8 (1906–7): 8–9. However, for a recent analysis which stresses the differences between Artois and a more moderate Marie-Antoinette, see M. Price, "The 'Ministry of the Hundred Hours': A Reappraisal," *French History* 4 (1990): 317–39.

2 *Les Correspondances des agents diplomatiques étrangers en France avant la Révolution*, ed. J. Flammermont, (Paris, 1896), 232–3. For d'Eprémesnil's relations with Artois at this time, see H. Carré, *La Noblesse de France et l'opinion publique au XVIIIe siècle*, (Geneva, 1977), 363.

3 *Mémoires du Duc des Cars*, (Paris, 1890), II: 67.

4 *Correspondance secrète du Comte de Mercy-Argenteau avec l'Empereur Joseph II et le Prince de Kaunitz*, eds. A. Arneth and J. Flammermont, (Paris, 1891), II: 255. For other repressive plans being discussed within the Court at this time, see *Mémoires du Comte de Paroy*, (Paris, 1895), 54; and E. Vingtrinier, *La Contre-Révolution: Première période, 1789–1791*, (Paris, 1924), I: 14.

5 For Besenval's friendships with Artois and Marie-Antoinette, see *Mémoires du Baron de Besenval*, (Paris, 1883), 310–11; *Mémoires du Comte de Saint-Priest*, (Paris, 1929), II: 65; and J. Flammermont, *La Journée du 14 juillet 1789*, (Paris, 1892), clv–clvi.

6 Caron, "La Tentative," 653.

7 J. Necker, *Histoire de la Révolution française*, (Paris, 1821), II: 14.

8 *Mémoires du Duc des Cars*, II: 67.

9 Caron, "La Tentative," 33; and Vingtrinier, *La Contre-Révolution*, I: 17. The phrase on "unsheathing the sword" is from P. V. Malouet, *Mémoires*, (Paris, 1868), I: 343.

10 Flammermont (ed.), *Correspondances des agents diplomatiques*, 234.

11 J. de Campan, *The Private Life of Marie-Antoinette*, (London, 1883), II: 162; G. de Staël, *Considérations sur les principaux événements de la Révolution française*, (Paris, 1818), I: 339; and Sallier, *Annales françaises*, I: 333.

12 The most significant skirmish of July 12 was a charge into the Tuileries gardens by a cavalry unit led by the Prince de Lambesc. One of the earliest of the *émigrés*, Lambesc was tried *in absentia* by the Châtelet, and

although Lafayette later wrote that he was acquitted, it actually appears that no final judgment was ever rendered in the case. (See Lambesc dossier, AN BB 3 221, esp. Besenval deposition, Addition d'Information, no. 36; J. Godechot, *La Prise de la Bastille*, [Paris, 1965], 236–9; *PF*, December 18, 1790, 2; and Lafayette, *Mémoires*, II: 390.)

13 See Caron, "La Tentative," 14, 653; and Flammermont (ed.), *Correspondances des agents diplomatiques*, 241.

14 See Caron, "La Tentative," 662; and Besenval, *Mémoires*, 365.

15 *The Coming of the French Revolution*, tr. R. R. Palmer, (Princeton, 1967), 67.

16 For the fears of troop disaffection, see Caron, "La Tentative," 653–5, 663–4; Besenval, *Mémoires*, 365; and *Correspondance de Mercy*, II: 252.

17 See de Staël, *Considérations*, I: 226: "Although hardly disposed by character to want absolute power, [Louis XVI] never renounced his claim to it."

18 C. Rogers, *The Spirit of Revolution in 1789*, (Princeton, 1949), 156.

19 See S. Scott, *The Response of the Royal Army to the French Revolution*, (Oxford, 1978), 58–9.

20 Flammermont (ed.), *Correspondances des agents diplomatiques*, 238–9. For rumors of plans to dissolve the Assembly and arrest some of its leaders, see Bailly, *Mémoires*, I: 361; *Journal de DuQuesnoy*, I: 184; G. Morris, *A Diary of the French Revolution*, (Boston, 1939), I: 151; Caron, "La Tentative," 676; and AN BB 30 161, Besenval dossier.

21 See Caron, "La Tentative," 22; *Procès-verbal de l'Assemblée Nationale*, (Paris, 1789), annex to July 14 meeting, 2; and *Moniteur*, July 13–15, 1789, 158.

22 *PV*, I: 274. Also see *ibid.*, I: 279, 297–8, 304, 376–7; and Bailly, *Mémoires*, I: 368–9.

23 *PF*, August 5, 1789, 2.

24 *Ibid.*, August 5, 1789, 2–3 (my emphasis); and July 30, 1789, 4.

25 See *De la vérité, ou méditations sur les moyens de parvenir à la vérité dans toutes les connaissances humaines*, (Neufchâtel, 1782).

26 *PF*, August 4, 1789, 3–4.

27 *PF*, August 5, 1789, 2–3. The original of Besenval's order can be found in AN BB 30 161, Besenval dossier.

28 See pp. 19–20 above.

29 See *CdV*, August 16, 1789, 302–5; and *Les crimes dévoilés*, (Paris, 1789), BN LB 39 1977. For reports on the circulation of rumors about the plan, see *RdP*, July 26–August 1, 1789, 16–17; and *Correspondance secrète inédite sur Louis XVI, Marie-Antoinette. la Cour et la Ville*, ed. M. Lescure, (Paris, 1866), II: 373.

30 See note 13 above.

31 See G. Lefebvre, *La grande peur*, (Paris, 1932), 69–78.

32 J. J. Mounier, *Exposé de la conduite de M. Mounier dans l'Assemblée Nationale*,

(Paris, 1789), sec. I, 7; and C. E. de Ferrières, *Correspondance inédite*, (Paris, 1932), 76. "P" here refers to *proscrit*.

33 For example, though it is often thought of as a particularly fertile arena for revolutionary blood-letting, there were apparently only five deaths during the Great Fear of summer 1789. (See Vovelle, *Mentalité révolutionnaire*, 84.)

34 *Mémoire de M. le Comte de Lally-Tolendal ou seconde lettre à ses commettants*, (Paris, 1790), 141.

35 A. de Lamartine, *Histoire des Constituants*, (Paris, 1855), I: 368.

36 *Moniteur*, July 13–15, 1789, 156.

37 See *Histoire de la Révolution de 1789 par Deux Amis de la Liberté*, (Paris, 1790), II: 184; *Le ministère de trente-six heures, quarante-quatre minutes, et vingt-cinq secondes*, (n.p., n.d.), BN LB 39 1988; and Carré, *La Noblesse*, 364–9.

38 See LaCroix, I: 68–9; and M. Sepet, "La Révolution de juillet 1789," *Revue des questions historiques* (1891): 501.

39 See *PV*, I: 256–8, 294–7, 314–17, 326–7, 344–7; J. Peuchet, *Mémoires tirés des archives de la police de Paris*, (Paris, 1838), IV: 103–12; and AN BB 30 161, Besenval Information, witnesses nos. 40 and 43.

40 *Moniteur*, July 28, 1789, 217. While rumors about this note certainly helped determine Flesselles' fate, there is a good chance that it actually never existed. See M. Dusaulx, *De l'insurrection parisienne et de la prise de la Bastille*, (Paris, 1790), 42; and L. G. Pitra, "La journée du 14 juillet," in Flammermont, *La Journée*, 29.

41 *Biographie Universelle*, XV: 603. Also see F. L. Montjoie, *Histoire de la Révolution de France et de l'Assemblée Nationale*, (Paris, 1791), sec. 3, ch. 46, 124; C. Beaulieu, *Essais historiques sur les causes et les effets de la Révolution de France*, (Paris, 1801), I: 335; P. Buchez and P. Roux, *Histoire parlementaire de la Révolution française*, (Paris, 1834), II: 104; and J. Claretie, ed. notes to C. Desmoulins, *Discours de la lanterne*, (Paris, 1869), 113.

42 Compare Bord, *La conspiration*, 153 with *PV*, I: 344. Without mentioning Garran, the *Procès-verbal* does name two of Flesselles' earlier denunciators. (*PV*, I: 297, 326.)

43 Compare Bord, *La conspiration*, 282–3 with *PV*, II: 238.

44 See Bord, *La conspiration*, 30.

45 *Ibid.*, 389.

46 *Ibid.*, 387.

47 *PV*, I: 360–1.

48 See *RdP*, July 12–17, 1789, 12; Dusaulx, *De l'insurrection*, 126–7; and Restif de la Bretonne, "Les Nuits de Paris," *Oeuvres*, (Paris, 1930), I: 210.

49 *PV*, I: 341–2. The so-called Permanent Committee was a group of Electors temporarily administering municipal affairs. For other accounts of the invasion of the Hôtel-de-Ville, see Peuchet, *Mémoires*, IV: 112; and Pitra, "La journée," in Flammermont, *La Journée*, 16–17.

50 *PV*, I: 320, 355, 358–9, 362. For other situations during the day which

pitted an indulgent elite against a punitive crowd, see *PV*, 1: 264–5 (the release of two leaders of the Parlement de Paris), and 364–5 (the release of the commander of the Arsenal and his wife).

51 *PV*, 1: 235.
52 Restif de la Bretonne, *Oeuvres*, 1: 211.
53 *Mémoires*, 1: 372. Bailly's phrase "le peuple assemblé" combines the abstraction "le peuple" with the tangible individuals surrounding the Electors at the Hôtel-de-Ville in an interesting way. For if he had only meant to refer to tangible individuals, would he not have written "les gens assemblés"?
54 Dusaulx, *De l'insurrection*, 40. Also see Bancal's report to the National Assembly, as found in *PV*, 1: 400.
55 See *PV*, 1: 348–9; and Dusaulx, *De l'insurrection*, 111–12.
56 *PV*, 1: 395–6.
57 *PV*, 1: 423–5.
58 "Continual alarms" were, in fact, being voiced all day and a rumor that troops based in Saint-Denis were about to attack Paris was being circulated immediately before Ogny's arrival at the Hôtel-de-Ville. (See *PV*, 1: 417–18.)
59 *Mémoires de Talleyrand*, (Paris, 1982), 176.
60 See Bibliothèque Historique de la Ville de Paris, MS 741, piece 54.
61 Duc de Castres, *Mirabeau*, (Paris, 1986), 189.
62 For the hostility between the Electors and the districts, see LaCroix, 1: xii–xvii and Garrigues, *Les Districts*, 128–9.
63 *PV*, II: 248. Also see *PV*, II: 228, 277–8.
64 See Bailly, *Mémoires*, II: 139–40. The comment on Liancourt's "delicacy" is from *Histoire par Deux Amis*, II: 184.
65 *Moniteur*, July 25, 1789, 205.
66 *PdJ*, July 27, 1789, 303; and *Moniteur*, July 25–27, 1789, 206.
67 The first section of this citation is from *CdV*, July 28, 1789, 7–8. The second section is from *PdJ*, July 28, 1789, 314.
68 *PdJ*, July 27, 1789, 302; and *Moniteur*, July 25–27, 1789, 206–7. Also see A. Lameth, *Histoire de l'Assemblée Constituante*, (Paris, 1828), 1: 82–3.
69 *PdJ*, July 27, 1789, 301; and *Moniteur*, July 25–27, 1789, 206.
70 *Moniteur*, July 25–27, 1789, 210. For a persuasive argument that this unnamed deputy was Robespierre, see G. Rouanet, "Robespierre à la Constituante," *Annales révolutionnaires* 10 (1918): 180–1.
71 *PdJ*, July 28, 1789, 314.
72 *Journal de Paris*, July 29, 1789, 943.
73 *Moniteur*, July 25–27, 1789, 210. ("Je ne le crois pas. Les ménagements pour les conspirateurs sont une trahison envers le peuple." My emphasis.)
74 For Robespierre as revolutionary "alchemist," see Furet, *Interpreting the French Revolution*, 56.
75 See Bailly, *Mémoires*, II: 139.

76 *Bulletin de l'Assemblée Nationale*, July 27, 1789, supplement, 2. Also see *PF*, July 29, 1789, 3; *RdP*, July 26–August 1, 1789, 12; and *Courrier national*, July 27, 1789, 3.

77 See *Mémoires du Prince de Talleyrand*, ed. Duc de Broglie, (Paris, 1891), 1: 125–6, 137–41; *Mémoires de Vitrolles*, (Paris, 1950), 1: 338–9; and Marquis de Clermont-Gallerande, *Mémoires*, (Paris, 1826), 1: 134. For another example of the kind of information that might have been kept secret in this period, see Bailly, *Mémoires*, 1: 359. Bailly explains here that he had written to Breteuil concerning some "routine" matter during the July crisis: "My intentions were pure, but if that [the very fact he had been corresponding with Breteuil] had been known then, it could have exposed me to suspicion." Also see Price, "Ministry of the Hundred Hours," 333–4.

78 Brissot's willingness to co-operate with the policies of the newly established Fayettist municipality during this period is reflected in his acceptance of the "official report" on the Castelnau correspondence. (See note 76 above.) As one of the sponsors of Lafayette's election as National Guard Commander, was he already influential enough at the Hôtel-de-Ville to have actively participated in the decision to suppress its contents?

79 *Courrier national*, July 27, 1789, 3.

80 *Le Juif errant*, no. 1, March 1790, BN LC 2 2346, 3.

81 See *PdJ*, July 28, 1789, 315; and *Journal des débats*, July 27, 1789, 264.

82 For the connection between the rejection of the postal committee and the creation of the Comité des Recherches, see Lameth, *Histoire de l'Assemblée Constituante*, 1: 82–3.

83 See *Gazette de Leyde*, July 31, 1789, supplement; Ferrières, *Mémoires*, (Paris, 1822), 1: 136; *Histoire par Deux Amis*, 11: 75; Buchez and Roux, *Histoire parlementaire*, 11: 100; and *The Times Reports the French Revolution*, ed. N. Ascherson, (London, 1975), 9.

84 *La chasse aux bêtes puantes et féroces*, (Paris, 1789), BN LB 39 1990, 4, 5, 7.

85 *La grande peur*, 105.

86 *Gazette de Leyde*, August 7, 1789, supplement. The same story can also be found in Clermont-Gallerande, *Mémoires*, 1: 141–2; and *Mémoires de Paroy*, 43.

87 *La grande peur*, 105.

88 AN D XXIX bis 44, 417, piece 15.

89 *Ibid.*, piece 16. Liancourt's letter was counter-signed by two members of the just-appointed national Comité des Recherches.

90 See *Biographie Universelle*, V: 493; and V. Fournel, *L'événement de Varennes*, (Paris, 1890), 48–9.

91 See *Moniteur*, July 30, 1789, 242; *Mémoires de Paroy*, 41; Carré, *La Noblesse*, 366–7; and M. Bouloiseau, "Le Royal-Allemand cavalerie en juillet 1789," *Actes du 92e congrès des sociétés savantes: Strasbourg et Colmar* (1967): 309.

92 See Carré, *La Noblesse*, 364–9; and *Biographie Universelle*, III: 86–7, and V: 493.
93 See *PV*, II: 456–8; *Gazette de Leyde*, August 4, 1789; and Lafayette, *Mémoires*, II, 264.
94 See *Moniteur*, June 20–24, 1789, 95.
95 *PF*, July 29, 1789, 2. On Maury and Calonne, see *Moniteur*, July 25–27, 1789, 210–11; *PdJ*, July 28, 1789, 315–17; and AN C 28 225, pieces 1–4. Curiously, the only deputy reported as opposed to either of these releases was the Monarchien Clermont-Tonnerre, who argued that Calonne had been arrested legally and should be tried by the relevant local tribunal. Was he hoping to bolster the authority of the existing judicial institutions? (See p. 26 above.)
96 See *Moniteur*, August 1, 1789, 257, and August 5, 1789, 296; *PdJ*, August 8, 1789, 57; and Rouanet, "Robespierre à la Constituante," 294–7. The only deputies identified as opposing Vauguyon's release were Robespierre, Glezen, and Desmeuniers. Brissot also opposed it. (See *PF*, August 8, 1789, 3.) In leaving Vauguyon's fate in the King's hands, the Assembly seems to have disregarded its own July 13 decree declaring ministers "responsible" for all attacks on the rights of the Nation. No one, however, seems to have pointed out this discrepancy.

3 THE BESENVAL AFFAIR: AMNESTY OR PROSECUTION?

1 See Besenval, *Mémoires*, 368–9. The most reasonable estimate for the date of this departure is July 25 or 26, though Besenval's claim that he didn't learn about the July 22 Foulon–Berthier massacres until after his arrest is puzzling.
2 See Carré, *La Noblesse*, 366; and Bouloiseau, "Le Royal-Allemand," 408.
3 *Journal Politique National*, 1790 re-edition, no. 7, 73. Also see Saint-Priest, *Mémoires*, II: 234.
4 Montjoie, *Histoire de la Révolution*, sec. 4, ch. 51, 122; and *Histoire authentique et suivie*, as cited by Flammermont, *La Journée*, cxxxii. For similar comments from an officer who served under Besenval, see Marquis de Maleissye, *Mémoires d'un officier aux gardes-françaises*, (Paris, 1897), 50.
5 Besenval, *Mémoires*, 368–9.
6 Besenval had already been losing favor at the Court in the period immediately prior to the July crisis, as is indicated by the recall from retirement of his old rival Broglie, who, in being named War Minister, assumed command over him. (See *ibid.*, 363–4.)
7 AN BB 30 161, Besenval Information, witnesses nos. 99, 107, 108. Also see Besenval, *Mémoires*, 370.

8 AN D xxix bis, 2, 13, piece 16; AN BB 30 161, Information, no. 3; and Besenval, *Mémoires*, 370. For the municipal transition, see LaCroix, I: 10–12.

9 Bailly, *Mémoires*, II: 166. Considering the events that will be described below, there may well have been another reason for the Police Committee's secrecy: fear that either the Electors or the Représentants would order Besenval's release, or at least ask the National Assembly to intervene.

10 For the use of secrecy a week earlier by the Electors in an ultimately futile effort to protect Foulon and Berthier, see *PV*, II: 290.

11 Besenval, *Mémoires*, 370. But see note 1 above.

12 See LaCroix, I: 48–9. Necker revealed these details in his July 30 speech at the Paris Hôtel-de-Ville, reprinted here by LaCroix. Among numerous other places, the text of this key speech can also be found in *Moniteur*, July 30, 1789, 244–5, and July 31, 1789, 249.

13 See LaCroix, I: 46; and *RdP*, July 26–August 1, 1789, 31.

14 Necker, *Histoire de la Révolution*, II: 36–7.

15 LaCroix, I: 47. For "capitalist" support of Necker, see Caron, "La Tentative," 666–8.

16 LaCroix, I: 47–8.

17 *Ibid.*, I: 49.

18 *Ibid.*, I: 50.

19 *Ibid.*, I: 50.

20 *Histoire authentique*, as cited by Flammermont, *La Journée*, cxxxii. Also see Montjoie, *Histoire de la Révolution*, sec. 4, ch. 51, 122.

21 J. J. Rutledge, *L'astuce dévoilée*, (Paris, 1790), 85–6. Also see the apocryphal *Réponse de M. le baron de Besenal à M. le marquis de Favras*, (Paris, 1790), BN LB 39 8406, 9–10.

22 *Necker: Fourrier de la Révolution*, (Paris, 1933), 306.

23 *Ibid.*, 179.

24 *Sur l'administration de M. Necker*, 92.

25 *Ibid.*, 87, 91–2; and Necker, *Histoire de la Révolution*, II: 38. For Necker as a financial "juggler," see Rutledge, *L'astuce dévoilée*, 86.

26 See Malouet, *Mémoires*, I: 311–17; and J. Egret, *Necker: Ministre de Louis XVI*, (Paris, 1975), 286–7. For the pre-revolutionary enmity between Necker and Mirabeau, see Bénétruy, *L'Atelier de Mirabeau*, 228–32.

27 Malouet, *Mémoires*, I: 316–17.

28 Bailly, *Mémoires*, II: 172. For confirmation of Bailly's story, see Necker, *Histoire de la Révolution*, II: 37.

29 Lameth, *Histoire de l'Assemblée Constituante*, I: 84–5. The comment on Necker's "exaggerated opinion" is from Malouet, *Mémoires*, I: 246. Also see Egret, *Necker*, 46: "All the sources report his total confidence in the persuasive force of his presence."

30 Letter to Maurepas, as cited by Egret, *Necker*, 47.

31 LaCroix, I: 51–2. Also see Bailly, *Mémoires*, I: 174; *Journal de Duquesnoy*, I:

246; *PF*, July 31, 1789, 3–4; and AN BB 30 161, Information, no. 30. One of the Représentants, De Joly, later claimed to have opposed the release order and Clermont also reported one objection. (See "Mémoires de De Joly," *AHRF* 18 [1946]: 309; and Clermont-Tonnerre, *Oeuvres*, I: xxi–xxii). However, none of the other sources mentions any opposition.

32 *PV*, II: 521–2. Also see Bailly, *Mémoires*, II: 177; and *RdP*, July 26–August 1, 1789, 33.

33 *Sur l'administration de M. Necker*, 87, 90; *PV*, II: 523; and Clermont-Tonnerre, *Oeuvres*, I: xx.

34 See "Mémoires de De Joly," 309; and *Histoire par Deux Amis*, II: 251.

35 Lameth, *Histoire de l'Assemblée Constituante*, I: 86–7.

36 J. J. Godard, speech to National Assembly, *Extrait des régistres des délibérations du district des Blancs-Manteaux*, (Paris, 1789), BN LB 40 234, 2.

37 *Histoire par Deux Amis*, II: 251.

38 See AN C 28, 225, piece 42; and *CdV*, August 1, 1789, 72.

39 District de l'Oratoire, *Extrait de la délibération du 30 juillet*, (Paris, 1789). For reports of armed men being sent to arrest Besenval, see AN C 28, 225, piece 41; and AN BB 30 161, Information, witness no. 30. Though neither source identifies them, these men were, in all likelihood, from the Oratoire District.

40 See LaCroix, I: 53–4; "Mémoires de De Joly," 310–11; *CdV*, August 1, 1789, 73; and Droz, *Histoire de Louis XVI*, II: 395.

41 LaCroix, I: 53–4; *PF*, August 1, 1789, 2; *Journal de Paris*, August 2, 1789, 960; *RdP*, July 26–August 1, 1789, 39; *CdV*, August 3, 1789, 99; and Droz, *Histoire de Louis XVI*, II: 399.

42 For reports of unrest in virtually all the districts, see AN C 28 225, piece 41; and *PF*, August 1, 1789, 1.

43 *Extrait des Blancs-Manteaux*, 6.

44 *CdV*, August 3, 1789, 99.

45 LaCroix, I: 54; and Oratoire, *Extrait du 30 juillet*.

46 *PV*, II: 534–5.

47 De Staël, *Considérations*, I: 258; Necker, *Histoire de la Révolution*, II: 43; and Beaulieu, *Essais historiques*, II: 61.

48 *Histoire par Deux Amis*, II: 251; Ferrières, *Mémoires*, I: 169; and *Sur l'administration de M. Necker*, 39–40. Also see Bailly, *Mémoires*, II: 180–1; Lameth, *Histoire de l'Assemblée Constituante*, I: 88; and Droz, *Histoire de Louis XVI*, II: 394–5.

49 See Bailly, *Mémoires* II: 154; *Moniteur*, July 23, 1789, 190–1; and Duc de Castries, *Mirabeau*, 346.

50 See *Histoire par Deux Amis*, II: 243–50; and Clermont-Tonnerre, *Oeuvres*, I: xx–xxi.

51 Bailly, *Mémoires*, II: 174; *Versailles et Paris*, August 1, 1789, 2–3; *Lettre à M. le Comte de Clermont-Tonnerre sur sa motion en faveur du sr. de Besenval et des autres coupables*, (Paris, 1789), BN LB 39 7538, 2; and *Extrait des*

délibérations du district des Petits-Pères, (Paris, 1789), BN LB 40 1505. Also see the Electors' self-described "involuntary impulse," p. 67 above.

52 *Réponse de la nation à la demande qu'a faite M. Necker de pardonner à ceux qui avaient médité sa ruine et celle de l'état*, (Paris, 1789), BN LB 39 7539, 5; and *Tribut d'un Parisien à Monsieur Necker*, (Paris, 1789), BN LB 39 7594, 6.

53 *CdV*, July 31, 1789, 50–1; August 1, 1789, 66, 71–2; and August 3, 1789, 97–8 (his emphasis). Also see *CdV*, August 3, 1789, 98–9: "The amnesty was accorded by MM. les Electeurs in a moment of enthusiasm, an enthusiasm no doubt honorable but misplaced under the circumstances."

54 *CdV*, July 25, 1789, 295.

55 See *CdV*, July 16, 1789, 16; and July 24, 1789, 290.

56 *CdV*, July 28, 1789, 12.

57 *Lettre à Clermont-Tonnerre*, 3.

58 See M. Dorigny, "Violence et révolution: Les Girondins et les massacres de septembre," *Actes du Colloque Girondins et Montagnards*, (Paris, 1980), 105–6.

59 See comments of G. Lefebvre, M. Bouloiseau, and A. Soboul, *Oeuvres Complètes de Maximilien Robespierre*, (Paris, 1958), II: 48; and Rouanet, "Robespierre à la Constituante," 188.

60 *J. P. Brissot à Stanislas Clermont*, 50.

61 *PF*, July 31, 1789, 3–4.

62 *PF*, August 1, 1789, 1–2.

63 *PF*, August 4, 1789, 3–4.

64 *PF*, August 5, 1789, 2–4.

65 *PF*, August 10, 1789, 6.

66 *PF*, August 10, 1789, 4.

67 *Lettres à M. le Chevalier de Pange*, (Paris, 1790), 13–14; and De Pange, *Oeuvres*, 57.

68 See the comments on the Girondins' "half-hearted use of the language of the Revolution" in Furet, *Interpreting the French Revolution*, 68.

69 Popular support for judicial severity often extended beyond political cases. For examples of popular opposition to leniency for ordinary criminals, see *Moniteur*, May 26, 1790, 460, May 27, 1790, 468, and May 28, 1790, 472; LaCroix, V: 545–8; and *Le Châtelet démasqué*, BN LC 2 2395, no. 2, 2–3.

70 *Bulletin de l'Assemblée Nationale*, July 31, 1789, supplement, 2–3.

71 *Moniteur*, July 31, 1789, 255.

72 Necker, *Histoire de la Révolution*, II: 42.

73 See *Journal Logographique*, July 31, 1789, 288–90; and *PdJ*, August 1, 1789, 365.

74 *Moniteur*, July 31, 1789, 255.

75 See *Bulletin de l'Assemblée Nationale*, July 31, 1789, supplement, 1.

76 See comments of Barnave and Robespierre, *Moniteur*, July 31, 1789, 255–6.

77 *Ibid.*, July 31, 1789, 255.
78 *Ibid.*, August 1, 1789, 257.
79 Since they began their evening sessions at 5 p.m. and since the news about Brie is contained in the minutes for their day session, it is clear that the Représentants learned Besenval was at Brie sometime before late afternoon. Certainly the National Assembly could not have received this information much later, even allowing for the distance between Paris and Versailles. Putting the matter with perhaps too much certainty, LaCroix stated that the Assembly "knew quite well he was under arrest." (I: 62–3, 73.)
80 *Journal de DuQuesnoy*, I: 252 (my emphasis). Also see Bailly, *Mémoires*, II: 190.
81 See AN BB 30 161, Information, witnesses nos. 30, 45.
82 LaCroix, I: 61–2, 81. Also see G. Lefebvre, "La première proposition d'instituer un tribunal révolutionnaire," *AHRF* 10 (1933): 354–6.
83 LaCroix, I: 464; II: 121–3.
84 *AdP*, September 28, 1789, 156; September 18, 1789, 73–4; and September 17, 1789, 68.
85 Besenval, *Mémoires*, 372. Also see LaCroix, I: 174.
86 *CdV*, October 17, 1789, 244.
87 See LaCroix, II: 407–8; and *Moniteur*, December 1, 1789, 275.

4 LAFAYETTE, ORLÉANS, AND THE OCTOBER DAYS

1 See Sallier, *Annales françaises*, II: 63: "Woe to vanquished governments! The impotent efforts by which they seek to reaffirm their shaken authority are always seen as crime and conspiracy."
2 See *Procédure criminelle instruite au Châtelet de Paris sur la dénonciation des faits arrivés à Versailles dans la journée du 6 octobre 1789*, (Paris, 1790), BN LE 29 980, witness no. 214, sec. 2, 68; no. 236, sec. 2, 97; no. 237, sec. 2, 105; and no. 377, sec. 3, 35. This is the transcript of the Châtelet's investigation of the October Days.
3 *Ibid.*, no. 211, sec. 2, 63; and no. 344, sec. 2, 217. The phrase "indescribable procession" is from G. Lefebvre, *La Révolution Française*, (Paris, 1957), 144. For Orléans as "the Red Prince," see A. Castelot, *Philippe-Egalité, Le Prince Rouge*, (Paris, 1950).
4 See *Moniteur*, September 4, 1789, 417–20; LaCroix, I: 446–7, 552–4, 557, 584; H. Furgeot, *Le Marquis de Saint-Huruge: Généralissime des sans-culottes (1738–1801)*, (Paris, 1908), 122–78; and Gottschalk and Maddox, *Lafayette: Through the October Days*, 231–7. The two most prominent of those arrested, Saint-Huruge and the abbé Bernard, were released after two months in prison. As for the others, one man was sent to the galleys until May 1790, another was banished from Paris for three months, and the three remaining were released after a few days. These cases were

handled by the Châtelet in its capacity as ordinary criminal court for the Paris area.

5 See *Moniteur*, August 28–31, 1789, 399–400; *Bulletin de l'Assemblée Nationale*, August 31, 1789, 2–4; and Furgeot, *Saint-Huruge*, 128.

6 The most insightful and well-balanced study of the October Days is still A. Mathiez, *Etude critique sur les journées des 5 et 6 octobre 1789*, (Paris, 1899). For other good general studies, see P. Dominique, *Paris enlève le roi: octobre 1789*, (Paris, 1973); and M. de Villiers, *Les 5 et 6 octobre 1789: Reine Audu*, (Paris, 1917).

7 On the number of marchers, see LaCroix, II: 183; and *Procédure criminelle*, no. 81, sec. 1, 122.

8 See Saint-Priest, *Mémoires*, II: 9–11; and *Mémoires de Madame la Duchesse de Tourzel*, (Paris, 1883), I: 7–8.

9 See *Procédure criminelle*, no. 18, sec. 1, 38. Also see *Mémoires de Tourzel*, I: 8; and *Louis XVI, Marie-Antoinette, et Madame Elisabeth: Lettres et documents inédits*, ed. Feuillet de Conches, (Paris, 1864), I: 273.

10 See Malouet, *Mémoires*, I: 340–3; J. Egret, *La Révolution des notables: Mounier et les Monarchiens*, (Paris, 1950), 169–72; and Mathiez, *Etude critique*, 96–8. According to Malouet, the Monarchiens suggested that the King "order" the transfer of the National Assembly to Soissons or Compiègne, a step which presumably would also have entailed the movement of the royal government itself. As for Necker, Malouet states that he claimed to support the Monarchien plan, but, in reality, added his own "hesitations" to those of the King. On the other hand, Necker was clearly opposed to flight in October. (See Saint-Priest, *Mémoires*, II: 16; *Mémoires de Tourzel*, I: 8; and *Sur l'administration de M. Necker*, 137–42.)

11 See Saint-Priest, *Mémoires*, II: 14–16.

12 Dominique, *Paris enlève le roi*, 159. The phrase on "passive courage" is from Malouet, *Mémoires*, I: 342.

13 "Irruption soudaine" and "bandits" are from the Comité des Recherches' official October Days denunciation, *Procédure criminelle*, sec. 1, 6. Among numerous other places, this document can be found in *Moniteur*, December 1, 1789, 274–5.

14 G. Rudé, *The Crowd in the French Revolution*, (London, 1971), 61.

15 Mathiez, *Etude critique*, 95–6.

16 Rudé, *The Crowd*, 61.

17 G. A. Kelly, *Victims, Authority, and Terror*, (Chapel Hill, 1982), 61. Also see Gottschalk and Maddox, *Lafayette: Through the Federation*, 3–4.

18 Mathiez, *Etude critique*, 48.

19 See Gottschalk and Maddox, *Lafayette: Through the Federation*, 139–42, 147–52. The four deputies who worked most closely with Lafayette in attempting to reach an accommodation with the Monarchiens were Latour-Maubourg, LaRochefoucauld, Liancourt, and the Marquis de Lacoste.

20 For a wave of arrests of protesters in August and September, see Rudé, *The Crowd*, 71.

21 *RdP*, October 3–10, 1789, 4. Also see *RdP*, September 26–October 2, 1789, 22.

22 *AdP*, September 28, 1789, 154; and September 29, 1789, 164.

23 *Le Fouet national*, September 29, 1789, 25–6; and *Mémoire à consulter et consultation pour le Marquis de Saint-Huruge contre les sieurs Bailly et Lafayette*, (n.p., 1789), BN LB 39 2377, 4.

24 See *RdP*, September 26–October 2, 1789, 32; and Bailly, *Mémoires*, II: 403–4. For the general conflict between Lafayette and the popular movement concerning the structure and nature of the National Guard, see Garrigues, *Les Districts*, 169–92; D. L. Clifford, "Command Over Equals: The Officer Corps of the Parisian National Guard," *Proceedings of the Annual Meeting of the Western Society for French History* 18 (1991): 157–61; and M. Coqueau, *Très sérieuses observations sur la mauvaise organisation de la Garde Nationale Parisienne*, (Paris, 1789).

25 *AdP*, September 25, 1789, 132.

26 *RdP*, September 12–18, 1789, 3. Also see *AdP*, September 25, 1789, 132–3; September 30, 1789, 169–70; and October 4, 1789, 208.

27 *RdP*, September 6–11, 1789, 6. For Brissot's municipal plan, see Kates, *Cercle Social*, 34–7; and M. Genty, "Mandataires ou représentants: Un Problème de la démocratie municipale à Paris, en 1789–1790," *AHRF* 44 (1972): 1–15.

28 *Quand aurons-nous du pain*, (n.p., n.d.), BN LB 39 2344, 1. Gorsas reported that this pamphlet appeared just before October 5. (*CdV*, October 8, 1789, 96.) Also see the violent denunciation of the municipal regime in *Le Furet parisien*, no. 2, 13: "You must slit the throats of these beings who are so dear to you."

29 See LaCroix, II: 165–7; Bailly, *Mémoires*, III: 84–5; Lafayette, *Mémoires*, III: 235; and *Procédure criminelle*, no. 12, sec. 1, 30–1; no. 35, sec. 1, 67–8; and no. 39, sec. 1, 73–4. Also see Flammermont, *Correspondances des agents diplomatiques*, 260–1, where Bailly is reported to have resigned. Though false, this report indicates that contemporaries thought of the day's events in terms of an attack on the municipality.

30 LaCroix, II: 166–7.

31 *Procédure criminelle*, no. 81, sec. 1, 118. Maillard seemed to specialize in situations in which he served as a kind of "mediator" between popular and elite culture. Three years later, he would turn up as a "judge" on one of the impromptu "courts" set up during the September Massacres. (See Seligman, *La Justice*, II: 250–2.)

32 Letter of July 16, 1789, Lafayette, *Mémoires*, II: 317. For other incidents in which Lafayette was able to charm a hostile crowd, see Gottschalk and Maddox, *Lafayette: Through the October Days*, 115–16, 179–81, 196–7.

33 See *Procédure criminelle*, no. 35, sec. 1, 68; Lafayette, *Mémoires*, II: 336; and Gottschalk and Maddox, *Lafayette: Through the October Days*, 336–7.

34 Mathiez, *Etude critique*, 88.
35 Lafayette, *Mémoires*, III: 236.
36 *PF*, October 6, 1789, 2.
37 See H. von Sybel, *History of the French Revolution*, tr. W. C. Perry, (London: 1867), I: 122–32; and Lefebvre, *Coming of the Revolution*, 194–5. For a more complete discussion of this argument by historians who reject it, see Mathiez, *Etude critique*, 87–8; and Gottschalk and Maddox, *Lafayette: Through the October Days*, 350–1.
38 *CdP*, October 7, 1789, 179; and October 6, 1789, 175.
39 See Rudé, *The Crowd*, 61.
40 *PF*, October 8, 1789, 1, 4.
41 *CdV*, October 8, 1789, 93, 95; October 10, 1789, 136; and October 12, 1789, 160. These remarks on Marat initiated a wild four year polemic between Gorsas and Marat. For a similar interpretation of the October uprising by another future Girondin, Carra, see *APL*, October 9, 1789, 3.
42 For the attempts to form a new ministry, see Gottschalk and Maddox, *Lafayette: Through the October Days*, 26–46, 70–89.
43 Mathiez, *Etude critique*, 91–2. Also see J. Michelet, *History of the French Revolution*, tr. C. Cocks, (Chicago, 1967), 321–7; and R. Griffiths, *Le Centre perdu: Malouet et le "monarchiens" dans la Révolution française*, (Grenoble, 1988), 82–5.
44 Rudé, *The Crowd*, 79. Also see Garrigues, *Les Districts*, 232.
45 *PF*, August 7, 1789, 3; and October 8, 1789, 4. Public apologias for popular violence, which were virtually non-existent after the October Days, had been quite common during the summer. The most celebrated of them was by Barnave, who, on the day after the Foulon–Berthier massacres, declared: "They are asking us to feel sorry for those whose blood was spilled in Paris yesterday. But was this blood so pure?" (Cited by J. J. Chevallier, *Barnave ou les deux faces de la Révolution*, [Paris, 1936], 81.)
46 *Journal de Duquesnoy*, I: 462.
47 *Domine salvum fac regum*, (Paris, 1789), BN LB 39 2473, I, 31 (my emphasis).
48 Lafayette, *Mémoires*, II: 313.
49 As cited by Rudé, *The Crowd*, 47. In Rudé's view, Orleanist "directives" had indeed played a large part in determining the course of events during the summer crisis.
50 Lafayette, *Mémoires*, II: 357–8; and III: 201.
51 For an account which stresses the importance of Orleanist activity in October, see Mathiez, *Etude critique*, 58–9.
52 *Moniteur*, October 4, 1790, 31.
53 Lafayette, *Mémoires*, II: 357. Officially Orléans was sent to London on a diplomatic mission.
54 *Ibid.*, II: 358, 416.

55 See Pelletier, *Domine salvum*, 15; and Gottschalk and Maddox, *Lafayette: Through the Federation*, 15–16.
56 *Moniteur*, October 4, 1790, 31.
57 See p. 19 above.
58 See Gottschalk and Maddox, *Lafayette: Through the October Days*, 320.
59 *Moniteur*, October 4, 1790, 31, 33; and *Correspondance entre Mirabeau et LaMarck*, I: 127–8. For another interesting comment on Orléans by Mirabeau, see Duc de Castries, *Mirabeau*, 377: "He wants to, but he can't. He is a eunuch when it comes to crime."
60 *RdP*, October 17–24, 1789, 32; and *PF*, October 19, 1789, 1.
61 Ironically, the moment of Orleanism's greatest triumph, the crowning of Orléans' son Louis Philippe in 1830, would be blessed by the venerable patriarch of French liberalism, the septuagenarian General Lafayette.

5 THE POST-OCTOBER DAYS CAMPAIGN AGAINST THE LEFT

1 See *AdP*, September 25, 1789, 133; September 28, 1789, 151–2; and LaCroix, II: 69.
2 *AdP*, September 28, 1789, 152–3; October 2, 1789, 194; and October 7, 1789, 228.
3 See AN D XXIX 63, Marat-Danton dossier; and *AdP*, October 7, 1789, 232.
4 Though even more violent than Marat's journal, both the *Fouet national* and the *Furet parisien* (see chapter 4, notes 23 and 28 above) were distinctly less compelling in style. Moreover, neither of these papers was a daily, and most importantly, their authors were anonymous. In any case, both these journals were very short-lived, perhaps due to some form of governmental harassment. (For a denunciation of the *Furet*, the outcome of which I was unable to determine, see LaCroix, II: 125.)
5 *PF*, September 28, 1789, 2; and LaCroix, II: 202.
6 For Assembly policy on press freedom, see C. Berranger, *et al.*, *Histoire générale de la presse française*, (Paris, 1969), I: 432–4.
7 See LaCroix, I: 432–3; II: 215–16; and *RdP*, October 17–24, 1789, 6–7. The new-found royalism of these market-women was an important part of the post-October Days popularity of the royal family discussed earlier. (See A. Mathiez, *The French Revolution*, tr. C. Phillips, [New York, 1929], 66.)
8 *RdP*, October 17–24, 1789, 8. Also see *Ami du Peuple ou le vrai citoyen*, no. 1, 6–7; and no. 7, 7–8. (This is a "counterfeit Marat" which appeared in October 1789 while Marat himself was in hiding.)
9 Letter to *PF*, October 20, 1789, 3. For Brissot's more guarded criticism of this campaign, see *PF*, October 14, 1789, 3.

10 *RdP*, October 10–17, 1789, 31–2; and October 17–24, 1789, 6. For Marat's "confession," see letter to *Journal d'état et du citoyen*, October 26, 1789, 243.

11 See *Lettre de M. Marat à M. Joly*, October 15, 1789, (n.p., 1789), BN LB 39 2451, 2: "Les noms propres et les dates sont l'écueil de ma mémoire."

12 *AdP*, December 19, 1789, 4–6.

13 *AdP*, January 4, 1790, 8.

14 See *AdP*, January 14, 1790, 4–8; and January 20, 1790, 3–5.

15 For the January 18 publication of the devastating pamphlet, *Dénonciation contre Necker*, see L. Gottschalk, *Jean-Paul Marat: A Study in Radicalism*, (New York, 1966), 61.

16 The best study of the events of January 22 is E. Babut, "Une Journée au District des Cordeliers: le 22 Janvier 1790," *Revue historique* 81 (March 1903): 279–300. Also see Gottschalk and Maddox, *Lafayette: Through the Federation*, 181–5. The close links between radical districts and radical journalists are stressed in J. Censer, *Prelude to Power: The Parisian Radical Press, 1789–1791*, (Baltimore, 1976), 1–12.

17 See "C'en est fait de nous," *Les Pamphlets de Marat*, ed. C. Vellay, (Paris, 1911), 209.

18 See H. LeClerq, *Les journées d'octobre et la fin de l'année 1789*, (Paris, 1924), 197–8; and *CdP*, October 22, 1789, 45–6. For the eventual effectiveness of the new supply system, see Rudé, *The Crowd*, 78–9.

19 For Garran's attempt to save François, see Dusaulx, *De l'insurrection*, 203. Garran's legalistic approach in this case contrasts sharply with the role attributed to him in the Flesselles affair, a contrast which again highlights the difference in political climate between July and October.

20 For the François killing, see *PF*, October 22, 1789, 2–4, October 23, 1789, 4; *Moniteur*, October 26–28, 1789, 89–91; LaCroix, II: 370–2; Gottschalk and Maddox, *Lafayette: Through the Federation*, 57–61; and LeClerq, *Les journées d'octobre*, 197–204. For the parading of François' head, see *Mort du boulanger*, (Paris, n.d.), BN LB 39 8013, 5: "On lui accorde . . . les honneurs de la pique." Also see *Le cacheur de pain dans la cave*, (n.p., n.d.), BN LB 39 8012.

21 See *RdP*, October 17–24, 1789, 26.

22 For the use of cannon, see *PF*, October 22, 1789, 4.

23 See AN Y 10530, fol. 157; and *Jugement prévôtal*, (Paris, 1789), BN LB 39 2501. Three other persons were also tried in connection with the François murder. Two were acquitted, and a metal-worker charged with having cut off the head of the already dead baker was banished from Paris for nine years. (See AN Y 10530, fol. 167; and *Jugement prévôtal*, [Paris, 1789], BN LB 39 2546.)

24 Lafayette, *Mémoires*, II: 375–6.

25 *Lafayette: Through the Federation*, 59. Lafayette's *Mémoires* seems to be Gottschalk and Maddox's only source for their account of this incident.

Notes to pages 104–9

The other sources cited for the paragraph in which the incident is described speak to other events mentioned in the paragraph.

26 AN y 18768, Adrien dossier (my emphasis).

27 See *Jugement prévôtal*, (Paris, 1789), BN LB 39 2502.

28 AN y 18768, Adrien dossier.

29 For the Bourguignon arrest warrant, see *Jugement prévôtal*, BN LB 39 2502. (I have been unable to determine whether he was ever found.)

30 See Talon to LaMarck, October 22, 1789, *Correspondance entre Mirabeau et LaMarck*, I: 402: "Voilà, enfin un exemple."

31 In addition to abolishing judicial secrecy and requiring counsel for defendants, this decree also provided that a four-fifths vote of the judges present was needed for a death sentence. (See *Collection complète des lois*, ed. Duvergier, [Paris, 1834], I: 50.)

32 *PF*, October 23, 1789, 4.

33 See *RdP*, October 24–31, 1789, 31. The case against the Evêque de Tréguier was eventually annulled by the National Assembly. (See LaCroix, III: 84–5.)

34 *RFB*, no. 14, 7.

35 AN F7 4767. (Also see Mortimer-Ternaux, *Histoire de la Terreur*, I: 427.)

36 There were, however, many executions of rioters outside of Paris, where traditional judicial institutions operated with fewer constraints. (See, for example, Rudé, *The Crowd*, 87; P. Vaissière, *Lettres d'"Aristocrates"*, [Paris, 1907], 19, 90; and M. Wahl, *Les premières années de la Révolution à Lyon*, [Paris, 1894], 200.)

37 See AN y 10530, fols. 154, 160, 163, 164, 167. Other cases in which relatively light sentences were given to defendants charged with various forms of sedition can be found in fols. 159, 160, and 163–4.

38 For the Pont Notre-Dame disturbance, see *PF*, October 23, 1789, 4; and LaCroix, II: 364, 369.

39 For the passage of the Loi Martiale, see *Moniteur*, October 20–22, 1789, 77–80.

40 See AN y 10508 B, Martin-Duval dossier; *Délibérations de l'assemblée générale des volontaires du bataillon de Saint-Martin des Champs*, (Paris, 1789), BN LB 40 358, 7; *Appel des sieurs Martin et Duval de Stains à la justice et à la vérité*, (Paris, 1789), BN LB 39 8066, 8; *PF*, October 26, 1789, 3; *RdP*, October 24–31, 1789, 3; and LaCroix, II: 431.

41 For a protest by the Bonne-Nouvelle District, see AN 32 271. For a report of protests by the Trinité and the Petit-Pères Districts, see *Chronique*, October 27, 1789, 259. However, the Petit-Pères District denied this report and proclaimed its support for the new law. (See *Chronique*, October 29, 1789, 267.)

42 See *Délibérations du bataillon de Saint-Martin*, 2.

43 *PF*, October 26, 1789, 3.

44 The districts were replaced by sections in May 1790.

45 See LaCroix, II: 433–5, 495; *Journal de Paris*, October 31, 1789, 1401–2; and *District de Saint-Martin*, (Paris, 1789), BN LB 40 359.

46 AN Y 10508 B. After their release, both men remained active in the popular movement, and both turned up as members of the Revolutionary Commune of August 1792. (See Braesch, *Commune du dix août*, 252, 258.)

47 For Rutledge's literary career, see A. de Gallier, "Les émeutiers de 1789," *Revue des questions historiques* (1883): 143–5. According to Brissot, the authorship of many of Rutledge's never-performed plays was disputed because "no one dared take responsibility for them." (*Mémoires*, ed. Perroud, I: 130.) For Rutledge's pre-revolutionary activities as an informer, see Interrogatoire au Châtelet, December 1, 1789, as found in *Procès fait au Chevalier Rutledge, Baronet, avec des pièces justificatives et sa correspondance avec M. Necker*, (Paris, 1790), BN LN 27 18148, 37. (This volume reprinted most of the transcript of Rutledge's trial. The transcript itself can be found in AN Y 10506.)

48 See *Procès fait*, 39, 106; J. J. Rutledge, *Second mémoire pour les maîtres boulangers*, (Paris, 1789), 35; and Rutledge, *Mémoire pour la communauté des maîtres boulangers de la ville et faubourgs de Paris*, (Paris, 1789), esp. 7.

49 For the suppression of the first *Mémoire*, see "Extrait des registres du conseil d'état du roi," as found in G. Bord, *Le pacte de famine*, (Paris, 1887), sec. 2, 5. For rumors that Rutledge would be arrested, see *Correspondance secrète*, March 27, 1789, II: 339. For Rutledge's continued defense of Necker in a new pamphlet published in July, see *Second mémoire*, 38.

50 Letters of August 1 and October 7, 1789, *Procès fait*, 134, 138.

51 See *ibid.*, 111–12, 137–8.

52 See *ibid.*, 112, 114–16. This is the same de Lessart who would serve as Interior and Foreign Minister in 1791–2.

53 Réquisitoire du Procureur du Roi, *ibid.*, 33–4. The arrest order can be found in AN Y 10506, Rutledge dossier.

54 *Procès fait*, 112, 114.

55 Rutledge, *Dénonciation sommaire faite au Comité des Recherches de l'Assemblée Nationale contre M. Necker*, (Paris, 1790), 13. For a study which traces the history of accusations of collusion between the French government and grain monopolists, see Kaplan, *The Famine Plot Persuasion*.

56 Rutledge's Comité de Police interrogators told him that "he should have known that, in a moment of unrest, inciting the bakers was not permitted." They also told him that his activities had led to "the violent and seditious words that some bakers have dared to express." (*Procès fait*, 21.) These points, however, were not pursued at the trial itself.

57 *RdP*, January 2–9, 1790, 24; and *JCV*, December 6, 1789, 631; December 9, 1789, 653–5. (Similar reports can also be found in *Courrier français*, December 8, 1789, 550; December 10, 1789, 566–8.). Apart from the *APL*, which reprinted some of the *Courrier français*' reports, coverage of

the Rutledge trial is almost totally absent from the rest of the revolutionary press.

58 For the release order, see AN y 10506.
59 See *Moniteur*, January 25, 1790, 199–200; and *Correspondance secrète*, ii: 418. The first of the anti-Necker pamphlets was *Projet d'une législation des substances composée pour M. Necker par James Rutledge*, (Paris, 1790). This was quickly followed by *Dénonciation sommaire; L'Astuce dévoilée; Vie privée et ministérielle de M. Necker*, (Geneva, 1790); and *Supplément à la vie privée et ministérielle de M. Necker*, (Geneva, 1790).
60 See his journal *Le Creuset*, published from January–August 1791. For his participation in the sectional movement, see *Procès-verbal de l'Assemblée Nationale*, (Paris, 1793), xxii: 246.
61 Many people assumed that Rutledge was mad, and rumors to that effect were common. (See *Courrier français*, December 20, 1789, 646.)
62 See annex to Réquisitoire, *Procès fait*, 36. This charge, however, did not surface at the trial itself, undoubtedly because, as already indicated, the authorities sought to avoid substantive grain policy issues.
63 *Ibid.*, 91. Also see *ibid.*, 80; and Rutledge letter to *AdP*, January 3, 1790, 3.
64 *Moniteur*, December 1, 1789, 274–5.
65 The Comité spoke of the "excess to which these brigands devoted themselves." (*Ibid.*, December 1, 1789, 274.)
66 *PF*, October 8, 1789, 4.
67 Agier, *Compte-rendu*, 15.
68 *PF*, October 8, 1789, 4.
69 LaCroix, ii: 366.
70 See *Moniteur*, December 1, 1789, 274.
71 For the October 29 denunciation of Augeard, see AN d xxix bis, 37, 384. For the denunciation of the abbé Douglas and associates, see A. Tuetey, *Répertoire général des sources manuscrites de l'histoire de Paris pendant la Révolution française*, (Paris, 1890), i: 128. (Tuetey gives October 4 as the date of this denunciation, but there was no Paris Comité des Recherches at that time. Perhaps the correct date is November 4.)
72 *Mercure de France*, November 21, 1789, 246–7; and Mounier, *Exposé*, sec. 3, 37.
73 Letter to Mounier, October 23, 1789, Lafayette, *Mémoires*, ii: 416. In the same letter, Lafayette spoke of "the desertion of those whose return would save us and whose opposition could ruin everything." (*Ibid.*, ii: 420.)
74 *Ibid.*, ii: 362; and Brissot, "Projet de défense devant la Tribunal révolutionnaire," *Mémoires*, ed. Perroud, ii: 280. Also see letter of Blonde, *Moniteur*, January 2, 1790, 15.
75 *Moniteur*, December 1, 1789, 274.
76 *Correspondance secrète*, ii: 406; and Brissot, *Mémoires*, ed. Perroud, ii: 280.

77 AN Y 10598, fol. 139, as cited by Tuetey, *Répertoire général*, I: 109, no. 1015.
78 *Domine salvum*, 9.
79 *Procédure criminelle*, witness no. 1, sec. 1, 11.
80 See *ibid.*, sec. 1, 11–17.
81 *Ibid.*, sec. 1, 14, 16.
82 For other testimony directed against the Triumvirate, see *ibid.*, no. 17, sec. 1, 37; no. 98, sec 1, 153; no. 147, sec. 1, 227; no. 194, sec. 2, 39; no. 226, sec. 2, 83; and no. 373, sec. 3, 30–1.
83 See G. Michon, *Essai sur l'histoire du parti feuillant: Adrien Duport*, (Paris, 1924), 72–9; Lafayette, *Mémoires*, II: 370–1; and T. Lameth, *Mémoires*, (Paris, 1913), 113–15.
84 For a detailed discussion of secrecy and publicity under the new regulations, see Seligman, *La Justice*, I: 202–3.
85 *Gazette universelle*, April 11, 1790, 526; and *Ami du Peuple*, BN LC 2 234, April 24, 1790, 7. The latter was another "counterfeit Marat," one of several that appeared during Marat's absence in winter–spring 1790.
86 See *Procédure criminelle*, no. 1, sec. 1, 14–15. For other testimony on Orleanist plotting in spring–summer 1789, see *ibid.*, no. 4, sec. 1, 20; no. 5, sec. 1, 21; no. 124, sec. 1, 185–6; no. 126, sec. 1, 190–1; no. 140, sec. 1, 213–16; no. 224, sec. 2, 80–1; and no. 232, sec. 2, 90–1.
87 See *ibid.*, no. 104, sec. 1, 160; and no. 109, sec. 1, 165. The latter, a locksmith employed by Orléans, said these pikes had been ordered by the Filles-Saint-Thomas District. Since the president of that district at that time had been Brissot, this little sub-plot may have been an attempt by the Châtelet to put some heat on an uncooperative Comité des Recherches.
88 See, for example, Dominique, *Paris enlève le roi*, 77–8; Gottschalk and Maddox, *Lafayette: Through the October Days*, 288–9; and Maleissye, *Mémoires*, 97–100.
89 *AP*, XIX: 390–1.
90 Gottschalk and Maddox suggest that Lafayette's intention in speaking to d'Estaing was to have a warning conveyed to the Queen, who was generally suspected of being the ultimate sponsor of the Metz plot. (See *Lafayette: Through the October Days*, 289.) As we will see in the next chapter, one of Lafayette's informants (though admittedly a not very reliable one) reported that d'Estaing himself was involved in the Metz conspiracy.
91 For the Gardes de la Régénération Française, see Mathiez, *Etude critique*, 70–1.
92 See AN D XXIX bis, 2, 13; *Faits justificatifs du sieur de Livron*, (Paris, 1790), BN LB 39 3902; *RdP*, October 24–31, 1789, 20, and November 21–28, 1789, 32; *APL*, October 9, 1789, 3; *Modérateur*, February 11, 1790, 166–7; Mathiez, *Etude critique*, 101–3; and Tuetey, *Répertoire général*, I: 128–9.

93 See *Mémoires secrets de J. M. Augeard*, (Paris, 1866), 204–30; Letter of Blonde, *Moniteur*, January 2, 1790, 15; Agier, *Eclaircissements donnés à un de MM. de l'Assemblée Nationale par M. Agier*, (Paris, 1790); *Réponse de M. Blonde aux éclaircissements donnés par M. Agier dans l'affaire de M. Augeard*, (n.p., 1790); and M. de Bonnières, *Plaidoyer pour M. Augeard*, (Paris, 1790).

94 See p. 86 above. In addition, on October 5 itself, Mounier had advised the King to leave for Rouen, a suggestion which might also be construed as seditious. (See Egret, *La Révolution des notables*, 183–4.) However, the pre-October Days initiative, which was the premeditated proposal of an entire faction, must be regarded as more serious than Mounier's spontaneous and apparently individual Rouen suggestion.

6   THE FAVRAS CONSPIRACY

1 Lafayette, *Mémoires*, II: 388. Note the class-based nature of Lafayette's concept of "crimes against the state," which apparently did not include seditions committed by *émeutiers* like Adrien. The comment on "more titles than assets" is from A. de Valon, "Le Marquis de Favras," *Revue des deux mondes* 10 (April–June 1851): 1032.

2 See Lafayette, *Mémoires*, II: 329–30; and Morel deposition, as found in G. F. Mahy de Cormère, *Justification du Marquis de Favras*, (Paris, 1791), sec. 2, 2–3. Section 2 of this work contains the entire Favras trial transcript along with other documents relating to the case. (Cormère was Favras' brother and section 1 of this work is a defense of the accused.) The original Châtelet transcript can be found in AN BB 3 221.

3 Lafayette, *Mémoires*, II: 330.

4 A document bestowing this commission was published in *RdP*, February 6–14, 1790, 34–5.

5 *Justification*, sec. 2, 2.

6 *Ibid.*, sec. 2, 30–3. Both Morel and Favras also testified that their first meeting only took place in November. (*Ibid.*, sec. 2, 3, 228.)

7 Without providing any sources, Georges Lefebvre connected Favras to the Régénération Française plot discussed in the last chapter. However, I have not uncovered any evidence linking Favras to this plot, and Lefebvre may have mistakenly combined two separate but similar plots into one. (See *Coming of the Revolution*, 194.)

8 See *Justification*, sec. 2, 222; Cormère, *Plaidoyer pour Thomas Mahy de Favras*, (Paris, 1790), 4; and Favras, *Le déficit des finances de la France vaincue*, (n.p., 1789).

9 See Favras, "Mémoire pour Thomas de Mahy, Marquis de Favras, accusé," as found in *Recueil dédié a M. de Favras*, (n.p., 1790), sec. 1, 8–9; *Justification*, sec. 2, 116–17, 223–6; and Saint-Priest, *Mémoires*, II: 15.

10 *Justification*, sec. 2, 116–17. Also see *Moniteur*, January 20, 1790, 160.

11 The future co-ordinator of a major counter-revolutionary intelligence network, d'Antraigues lost his father at a very young age and was extremely close to his uncle. He left France soon after Morel testified that Favras had stated that d'Antraigues was "totally committed to us." (See *Justification*, sec. 2, 12; and L. Pinguad, *Le Comte d'Antraigues: Un agent secret sous la Révolution et l'Empire*, [Paris, 1894], 73–4.)

12 Favras, "Mémoire," *Recueil*, sec. 1, 15–16. Just before his execution, Favras revealed that he reported to "un grand seigneur" from "a house just below that of our princes." (Favras, *Testament de mort*, [Paris, 1790], 9.)

13 See, for example, Cormère, *Justification*, sec. 1, 81; Comte de Bouillé, *Souvenirs et fragments*, (Paris, 1906), I: 123–4; and T. Lameth, *Notes et souvenirs*, (Paris, 1914), 192–3.

14 *Mémoires d'Augeard*, 218–19. Favras' wife was arrested the same night he was and released the day after his execution.

15 Morris, *Diary*, I: 294, 305.

16 *Mémoires d'Augeard*, 218. This story was told to Augeard by Morris in 1798. The same story is also related in Maleissye, *Mémoires*, 121–2.

17 See *Moniteur*, December 28, 1789, 496; and Cormère, *Plaidoyer pour Favras*, 6.

18 See G. Walter, *Le Comte de Provence*, (Paris, 1950), 113–14; and P. Mansel, *Louis XVIII*, (London, 1981), 44.

19 "Notes de lecture: A travers les papiers de Louis XVIII," *Le Correspondant* 10 (January 1910): 45. According to Walter, the authenticity of these papers is beyond dispute. (*Le Comte de Provence*, 155.)

20 The comment on Mirabeau is from Droz, *Histoire de Louis XVI*, III: 8.

21 *Correspondance entre Mirabeau et LaMarck*, I: 119.

22 *Ibid.*, I: 125, 369, 374. The complete text of Mirabeau's plan can be found in *ibid.*, I: 364–82.

23 See Mathiez, *The French Revolution*, 68. Though he did not document his assertion, Mathiez was probably relying on the testimony of Morel, who implicated Mirabeau in the Favras plot at the same point that he implicated d'Antraigues. (See note 11 above.) However, as we have already seen, Morel was hardly the most trustworthy source.

24 See *Correspondance entre Mirabeau et LaMarck*, I: 129, 423; and Lafayette, *Mémoires*, II: 391.

25 A. Vallentin, *Mirabeau*, tr. E. Dickes, (New York, 1948), 399. Vallentin did not indicate her source for this letter and stated that its authenticity "is not definitely established."

26 See Droz, *Histoire de Louis XVI*, III: 72–5. Though Droz did not name him, there is unanimous agreement that Sémonville, who was still alive when this book was first published, was the source for this much-discussed vignette. (See, for example, Walter, *Le Comte de Provence*, 421; and Comte d'Hérisson, *Autour d'une Révolution*, [Paris, 1888], 70–88.) As for the story itself, while Monsieur's involvement in the Favras plot is

indisputable, Marie-Antoinette's must be considered highly problematic: besides the Sémonville–Droz account, the only other indication of it is Morel's quite unreliable pre-October Days report to Lafayette. Yet, regardless of whether or not the Queen was actually involved in the plot, it does seem to be true that she was mentioned in the Favras declaration. For it was probably this document that LaMarck was referring to when he notified Marie-Antoinette in December 1790 that Talon had shown him the original of a document which "could compromise Your Majesty." (See *Correspondance entre Mirabeau et LaMarck*, II: 515, 521.)

27 Droz, *Histoire de Louis XVI*, III: 73–4. Talon's possession of a secret document in the Favras case was widely known, and was reported by several contemporaries. (See Bouillé, *Souvenirs et fragments*, I: 123; Lameth, *Notes et souvenirs*, 193; *Mémoires du Général Thiébault*, [Paris, 1893], I: 272–3; and Lafayette, *Mémoires*, II: 394.) (Lafayette denied any knowledge of Talon's maneuvers in the Favras case, but, for reasons that will become clearer as this chapter proceeds, I don't think we can take this denial seriously.)

28 See P. Gaulot, *Amours d'autrefois*, (Paris, 1903), 240–8; Droz, *Histoire de Louis XVI*, III: 75; and Lafayette, *Mémoires*, II: 395.

29 *Mémoires de Thiébault*, I: 269, 272. According to Walter, the abbé LeDuc, who was also known as the "abbé de Bourbon," may have been assigned the task of being one of Favras' pre-execution confessors. If so, this was probably another deliciously cynical step taken by Talon to insure Favras' silence. (See *Le Comte de Provence*, 421.)

30 Bouillé, *Souvenirs et fragments*, I: 122. Bouillé's father, garrison commander at Metz during this period, may also have provided him with some information on the case.

31 See E. Cleray, *L'Affaire Favras*, (Paris, 1932), 37–53; and *Justification*, sec. 2, 168–78.

32 See *Justification*, sec. 2, 122–5, 136–8, 209–10.

33 See *ibid.*, sec. 1, 15, and sec. 2, 479; and *Mémoires d'Augeard*, 217–19.

34 See *Justification*, sec. 2, 113–14; and *Recueil*, sec. 1, 9.

35 Morris, *Diary*, I: 346. For other reports that documents implicating Monsieur were found either on Favras or at his apartment, see Bouillé, *Souvenirs et fragments*, I: 122; and A. Dumas père, *Mes Mémoires*, (Paris, 1967), IV: 56–7.

36 This meeting will be discussed in more detail shortly. Monsieur lamely claimed at the meeting that the loan was designed to cover some personal debts, but Walter argues that anyone with any knowledge of how royal family financial operations were conducted would have known that this could not have been true. (See *Le Comte de Provence*, 419.)

37 Cleray, *L'Affaire Favras*, 169–70.

38 See *ibid.*, 171–5; F. Braesch, "Un faux historique prétendue lettre du

Comte de Provence à Favras," *La Révolution française* 72 (1919): 201–20; and Feuillet de Conches, *Louis XVI*, III: 471–7.

39 See Lafayette, *Mémoires*, II: 391–2; *Mémoires d'Augeard*, 214–15; and Walter, *Le Comte de Provence*, 137.

40 See Agier, *Eclaircissements donnés*; Agier, *Compte-rendu;* Garran, *Rapport sur la conspiration des mois de mai, juin, et juillet derniers*, (Paris, 1789); Garran, *Réponse aux observations pour le Baron de Besenval et au mémoire de M. Barentin*, (Paris, 1790); Garran, *Rapport fait au comité des recherches de la municipalité de Paris par Jean Philippe Garran suivi des pièces justificatives et l'arrêté du comité tendant à dénoncer MM. Maillebois, Bonne-Savardin, et Guignard Saint-Priest*; and Garran, *Réponse au mémoire à consulter et consultation pour M. Guignard Saint-Priest*, (Paris, 1790).

41 For the denunciation of Favras, see *Moniteur*, December 31, 1789, 515. The other documents released by the Comité were a statement exonerating an Intendant of Monsieur who took part in the Chomel loan negotiations (he was arrested the same night as Favras but released almost immediately); and a statement on an assault on a National Guardsman, an incident that will be discussed in the next chapter. (See *Moniteur*, January 9, 1790, 71; and LaCroix, III: 294.)

42 *PF*, November 7, 1789, 2–3; and January 14, 1790, 2–3.

43 See, for example, *PF*, December 9, 1789, 2–4; December 24, 1789, 5–6; January 8, 1790, 2; February 19, 1790, 3–4; and February 25, 1790, 5–8.

44 Prospectus for *PF*, March 16, 1789, 5. Brissot's first attempt to publish his journal was suppressed by the royal censors in April 1789, and it did not actually appear until July 28. (See Berranger, *Histoire de la presse*, I: 425–7.)

45 Lacretelle did not sign any of the publicly issued Comité documents on the Besenval, October Days, and Maillebois affairs. Yet, he signed all three documents cited in note 41 above, as well as the Comité's order for the arrest of two men in the "Barauz" incident that will be discussed shortly. (See AN Y 10506, Potel-Jouve dossier.) While he never formally resigned from the Comité, Lacretelle's alienation from it would eventually become so complete that he would cease to be regarded as a member. (See Comité letter of June 1790, which speaks of "the five members of the Comité," *Discours prononcé à la barre de l'Assemblée Nationale par M. Oudart*, [n.p., 1790], 14.)

46 J. Peuchet, *Mémoires tirés des archives de la police de Paris*, (Paris, 1838), IV: 38–40. Apparently worried that the Comité might go beyond "official policy" and denounce Monsieur or part of his entourage, some of the more conservative Représentants proposed on December 26 that the Comité be required to get the approval of the full Assemblée des Représentants before issuing a denunciation. But this proposal did not make any headway, and the Comité soon proved its reliability later that day by denouncing only Favras. (See *ibid.*, IV: 49–50; and LaCroix, III: 286.)

47 See *PF*, January 1, 1791, 4.

48 *Moniteur*, December 28, 1789, 496. For Mirabeau's part in composing this speech, see Hérisson, *Autour d'une Révolution*, 50–9.

49 See LaCroix, III: 284, Peuchet, *Mémoires de la police*, IV: 41; and *Moniteur*, December 29, 1789, 499.

50 *CdP*, January 19, 1790, 170. For similar reactions by other "left Fayettist" journals, see *APL*, December 30, 1789, 3; and *Chronique*, December 28, 1789, 507. As for Brissot, in spite of the "delicacy" of his position, he managed to praise Monsieur's "noble simplicity." (*PF*, December 27, 1789, 2.)

51 In surveying the radical press reaction to Favras' arrest, I will follow five of the six major early revolutionary radical journals examined in Censer, *Prelude to Power*. (The sixth, Fréron's *Orateur du Peuple*, only began publishing in spring 1790.) For an exoneration of Monsieur by two other radical papers, see *L'Observateur*, December 30, 1789, 526; and *Révolutions de Paris* (Tournon), no. 24, 24.

52 *RdP*, December 26, 1789–January 2, 1790, 15; *JU*, December 28, 1789, 281–2; *Journal d'état et du citoyen*, December 31, 1789, 17; and *RFB*, no. 6, 270.

53 *AdP*, December 30, 1789, 4–6; and December 31, 1789, 4–5.

54 *JU*, February 8, 1790, 642, and February 9, 1790, 645; and *RFB*, no. 8, 353, 363.

55 *RdP*, February 20–27, 1790, 23–4; and January 9–16, 1790, 14.

56 See the apocryphal *Lettre du Marquis de Favras au Baron de Besenval*, (Paris, 1790), BN LB 39 2930, 9; the equally apocryphal *Résponse de M. le Baron de Besenval au Marquis de Favras*, (Paris, 1790), BN LB 39 8406, 5; and *Réflexions impartiales sur le mort du Marquis de Favras*, (Paris, 1790), BN LB 39 8478, 4.

57 See AN Y 10506, Potel-Jouve dossier.

58 *Le Comte de Provence*, 138.

59 *RdP*, December 26, 1789–January 2, 1790, 13.

60 See Van Kley, *The Damiens Affair and the Unraveling of the Old Regime*, (Princeton, 1984), 246.

61 Perhaps revealing more of a sense of relief than he had intended, Brissot wrote that "his affair terminates with him." (*PF*, February 23, 1790, 3.)

62 *Justification*, sec. 2, 328.

63 *RdP*, March 6–13, 1790, 20–1. In this passage, Loustalot intermingled the formal charges against Augeard (which had to do with a scheme to extract the King from his post-October Days situation) with some comments he made concerning what the King should have done in July. (See Agier, *Eclaircissements donnés*, 8, 13.)

64 Not surprisingly, Favras' defenders also contended that his so-called "projects" were nothing more than "speculations," "thoughtless words," and "whims." (See Thilorier, "Plaidoyer pour M. de Favras,"

Recueil, sec. 3, 7, 87; Cormère, *Justification*, sec. 1, 79; and L. A. Pitou, *Réflexions sur le jugement et la mort de M. de Favras*, [n.p., n.d.], 7–9.)

65 See Cormère, *Justification*, sec. 2, 7–8, 54–5.

66 *Ibid.*, sec. 2, 56–7. For the general problems involved in merging the Gardes-Françaises into the National Guard, see Gottschalk and Maddox, *Lafayette: Through the Federation*, 162, 193–4.

67 *Ouvrez donc les yeux*, (n.p., n.d.), BN LB 39 2728, 51 (emphasis in original).

68 See *Justification*, sec. 2, 25–6, 58, 62.

69 See *ibid.*, sec. 2, 61–4; *Testament de mort*, 13; and *Chronique*, February 23, 1790, 213. This revelation will be discussed in more detail in the next chapter.

70 See *Justification*, sec. 2, 64; and de Valon, "Le Marquis de Favras," 1107–8.

71 For this incident, see *Moniteur*, January 15, 1790, 120–1; *APL*, January 13, 1790, 3; *PF*, January 13, 1790, 3; *RdP*, January 9–16, 1790, 6–7, 10–14; *Journal de Paris*, January 16, 1790, 63–4; *Journal de DuQuesnoy*, II: 278; and Gottschalk and Maddox, *Lafayette: Through the Federation*, 173–7, 193–4. Twenty-two of the mutinous Guardsmen were sent before a military court, but I have not been able to determine the outcome of these cases. The rest were detained for three months and expelled from the Guard. (See *Assemblée Nationale*, April 22, 1790, 7–8; and LaCroix, III: 436–7.)

72 See Cormère, *Justification*, sec. 1, 93–5. On the other hand, the Monarchien Bergasse (who may have been envisioning himself as a future defendant) would soon argue that political defendants should be given legal protections which go "beyond those which apply to ordinary accusations." (*Discours sur les crimes et les tribunaux de haute-trahison*, [n.p., 1790], 32.)

73 Cormère, *Justification*, sec. 2, 313. Lafayette later claimed this statement named Morel as Favras' "dénonciateur." (*Mémoires*, II: 393.) However, the Parisian General had been adamantly opposed two weeks earlier to having anyone but the Commune's Procureur-Syndic named as Morel's denunciator and had used his influence within the National Assembly to insure that the Assembly didn't interfere in this matter. (See letter to Latour-Maubourg, AN F7 4767; also in *Le Curieux*, January 1, 1884, 95.) Besides, if the municipal authorities had wanted to take an unambiguous position on this issue, why didn't they use the word "dénonciateur" in their statement?

74 See *Moniteur*, January 21, 1790, 170. Whenever the Comité des Recherches issued a denunciation, it was forwarded to the Procureur-Syndic, who rubber-stamped it and sent it to the Châtelet.

75 Cormère, *Justification*, sec. 2, 6, 34–5.

76 *Ibid.*, sec. 2, 6–11, 35–6. According to Tourcaty, Favras had said that "if

the King didn't want to leave, they would use force to put him in the carriage intended for him."

77 See, for example, Cormère, *Justification*, sec. 2, 231, where an exasperated Favras asked: "Where are these 1,200 horses . . . where have I put them?"

78 *Ibid.*, sec. 2, 45.

79 *Ibid.*, sec. 2, 8. On December 19, Morel was arrested after boasting to a neighbor that he was going to assassinate Lafayette. Hastily explaining that he had not really meant what he had said, the prisoner stated that Lafayette would vouch for him and his "special mission." Lafayette did, and Morel was soon released. (See Tuetey, *Répertoire*, ii, part 2: 66, no. 620; and Cormère, *Justification*, sec. 1, 104.)

80 For the theory that the real goal of the Favras plot was to have Monsieur named as Regent, see Bouillé, *Souvenirs et fragments*, i: 121–2; Lameth, *Notes et souvenirs*, 192–3; and Dumas père, *Mes Mémoires*, iv: 56. (Dumas says he was told this by Lafayette in 1830.)

81 For the King's inclination to flee on July 15, see Vingtrinier, *La Contre-Révolution*, i: 32–3; and *Mémoires du Duc des Cars*, ii: 80. For a good summary of all the escape plans, see Fournel, *Evénement de Varennes*, 14–46, 263–308.

82 See Vingtrinier, *La Contre-Révolution*, i: 195–6.

83 See *ibid.*, i: 217–30; and S. Scott, "Problems of Law and Order during 1790, the 'Peaceful' Year of the French Revolution," *American Historical Review* 80 (1975): 873–6.

84 See Vingtrinier, *La Contre-Révolution*, ii: 24–5, 35–44, 302–3; Wahl, *La Révolution à Lyon*, 234–6; and *Lyon en 1791*, ed. A. Metzger and J. Vaesen, (Lyon, n.d.), 5–24.

85 See Vingtrinier, *La Contre-Révolution*, i: 325–34, ii: 335–77; and H. Le-Clerq, *La Fuite du Roi*, (Paris, 1936), 181–203.

86 See Vingtrinier, *La Contre-Révolution*, ii: 200–20, 260–1; Wahl, *La Révolution à Lyon*, 254–85; and A. Audin, *La Conspiration lyonnaise de 1790*, (Lyon, 1984).

87 See Vingtrinier, *La Contre-Révolution*, i: 331.

88 See *Moniteur*, January 21, 1790, 170; *PF*, January 20, 1790, 1; and *RdP*, January 16–23, 1790, 52. (Also see note 73 above.)

7 THE FAVRAS–BESENVAL JUDICIAL TRANSACTION

1 Even Samuel Scott, who has sought to revise traditional notions about the Revolution's "quiet period," agrees that Paris itself was remarkably peaceful in 1790. (See "Problems of Law and Order," 860–1.)

2 *RFB*, no. 6, 259; *RdP*, December 26, 1789–January 2, 1790, 2; *CdP*, December 26, 1789, 230; and Vingtrinier, *La Contre-Révolution*, i: 109–10. Also see *JCV*, December 25, 1789, 783; and *Le Rôdeur français*, December 24, 1789, 167–8.

3 *APL*, January 14, 1790, 3. Also see *Gazette universelle*, January 10, 1790, 162.

4 *JCV*, December 30, 1789, 822–3.

5 La Croix, III: 294. (The Comité des Recherches report on this incident, reprinted here, is one of the documents mentioned in chapter 6, note 41 above.) Also see *PF*, December 29, 1789, 3; *CdP*, December 29, 1789, 273; and *Révolutions de Paris* (Tournon), no. 25, 13–14.

6 See La Croix, III: 295–6; *JCV*, January 6, 1790, 44; *Journal d'état et du citoyen*, January 3, 1790, 3; and *RFB*, no. 8, 349–50.

7 *Moniteur*, January 19, 1790, 152. Also see *PF*, January 1, 1790, 2, and January 2, 1790, 2.

8 See *CdP*, January 1, 1790, 319, and January 2, 1790, 330; *JCV*, January 1, 1790, 7; and *Gazette universelle*, January 10, 1790, 162. For other similar rumors during this period, see *JU*, December 31, 1789, 307, and January 1, 1790, 317; *JCV*, January 6, 1790, 44; Tuetey, *Répertoire*, II: part 2, 67, no. 625; and A. Young, *Travels in France during the Years 1787, 1788, and 1789*, (London, 1889), 294.

9 See *PF*, January 11, 1790, 1; *RdP*, January 9–16, 1790, 3–4; *AdP*, January 9, 1790, 7; and LaCroix, III: 398–9.

10 LaCroix, III: 399; and *JCV*, January 12, 1790, 94–5. Also see *Révolutions de Paris* (Tournon), no. 27, 16–17.

11 See *PF*, January 14, 1790, 2.

12 *RdP*, January 9–16, 1790, 14. For other reports of disorder at Besenval's trial at this time, see *Chronique*, January 9, 1790, 35; *CdP*, January 11, 1790, 51–2; *AdP*, January 8, 1790, 7; and *Mercure de France*, January 23, 1790, 305.

13 *Moniteur*, January 14, 1790, 112.

14 See *ibid.*, January 13, 1790, 104, and January 14, 1790, 112–13; *JU*, January 9, 1790, 37–8; *JCV*, January 13, 1790, 98–100; *CdP*, January 13, 1790, 82–7; *Chronique*, January 13, 1790, 51–2; *RdP*, January 9–16, 1790, 4–6; *Mercure de France*, January 23, 1790, 304–5; and LaCroix, III: 435. The figure of 10,000 protesters on January 11 is from *Révolutions de Paris* (Tournon), no. 27, 23–4.

15 See *Moniteur*, January 14, 1790, 112–13; and p. 34 above.

16 *JU*, January 14, 1790, 420.

17 *CdP*, January 13, 1790, 85–6; and January 15, 1790, 119–20. For a similar approach in other "left Fayettist" journals, see *Chronique*, January 13, 1790, 51–2; and *APL*, January 13, 1790, 3.

18 *PF*, January 14, 1790, 2. For a virtually identical passage, see *RFB*, no. 8, 353. The "open insurrection" referred to here was the Parlement de Rennes' refusal to register an Assembly decree which had, in effect, placed the Parlements on "permanent vacation." Though some deputies argued these magistrates should be indicted for *lèse-nation*, it was decided instead that their political rights would be suspended until they

pledged their loyalty to the Assembly. (See H. Carré, *La Fin des Parlements*, [Paris, 1912].)

19 *PF*, January 13, 1790, 4.

20 *RdP*, January 9–16, 1790, 3–14. For similar accounts of the origins of the Châtelet riots, see *JCV*, January 14, 1790, 109, and January 15, 1790, 115; *APL*, January 13, 1790, 3; *JU*, January 14, 1790, 420–1; *Chronique*, January 13, 1790, 51–2; *CdP*, January 15, 1790, 118–20; and *Moniteur*, January 15, 1790, 121.

21 *JU*, January 9, 1790, 380.

22 Buchez and Roux, *Histoire parlementaire*, iv: 290.

23 *RdP*, January 2–9, 1790, 16; and *JU*, December 26, 1789, 269.

24 *APL*, January 1, 1790, 4. Also see *RFB*, no. 7, 326–30.

25 See *AdP*, January 9, 1790, 7; and January 11, 1790, 8. Sounding for all the world like a modern-day critic of "bleeding-heart liberals," Loustalot attacked the "timid compliance" of the Versailles municipality for temporarily lowering bread prices. (*RdP*, January 9–16, 1790, 4.) Similarly, Audouin showed little sympathy for the idea that National Guardsmen were underpaid. (*JU*, January 17, 1790, 442.)

26 Malouet, *Mémoires*, i: 393.

27 See *ibid.*, i: 388–97; and *Mercure de France*, January 9, 1790, 164, and March 6, 1790, 77–81. Also see chapter 4, note 19 above. For the alienation between the Monarchiens and the "hard-right" which resulted from these meetings, see *Mémoires de Tourzel*, 50–1.

28 *PF*, January 20, 1790, 2; *RdP*, January 23–30, 1790, 17; and *RFB*, no. 8, 355–6. Also see *Chronique*, February 1, 1790, 127; and *Révolutions de Paris* (Tournon), no. 32, 10.

29 See LaCroix, iii: 429.

30 *AdP*, December 29, 1789, 8; and January 11, 1790, 8.

31 See *Moniteur*, December 1, 1789, 275; and *RdP*, December 12–19, 1789, 54.

32 *Le Rôdeur français*, January 10, 1790, 246. Clearly this anecdote refers to an earlier period in the trial. By January 10, it is highly unlikely that the ladies of the Court were still having dinner parties at the Châtelet.

33 Comité des Recherches denunciation, *Moniteur*, December 1, 1789, 274.

34 Besenval claimed the purpose of the troops was "to guarantee secure provisioning." (Third Interrogation, AN bb 30 161.) But see Garran's persuasive argument that they could not possibly have been summoned for that purpose alone, *Réponse aux observations*, 43–6, 59–60.

35 Garran, *Réponse aux observations*, 26.

36 See Morris, *Diary*, i: 9; and Campan, *Private Life*, i: 178.

37 Technically, a fourth co-conspirator, the ex-War Minister Puységur, who had been replaced by Broglie on July 11, was also on trial. However, there was little public antagonism against him, and unlike the other defendants, he had not fled after July 14. When he learned he had been indicted (largely on the basis of having signed orders summoning

troops to the Paris–Versailles area), Puységur came to Paris and was interrogated by the Comité, which subsequently praised his "frank and loyal behavior." (See LaCroix, III: 79.) With the Comité thus satisfied and with no one else particularly interested in him, Puységur was almost totally ignored during the Besenval trial.

38 AN BB 30, 161, Besenval Information, witnesses nos. 178, and 180–4. Also see *Moniteur*, January 28, 1790, 222–3; and January 29, 1790, 232–3. (These were the events connected with the Tennis Court Oath and the June 23 Royal Session.)

39 For a general discussion of such trials, see Kirchheimer, *Political Justice*, 304–47.

40 *JCV*, January 27, 1790, 210. This journal would soon begin a sharp move to the right, but in January 1790, it was still solidly patriotic. (See Berranger, *Histoire de la presse*, I: 471.)

41 See *Chronique*, January 27, 1790, 107 ("they testified about the problems the National Assembly experienced in its meeting-room"); and Garran, *Rapport sur la conspiration*, as found in *Moniteur*, December 27, 1789, 488.

42 On the other hand, it might be argued that it was not a question of ignoring strategy in formulating religious policy, but rather a matter of a gigantic political miscalculation: as immersed as they were in secular Enlightenment culture, the deputies may simply not have realized how much profound political support might still be mobilized on behalf of the old religion. (See N. Hampson, *Prelude to Terror*, [New York, 1988], 139–55.)

43 *Chronique*, November 24, 1789, 370; and December 12, 1789, 442. Actually, Besenval's attorneys never argued that their client was "only following orders," for to do so would have implied there was something wrong with his orders, thereby directing attention towards their ultimate source, the King. Instead, the general line taken by the Besenval defense team was simply to deny that the Court had any aggressive intentions. (See note 34 above, and R. de Sèze, *Observations pour le Baron de Besenval*, as found in *Moniteur*, January 4, 1790, 33.)

44 *Chronique*, December 31, 1789, 519; and January 14, 1790, 55.

45 *CdP*, January 2, 1790, 331.

46 *Moniteur*, January 25, 1790, 199; and February 3, 1790, 273.

47 *JCV*, January 16, 1790, 125–6. For other moderately patriotic journals which made a sharp distinction between an innocent Besenval and a guilty Favras, see *Assemblée Nationale*, January 15, 1790, 6–8; and *Assemblée Nationale et Commune de Paris*, January 14, 1790, 6–7. On the other hand, one "left Fayettist" journalist, Carra, remained consistently hostile to Besenval until the end. (See *APL*, January 1, 1790, 4; and January 29, 1790, 3.) But then Carra is usually described as one of the most radical of the Girondins. (See, for example, M. Reinhard, *La Chute de la royauté*, [Paris, 1969], 369.)

48 Morris, *Diary*, I: 355; Also see *Correspondance secrète*, January 23, 1790, II:

268 *Notes to pages 160–5*

418: "[The depositions against Besenval] are insignificant, and this monstrous proceeding is fatiguing for respectable citizens. 'It is not through tyranny,' they are saying, 'that we can be made to love liberty.'"

49 Garran, *Réponse aux observations*, 27.

50 *Ibid.*, 14 (his emphasis). For accusations that the Comité had incited hatred against the defendant, see de Sèze, *Observations*, as found in *Moniteur*, January 4, 1790, 32; and letter of Bruges to *Journal de Paris*, January 25, 1790, 98.

51 *JU*, December 26, 1789, 269.

52 *RFB*, no. 7, 326.

53 *RdP*, January 2–9, 1790, 17 (his emphasis).

54 Young, *Travels in France*, 298–9; Vaissière, *Lettres d'"Aristocrates"*, 34–5; and *Correspondance secrète*, II: 417.

55 See *Journal de Paris*, January 31, 1790, 133; *Mercure de France*, February 6, 1790, 56; and *JU*, February 1, 1790, 582–3. Technically, Besenval's release, which was based on a finding that there were no grounds for issuing a formal arrest warrant against him, was only provisional. He and his absent co-defendants were officially acquitted on March 1. (See *Jugement en dernier ressort qui décharge le Baron de Besenval, et al.*, [Paris, 1790], BN LB 39 3050.)

56 *RdP*, January 30–February 6, 1790, 20–1 (his emphasis).

57 *CdP*, February 1, 1790, 370.

58 Most of the sources do not give any figures on the voting that night. Those that do are *RFB*, no. 11, 498: 29 for death; *Correspondance de Thomas Lindet pendant la Constituante et la Législative*, (Paris, 1899), 48–9: 28; C. G. de Clermont-Gallerande, *Mémoires*, (Paris, 1826), I: 306: 28; *Journal de DuQuesnoy*, II: 342: 26; *Courrier français*, February 2, 1790, 261: 21; *Assemblée Nationale et Commune de Paris*, February 2, 1790, 2: a slight majority for death; and *RdP*, January 30–February 6, 1790, 21: a slight majority against death. For the text of the decision released that night, see *Justification*, sec. 2, 324.

59 The best evidence that Paris was remarkably calm is the total absence in the sources of any reports of unrest. For explicit mention of the prevailing calm, see *CdP*, January 31 1790, 359; and *Journal de DuQuesnoy*, II: 339. For a report that extra National Guard troops were sent to the Châtelet and then withdrawn because they were unnecessary, see *Lettere di Filippo Mazzei alla Corte di Polonia 1788–1792*, ed. R. Ciampini, (Bologna, 1937), I: 270. For Besenval's reception at the Tuileries, see *CdP*, January 31, 1790, 358–9; *JCV*, February 1, 1790, 250; and *APL*, February 14, 1790, 2.

60 See *JU*, January 31, 1790, 573–4. (All other radical journals then publishing were either weeklies or twice-weeklies. Marat's paper was a daily, but he had fled to England a week earlier.) Gorsas' paper was the only major one that actually reported Favras' *condemnation* in its January

31 issue (p. 368). However, the *PF* (p. 2), the *JCV* (pp. 242–3), and the *Journal de Paris* (p. 123) all reported Besenval's release and Flandre's recommendation that Favras be condemned in their January 31 issue without reporting that the final judgment had been suspended. And the *APL* (p. 2), the *Chronique* (p. 123), and the *Moniteur* (p. 249) all reported Besenval's release in their January 31 issue without reporting any late information on the Favras case.

61 *Correspondance de Lindet*, 70, 81.

62 For reports of twenty-eight votes for death, see *Mercure de France*, February 27, 1790, 304; and M. LeCoq, *La Conspiration de Favras*, (Paris, 1955), 153. On the other hand, for reports that thirty-two of thirty-eight voted for death, see *RFB*, no. 14, 7; and *Journal de DuQuesnoy*, ii: 404. Sallier (*Annales françaises*, ii: 248–9) also reported thirty-two votes for death, but indicated there were two votes taken that day, with a smaller number for death (twenty-eight?) on the first ballot. None of the other sources gives figures on the voting. Though it may appear arbitrary to prefer the figure of twenty-eight votes to thirty-two, it does seem reasonable to assume that some of those who voted against death on January 30 would have been more likely to be absent or otherwise disqualify themselves than to actually change their vote. In any case, another question that remains unanswered is how the number of judges taking part in the final decision was determined. The *Almanach royal* ([Paris, 1789], 388–90) lists fifty-nine Conseillers au Châtelet plus four officers. Were they all eligible to participate? Might the Châtelet leaders have found ways to discourage some of the more intransigent reactionaries from participating? (For the final judgment signed by thirty-eight judges, see Cormère, *Justification*, sec. 2, 329.)

63 *Souvenirs d'un historien de Napoléon: Mémorial de J. Norvins*, ed. L. Lanzac de Laborie, (Paris, 1896), i: 238, editor's note.

64 *Révolutions de Paris* (Tournon), no. 32, 26–7. Also see *Chronique*, February 20, 1790, 202; *CdP*, February 19, 1790, 251; and *RFB*, no. 14, 7.

65 Maleissye, *Mémoires*, 124. Also see Clermont-Gallerande, *Mémoires*, i: 307; and *Mémoires de Paroy*, 143. For Lafayette's disclaimer, see his *Mémoires*, ii: 394.

66 *CdP*, February 21, 1790, 283–4. For the reaction of the spectators, also see *JU*, February 19, 1790, 726; *Chronique*, February 21, 1790, 407; and *Mercure de France*, February 27, 1790, 306.

67 *RFB*, no. 14, 7–8.

68 *RFB*, no. 14, 8, 10.

69 See *CdP*, February 21, 1790, 206; *Journal de Paris*, February 20, 1790, 202, and February 22, 1790, 209; *Mercure de France*, February 27, 1790, 306; and *Moniteur*, February 24, 1790, 444.

70 *Testament de mort*, 12, 13–14, 17.

71 *Ibid.*, 18–19. For Favras' "fermeté," see *RdP*, February 13–20, 1790, 3; *CdP*, February 22, 1790, 307; and *Moniteur*, February 21, 1790, 421.

72 *RFB*, no. 14, 18–19. For slightly different versions, see *RdP*, February 20–27, 1790, 48; and *Testament de mort*, 19. For Monsieur's vigil, see *Mémoires de Thiébault*, I: 272; and Bouillé, *Souvenirs et fragments*, I: 124–5. For Talon's preparations, see Sémonville letter, Hérisson, *Autour d'une Révolution*, 78.

73 *Moniteur*, December 1, 1790, 280.

74 See *RdP*, February 20–27, 1790, 21; *RFB*, no. 14, 8; *JCV*, February 23, 1790, 429; Sallier, *Annales françaises*, II: 84; and G. Touchard-LaFosse, *Souvenirs d'un demi-siècle*, (Paris, 1836), I: 141. The crowd count given here is from *Histoire par Deux Amis*, IV: 419. For the double meaning of *sauter* in this epoque ("jump" and "derogate"), see LeCoq, *La Conspiration de Favras*, 168.

75 For a royalist version of the same point, see Pitou, *Réflexions*: "The tigers of the People have devoured him. These ferocious beasts had to be fed, and their screams signalled their hunger. Lafayette and Bailly thought that spilling blood for them would consolidate their own power. They have slaughtered him and their tigers have eaten him."

76 *Chronique*, February 21, 1790, 207.

77 R. de Sèze, *Plaidoyer pour le Baron de Besenval*, (Paris, 1790), 70–1.

78 Walzer, *Regicide and Revolution*, (London, 1974), 70.

79 See *Moniteur*, February 6, 1790, 297–9; LaCroix, IV: 5; and Gottschalk and Maddox, *Lafayette: Through the Federation*, 206–9.

80 *RFB*, no. 11, 496–8; and no. 14, 19.

81 *JU*, January 27, 1790, 526; February 20, 1790, 734; and February 24, 1790, 767. Also see *Révolutions de Paris* (Tournon), no. 30, 7: "They sensed they could not convict you [Besenval] without exiling and sullying forever the fugitives who, like you, have outraged the Nation. They sensed such a course would have renewed or at least perpetuated our divisions and blocked public prosperity. Thus, they preferred to pardon you."

82 *RdP*, January 30–February 6, 1790, 20; February 13–20, 1790, 22; February 20–27, 1790, 23; and March 6–13, 1790, 28.

83 See *RdP*, March 13–20, 1790, 2–4.

84 See *Correspondance de Lindet*, 82.

85 *Nouvelle trahison de Monsieur le Baron de Besenval et son emprisonnement*, (Paris, 1790), BN LB 39 8508, 2.

86 See Morris, *Diary*, II: 216.

8 THE MAILLEBOIS CONSPIRACY

1 See Garran, *Rapport fait*, sec. 1, 7; and sec. 2, 6, 19, 24–5, 141–3. The "Conseil de l'Emigration" is discussed in Vingtrinier, *La Contre-Révolution*, I: 80. For a reference to Bonne as a "second Favras," see *Mémoire de Bertrand de Bonne-Savardin*, (Paris, 1790), BN LB 39 8747, 1.

2 See *Correspondance de Mercy*, II: 277–9; *Correspondance intime du Comte de Vaudreuil et du Comte d'Artois pendant l'émigration 1789–1815*, (Paris, 1889), I: 111; D. Carutti, *Storia della corte di Savoia durante La Rivoluzione e l'Impero francese*, (Turin, 1892), I: 140; and Vingtrinier, *La Contre-Révolution*, I: 125.

3 Condé to de la Rouzière, March 3, 1790, as found in E. Daudet, *Histoire de l'émigration*, (Paris, 1907), I: 26; and Vaudreuil to Artois, April 10 and April 17, 1790, *Correspondance intime*, I: 164, 168. On the lack of co-operation between the King and the fugitive Princes, see "Note du Marquis de Bombelles sur les causes du désaccord qui existe entre le Roi de France et les Princes," Feuillet de Conches, *Louis XVI*, V: 179–99.

4 Maillebois' father had been one of the leading generals of eighteenth-century France, and his grandfather, Nicolas Desmarets (a nephew of Colbert) had been Louis XIV's last Finance Minister. (See *Biographie Universelle*, X: 520–1, and XXVI: 124–5.) For Maillebois' military talents and checkered career, see Saint-Priest, *Mémoires*, I: 210; *Journal d'émigration du Comte d'Espinchal*, (Paris, 1912), 254; *Histoire par Deux Amis*, V: 195; C. Rousset, *Le Comte de Gisors*, (Paris, 1868), 447–52; P. Le Bas, *France: Dictionnaire encyclopédique* (Paris, 1843), X: 485–6; *Biographie Universelle* XXVI: 125; and *Mémoire de Monsieur le Comte de Maillebois, lieutenant-général des armées du roi*, (n.p., 1758), BN LB 38 755.

5 See *Journal d'Espinchal*, 255; and *Mémoire de Bonne-Savardin*, 4. For Maillebois' activities in Holland, see H. de Peyster, *Les Troubles de Hollande à la veille de la Révolution française*, (Paris, 1905), 108–52.

6 *Rapport fait*, sec. 2, 21–2.

7 See Grandmaison deposition, *ibid.*, sec. 2, 2–4.

8 See deposition of Maillebois' valet, *ibid.*, sec. 2, 12–16. Also see *Chronique*, April 4, 1790, 375; and *Gazette de Leyde*, supplement to no. 29, April 9, 1790.

9 See *Rapport fait*, sec. 2, 6, 18–25. Although Garran asserted that these reports were unsolicited, it seems more reasonable to assume that the revolutionary regime had established some form of organized intelligence network in the Sardinian capital. (See *ibid.*, sec. 1, 17.)

10 See *ibid.*, sec. 2, 143; *Chronique*, March 28, 1790, 346–7; and *L'Observateur*, March 28, 1790, 715–19. The *Chronique*'s March 28 dispatch was reprinted on March 29 by *CdP*, 369–70; *JCV*, 700; *Courrier national*, 8; and *Assemblée Nationale*, 7–8. For similar reports, see *APL*, March 29, 1790, 3; *JU*, March 30, 1790, 1020–22; and *PF*, April 1, 1790, 4.

11 *Lafayette: Through the Federation*, 309–10.

12 *Chronique*, March 28, 1790, 347 (my emphasis); and March 31, 1790, 359.

13 *JCV*, April 3, 1790, 24.

14 See Ferrières, *Mémoires sur les Assemblées parlementaires de la Révolution*, ed. M. Lescure, (Paris, 1880), I: 279: "Of all the King's ministers, the Comte de Saint-Priest was the one the revolutionaries feared most.

Thus, it was he whom they most relentlessly sought to de-popularize."
In contrast, though he remained in office until September 1790, Necker
was, politically speaking, a rather insignificant figure by this point.

15 *Révolutions de Paris* (Tournon), no. 38, 13–14; *RFB*, no. 18, 139–40; and
RdP, March 30–April 6, 1790, 6.

16 *Chronique*, April 4, 1790, 375; and April 13, 1790, 410. Compare the
statement here on Lafayette with one that had appeared five days
earlier: "Brave comrades, we must, above all, watch over the precious
life of our general . . . May this virtuous citizen continue to enjoy at every
moment the testimony of our recognition, our esteem, and our love."
(*Ibid.*, March 30, 1790, 355.)

17 *APL*, March 23, 1790, 2, and March 30, 1790, 4; and *PF*, April 20, 1790,
3. For an attack on the ministers by another "left Fayettist" journal, see
Bouche de fer, no. 53, 338–9. For Brissot's vision of war as a means of
unmasking traitors, see Furet, *Interpreting the French Revolution*, 66.

18 See *Rapport fait*, sec. 1, 8–9, and sec. 2, 29–31, 34–5, 65–6, 71, 80, 143–4;
Chronique, May 14, 1790, 533, and May 20, 1790, 559; and *PF*, May 20,
1790, 3.

19 See *Rapport fait*, sec. 2, 128–9. For Bonne's boast about deceiving the
Comité, see letter to Maillebois, December 6, 1789, *ibid.*, sec. 2, 134.

20 "Récit fait par M. Bonne-Savardin, de sa conversation avec Farcy,"
ibid., sec. 2, 136–8.

21 See "livre de raison", *ibid*, sec. 2, 139; and Saint-Priest, *Mémoires*, II: 33.
For the comment on the usual practices of conspirators, see *Histoire par
Deux Amis*, V: 206.

22 See *Mémoires*, II: 33. Saint-Priest did not, however, provide any clari-
fication here on the nature of "Farcy's" activities during this period.

23 *Moniteur*, July 14, 1790, 117. Saint-Priest, who had come into contact
with Maillebois and Bonne during a stint as French Ambassador to The
Hague from 1787–8, also denied that he had ever had "any kind of close
relationship with MM. de Maillebois and Bonne-Savardin, although I
have known them for a long time."

24 See *Mémoire à consulter et consultation pour M. Guignard Saint-Priest*, (Paris,
1790), 15–16, 31–2.

25 See *Rapport fait*, sec. 2, 86, 103.

26 *Ibid.*, sec. 2, 111 (capitals and emphasis in original).

27 See *ibid.*, sec. 2, 112–15.

28 Garran, *Réponse au mémoire à consulter*, 38.

29 See Saint-Priest, *Mémoires*, I: 227–43; and *Rapport fait*, sec. 1, 42.

30 For the Saint-Philippe du Roule episode, see *Mémoire à consulter*, 3; and
Tourneux, *Bibliographie de l'histoire de Paris pendant la Révolution française*,
(Paris, 1890), II: 247, no. 7764. Tourneux signals an October 7 Saint-
Philippe du Roule decree expressing confidence in Saint-Priest as being
located in BN MSS N.A.F. 2697, fol. 58. This piece might provide some

indication of the nature of the accusation made against the minister, but I have been unable to locate it.

31 See, for example, *APL*, July 22, 1790, 172; and *Orateur du Peuple*, no. 49, 395–6. The same title was also routinely bestowed on Saint-Priest by a number of historians who have written on the Maillebois affair. (See G. Bord, *Autour du Temple*, [Paris, 1912], 387; H. LeClerq, *La Propagande révolutionnaire: Juillet 1790–Décembre 1790*, [Paris, 1931], 138; and Ving-trinier, *La Contre-Révolution*, i: 143.)

32 Comité denunciation, July 9, 1790, *Rapport fait*, sec. i, 50–1 (my emphasis).

33 See Mansel, *Louis XVIII*, 92–3; and Walter, *Le Comte de Provence*, 297–8. If Farcy-Saint-Priest was indeed acting as an agent of Monsieur, this may help explain why he did not divulge anything about Farcy's projects in his *Mémoires*, which were written while Louis XVIII was still on the throne. Moreover, some support for the hypothesis that Saint-Priest was more involved in the Favras plot than in the Maillebois–Turin plot is also provided by the Vaudreuil–Artois correspondence. Though Vaudreuil's letters express a growing appreciation of Saint-Priest's anti-revolutionary qualities, they give no indication of any communication between the Minister and the Princes at Turin during this period. (See *Correspondance intime*, March 25, 1790, 152; and July 24, 1790, 241.) In addition, the fact that a letter written by the Comte de la Châtre, a top aide of Monsieur, was found in Bonne's possession when he was arrested also points to the possibility of a connection between Monsieur and the Saint-Priest–Maillebois network. (This letter will be discussed in more detail in chapter 10 below.) Finally, the flight of Saint-Priest's nephew d'Antraigues might also be recalled at this point. (See p. 127 above.) On the other hand, it is also possible that Saint-Priest was actually working for both Artois and Monsieur and perhaps serving as a connecting point between them. In this case, both the Favras plot and the Maillebois plot could be seen as emanating from a single counter-revolutionary network co-directed by the King's two brothers.

34 Mirabeau, *Lettre du Comte de Mirabeau au comité des recherches*, (Paris, 1789), 4. Also see *Moniteur*, October 10–11, 1789, 36–7; *Mémoire à consulter*, 3–4; Garran, *Réponse au mémoire à consulter*, 56–7; Saint-Priest, *Mémoires*, ii: 29–31; and Lally-Tolendal, *Observations du Comte de Lally-Tolendal sur la lettre écrite par M. le Comte de Mirabeau contre M. le Comte de Saint-Priest*, (Paris, 1789).

35 *Correspondance secrète*, April 10, 1790, ii: 438.

36 For the Marseilles affair, see Vingtrinier, *La Contre-Révolution*, i: 164–73; Gottschalk and Maddox, *Lafayette: Through the Federation*, 346–52; *RFB*, no. 25, 560–8; and *RdP*, May 8–15, 1790, 301–9.

37 *PF*, May 13, 1790, 3.

9 THE OCTOBER DAYS AFFAIR AND THE RADICALIZATION OF THE COMITÉ DES RECHERCHES

1 Garran's second report on the July Conspiracy, published in February 1790, did express some dissatisfaction with the Châtelet for withholding evidence in the Besenval case from the Comité. However, as we saw in chapter 7, the most significant thing about this report was the fact that it did not in any way attack the decision to release the defendant. (See *Réponse aux observations*, 28.)

2 See *Chronique*, January 14, 1790, 55; February 27, 1790, 207; March 4, 1790, 252; March 6, 1790, 258; and March 7, 1790, 262.

3 See *ibid.*, March 11, 1790, 278–9; March 13, 1790, 286; and March 17, 1790, 303. For the Laizer affair, see *RFB*, no. 16, 113–16; *Extrait des délibérations du district des Minimes*, (Paris, 1790), BN LB 40 1459; *Extrait des registres des délibérations de l'Assemblée Générale du district des Minimes*, (Paris, 1790), BN LB 40 1460; and Tuetey, *Répertoire général*, I: 151–3. For the Curé case, see AN Y 10506, Curé dossier; and *RdP*, March 13–20, 1790, 5–6.

4 See Anthoine report, as found in D. Robinet, *Danton: Homme d'Etat*, (Paris, 1889), 267; and Babut, "Une Journée aux Cordeliers," 299.

5 See *CdP*, March 22, 1790, 259; *RdP*, March 13–20, 1790, 31; and Babut, "Une Journée aux Cordeliers," 300. For Danton as the Cordeliers' "illustrious president," see *RFB*, no. 18, 109.

6 On May 18, 1790, the National Assembly's Comité des Rapports recommended that the Danton warrant be annulled, but no action was ever taken on this recommendation. Instead, the case against Danton was simply never pursued any further. (See LaCroix, IV: 477; *Procès-verbal de l'Assemblée Nationale*, no. 293, May 18, 1790, 7; and *Chronique*, May 20, 1790, 559.)

7 *Bouche de fer*, no. 40, 216, 221.

8 See *Moniteur*, February 6, 1790, 295; and LaCroix, III: 695, 708–11. Ridiculing this proposal, Loustalot pointed out Fauchet's pre-revolutionary connections with Lafayette's in-laws, the powerful Noailles family. (*RdP*, February 13–20, 1790, 16–21.) The scorn heaped on Fauchet in this period continued to haunt him through the entire Revolution. For the Montagnards, he was always the "flagorneur" Fauchet.

9 *Chronique*, March 24, 1790, 330. Brissot also argued that Danton could not be prosecuted for remarks made at a district assembly meeting, a right that he had neglected to grant to Martin and Duval the previous October. (See *PF*, March 26, 1790, 2.) For other reports on the March 19 Représentants' meeting, see *Moniteur*, March 28, 1790, 714–15; *RdP*, March 20–30, 1790, 16; *CdP*, March 22, 1790, 260; and LaCroix, IV: 451–2, 460–2.

10 *Chronique*, April 4, 1790, 375; and April 22, 1790, 446.

11 See *Moniteur*, February 6, 1790, 299.

12 As one anonymous rhyme-maker put it: "Pensez-vous que notre in-dulgence / Voyant sauver nos ennemis / Vous laisse mettre à la potence / Nos défenseurs et nos amis." (*L'Observateur*, April 20, 1790, 885.) [Do you think the indulgence we have shown while seeing our enemies escape will allow you to hang our defenders and friends?]

13 *CdP*, March 22, 1790, 258–9.

14 *CdP*, April 17, 1790, 178. ("You who whitewash Broglie, Augeard, and Besenval, and who would even whitewash the plague, you are like erasing paper, you take off the spot, and the spot remains with you.") The same verse can also be found in *APL*, April 16, 1790, 4; *RFP*, no. 21, 375; and *Ami du Peuple* ("counterfeit Marat"), BN LC 2 234, April 17, 1790, 8. Also see *Correspondance secrète*, II: 441. For other anti-Châtelet sorties by Gorsas, see *CdP*, April 10, 1790, 73–4; April 21, 1790, 248–51; April 24, 1790, 293–4; April 28, 1790, 359; and April 29, 1790, 372–4. For Gorsas' approval of Augeard's release, see *CdP*, March 11, 1790, 81–2.

15 The phrase on the "spirit of toleration" is taken from Peuchet's explanation of why he supported Danton at the March 19 Représentants meeting. (See *Moniteur*, March 28, 1790, 715.)

16 See LaCroix, IV: i–xv; Garrigues, *Les Districts*, 143–57; Rose, *The Making of the Sans-culottes*, 76–80; and Genty, "Mandataires ou Représentants," 15–27. According to Garrigues, fifty-three of the sixty districts sent delegates to the alternative assembly and forty of these formally ad-hered to the municipal plan it formulated.

17 See Anthoine report, Robinet, *Danton: Homme d'Etat*, 267.

18 *PF*, March 26, 1790, 2; and March 25, 1790, 2. Also see *PF*, May 8, 1790, 2–3. For the parts played by Brissot and Fauchet in drafting the Représentants' plan, see LaCroix, III: iii–vi; and Garrigues, *Les Districts*, 144–6. For Brissot's responsibility for an earlier version of this plan, see chapter 4, note 27 above.

19 *APL*, April 22, 1790, 3. For similar statements, see *Chronique*, April 27, 1790, 446; and *RFB*, no. 22, 415.

20 Undated Comité letter to Flandre, piece 5 appended to *Discours prononcé à la barre de l'Assemblée Nationale par M. Oudart, au nom et en présence des membres du comité des recherches de la municipalité de Paris*, August 10, 1789, (n.p., 1790), BN LE 29 834, 14. The reference to "a few months after" is from Oudart's speech, *ibid.*, 3.

21 Flandre's undated reply to Comité, *ibid.*, piece 6, 17.

22 See *Procédure criminelle*, sec. 1, 9.

23 See chapter 5, note 86 above.

24 *Discours prononcé par M. Oudart*, piece 6, 19.

25 *Ibid.*, piece 6, 18, note 3.

26 *Ibid.*, 4.

27 *APL*, April 22, 1790, 3; and *Révolutions de Paris* (Tournon), no. 39, 17. Also see *Chronique*, April 22, 1790, 446; and *RFB*, no. 22, 415.

28 *JCV*, April 7, 1790, 51; and *Gazette universelle*, April 11, 1790, 51. Also see *Modérateur*, April 9, 1790, 395; and *Mercure de France*, May 8, 1790, 140–1.

29 See *L'Observateur*, April 20, 1790, 884; *AdP*, May 20, 1790, 4; and *Correspondance secrète*, II: 439, 445.

30 *APL*, April 24, 1790, 4; and *Chronique*, May 1, 1790, 482.

31 *RdP*, April 24–May 1, 1790, 210; and *Ami du Peuple*, LC 2 234, April 24, 1790, 5–7. For other efforts to link the Châtelet's maneuvers with a general counter-revolutionary offensive, see *Orateur du Peuple*, no. 4, 25–9; *Révolutions de Paris* (Tournon), no. 39, 17–25; and *JU*, April 28, 1790, 1249–52.

32 See *Extrait du registre des délibérations de l'Assemblée Générale du District des Cordeliers*, April 20, 1790, (Paris, 1790), BN LB 40 258.

33 District des Carmelites, *Extrait des procès-verbaux des délibérations de l'Assemblée Générale du District*, (Paris, 1790), BN LB 40 1361, 5.

34 See *Adresse à l'Assemblée Nationale rédigée par le District des Cordeliers d'après le voeu de la Commune de Paris*, May 10, 1790, (Paris, 1790), BN LB 40 1387, 14–15.

35 See LaCroix, V: 146–7, 294–7. In addition to the demand for punishment issued by the Oratoire District, the Cordeliers (which suggested that the judges should "perhaps" be punished) stated that "other" districts had also demanded the prosecution of the Châtelet. (See *Adresse à l'Assemblée Nationale*, 13, 15.)

36 See Seligman, *La Justice*, I: 280–328.

37 For the Cordeliers' contention that the King had proclaimed a "universal amnesty" in his February 4 speech, see *Adresse à l'Assemblée Nationale*, 10–11.

38 See *Révolutions de Paris* (Tournon), no. 39, 21.

39 *Moniteur*, July 3, 1790, 22. Talon had been elected as an alternate deputy in spring 1789. His seating in the Assembly is signalled in *Procès-verbal de l'Assemblée Nationale*, December 16, 1789, 1–2.

40 See *Moniteur*, July 3, 1790, 22; and AN BB 30 82.

41 See Charavay, *L'Assemblée électorale de Paris: 18 novembre 1790–15 juin 1791*, 121–216; and Seligman, *La Justice*, I: 343–4. By contrast, it will be recalled that three members of the Comité des Recherches (Garran, Agier, and Oudart) were elected to the new tribunals.

42 *Modérateur*, April 7, 1790, 395. Also see *Gazette universelle*, April 11, 1790, 526; and District des Carmelites, *Extrait des procès-verbaux*, 4–5.

43 See *L'Observateur*, April 20, 1790, 885; and *Orateur du Peuple*, no. 4, 25.

44 *Discours prononcé par M. Oudart*, 4.

45 *Moniteur*, May 1, 1790, 246; and *Mercure de France*, May 8, 1790, 141.

46 See *PF*, April 27, 1790, 3; and Brissot statement to Représentants, LaCroix, V: 134.

47 *RdP*, April 24–May 1, 1790, 214 (his emphasis). For the controversy

surrounding the death of this demonstrator, see Mathiez, "Etude critique sur les journées des 5 et 6 octobre 1789", *Revue historique* 67: 243; and Marc de Villiers, *Les 5 et 6 octobre*, 205–24.

48 *AdP*, May 20, 1790, 3; and *L'Observateur*, April 27, 1790, 909, and April 29, 1790, 910–11.

49 For testimony concerning evidence being held by the Comité, see *Procédure criminelle*, no. 8, sec. 1, 24–5; no. 126, sec. 1, 191–2; no. 155, sec. 1, 245–6; no. 162, sec. 1, 256–7; no. 170, sec. 1, 269–70; and no. 211, sec. 2, 64. For the Comité's interception of Orleanist correspondence, see p. 49 above.

50 *Moniteur*, August 8, 1790, 336.

51 *Discours prononcé par M. Oudart*, 5.

52 Witnesses nos. 126, 155, 162, and 170 mentioned in note 49 above were all deputies who had been members of the Assembly's Comité des Recherches.

10   THE MAILLEBOIS AND OCTOBER DAYS AFFAIRS

1 This phrase, taken from a letter of American diplomat William Short, is used as the title of Gottschalk and Maddox's chapter on the Federation. (See *Lafayette: Through the Federation*, 551–2.) Also see Lefebvre, *The French Revolution*, 1: 139–40; O. Bernier, *Lafayette*, (New York, 1983), 218–19) and P. Bruckman, *Lafayette*, (New York, 1977), 185–7.

2 For other Fayettist overtures to the Monarchiens during this period, see F. Acomb, *Mallet du Pan*, (Durham, N.C., 1973), 223–4.

3 For this series of incidents, which culminated in the Nancy massacre of August 1790, see Scott, *The Response of the Royal Army*, 81–97.

4 See *Procédure criminelle*, sec. 1, 20 (Bergasse); sec. 2, 80–1 (Clermont-Tonnerre); and sec. 3, 70–9 (Mounier).

5 See *Rapport fait*, sec. 2, 6–7, 19, 24.

6 The proposed manifesto was to have been based on the principles enunciated at the June 23, 1789 royal session, principles to which Mounier and Lally were unalterably opposed. (See Lanzac de Laborie, *Un Royaliste libéral en 1789: Jean-Joseph Mounier*, [Paris, 1887], 94–6; and Egret, *La Révolution des notables*, 75–6.)

7 *Rapport fait*, sec. 2, 127.

8 *Ibid.*, sec. 1, 15–16.

9 *Ibid.*, sec. 1, 45.

10 See *Mercure de France*, July 31, 1790, 376; Lanzac de Laborie, *Un Royaliste libéral*, 245–6; and Egret, *La Révolution des notables*, 221–2.

11 Deposition given to Paris Comité des Recherches, as found in Buchez and Roux, *Histoire parlementaire*, III: 114–15. For the incident described by Lecointre, see Dominique, *Paris enlève le roi*, 176.

12 *Chronique*, April 22, 1790, 446–7.

13 *RFB*, no. 22, 415–16.
14 See Garran, *Réponse au mémoire*, 50; and Saint-Priest, *Mémoires*, ii: 16–17.
15 *Réplique de J. P. Brissot à Stanislas Clermont*, October 8, 1790, (Paris, 1790), 43–4.
16 *Ibid.*, 44.
17 Agier, *Eclaircissements donnés*, 52.
18 For the fall of de Lessart, see M. J. Sydenham, *The French Revolution*, (New York, 1966), 94.
19 See *AP*, xviii: 229; *PF*, July 16, 1790, 4; *Chronique*, July 31, 1790, 847.
20 *Les Pamphlets de Marat*, 203–4, 207–8, 209. In a letter to Brissot's journal, Garran acknowledged that two unnamed accused agents of Artois had been denounced to the Comité. He insisted, however, that their papers could not be seized because the evidence provided was not sufficient to warrant violating their privacy. (See *PF*, August 3, 1790, 2–3.)
21 *RFB*, no. 37, 602; and *RdP*, July 31–August 7, 1790, 185–7, and July 10–17, 1790, 14–15.
22 See *Les Pamphlets de Marat*, 208.
23 For the arrest and return to Paris of Barmond and Bonne, see *AP*, xviii: 229–33; and *Chronique*, July 31, 1790, 847, and August 18, 1790, 918.
24 *Moniteur*, August 19, 1790, 425–6.
25 For Foucault's "confession," see *ibid.*, August 24, 1790, 464. Echoing Barmond, Foucault explained that "humanity and religion commanded me to come to the aid of a helpless unfortunate."
26 Ferrières, *Correspondance inédite*, 262.
27 See *Moniteur*, June 27, 1790, 724–5. For the Lautrec case, see p. 146 above.
28 See *Moniteur*, August 8, 1790, 333–6, and August 9, 1790, 339–41. Actually Boucher d'Argis announced only that two unnamed deputies were being charged. However, it was common knowledge that it was a question of Orléans and Mirabeau.
29 *Rapport de la procédure du Châtelet sur l'affaire des 5 et 6 octobre 1789, fait les 30 septembre et 1 octobre 1789, à l'Assemblée Nationale, par M. Charles Chabroud*, as reprinted in *AP*, xix: 339, 366–7. For Chabroud's connection to Barnave, see Egret, *La Révolution des notables*, 205.
30 *Moniteur*, October 4, 1790, 34. Some idea of the extent of opposition to the Chabroud report can be ascertained from the fact that 117 rightist deputies signed a joint protest against it, and twenty-nine others (including the abbé Barmond) declared that they partially adhered to this protest. In addition, forty other deputies, many of them Monarchiens, had testified in the Châtelet probe and had thereby been barred from participating in the vote on the report. (See *AP*, xix: 416–20.) Assuming, as seems likely, that almost all of these deputies would also have opposed the report, we are left with an opposition total of about 175 deputies, or somewhere between one-sixth and one-fifth of the Assembly.

31 See *Moniteur*, August 24, 1790, 466.
32 *Ibid.*, August 24, 1790, 465.
33 See Archives du Loiret, Haute Cour Nationale, Bonne-Savardin dossier, Châtelet Information of September 10, 1790, 51. Although the case against Barmond was not formally dropped when he was released from house arrest, there do not seem to have been any further steps taken to pursue it. In the mean time, no proceedings were ever initiated against Foucault. For Pétion's expression of confidence in the Châtelet, see *Moniteur*, August 24, 1790, 466.
34 *AP*, XVIII: 149.
35 See Archives du Loiret, Haute Cour Nationale, Bonne-Savardin dossier, Châtelet Informations of July 26, 1790 and September 10, 1790. Flandre's recommendation and the October 8 judgment can be found at the end of the Information of September 10, 50–1. In addition to simply ignoring Saint-Priest and ordering Barmond's release from house arrest, this judgment also provided for the token issuance of arrest warrants against the already-escaped Maillebois and the already-jailed Bonne. It also included orders for the release of three other individuals who had been arrested in connection with Bonne's escape from the Abbaye Prison. For Saint-Priest's resignation and emigration, see Saint-Priest, *Mémoires*, II: 56–8, 100–1; and LaCroix, VI: 601.
36 See *Correspondance entre Mirabeau et LaMarck*, II: 202.
37 According to Keith Baker, a series of meetings were held in late August and September in an attempt to arrange a rapprochement between Lafayette's 1789 Club and the Triumvirate-dominated Jacobin Club, and it can probably be assumed that the judicial issues being discussed here were an important element in these negotiations. (See *Condorcet*, [Chicago, 1975], 283–4.) Incidentally, neither Lafayette nor any of his closest associates in the Assembly (i.e., Liancourt, LaRochefoucauld, Latour-Maubourg, Lacoste, or Emmery) appears on the lists of those who protested the Chabroud report. (See note 30 above.)
38 The only explicit attack on this judgment that I have found was by Marat. (See *AdP*, October 12, 1790, 8.)
39 See de Villiers, *Les 5 et 6 octobre*, 307, 315, 326–38.
40 *AdP*, October 12, 1790, 8.
41 See Tuety, *Répertoire des sources manuscrites*, I: 165, nos. 1444–5; and *Dictionnaire de biographie française*, VI: 991.
42 *RFB*, no. 48, as cited by Buchez and Roux, *Histoire parlementaire*, VII: 379.
43 *APL*, October 29, 1789, as cited by Baker, *Condorcet*, 284.
44 *PF*, October 3, 1790, 4.
45 See, for example, DiPadova, "The Girondins and the Question of Revolutionary Government."
46 See *Moniteur*, October 27, 1790, 215.
47 See Seligman, *La Justice*, I: 338–40, 351–2.
48 See *Moniteur*, March 6, 1791, 554–5. For the connection between the

popular unrest of late February and the creation of the Haute Cour Provisoire, see Seligman, *La Justice*, II: 16–20. The newly created Parisian tribunals, it should be noted, took on the Châtelet's general authority in the capital area, not the special authority it had held over all *lèse-nation* cases in France.

49 See remarks of d'André, as cited by Seligman, *La Justice*, II: 4–5. Also see Robespierre's unsuccessful counter-argument: "The High Court will have to decide the fate of powerful individuals, for the weak do not conspire. It is therefore necessary that it be surrounded by the massive power of public opinion, an indispensable counter-weight to the imminent danger of complacency." (*Ibid.*, II: 5.)

50 For the indulgent record of these two courts, see *ibid.*, II: 20–1, 52–3, 100–15, 135–42. The first and only death sentence pronounced by either court was handed down in the last week of August of 1792. (See *ibid.*, II: 266–7.) Incidentally, the cases of both Bonne and Reine Audu were sent to the Haute Cour Provisoire, but the amnesty of September 1791 intervened before a judgment was rendered in either case.

CONCLUSION

1 This distinction was made by radical historians who praised the Jacobin Revolution as well as by liberals who abhorred it. (See F. Furet, "La Révolution sans la terreur?: Le débat des historiens du XIXe siècle," *Le Débat* no. 13 (1981): 40–54.

2 Furet, *Interpreting the French Revolution*, 55, 62–3.

3 See Lefebvre, *Coming of the Revolution*, 120–1, 212; and A. Soboul, *A Short History of the French Revolution*, tr. G. Symcox, (Berkeley, 1977), 46.

4 See Schama, *Citizens*, 448–9.

5 See Lefebvre, *The French Revolution*, 135; and Furet, "La Révolution dans l'imaginaire politique français," *Le Débat* no. 26 (1983): 174–5.

6 For a recent study which stresses the mutual interaction between Revolution and Counter-revolution, see D. Sutherland, *France, 1789–1815*, (New York, 1986).

7 See Furet, *Interpreting the French Revolution*, 37–9, 43–4.

8 Of course, the authorities were motivated, to at least some degree, by a recognition of the physical power of the revolutionary crowd. It seems clear, however, that there was also a measure of genuine recognition of "the People" as a legitimate and valid political force.

Select bibliography

I ARCHIVAL MATERIAL

ARCHIVES NATIONALES

AP 446. Brissot Papers

BB 30 82. Favras dossier and other assorted Châtelet and Ministry of Justice material

BB 30 161. Besenval dossier

BB 30 178 and BB 3 31. Material relating to the amnesty of September 1791

BB 3 221. Favras and Lambesc dossiers

C 28 211, 220, and 225. National Assembly documents from July 1789

D XXIX 63. Marat–Danton dossier

D XXIX bis. Archives of the National Assembly's Comité des Recherches

F 7 4774 60. Oudart dossier

Y 10506. Rutledge, Cordon, Potel–Jouve, and Curé dossiers

Y 10508. Duval–Martin and Delcros dossiers

Y 10530. Records of the Châtelet's prévôtal court

Y 18768. Adrien dossier

ARCHIVES DU LOIRET

Records of the Haute Cour Nationale Provisoire. Bonne-Savardin dossier.

BIBLIOTHEQUE NATIONALE

Nouvelles acquisitions françaises 2658, 2683, and 2696. Records of Parisian districts

Françaises 11697. Lafayette–Bailly Correspondence

BIBLIOTHEQUE HISTORIQUE DE LA VILLE DE PARIS

MS 741, piece 54. Order from the Paris Comité des Recherches

281

2 PRINTED JUDICIAL PROCEEDINGS

Justification du Marquis de Favras, ed. G. F. Mahy de Cormère, (Paris, 1791), BN LB 39 3009

Procédure criminelle instruite au Châtelet de Paris sur la dénonciation des faits arrivés à Versailles dans la journée du 6 octobre 1789, (Paris, 1790), BN LE 29 980

Procès fait au Chevalier Rutledge, Baronet, avec des pièces et sa correspondance avec M. Necker, (Paris, 1790), BN LN 27 18148

3 PROCEEDINGS OF REVOLUTIONARY ASSEMBLIES

Actes de la Commune de Paris pendant la Révolution, ed. S. LaCroix, series I, (Paris, 1895–1914)

Archives parlementaires de 1787 à 1860, series I (1787–99), ed. M. J. Mavidal and M. E. Laurent, (Paris, 1867–96)

Histoire parlementaire de la Révolution française, ed. P. J. Buchez and P. C. Roux, (Paris, 1834–8)

Procès-verbal de l'Assemblée Nationale, (Paris, 1789–91)

Procès-verbal des séances et délibérations de l'Assemblée Générale des Electeurs de Paris, (Paris, 1790)

4 OTHER COLLECTIONS OF REVOLUTIONARY DOCUMENTS

Recueil de documents relatifs à la convocation des Etats-Généraux, ed. A. Brette, (Paris, 1896)

L'Assemblée électorale de Paris: 18 novembre 1790–15 juin 1791, ed. E. Charavay, (Paris, 1894)

L'Assemblée électorale de Paris: 26 août 1791–12 août 1792, ed. E. Charavay, (Paris, 1894)

L'Assemblée électorale de Paris: 2 septembre 1792–17 frimaire an II, ed. E. Charavay, (Paris, 1905)

Les Elections et les Cahiers de Paris en 1789, ed. C. Chassin, (Paris 1888)

Collection complète des Lois, ed. J. B. Duvergier, (Paris, 1834)

Le Personnel Municipal de Paris pendant le Révolution: Période Constitutionelle, ed. P. Robiquet, (Paris, 1890)

5 PROCEEDINGS OF PARISIAN DISTRICTS

Extrait des registres des délibérations du District des Blancs-Manteaux, (Paris, 1789), BN LB 40 234

District des Carmelites, *Extrait des Procès-verbaux des délibérations de l'Assemblée Générale du District*, (Paris, 1790), BN LB 40 1361

Adresse à l'Assemblée Nationale rédigée par le District des Cordeliers d'après le voeu de la Commune de Paris, (Paris, 1790), BN LB 40 1387

Extrait du registre des délibérations de l'Assemblée Générale du District des Cordeliers, (Paris, 1790), BN LB 40 258
Arrêté du Comité Général des Filles-Saint-Thomas, (Paris, 1789), BN LB 40 267
Extrait des délibérations du District des Minimes, (Paris, 1790), BN LB 40 1459
Extrait des registres des délibérations de l'Assemblée Générale du District des Minimes, (Paris, 1790), BN LB 40 1460
District de l'Oratoire, *Extrait de la délibération du 30 juillet,* (Paris, 1789), BN LB 40 1479
Extrait des délibérations du District des Petits-Pères, (Paris, 1789), BN LB 40 1505
Délibération de l'Assemblée Générale des Voluntaires du Bataillon de Saint-Martin des Champs, (Paris, 1789), BN LB 40 358
Saint-Martin District: Deliberation of October 26, 1789, (Paris, 1789), BN LB 40 359

6 REVOLUTIONARY PRESS

(A) RADICAL JOURNALS

Ami du Peuple (Marat)
Ami de Peuple ("false Marat"), BN LC 2 234
Ami du Peuple ou le vrai citoyen (another "false Marat"), BN LC 2 2283
Fouet national
Furet parisien
Journal d'état et du citoyen (Keralio)
Journal universel (Audouin)
L'Observateur
Orateur du Peuple (Fréron)
Révolutions de France et de Brabant (Desmoulins)
Révolutions de Paris (Prudhomme–Loustalot)
Révolutions de Paris (Tournon)

(B) "LEFT FAYETTIST" JOURNALS

Annales patriotiques et littéraires (Mercier–Carra)
Bouche de fer (Bonneville–Fauchet)
Chronique de Paris (Noël–Millin)
Courrier de Paris (Gorsas) (Known as *Courrier de Versailles* prior to the October Days)
Patriote français (Brissot)

(C) MAINSTREAM CONSTITUTIONAL MONARCHIST JOURNALS

Assemblée Nationale
Assemblée Nationale et Commune de Paris
Courrier français
Journal de Paris

Journal général de la cour et de la ville (Began to move towards the right in February 1790)
Moniteur

(D) MONARCHIEN-ORIENTED JOURNALS

Gazette Universelle
Modérateur
Mercure de France (Mallet du Pan)

(E) JOURNALS OF THE EXTREME RIGHT

Gazette de Paris
Journal Politique-National (Sabatier de Castres–Rivarol)

(F) OTHER JOURNALS CITED

Bulletin de l'Assemblée Nationale
Le Châtelet démasqué
Courrier national
Gazette de Leyde
Le Juif errant
Journal des débats
Journal logographique
Point du jour (Barère)
Le Rôdeur français
Le Spectateur national
Versailles et Paris

7 COMITE DES RECHERCHES BRIEFS AND REPORTS

Compte-rendu à l'Assemblée des Représentants de la Commune par M. Agier au nom du Comité des Recherches, (Paris, 1789), BN LB 40 41
Eclaircissements donnés à un de MM. de l'Assemblée Nationale par M. Agier au sujet de la lettre de M. Blonde, (Paris, 1790), BN LB 39 2866
Jacques–Pierre Brissot, membre du Comité des Recherches de la Municipalité à Stanislas Clermont, (Paris, 1790), BN LB 39 3974
Brissot, J. P., *Lettres à M. le Chevalier de Pange*, (Paris, 1790), BN LB 39 3200
Rapport dans l'affaire de MM. Dhosier et Petitjean, lu aux comités des recherches de l'Assemblée Nationale et de la municipalité de Paris, le 29 Juillet 1790, (Paris, 1790), BN LB 40 120
Réplique de J. P. Brissot à Stanislas Clermont, (Paris, 1790), BN LB 39 4206
Rapport fait au comité des recherches de la municipalité de Paris par Jean Philippe Garran, suivi des pièces justificatives et l'arrêté du comité tendant à dénoncer MM. Maillebois, Bonne-Savardin, et Guignard Saint-Priest, (Paris, 1790), BN LB 40 114

Garran, J. P., *Rapport sur la conspiration des mois de mai, juin, et juillet derniers,* (Paris, 1789), BN LB 40 9

Réponse au mémoire à consulter et consultation pour M. Guignard Saint-Priest, (Paris, 1790), BN LB 40 116

Réponse aux Observations pour le Baron de Besenval et au Mémoire de M. Barentin, (Paris, 1790), BN LB 39 2825

Discours prononcé à la barre de l'Assemblée Nationale par M. Oudart, au nom et en présence des membres du comité des recherches de la municipalité de Paris, (n.p., 1790), BN LE 29 834

8 OTHER PRINTED MATERIAL ON THE AFFAIRS EXAMINED

(A) BESENVAL AFFAIR

La Chasse aux bêtes puantes et féroces, (Paris, 1789), BN LB 39 1990

Le Fuyard ou le Baron de Besenval, Général sans armée, (n.p., 1789), BN LB 39 7405

Jugement en dernier ressort qui décharge le Baron de Besenval, et al., (Paris, 1790), BN LB 39 3050

Lettre à M. le Comte de Clermont-Tonnerre sur sa motion en faveur du Sr. de Besenval et des autres coupables, (Paris, 1789), BN LB 39 7538

Mémoire pour M. Barentin, Ancien Garde-des-Sceaux de France, (Paris, 1790), BN LB 39 8302

Le Ministère de trente-six heures, quarante-quatre minutes, et vingt-cinq secondes, (n.p., n.d.), BN LB 39 1988

Nouvelle trahison de Monsieur le Baron de Besenval et son emprisonnement, (Paris, 1790), BN LB 39 8508

Réponse de la Nation à la demande qu'a faite M. Necker de pardonner à ceux qui avaient médité sa ruine et celle de l'Etat, (Paris, 1789), BN LB 39 7539

R. de Sèze, *Observations pour le Baron de Besenval,* (Paris, 1790), BN LB 39 2824

Plaidoyer pour le Baron de Besenval, (Paris, 1790), BN LB 39 8509

Tribut d'un Parisien à Monsieur Necker, (Paris, 1789), BN LB 39 7594

(B) OCTOBER DAYS AFFAIR

Chabroud, C., *Rapport de la procédure du Châtelet sur l'affaire des 5 et 6 octobre 1789, fait les 30 septembre et 1 octobre 1790, à l'Assemblée Nationale,* (Paris, 1790), BN LE 29 981

Exposé de la conduite de M. le Duc d'Orléans dans la Révolution française rédigé par lui-même, à Londres, (Paris, 1790), BN LB 39 2664

Faits et gestes de l'Hon. Ch. Chabroud, (Paris, n.d.), BN LN 27 3804

Discours de M. Mirabeau l'aîné sur la procédure du Châtelet, (Paris, 1790), BN LE 29 983

Mounier, J. J., *Appel au tribunal de l'opinion publique,* (Geneva, 1790), BN LE 39 Y 2652

Quand-aurons-nous du Pain, (n.p., n.d.), BN LB 39 2344

Pelletier, J., *Domine salvum fac regum,* (Paris, 1789), BN LB 39 2473

(C) MARAT AFFAIR

Lettre de M. Marat à M. Joly, (n.p., n.d.), BN LB 39 2451
Les Pamphlets de Marat, ed. C. Vellay, (Paris, 1911)

(D) ADRIEN AFFAIR

Le Cacheur de pain dans la cave, (n.p., n.d.), BN LB 39 8012
Jugements prévôtaux, (Paris, 1789), BN LB 39 2501, 2502, 2546
Mort du boulanger, (Paris, n.d.), BN LB 39 8013

(E) MARTIN–DUVAL AFFAIR

Appel des Sieurs Martin et Duval de Stains à la justice et à la vérité, (Paris, 1789),
BN LB 39 8066

(F) RUTLEDGE AFFAIR

Rutledge, J. J., *Mémoire pour la communauté des maîtres boulangers de la ville et
faubourgs de Paris*, (Paris, 1789), BN VP 3194
L'Astuce dévoilée, (Paris, 1790), BN LB 39 4073
*Dénonciation sommaire faite au comité des recherches de l'Assemblée Nationale
contre M. Necker*, (Paris, 1790), BN LB 39 3062
Project d'une législation des substances composée pour M. Necker, (Paris, 1790),
BN LB 39 2864
Second mémoire pour les maîtres boulangers, (Paris, 1790), BN VP 3507
Supplément à la vie privée et ministérielle de M. Necker, (Geneva, 1790), BN LB
39 3356
Vie privée et ministérielle de M. Necker, (Geneva, 1790), BN LB 39 3355

(G) FAVRAS AFFAIR

Adresse aux Parisiens dites la Nation, par les mânes du Marquis de Favras, (Paris,
n.d.)
Cormère, G. F. Mahy de, *Plaidoyer pour Thomas Mahy de Favras*, (Paris, 1790),
BN LB 39 2994
Favras, T. Mahy de, *Adresse à l'ordre de la noblesse de la prévôté et vicomté de Paris*,
(n.p., 1789), BN LB 39 1630
Le Déficit des finances de la France vaincue, (n.p., 1789), BN LB 39 7242
Testament de mort, (Paris, 1790), BN LB 39 3000
Lettre du Marquis de Favras au Baron de Besenval (apocryphal), (Paris, 1790),
BN LB 39 2930
Ouvrez donc les yeux, (n.p., n.d.), BN LB 39 2728
Pitou, L. A., *Réflexions sur le jugement et la mort de M. de Favras*, (n.p., n.d.), BN
LB 39 300
Recueil dédié à M. de Favras, (n.p., 1790), BN LB 8474
Réflexions impartiales sur la mort du Marquis de Favras, (Paris, 1790), BN LB 39
8478

Réponse de M. le Baron de Besenval au Marquis de Favras (apocryphal), (Paris, 1790), BN LB 39 8406

(H) MAILLEBOIS AFFAIR

Lettre du Comte de Mirabeau au comité des recherches, (Paris, 1789), BN LB 39 2441
Mémoire à consulter et consultation pour M. Guignard Saint-Priest, (Paris, 1790), BN LB 39 3858
Mémoire de Bertrand de Bonne-Savardin, (Paris, 1790), BN LB 39 8747
Mémoire de Monsieur le Comte de Maillebois, Lieutenant-Général des armées du Roi, (n.p., 1758), BN LB 38 755
Observations du Comte de Lally-Tolendal sur la lettre écrite par M. le Comte de Mirabeau contre M. Le Comte de Saint-Priest, (Paris, 1789), BN LB 39 2581
Relation des circonstances relatives à la capture du Chevalier de Bonne-Savardin, (n.p., n.d.), BN LN 27 21208

9 OTHER REVOLUTIONARY PAMPHLETS AND COMMENTARIES

Agier, P. L., *Le Jurisconsulte national*, (n.p., 1788), BN LB 39 1287
Réponse de M. Blonde aux éclaircissements donnés par M. Agier dans l'affaire de M. Augeard, (n.p., 1790), BN LB 39 2867
Bergasse, N., *Discours sur les crimes et les tribunaux de haute trahison*, (n.p., 1790), BN LB 39 3312 C
Bonnières, M.de, *Plaidoyer pour M. Augeard*, (Paris, 1790), BN LB 39 8595
Clermont-Tonnerre, S., *Oeuvres*, (Paris, an III)
Coquéau, M., *Très sérieuses observations sur la mauvaise organisation de la Garde Nationale Parisienne*, (Paris, 1789), BN LB 39 7837
Dénonciation à la Nation et à l'opinion publique de trois décrets de l'Assemblée Nationale, (Paris, 1790), BN LB 39 3947
Desmoulins, C., *Discours de la lanterne*, (Paris, 1869)
Dusaulx, J., *De l'insurrection parisienne et de la prise de la bastille*, (Paris, 1790)
Histoire de la Révolution de 1789 par Deux Amis de la Liberté, (Paris, 1790)
Mémoire de M. le Comte de Lally-Tolendal ou seconde lettre à ses commettants, (Paris, 1790)
Faits justificatifs du sieur de Livron, (Paris, 1790), BN LB 39 3902
Montjoie, F. L., *Histoire de la conjuration de Louis-Philippe-Joseph d'Orléans*, (Paris, 1834)
Histoire de la Révolution de France et de l'Assemblée Nationale, (Paris, 1791)
Exposé de la conduite de M. Mounier dans l'Assemblée Nationale, (Paris, 1789)
Necker, J., *Sur l'administration de M. Necker*, (Amsterdam, 1791)

Pange, F. de, *Oeuvres*, (Paris, 1832)
Pitra, L. G., "La journée du 14 juillet," in J. Flammermont, *La journée du 14 juillet*, (Paris, 1892)
Mémoire à consulter et consultation pour le Marquis de Saint-Huruge contre les sieurs Bailly et Lafayette, (n.p., 1789), BN LB 39 2377

10 CONTEMPORARY COMMENTARIES ON CRIMINAL JUSTICE

Beccaria, C., *Traité des délits et des peines*, tr. Morellet, (Lausanne, 1766)
Bernardi, J. E., "Les moyens d'adoucir les lois pénales en France," *Les moyens d'adoucir la rigueur des lois pénales en France sans nuire à la sûreté publique*, (Châlons-sur-Marne, 1781)
Boucher d'Argis, A. J., *Observations sur les lois criminelles de France*, (Amsterdam, 1781)
Brissot, J. P., "Les moyens d'adoucir la rigueur des lois pénales en France," *Les moyens d'adoucir la rigueur des lois pénales en France sans nuire à la sûreté publique*, (Châlons-sur-Marne, 1781)
Le sang innocent vengé, (Paris, 1781)
Théorie des lois criminelles, (Paris, 1836)
Carrard, B., *De la jurisprudence criminelle*, (Geneva, 1785)
Chaussard, P., *Théorie des lois criminelles*, (Auxerre, 1789)
Delacroix, J. V., *Réflexions philosophiques sur l'origine de la civilisation*, (Amsterdam, 1778)
Observations sur la société, (Paris, 1787)
Desgranges, M., *Essais sur le droit et le besoin d'être défendu quand on est accusé*, (Paris, 1785)
Dupaty, C. M., *Lettres sur la procédure criminelle de la France, dans lesquelles on montre sa conformité avec celle de l'Inquisition*, (n.p., 1788)
Lacretelle, P. L., *Discours sur le préjugé des peines infamantes*, (Paris, 1784)
Mélanges de jurisprudence, (Paris, 1788)
Landreau de Maine-au-Piq, *Législation philosophique, politique et morale*, (Geneva, 1787)
Marat, J. P., *Plan de législation criminelle*, (Paris, 1790)
Mercier, L. S., *Memoirs of the Year 2,500*, (Boston, 1977)
Mirabeau, G. H., *Essai sur le despotisme*, (London, 1775)
Pastoret, C. E., *Des lois pénales*, (Paris, 1790)
Robespierre, M., *Mémoire pour le sieur L. M. H. Dupond*, (Arras, 1789)
"Discours sur les peines infamantes couronné par l'Académie de Metz en 1784," *Oeuvres complètes de Maximilien Robespierre*, (Paris, 1912)
Roussel de la Bérardière, J. H., *Dissertation sur la composition des lois criminelles*, (Leyden, 1775)
Servan, J. M., *Discours sur l'administration de la justice criminelle*, (Geneva, 1767)

Servin, M., *De la législation criminelle*, (Basle, 1782)
Valazé, C. F., *Lois pénales*, (Alençon, 1784)

11 MEMOIRS AND CORRESPONDENCE

Mémoires secrets de J. M. Augeard, (Paris, 1866)
Bailly, J. S., *Mémoires*, (Paris, 1821)
Beaulieu, J., *Essais historiques sur les causes et les effets de la Révolution française*, (Paris, 1801)
Mémoires du Baron de Besenval, (Paris, 1883)
Bouillé, Comte de, *Souvenirs et fragments*, (Paris, 1906)
Brissot, J. P., *Correspondance et papiers*, (Paris, 1912)
Mémoires de J. P. Brissot, ed. C. Perroud, (Paris, n.d.)
Mémoires de Brissot, ed. M. Lescure, (Paris, 1876)
Campan, J., *The Private Life of Marie-Antoinette*, (London, 1833)
   Memoirs of Marie-Antoinette, (New York, 1910)
Clermont-Gallerande, Marquis de, *Mémoires*, (Paris, 1826)
"Les Grandes Journées de juin et de juillet 1789, d'après le 'journal' inédit de Creuzé-Latouche," *Revue des questions historiques* (1935)
Mémoires des Duc des Cars, (Paris, 1890)
Droz, J., *Histoire du règne de Louis XVI*, (Paris, 1858)
Dumas père, A., *Mes Mémoires*, (Paris, 1967)
Journal d'Adrien Du Quesnoy, (Paris, 1894)
Journal d'émigration du Comte d'Espinchal, (Paris, 1912)
Ferrand, A., *Mémoires*, (Paris, 1897)
Ferrières, Marquis de, *Mémoires*, (Paris, 1822)
   Correspondance inédite, (Paris, 1932)
Les correspondances des agents diplomatiques étrangers en France avant la Révolution, ed. J. Flammermont, (Paris, 1896)
"Mémoires de Garran de Coulon," *Revue des provinces de l'ouest* 2 (1890); 3 (1891); and 5 (1892)
"Papiers de Garran de Coulon (1756–1788)," *Revue d'archéologie poitevine* 3 (1900)
Mémoires, correspondance et manuscrits du Général Lafayette, (Paris, 1838)
Lameth, A., *Histoire de l'Assemblée Constituante*, (Paris, 1828)
Lameth, T., *Mémoires*, (Paris, 1913)
   Notes et souvenirs, (Paris, 1914)
Correspondance secrète inédite sur Louis XVI, Marie-Antoinette, la cour et la ville, ed. M. Lescure, (Paris, 1866)
Correspondance de Thomas Lindet pendant la Constituante et la Législative, (Paris, 1899)
Louis XVI, Marie-Antoinette, et Madame Elisabeth: Lettres et documents inédits, ed. Feuillet de Conches, (Paris, 1864)
"Notes de Lecture: A Travers les Papiers de Louis XVIII," ed. E. Daudet, *Le Correspondant* 10 (January 1910)

Maleissye, Marquis de, *Mémoires d'un officier aux gardes françaises*, (Paris, 1897)
Mémoires et correspondance de Mallet du Pan, (Paris, 1851)
Malouet, P. V., *Mémoires*, (Paris, 1868)
Correspondance secrète du Comte de Mercy Argenteau avec l'Empereur Joseph II et le Prince de Kaunitz, (Paris, 1891)
Correspondance entre le Comte de Mirabeau et le Comte de La Marck pendant les années 1789, 1790, et 1791, (Paris, 1851)
Morris, G., *A Diary of the French Revolution*, (Boston, 1939)
Necker, J., *Histoire de la Révolution française*, (Paris, 1821)
Souvenirs d'un historien de Napoléon: Mémorial de J. Norvins, (Paris, 1896)
Mémoires du Comte de Paroy, (Paris, 1895)
Peuchet, J., *Mémoires tirés des archives de la police de Paris*, (Paris, 1838)
Restif de la Bretonne, *Oeuvres* (Paris, 1930)
Mémoires authentiques du Maréchal de Richelieu, (Paris, 1918)
Mémoires du Comte de Saint-Priest, (Paris, 1929)
Sallier, G., *Annales françaises: mai 1789–mai 1790*, (Paris, 1832)
Staël, G. de., *Considérations sur les principaux événements de la Révolution française*, (Paris, 1818)
Mémoires du Prince de Talleyrand, ed. Duc de Broglie, (Paris, 1891)
Mémoires de Talleyrand, (Paris, 1982)
Mémoires du Général Thiébault, (Paris, 1893)
Touchard-LaFosse, G., *Souvenirs d'un demi-siècle*, (Paris, 1836)
Mémoires de Madame la Duchesse de Tourzel, (Paris, 1883)
Lettres d'"Aristocrates", ed. P. Vaissière, (Paris, 1907)
Correspondance intime du Comte de Vaudreuil et du Comte d'Artois pendant l'émigration 1789–1815, (Paris, 1889)
Young, A., *Travels in France during the Years 1787, 1788, and 1789*, (London, 1889)

12 SECONDARY WORKS

Acomb, F., *Mallet du Pan*, (Durham, N.C., 1973)
Andrews, R. H., "Boundaries of Citizenship: The Penal Regulation of Speech in Revolutionary France," *French Politics and Society* 7 (Summer 1989)
"The Cunning of Imagery: Rhetoric and Ideology in Cesare Beccaria's Treatise on 'Crimes and Punishments'," *Begetting Images: Studies in the Art and Science of Symbol Production*, ed. M. Campbell and M. Rollins, (New York, 1989)
Aubry, G., "La Juridiction criminelle du Châtelet de Paris sous le règne de Louis XVI," Thèse pour le Doctorat en Droit, Université de Paris, 1971

Audin, A., *La Conspiration Lyonnaise en 1790*, (Lyon, 1984)
Babut, E., "Une Journée au District des Cordeliers: le 22 janvier 1790," *Revue historique* 81 (1903)
Baker, K. M., *Condorcet*, (Chicago, 1975)
  Inventing the French Revolution, (Cambridge, 1990)
  ed., *The French Revolution and the Creation of Modern Political Culture: The Political Culture of the Old Regime*, (Oxford, 1987)
Beach, V., *Charles X of France*, (Boulder, Co., 1971)
Bénétruy, J., *L'Atelier de Mirabeau*, (Geneva, 1962)
Bernier, O., *Lafayette*, (New York, 1983)
Berranger, C., et al., *Histoire générale de la presse française*, (Paris, 1969)
Bluche, J. F., *Les Origines des magistrats du Parlement de Paris (1715–91)*, (Nogent, 1956)
Blum, C., *Rousseau and the Republic of Virtue: The Language of Politics in the French Revolution*, (Ithaca, 1986)
Bord, G., *Le Pacte de famine*, (Paris, 1887)
  La Conspiration révolutionnaire, (Paris, 1909)
Braesch, P., *La Commune du dix août*, (Paris, 1911)
  "Un Faux historique prétendue lettre du Comte de Provence à Favras," *La Révolution française* 72 (1919)
Bruckman, P., *Lafayette*, (New York, 1977)
Cahen, L., *Condorcet et la Révolution française*, (Paris, 1904)
Caron, P., "La Tentative de Contre-révolution de juin–juillet 1789," *Revue d'histoire moderne et contemporaine* 8 (1906–7)
  Les Massacres de septembre, (Paris, 1935)
Carré, H., *La Noblesse de France et l'opinion publique au XVIIIe siècle*, (Geneva, 1977)
Castelot, A., *Philippe-Egalité, Le prince rouge*, (Paris, 1950)
Castres, Duc de, *Mirabeau*, (Paris, 1986)
Cavallaro, G., *J. P. Brissot Criminalista, al Tramonto dell' Ancien Régime*, (Ferrara, 1981)
Censer, J. R., "The Coming of a New Interpretation of the French Revolution," *Journal of Social History* (Winter 1987)
  Prelude to Power: The Parisian Radical Press, 1789–1791, (Baltimore, 1976)
Champion, M., *Mémoire autographe de M. de Barentin*, (Paris, 1844)
Chevallier, J. S., *Barnave ou les deux faces de la Révolution*, (Paris, 1936)
  "The Failure of Mirabeau's Political Ideals," *Review of Politics* 13 (1951)
Church, W., *Richelieu and Reason of State*, (Princeton, 1972)
Cleray, E., *L'Affaire Favras*, (Paris, 1932)
Conein, B., "Le Tribunal et la terreur du 14 juillet 1789 aux 'massacres de septembre'," *Révoltes logiques* no. 11 (1979–80)
Dard, E., *Le Général Choderlos de Laclos*, (Paris, 1905)
Darnton, R., "The Grub Street Style of Revolution: J. P. Brissot, Police Spy," *Journal of Modern History* 40 (1968)
Daudet, E., *Histoire de l'émigration*, (Paris, 1904)

Desjardins, A., *Les Cahiers des Etats-Généraux et la législation criminelle*, (Paris, 1883)

Desmaze, C., *Le Châtelet de Paris*, (Paris, 1863)

D'Huart, S., *Brissot: La Gironde au pouvoir*, (Paris, 1986)

Di Padova, T., "The Girondins and the Question of Revolutionary Government," *French Historical Studies* 9 (1976)

Dominique, P., *Paris enlève le roi*, (Paris, 1973)

Dorigny, M., "Violence et révolution: Les Girondins et les massacres de septembre," *Actes du Colloque Girondins et Montagnards*, (Paris, 1980)

DuBus, C., *Stanislas de Clermont Tonnerre et l'échec de la Révolution monarchique*, (Paris, 1931)

Egret, J., *La Révolution des notables: Mounier et le Monarchiens*, (Paris, 1950)
Necker: Ministre de Louis XVI, (Paris, 1975)

Elias, N., *The Civilizing Process*, tr. E. Jephcott, (New York, 1978)

Ellery, E., *Brissot de Warville*, (Boston, 1915)

Fehér, F., *The Frozen Revolution: An Essay on Jacobinism*, (Cambridge, 1987)

Ferdinand-Dreyfus, "L'Association de Bienfaisance Judiciaire," *La Révolution française* 46 (1904)

Foucault, M., *Madness and Civilization*, tr. R. Howard, (New York, 1965)
Discipline and Punish: The Birth of the Prison, tr. A. Sheridan, (New York, 1977)

Fournel, V., *L'Evénement de Varennes*, (Paris, 1980)

Furet, F., *Interpreting the French Revolution*, tr. E. Forster, (Cambridge, 1981)
"La Révolution sans la terreur?: Le Débat des historiens du xixe siècle," *Le Débat*, no. 13 (June 1981)
"La Révolution dans l'imaginaire politique français," *Le Débat*, no. 26 (September 1983)

Furet, F., and Halévi, R., "L'Année 1789," *Annales E.S.C.* (January 1989)

Furet F., and Ozouf, M., eds., *A Critical Dictionary of the French Revolution*, tr. A. Goldhammer, (Cambridge, Mass., 1989)

Furgeot, H., *Le Marquis de Saint-Huruge: Généralissime des sans-culottes (1738–1801)*, (Paris, 1908)

Garrigues, G., *Les Districts parisiens pendant La Révolution française*, (Paris, n.d.)

Godechot, J., *Les Institutions de la France sous la Révolution et l'Empire*, (Paris, 1962)
La Prise de la Bastille, (Paris, 1965)

Gottschalk, L., *Jean-Paul Marat*, (New York, 1927)
Lafayette Between the American and the French Revolution, (Chicago, 1950)

Gottschalk, L., and Maddox, M., *Lafayette in the French Revolution: Through the October Days*, (Chicago, 1969)
Lafayette in the French Revolution: From the October Days Through the Federation, (Chicago, 1973)

Griffiths, R., *Le Centre perdu: Malouet et les "monarchiens" dans la Révolution française*, (Grenoble, 1988)

Hérisson, Comte d', *Autour d'une Révolution*, (Paris, 1888)
  Les Girouettes politiques: Une Constituante, (Paris, 1892)
Higonnet, P., *Class, Ideology, and the Rights of Nobles During the French Revolution*, (Oxford, 1981)
Hunt, L., *Politics, Culture, and Class in the French Revolution*, (Berkeley, 1984)
Ignatieff, M., *A Just Measure of Pain: The Penitentiary in the Industrial Revolution, 1750–1850*, (New York, 1978)
Kaplan, S. L., *The Famine Plot Persuasion in Eighteenth Century France*, (Philadelphia, 1982)
Kates, G., *The Cercle Social, the Girondins, and the French Revolution*, (Princeton, 1985)
Kaufmann, J., "The Critique of Criminal Justice in Late Eighteenth Century France: A Study of the Changing Social Ethics of Crime and Punishment," Ph.D. dissertation, Department of History, Harvard University, 1976
  "In Search of Obedience: The Critique of Criminal Justice in Late Eighteenth Century France," *Proceedings of the Sixth Annual Meeting of the Western Society for French History* (1979)
Kelly, G. A., "From Lèse-majesté to Lèse-nation: Treason in Eighteenth-Century France, *Journal of the History of Ideas* 42 (1981)
  Victims, Authority, and Terror, (Chapel Hill, 1982)
Kirchheimer, O., *Political Justice: The Use of Legal Procedure for Political Ends*, (Princeton, 1961)
Langbein, J. H., *Torture and the Law of Proof*, (Chicago, 1977)
Lanzac de Laborie, L., *Un Royaliste libéral en 1789: Jean-Joseph Mounier*, (Paris, 1887)
Lavaquery, E., *Necker: Fourrier de la Révolution*, (Paris, 1933)
LeClerq, H., *Les Journées d'octobre et la fin de l'année 1789*, (Paris, 1924)
  La Propagande révolutionnaire: juillet 1790–décembre 1790, (Paris, 1931)
Lefebvre, G., *La Grande peur de 1789*, (Paris, 1932)
  "La Première proposition d'instituer un tribunal révolutionnaire," *Annales historiques de la Révolution française* 10 (1934)
Lemay, E., "Une Voix dissonante à l'Assemblée Constituante: Le prosélytisme de Robespierre, *Annales historiques de la Révolution française* 53 (1981)
Lucas, C., ed., *The French Revolution and the Creation of Modern Political Culture: The Political Culture of the French Revolution*, (Oxford, 1988)
Mansel, P., *Louis XVIII*, (London, 1981)
Mathiez, A., *Etude critique sur les journées des 5 et 6 octobre 1789*, (Paris, 1899)
  "Brissot électeur de Lafayette," *Annales révolutionnaires* 14 (1922)
  Etudes sur Robespierre, (Paris, 1973)
Maza, S., "Le Tribunal de la nation: Les mémoires judiciaires et l'opinion publique à la fin de l'ancien régime," *Annales E.S.C.*, (January–February 1987)

McCloy, S. T., *The Humanitarian Movement in Eighteenth-Century France*, (Lexington, Ky., 1957)

Metzger, A., and Vaesen, J., eds., *Lyon en 1791*, (Lyon, n.d.).

Michon, G., *Essai sur l'histoire du parti feuillant: Adrien Duport*, (Paris, 1924)

Morgan, R., "Divine Philanthropy: John Howard Reconsidered," *History* 62 (1977)

Patrick, A., *The Men of the First French Republic*, (Baltimore, 1972)

Perrod, P., *L'Affaire Lally-Tolendal: Une erreur judiciaire au XVIIIe siècle*, (Paris, 1972)

Perroud, C., "La Société Française des Amis des Noirs," *Révolution française* 69 (1916)

Peyster, H. de, *Les Troubles de Hollande á la veille de la Révolution française*, (Paris, 1905)

Pingaud, L., *Le Comte d'Antraigues: Un agent secret sous la Révolution et l'Empire*, (Paris, 1894)

Robinet, D., *Danton: Homme d'Etat*, (Paris, 1889)

Rogers, C., *The Spirit of Revolution in 1789*, (Princeton, 1949)

Rouanet, G., "Robespierre à la Constituante," *Annales révolutionnaires* 10 (1918)

Rousset, C., *Le Comte de Gisors*, (Paris, 1868)

Rudé, G., *The Crowd in the French Revolution*, (London, 1971)

Schama, S., *Citizens: A Chronicle of the French Revolution*, (New York, 1989)

Schmid, O., "Der Baron von Besenval," Thesis, University of Basel, 1913

Scott, S., "Problems of Law and Order During 1790, the 'Peaceful' Year of the French Revolution," *American Historical Review* 80 (1975)

The Response of the Royal Army to the French Revolution, (Oxford, 1978)

Seligman, E., "Le Dossier d'un magistrat au XVIIIe siècle," *Revue du Palais* 2 (February 1898)

La Justice en France pendant la Révolution, (Paris, 1901)

Spink, J. S., *French Free Thought From Gassendi to Voltaire*, (London, 1960)

Sutherland, D., *France, 1789–1815: Revolution and counter-revolution*, (New York, 1986)

Sybel, H. de, *Histoire de l'Europe pendant la Révolution française*, tr. M. Bosquet, (Paris, 1869)

Sydenham, M. J., *The Girondins*, (London, 1961)

Taillemite, E., *La Fayette*, (Paris, 1989)

Talmon, J., *The Origins of Totalitarian Democracy*, (London, 1952)

Tourneux, M., *Bibliographie de l'histoire de Paris pendant la Révolution française*, (Paris, 1890)

Tuetey, A., *Répertoire général des sources manuscrites de l'histoire de Paris pendant la Révolution française*, (Paris, 1890)

Vallentin, A., *Mirabeau*, tr. E. Dickes, (New York, 1948)

Valon, A. de, "Le Marquis de Favras," *Revue des deux mondes* 10 (April–June 1851)

Van Kley, D., *The Damiens Affair and the Unraveling of the Ancien Régime*, (Princeton, 1984)
Villiers, M. de, *Les 5 et 6 octobre 1789: Reine Audu*, (Paris, 1917)
Vingtrinier, E., *La Contre-révolution: Première période, 1789–1791*, (Paris, 1924)
Vovelle, M., *La Mentalité révolutionnaire*, (Paris, 1985)
Wahl, M., *Les Premières années de la Révolution à Lyon*, (Paris, 1894)
Walter, G., *Le Comte de Provence*, (Paris, 1946)
Walzer, M., *Regicide and Revolution*, (London, 1974)
Williams, A., *The Police of Paris: 1718–1789*, (Baton Rouge, La., 1979)

Index

Adrien, Michel, execution of, 104–8
Agier, Pierre-Louis, 12–13, 18, 23–4, 25,
  115, 209
Alleray, Angran d', 31
Andrews, Richard, 3
Anthoine, 27
Antraigues, Comte d', 127
Artois, Comte d', 36, 37, 38, 39, 42, 44, 50,
  53, 54, 55, 57, 83, 128
  agents of, 146
  and Lafayette, 95
  and the Maillebois affair, 178, 182
  rumors of plots by, 148
  in Turin, 175
Assemblée des Représentants, 21, 28, 50,
  61, 132
  and the Besenval affair, 64, 67, 69–70,
  71, 72, 79, 82, 83
  and the Danton affair, 190, 191
  and the Favras affair, 136–7
  and Marat, 99–101
  and the October Days, 89
Assembly of Electors, 30, 44, 46–8, 61
  and the Besenval affair, 67–8, 70, 71
Association de Bienfaisance Judiciaire,
  32–3
Audouin, 137, 151, 152, 153, 161, 165, 173
Audu, Reine, 215
Augeard, Jacques, 121–2, 127, 133, 134,
  135, 140–1, 144, 189, 191, 192
Autichamp, Maréchal d', 157

Babut, 190
Bailly, Jean-Sylvain, 23, 48
  and the Assembly of Electors, 30
  and the Besenval affair, 61, 66, 71, 72,
  73–4
  and the Châtelet, 26
  and the Comité des Recherches, 17, 181

  and the Favras affair, 132, 143
  and the Metz plot, 125
  and the October Days, 85, 87, 90, 116
  and postal surveillance, 50, 51, 53
Balbi, Madame de, 131
Bancal des Issarts, 12
Barauz placard, 137, 138
Barentin (Minister of Justice), 31, 157
Barère de Vieuzac, Bertrand, 51
Barmond, Perrotin de, 211–12, 213–14, 215
Barnave, Antoine, 118–19, 136, 214
Bastille, fall of the, 43–4
Beccaria, C., 2, 6, 167
Belombre, Camusat de, 52
Bernardi, J. E., 4, 6, 12
Berthier, 26, 45, 46, 57, 61, 62
Besenval, Baron de, 15–16, 33, 34, 35, 36,
  37, 41, 44, 49, 57, 58
  affair of, 59–83, 84, 124, 134, 135, 147,
  179
  and the Chronique de Paris, 189
  and the Comité des Recherches, 115,
  188–9
  and the Favras affair, 138
  Favras–Besenval judicial transaction,
  148–74, 204, 216, 224
  release of, 163–4, 165, 191–2
  trial of, 156–62, 162–5
Biron, Duc de, 98
Blin (dock porter), execution of, 104, 106,
  107
Bonne-Savardin, Bertrand de, 175, 176–7,
  178, 179, 180, 181–4, 185–6, 206–7,
  215
  escape from prison, 210–12
Bord, Gustave, 45–7
Boucher d'Argis, André-Jean, 1, 30, 32–4,
  212
  and the campaign against the Châtelet,
  199, 202

and the Châtelet riots, 150–6
and Marat, 102
and the trial of Adrien, 105
Bouillé, Comte de, 131
Bourguignon, Pierre, 105
Breteuil, Baron de, 40, 56, 57
Brissot de Warville, Jacques-Pierre, 18–20, 28, 189, 204, 205
  and the Besenval affair, 69, 74–7, 80
  and the Châtelet, 16, 26, 151
  and the Comité des Recherches, 11, 12, 202
  and the Danton affair, 190, 193
  and the exile of Orléans, 98
  and the Favras affair, 135, 136, 139
  and the Favras–Besenval judicial compromise, 167
  and Garran, 21
  imprisonment of, 8
  on judicial practice, 8
  and Lafayette, 217
  and the Maillebois affair, 181, 206
  and Marat, 100, 102
  and the Monarchiens, 154–5
  and the October Days, 89, 91–2, 93–4, 115, 116, 117, 209
  October Days investigation, 200, 201
  and Perron, 24
  plan for attack on Paris, 40–2
  on the release of Maury and Calonne, 58
  and the repression of popular riots, 106, 108
  and Saint-Priest, 186–7
  on those unjustly accused of crimes, 3–4
  on treason, 5–6
Broglie, Victor-François, Duc de, 57, 59, 157, 171, 176, 182
Bruges (attorney), 160, 189
Brunville, Flandre de, 164, 194–5
Buchez, 153
Bussy, Comte de, 146

Calonne, abbé, 57–8, 61, 63, 73, 79, 80
Camp de Jalès, 146–7
Camus, Armand, 23, 52, 80
Caron, Pierre, 37
Carra, 9, 29, 153, 181, 194, 197, 217
Cars, Duc des, 36, 37
Castelnau, Baron de, 50–1, 52, 53–5, 56, 57, 80
Castres, Duc de, 50
Castries, Maréchal de, 57

Cavallaro, Giovanna, 6
Cayla, Madame du, 131
Cazalès, J., 212
Chabroud, Charles, 212–13, 214
Champ-de-Mars massacre, 134, 220
Châtelet court, 14–16, 25–34, 35, 94, 107, *see also* October Days: investigation
  and the Besenval affair, 83, 172
  campaign against, 194–203
  and the Comité des Recherches, 143, 188–9, 191, 194–6, 197
  and the Danton affair, 189–90, 190, 191, 192
  and the Favras affair, 138, 140
  and judicial reform, 34
  leaders of, 30–4
  Loustalot's attack on, 173–4
  and Marat, 100, 102
  and the National Assembly, 212–14, 217–20
  and Necker, 112
  riots, 150–5, 162
  and the trial of Adrien, 105, 106–7
  and the trial of Martin and Duval, 110
Chaussard, P., 7, 8
Chomel (banker), 132, 134, 136, 137, 145
Christmas 1789, rumors of counter-revolutionary uprising, 148–9, 178
Chronique de Paris, 142, 158, 159, 161, 170, 177–8, 189, 191, 197, 208
  and the Maillebois affair, 180–1
classical school of French revolutionary historiography, xii
Clermont-Tonnerre, 53, 54, 67, 68, 72, 74, 85
Comité des Recherches, 8–9, 11–13, 14–25, 35, 49, 222
  and the Besenval affair, 77, 82, 83, 157, 158, 160, 161, 172
  Bord on, 46
  and the Châtelet, 188–9, 191, 194–6, 197, 199–203, 219
  denunciation of Saint-Priest, 187
  and the Favras affair, 132, 134–138, 143, 179
  and Lafayette, 120
  left Fayettists of, 224
  and the Maillebois affair, 177, 181–5, 206–7, 210
  and Marat, 102, 103
  municipal versus national committee, 16–17
  National Assembly's, 55, 203, 222

and the prosecution of Augeard, 122
and the October Days investigation,
　114–17
and the repression of popular riots, 107
and Saint-Priest, 127, 208–9, 210
common faith, of Condorcet, xiv–xv, 1, 10
Condé, Prince de, 37, 57, 83, 175
Condorcet, M. J., xi, xiii, common faith,
　xiv–xv, 1, 10
conspiracies, and treason, 6
Constituent Assembly, 5
Constitutional Monarchists, 24, 202
constitutional monarchy, and Lacretelle, 23
Conti, Prince de, 173
Creuzé-Latouche, 21
criminal law reform *see* judicial reform
Curé, Pierre, 189

Danton, Georges-Jacques, 102–3, 109
　affair of, 189–94, 196, 197
Darnton, Robert, 20–1, 110
death penalty, 2, 6
Delacroix, F., 2, 7
democratic denunciation, 12
Desmoulins, Camille, 106, 148, 155, 161,
　167–8, 169, 173, 180, 208, 210, 216–17
Diderot, Denis, 8, 32
Douglas, abbé, 121, 122
Droz, 69
Duport, 118, 136
DuQuesnoy, 81, 94
Dusaulx, Elector, 48–9
Duval, Pierre, 108–10

Electors *see* Assembly of Electors
Elias, Norbert, 4
Eprémesnil, d', 36, 42
Estaing, Commander d', 121, 125
Estates-General
　and judicial reform, 1, 32–3
　and royal justice, 40
Estrées, Maréchal d', 176

'Farcy' (Saint-Priest), 182, 183, 185
Fauchet, abbé, 190–1, 192, 193
Favras, Thomas de Mahy, Marquis de, 106
　affair of, 123, 124–47, 177, 185, 188,
　191–2
　arrest, 148–9, 159, 178–9
　and the *Chronique de Paris*, 189

execution, 124, 140, 169–70, 174
Favras–Besenval judicial transaction,
　148–74, 204, 216, 224
trial of, 163–9
Fayettist regime, xv, 5, 10
Ferrières (National Assembly deputy), 43,
　70, 214
Flesselles, Jacques de, 44–5, 46–8, 197
Foucault (Barmond's friend), 211–12
Foucault, Michel, xiii–xiv, 2
Foulon, 26, 57, 61, 62
Fouquier-Tinville, Antoine-Quentin, 23
François (baker), execution of, 103–4, 107,
　113
Furet, François, xiv, 11, 221, 224

Garat, 52
Gardes de la Régénération Française, 121
Garran de Coulon, Jean-Philippe, 18, 21–2,
　45–8, 49, 103, 115, 157
　and Agier, 23, 24
　and the attack on press freedoms, 101
　and the Besenval affair, 160–1
　and the Maillebois affair, 185, 206–7
Garrigues, Georges, 29–30
Geoffrey (Comité agent), 132, 134
Girondins, 202, 217
　and Brissot, 20
　and the Paris Comité des Recherches, 17,
　18
Gorsas, 69, 72–4, 80, 92, 137
　and the Besenval affair, 156–7, 158, 159
　on counter-revolutionary agents, 151
　and the Danton affair, 190, 191, 192
　and the Favras–Besenval judicial
　compromise, 164, 167
　on the rumors of mid-December, 148,
　149
Gottschalk, Louis, 19, 88, 104, 177
Gouy d'Arcy, 9, 51
Grandmaison, Thomas-Jean, 176–7

Hardy (bookseller), 95
Haute Cour Provisoire, 218–19
humanitarianism, and the judicial reform
　movement, xiii–xiv

ideology of pure democracy, 11, 13
Ignatieff, Michael, xiv

imprisonment, as means of controlling
  individuals, xiv
inquisitorial justice, call for end to, 3
intrigue, and treason, 6

Jacobin Club, 119, 137
January 1790, disturbances of, 149–56
journals *see* press coverage
judicial reform, *see also* political crime
  and the Besenval affair, 162
  Boucher d'Argis on, 33–4
  and the Favras affair, 124–5
  Lafayette and Brissot on, 19–20
  and the National Assembly, 25, 33
  and political crime, 5–9
  pre-revolutionary movement, xiii–xv,
    1–13, 167, 223

Kates, Gary, 17–18, 21
Kaufmann, Joanne, xiii, 2, 3
Kelly, George A., 87
Keralio, Louise, 137
Kirchheimer, Otto, xv

La Châtre, Comte de, 139, 206
LaMarck, 31, 32, 129, 130
La Salle (National Guard Commander), 47
Laclos, Choderlos de, 98, 118
Lacretelle, Pierre-Louis, 8–9, 22–3, 34, 135
Lafayette, Marquis de, 14–16, 28, 31, 33,
    56
  and the administration of political
    justice, 224
  and the Besenval affair, 61, 83
  and Brissot, 18–20, 202
  and the Châtelet, 214–15, 219–20
  and the Comité des Recherches, 17, 116,
    209, 210
  and the Comte de Luxembourg, 127–8
  and the Danton affair, 190–1
  deterioration of position, 204, 205,
    216–17
  and the disturbances of January (1790),
    150, 153–4, 155
  and the exile of Orléans, 95–8
  and the Favras affair, 124, 131–4, 134,
    137, 138, 139, 141, 142, 143, 144, 149
  and the Favras–Besenval judicial
    compromise, 163–4, 166, 169–70, 172,
    174

  on the François killing, 104
  and the King, 176
  and Lacretelle, 22
  and the Loi Martiale, 109
  and the Maillebois affair, 180–1, 185
  and Marat, 102
  and the Marseilles insurrection, 186–7
  and the Metz plot, 125
  and Mirabeau, 129, 130
  Morel's plot to kill, 145
  and the National Assembly, 14, 28
  and Necker, 66, 114
  and the October Days, 85, 87–8, 90, 94,
    119, 195
  and the policy of forgiveness and
    reconciliation, 173
  and the post-October Days period, 120,
    121, 122, 123
  and the repression of popular riots, 106,
    108
Laizer, Chevalier de, 189
Lally-Tolendal, 43, 79, 205–6
Lamartine, A. de, 43–4
Lambert, 57
Lambesc, Prince de, 57, 59
Lameth, Alexandre, 66, 68, 119
Lameth, Charles, 119
Langres, Bishop de, 52
LaRochefoucauld, Duc de, 186–7
Launay, M. de (Bastille governor), 41, 45,
    197
Lavaquery, Eugène, 65
Lecointre (National Guard officer), 207–8
LeDuc, Abbé, 131
Lefebvre, Georges, 14, 38, 42, 55–6, 90,
    221–2, 224
left Fayettists, 15, 16, 20, 48, 115, 120, 204,
    205, 224
  and the Châtelet, 151, 154, 194, 196, 197,
    219
  and the Comité des Recherches, 189
  and the Danton affair, 189–94, 190–1
  and the Favras affair, 134, 135, 136, 188
  and the Maillebois affair, 181–2
  political agenda, 187
Leopold, Grand Duke of Tuscany, 7
lèse-majesté (high treason), crime of, 5–7
Lessart, Valdec de, 111, 210
letters, interception of, 48–55
Liancourt, Duc de, 50–1, 55, 56, 176
Liberty, Agier on Reign of, 12–13
Lindet, Thomas, 165, 166
Louis XVI, King, 14, 36, 37–40, 42, 59, 60,
    122, 172, 175

attempted flight of, 139–40
and the Besenval affair, 162
and the Favras affair, 144, 145
and the Metz plot, 125
and Mirabeau's Normandy plan, 129
and the October Days, 86
and Saint-Priest, 207, 208
Loustalot (radical journalist), 17, 29, 69,
101
and the campaign against the Châtelet,
197, 201
and the Châtelet riots, 150, 152, 153
and the exile of Orléans, 98
and the Favras affair, 137, 138, 139,
140–1
and the Favras–Besenval judicial
compromise, 164, 170, 173–4
and the Maillebois affair, 180, 210
and the Monarchiens, 155
and the October Days, 88–9
and the repression of popular riots, 106
on the rumors of mid-December, 148
and the trial of Besenval, 156, 159, 161–2
Luxembourg, Comte de, 127–8, 133, 142

Maddox, Margaret, 19, 88, 104, 177
Maillard (judicial clerk), 90
Maillebois affair, 9, 127, 134, 175–87, 197,
203
and the Monarchiens, 205–7
and the October Days investigation,
204–20
Maillebois, Yves-Marie Desmarets, Comte
de, 175, 176, 185–6
Malouet, 66, 154, 155
Marat, Jean-Paul, 10, 29, 33, 106, 109, 112,
151, 153, 173, 210
and the attack on press freedoms, 99–103
and the Besenval affair, 82–3
on the Comité des Recherches, 201
Danton's defense of, 190, 192
and the events of January, 155–6
and the Favras affair, 137
and the October Days, 89, 92
Marie-Antoinette, Queen, 32, 36, 55, 83,
121, 122, 125
and the Favras affair, 130
Marquié, Jean-Philippe, 141–3, 172
Marseilles insurrection, 186–7, 204
Martin, Jean-Marie, 108–10
Mathiez, Albert, xii, 87, 88, 91, 93, 129
Maury, Jean-Siffrein, 9, 57, 58, 61, 73, 79,
212, 217
Mercy-Argenteau (Austrian ambassador),
36

Metz plot, 121, 122, 125–6, 129
Mirabeau, Honoré-Gabriel Riqueti, Comte
de, 28, 29, 31–2, 52
and the Besenval affair, 66, 70–1, 80
and the Châtelet, 195, 197, 199, 203,
212–13, 214, 222
and the exile of Orléans, 95–8
and the Favras affair, 129–30, 136
and the October Days investigation, 119
and the prosecution of Orléans, 118
and Saint-Priest, 186
Monarchiens, 122, 204, 212
and the Fayettists, 154–5
and the Maillebois plot, 205–7
and the October days, 85, 86, 88, 93
monarchy *see* constitutional monarchy
Monsieur *see* Provence, Comte de
Montesquieu, C., on treason, 5, 7
Montjoie, 60
Morel, Jean-Philippe, 125–6, 127–5, 143–5,
172
Morris, Gouverneur, 127, 132, 160
Mounier (Monarchien leader), 42–3, 116,
119, 205–7
Mountain, the, 18, 33

National Assembly, 10
and the Besenval affair, 61, 63, 70, 79,
80, 81, 83, 157, 158–9, 162
and the campaign against the Châtelet,
198, 199, 202–3
and the Châtelet, 14, 25–30, 94, 188,
212–14, 217–20
and the Comité des Recherches, 16–17
and counter-revolutionary conspirators,
146, 147
and the Danton affair, 190, 193
debate on the privacy of letters, 54–5
and the exile of Orléans, 95, 97
and the fourteenth of July, 44
judicial reforms, 25, 33
and Lafayette, 14
and the Maillebois affair, 179
and the Monarchiens, 122
and political justice, 56–7
and the release of Maury and Calonne,
58
and the repression of popular riots,
103–4, 107–8, 108, 109
and royal justice, 40
transfer from Versailles to Paris, 28
National Guard
and the Besenval affair, 82
and Besenval's release, 165
and the Danton affair, 190

and the disturbances of January (1790), 149–50, 152, 153–4
and the Favras affair, 126, 141–3, 142, 144, 145
and the Marseilles insurrection, 186
and the October Days, 85, 86, 87, 88, 89, 90–1
and the repression of popular riots, 104, 106, 108
Necker, Jacques, 36, 37, 40, 50, 56, 86, 109, 204
and the Besenval affair, 60, 62–8, 69, 70, 71, 72, 74, 76
and the Chevalier de Rutledge, 110–12, 114
and the Favras affair, 143
and Lacretelle, 22
and Marat, 99, 102
and the October Days, 93, 94
and Saint-Priest, 184
Nemours, Dupont de, 51–2
newspapers *see* press coverage

October Days, 14, 20, 35, 83, 84–94, 100, 110, 148, 149
counter-inquest, 208
and the events of January, 153–4
and the Favras affair, 126, 127
investigation, 84, 86–7, 98, 114–20, 187, 188, 194, 195, 196, 197, 200, 201, 202, 203
and the Maillebois affair, 179, 204–20
and the Monarchiens, 205–6
and Saint-Priest, 207–10
judicial campaign following, 84
prosecution of the right after, 120–3
Ogny, Comte d', 49, 63
Orléans, Louis-Philippe-Joseph, Duc d', 28, 103, 128, 190
and the Châtelet, 195, 197, 199, 202, 203, 212–13, 214, 222
exile of, 95–8, 99
and the October Days, 84, 119
prosecution of, 117–20
Oudart, Nicolas, 24–5, 134, 191, 196, 200

Parlement de Paris
and judicial reform, 1, 25
Pelletier, Jean, 94, 118–20, 188
People, the
and the October Days, 91–2, 209
and revolutionary justice, 9–10, 12, 13, 77–9, 225–6
Perron, Alexandre-César, 18, 24

Pétion, J., 27, 213, 217
Peuchet, 135–6
Polignac, Duchesse de, 55–6
political crime
and judicial reform, 5–9, 171
non-punitive justice, 223–4
postal surveillance, 48–55
press coverage
anti-Châtelet campaign, 196–7, 200–2, 208
Besenval affair, 156–7, 158, 159–60, 173–4
Châtelet riots, 151, 154
Favras affair, 136–40
Maillebois affair, 177–8, 180–1
October Days, 89
press freedoms, attack on, 99–103
Prieur, 79
Provence, Comte de (Monsieur, later Louis XVIII), 28, 128–33, 136–7, 138, 139, 140, 145
and the Maillebois affair, 182, 185
public officials, execution of, 8
punishment: imprisonment, xiv
proportionality of, 2
and revolutionary regimes, 171

Quatremère, Judge, 168–9

radical journalists/press *see* press coverage
Représentants *see* Assemblée des Représentants
Reubell, 83
Revel, Antoine, 106–7
revisionist school of revolutionary historiography, xii–xv
right Fayettists, 15, 16, 205, 224
and the Châtelet, 194, 197
and the Favras affair, 134, 188
riots, repression of, 103–8
Rivarol, Antoine, 60
Robespierre, M., xii, 8, 10, 22, 23, 25, 29, 57, 58, 73, 80, 213, 217
and postal surveillance, 51, 53, 54
Rogers, Cornwall, 39
Rousseau, Jean-Jacques, 12, 225
Roussel de la Bérardière, J. H., 6–7
Roux, 153
Rudé, George, 87, 93
Rutledge, Chevalier de, 64, 110–14

Saint-Chamant, Marquis de, 61
Saint-Huruge, Marquis de, 85, 89

Saint-Priest, Comte de, 20, 86, 214, 215
    and the Favras affair, 125, 126–7, 133
    and the Maillebois affair, 180–7
    and the Marseilles affair, 204
    and the October Days, 93, 207–10
Sallier (magistrate), 38
Scott, Samuel, 39
Seligman, 218
Sémonville, 30, 31, 130
'sensitive souls', 4–5, 170
Seven Years War, 176
Sèze, de (attorney), 170–1, 189
Sieyès, abbé, 43
Soboul, Albert, 113, 222
Stäel, Madame de, 38, 70

Talleyrand, C., 49, 54
Talon, Antoine-Omer, 30–2, 33, 130–1,
    136, 189, 190, 194, 195, 199
    and the Favras–Besenval judicial
    compromise, 163, 164, 165, 166, 169
Target (jurist), 80
Tesse, Madame de, 118–19
Thiébault, General, 131
Thilorier (attorney), 160

Toulouse-Lautrec, Comte de, 146
Tourcaty (sergeant), 125–7, 143–5, 172
Tournon, 180, 196
treason, crime of, 5–7
trial procedures, length of, 3
Trudon (sentry), 149
Turin Council, 175

Valazé, C. E., 7
Valon, Alexis de, 142
Van Kley, Dale, 139
Varennes affair, 98, 145, 220
Vaudreuil, Comte de, 57, 175–6
Vauguyon, 58
Vergennes, 176
Vermont, abbé, 57
Vingtrinier, Emmanuel, 37
Virieu, Comte de, 26
Volny, 80
Voltaire, F., 7, 8

Walter, Gérard, 138
Walzer, Michael, 171

Young, Arthur, 163